Pierre-Yves Henin (Ed.)

Advances in Business Cycle Research

Springer
Berlin
Heidelberg
New York
Barcelona
Budapest
Hong Kong
London
Mailand
Paris
Tokyo

Pierre-Yves Henin (Ed.)

Advances in Business Cycle Research

With Application to the French and US Economies

With 60 Figures

Springer

Prof. Pierre-Yves Henin
CEPREMAP
142, rue du Chevaleret
F-75013 Paris
France

ISBN 3-540-59229-6 Springer-Verlag Berlin Heidelberg New York Tokyo

SPIN: 10500971 42/2202-543210 – Printed on acid-free paper.

Acknowledgments

This book has benefited greatly from the patient scrutiny of several of our colleagues of the MAD research unit, who read parts of the typescript and made detailed comments on previous versions of it. We have pleasure in thanking Antoine d'Autume, director of the MAD, Jean-François Jacques, Philippe Le Gall, Jean-Marc Tallon, Patrick Villieu and all the participants at the MAD workshop. We are particularly indebted to Jean-Marc Tallon for proof reading. At different point in time in the elaboration of the preliminary material of this book, the authors have benefited of financial and scientific support of University of Paris I, University of Paris IX, University of Evry, CEBI, CEME, CEPREMAP and CREST.

Finally, we thank the referee of this book and the editor, Dr. Werner A. Müller, who encouraged about this project.

Contents

On the Theoretical Relevance and Empirical Validity of Augmented Real Business Cycle Models: An Introduction

Pierre-Yves Hénin

Like the industrial technology, economic analysis proceeds through waves of innovations rather than through a continuous evolution. It may be however even more difficult to recognize a successful innovation in economics than in technology, as the process of empirical control is looser and the role of fashion or cultural a priori on the selection of new ideas is greater.

It is difficult to imagine a paradigm so disconcerting for European economists as the Real Business cycle one, such was its radical departure from the commonly accepted view on macroeconomic fluctuations. Its exclusive reliance on both optimal behavior and real -basically technological- shocks leads the common European economist -even more if French!- to consider this approach as basically irrelevant, if not as non sensible. Indeed, it is probably not by chance that the *RBC* paradigm did emerge at this very time which saw the apogee of supply side economics in the US. So, we can think of *RBC* as the Business cycle theory from the supply side perspective.

Does this mean that we have to be supply siders or stubborn liberals to take *RBC* seriously? This book arose from the conviction that discarding the *RBC* paradigm without further examination would probably involve "throwing the baby with the bath water".

1 Why to Consider Augmented Real Business Cycle Models?

Danthine [1989] was probably the first one, among European economists, to emphasize that the *RBC* paradigm provides a new, important, methodological framework for macroeconomics. With Donaldson, he delivered the pioneering message that *RBC*-like models can be extended to encompass non walrasian mechanisms (Danthine and Donaldson [1990] and Danthine and Donaldson [1993]).

At the same time, our interest resulted in the publication of a survey paper (Hénin [1989]) and in organizing the confrontation of *RBC* and alternative approaches to Business Cycles within the "Instability and Persistence" conference held in Paris in January 1990. A group of doctoral students joined a research program aiming at a theoretical assessment and an empirical evaluation of the *RBC* approach. This volume presents results from this three years program devoted to the derivation of progressively enriched *ARBC* ("Augmented *RBC*") models. Most of the collected material was presented at various annual meetings of the European Association or Econometric Society (ESEM). Related papers did appear in international or French journals, or are currently submitted for publication.

There is of course a major semantic problem on the extent to which we have to use the *RBC* expression to label models introducing new features within the initial general equilibrium, intertemporal, calibrated business cycle model ; what is the crucial change, which implies that a particular model does no longer belong to the *RBC* variety? Has it to be the introduction of new sources of impulses, like a demand shock and especially a monetary one? or the allowance for departure from exclusive walrasian, market clearing, propagation mechanism? or even the abandonment of the usual calibration strategy in favor of a structural estimation of parameters?

Rather than entering a quasi-theological debate on this point, we have to recognize the development of a burgeoning variety of augmented *RBC* models (*ARBC*) which may comfort part of the initial message but also oppose it as surely as the augmented Phillips curve contradicts the policy message delivered by the old Phillips curve. Every -but one- of the models presented in this volume belong to this wide "*ARBC*" family. The ten chapters are naturally divided in two parts, according to the major demarcation criteria which separates walrasian models from non walrasian models, which speak to us about a suboptimal world.

2 Walrasian *ARBC* Models

The first chapter -by Jean-Olivier Hairault- is devoted to a presentation of the canonical *RBC* model, in the formulation given by King, Plosser and Rebelo [1988]. It provides the reader with a precise indication of the assumptions, the derivation, the solution and simulation methods used by the *RBC* theorists and progressively enlarged in the following chapters. This presentation intends to be analytically self-contained and allows the interested reader to design its own version of the standard *RBC* model.

This first chapter presents also results from a comparative calibration performed on both the US and the French Economies. France is likely to be typical of an European economy, with a larger public sector and other institutional features which may partly insulate it from cyclical instability. However, it appears that the main failures of the canonical *RBC* model to replicate the main characteristics of French business cycles lies in labor market behavior, like in the US.

The labor market dynamics -especially the three well known "stylized facts" of a large employment volatility, a low employment-productivity correlation and a lead of productivity over employment (the so-called "productivity cycle") provides the matter of chapter two, by Xavier Fairise and François Langot. They consider a model which follows Christiano and Eichenbaum [1992] in introducing government expenditure, and Burnside, Eichenbaum and Rebelo [1993] in assuming labor hoarding. However, they depart from these references as they specify quadratic adjustment costs for labor which allow for a smoother response of employment to different impulses. Fairise and Langot's model results in an improved ability to reproduce the actual shape of productivity-hours correlation, both in the US and in France. However, it happens that labor adjustment costs excessively reduce the volatility of hours and output.

A decisive step from the canonical model is associated with this specification. Due to the labor input being predeterminated, the instantaneous response of output to unexpected shocks results from a variation in work effort, which is not observed by the econometrician when he computes the Solow residual. Thus, the computed -or naive- Solow residual is no longer a measure of technological factors but is "contaminated" by the government expenditures shock. This model explains how and why a pro-cyclical labor productivity is spuriously attributed to technological shocks by the canonical *RBC* model.

How does the introduction of money affects a *RBC* model? Such is the question addressed by Jean-Olivier Hairault and Franck Portier in chapter three. They consider a monetarized model which generalizes Cooley and Hansen [1989] by allowing a cash-in-advance constraint to affect both investment and consumption. This specification leads to a stronger real impact of monetary shocks that in Cooley and Hansen. However, an expanding money supply results in a contraction in real output rather than in a positive response. In fact, inflation tax is due both on consumption and investment which are cash goods, which provides an incentive to substitute leisure to worktime as the only way to avoid this tax.

Thus even if real and nominal features of the business cycle can be quite approximated by such a model, the interrelations between output and money or price dynamics are misrepresented. The counterfactual implications of the mechanism propagating monetary shocks to real variables disqualifies this kind of flexible price-cash in advance model as a sensible representation of monetary driven fluctuations in our economies.

The international transmission of business cycles is an important matter in the light of recent OECD experience. Various exercises in two country *RBC* modelling did show that a straightforward extension of the canonical model is able to reproduce some main features of the international business cycle. The main stylized fact resistant to explanation by *RBC* mechanisms is the moderate level of cross country correlation between consumption. Whereas the permanent income consumption behavior together with international capital mobility a priori implies a stronger international correlation for consumption than for output, this prediction is not supported by empirical data. In chapter four, Frédérique Bec presents a model which allows to reconcile this puzzling feature with the *RBC* approach. Her solution comes through the introduction of national government expenditure as an extra source of impulse, besides the usual technological shocks. However, while successful in accounting for the consumption correlation puzzle, F. Bec's model emphasizes the need for a high international correlation of productivity shocks to explain international business cycle in an *RBC* setting, which may suggest that the apparent success of *RBC* models on this matter may be to some extent considered as spurious.

An alternative approach to international business cycle builds on small open economy models. This framework is especially relevant to account for shocks in international interest rates or for oil shocks. In chapter five, Catherine Bruno and Frank Portier develop a small open economy *RBC* model, calibrated with French data. Oil is introduced as an imported input with exogenous price. World interest rate also follows a stochastic process. An imperfect international capital mobility is assumed and modelled as resulting from a preference for domestic assets.

After solving the model by usual methods, Bruno and Portier performs two different exercises aiming at the model validation. First, they consider the traditional comparison of simulated moments with empirical ones : Although they use a "decontaminated" measure of Solow residual, orthogonal to oil prices innovations, the model tends to overestimate the output variability, but the investment saving correlation is well reproduced.

As a second exercise in validating their model, Bruno and Portier compare the impulse response functions obtained from usual calibration to the IRF estimated from a 5-variables VAR which approximates the reduced form. By bootstrapping, they obtain confidence bands for estimated responses to which compare the theoretical ones. Results are disappointing, as the computed response barely fit the estimated ones. However, this comparison is not decisive, as the VAR estimation and the *RBC* calibration are conditional to an exogenous growth component that one would like to be endogenous.

3 Non Walrasian Models and Other Developments

Switching from competitive pricing to monopolistic competition means a decisive step apart from walrasian *RBC* modelling. Jean-Olivier Hairault and Frank Portier, in chapter six, consider an intertemporal extension of the standard new-keynesian Benassy [1987] and Blanchard and Kiyotaki [1987] models, allowing for capital accumulation and monetary dynamics. Their model thus includes three important analytical features : - a monopolistic competition *à la* Dixit and Stiglitz - money in the household utility function - "menu costs" of nominal price adjustments.

According to the responses from calibrated versions of the model, the monopolistic competition per se does not introduce much change, except for more investment variability. Similarly, price adjustment cost in a world of real shocks make markups pro-cyclical, which is counterfactual according to the (currently accepted) empirical evidence.

Again, monetary shocks in a flex price version of the model are unable to generate the positive price-output and money-output correlations which characterize the monetary business cycle.

Taken altogether, the three mechanisms are quite successful in reproducing the proper real responses to monetary shocks. The correct low (for the US, even negative for France) correlation between productivity and employment is obtained for a sensible calibration of real (productivity) and monetary shocks, using a Solow residual impulse "decontaminated" from (i.e. orthogonal to) monetary supply.

As satisfactory as it may appear according to the conformity of simulated responses to selected prices of empirical evidence, the Hairault and Portier's model maintains the walrasian assumption of a full employment, flex wage labor market. An alternative approach to labor market dynamics considers that wage are set according to contracts, which usually are not fully indexed. In chapter seven, Xavier Fairise combines nominal wage contracts with a richer specification of real adjustment costs, allowing for interrelated labor-capital adjustment costs. The empirical issue addressed by this chapter is the cyclical behavior of real wage, a feature usually not considered and unexplained in other *ARBC* models. In fact, while productivity is leading employment over the cycle, the real wage is lagging, which is inconsistent with standard market clearing.

Using calibrated versions of his model respectively with and without contracts and/or adjustment costs, Xavier Fairise shows how these two assumptions interact as to reproduce the correct pattern of cross time correlations. However, there is no consideration of unemployment in his model.

As it is well known, the hard core *RBC* models includes only a paradoxical kind of unemployment : under Hansen [1985] indivisible labor assumption, unemployed are better off than employed as they enjoy both the same consumption, due to full insurance, and more leisure time. For the relevance of the paradigm, it is important to formulate *ARBC* models in which unemployment involves social costs. Any model with preset wage may produce unemployment which may be considered as involuntary. However, in such a framework, the dynamics of unemployment is only a by product of wage dynamics.

Representing the labor market as a matching process allows for a richer dynamic view. Going beyond seminal papers by Mortensen [1990] or Andolfatto [1991] , François Langot introduces a matching process in a fully specified *ARBC* model, including capital accumulation. Langot's model, presented in chapter eight, maintains the assumption usual in this framework, that the wage rate is set according to some contractual sharing of the surplus from a match.

Results are encouraging, as the model is able to explain the pattern of correlation between employment, productivity and wage. However, it is difficult to obtain an empirical Beveridge curve, i.e. a contemporaneous correlation between unemployment and vacancies negative enough.

Introducing shocks in the labor market, to the matching function or to the separation rate makes things worse, as that induces more movements apart from the steady state Beveridge curve and thus more positive comouvements between unemployment and vacancies. An interesting message from the exercise, which is alike usual results in the empirical literature, is that specific labor market shocks are probably not an important source of business cycle impulses.

Although originating from the neoclassical growth model, as recurrently claimed by its proponents (e.g. Prescott [1986]), only stationary versions of the model are usually considered as relevant for explaining the business cycle phenomena, i.e. the (relatively) high frequency properties of the data. Thus, common *RBC* models can be seen as "castrated growth models". Some recent papers illustrates the interest of considering non stationary *ARBC* models, as to explore the interrelationship between cycles and growth. Due to the endogenous growth hypothesis, there is a new stake associated to the cycle-growth interaction, as transitory gaps from potential GNP do affect long run growth. Business cycle features, especially recessions, are not neutral for long run output.

However, there is a debate in recent literature on the nature of this persistence. Associated to the "creative destruction" view of growth, or the opportunity cost hypothesis, recessions are a time for greater improvement in long run productivity. For the Arrow-Kaldor view of learning by doing or "increasing dynamic return to scale", recessions involve a lasting loss of productive power and thus of output.

While Stadler [1990] considers these issues in an extended growth model allowing for a non stationary rate of growth, Fabrice Collard presents, in chapter IX, a simple, canonical, model of cyclical growth. In Collard's model, growth proceeds through human capital accumulation, which is a side product of activity. However, the relation between activity and human capital is two fold. On the one side, workers learn by doing, so the accumulation of human capital increases with the employment rate. However, on the other side, labor productivity is persistent. Workers more productive today are more productive for ever. Thus human capital accumulation gains from rationalizing, i.e. firing in recession as to maintain productivity.

Learning by doing and rationalizing imply conflicting effects on growth, and the calibration of one crucial parameter decides upon which effect dominates. Collard's model allows to analyze all the implications of different calibrations, supporting the alternative views.

Two empirical characterization of the growth cycle are considered, one in terms of Hodrick-Prescott stationary component, the other in terms of growth rate, an alternative reminiscent of Mintz [1969] distinction between "deviation cycles" and "step cycles". As a main empirical weakness of this cyclical growth model, it is worth noticing that it underpredicts the autocorrelation in the growth rate.

The last contribution to this volume, chapter ten, is devoted to one of the main improvements in recent *ARBC* modelling, the introduction of statistical estimation and testing of comprehensive dynamic models. Patrick Fève and François Langot follow Eichenbaum [1991] methodology, using GMM (Generalized Method of Moments) to estimate structural "deep" parameters, test restrictions but also to evaluate a selection of second order moments usually considered in the *RBC* literature. They do apply this methodology as an alternative assessment of the ability of the canonical *RBC* model to match the French business cycle experience.

4 Looking at the Future : Beyond *ARBC* Models

The ten chapters of this volume illustrate the recent trends in the literature and bring their original contribution to these trends. They show how the limits of early *RBC* models may be bypassed by building *ARBC* models, including new mechanisms, some of them non walrasians. Clearly, this achievement supports the view that the *RBC* paradigm provides a powerful framework, open to new developments. Does it mean that we may satisfy ourselves with the current state of the matter and accept the *RBC* approach as a paradigm? To this question, our answer is decisively no.

Several contributions in recent business cycle research point towards this statement of dissatisfaction. Using more precise, spectral analysis methods, to assess the contribution of *RBC* models to the explanation of persistence and cyclicity, Cogley and Nason [1993] find that these models actually do no more than to transfer to the output and other endogenous variables the persistence and pseudo-cyclicity built in the impulses and Cochrane [1994] concludes his systematic quest for sources of shocks able to account for output volatility by the disillusioned statement that he cannot find credible shocks of a sufficient quantitative importance.

Without adhering to a paradigm, we may learn a lot from it. We hope that this volume will convince the reader that it is worth to build small fully specified intertemporal general equilibrium models, to examine their properties by computing their response functions and other quantitative implications, to confront them to empirical data.

We think that most of the important features of real world dynamics are considered in one at least of the contributions to this book ; as sources of impulses : money, government expenditure, foreign interest rate, oil price, employment matching and separation as well as the standard "technological shock" ; as mechanisms of propagation : capital accumulation, adjustment costs on labor and capital, isolated or interrelated, cash in advance constraint, international capital mobility, monopolistic competition, nominal price rigidity and labor contracts, employment variations through matching, learning by doing and production rationalizing. However, none of the models presented here - neither in the literature- includes a satisfactory combination of the main features we think essential to account for actual business cycle.

The main problem is that business cycle -and especially recession as sharp as the one Europe is experiencing in the early nineties- cannot be seen only as fluctuations in the way people utilize resources, but more properly, as involving periods of huge underutilization of resources which can hardly been rationalized as Pareto optimal responses.

To account for this feature, we think necessary to go beyond *ARBC* towards *KRBC* (Keynesian Rational Business Cycles models) : - Keynesian, as to highlight that variations in the degree of resources utilization are more important than fluctuations in the way resources are allocated, not to disclaim for the shortcomings associated to the keynesian tradition. - Rational, rather than real, because we consider that, while the business cycle is not reducible to a real phenomenon, rationality has to be maintained as it provides a principle of intelligibility essential for economic analysis, macro as well as micro.

For building such a *KRBC* model, much can be done by bringing together some mechanisms considered in the various essays included in this volume, but further steps probably require designing new mechanisms.

Let us outline what we consider to be some of the priorities to write down in our research agenda. Intertemporal substitution in leisure is still an important mechanism in many *ARBC* models : we have rather to explain how the economy responds to shocks by varying the degree of utilization of equipment and labor, by adjusting operating time, effort, weekly hours and so on. Research on this way may follow on the pioneering work of Greenwood, Hercowitz and Huffman [1988] and Burnside, Eichenbaum and Rebelo [1993].

The motives to increase resources utilization in response to a demand shocks lies mainly upon some variety of nominal rigidity. Further work on deeper and stronger micro-foundations for those rigidities is still required, as well as the operational implications of demand externalities as an alternative explanation. As remarked by Lindbeck and Snower [1994] and exemplified by recent *ARBC* models (Deveureux, Head and Lapham [1993], Hornstein [1993] and Portier [1994]) the dynamics of entry of firms in an oligopolistic market is an interesting mechanism to explore.

It is relevant to remark, as Naish [1993] does, that mark up pricing may be near rational, and induce procyclical responses to monetary impulse, but the argument has still to be introduced into a fully specified intertemporal model with rational agents.

A better understanding of the transmission of demand shocks, together with the overwhelming corpus of analyses on non competitive wage setting may provide more light on the way unemployment arises and fluctuates. However, we are far from accounting satisfactorily for the consequences of unemployment on household behavior. It is important to acknowledge that unemployment risk is not fully insurable, due notably to moral hazard problems (Hansen and Imrohoroglu [1992]), and that human capital is both partly illiquid and depletable.

Recent work on endogenous participation with discouraged worker effect (Langot and Pucci [1994]) or a segmented labor market with different contractual or institutional rules (Danthine and Donaldson [1994]) provides good examples of promising line of research on labor market dynamics.

While a part of the seminal contribution of King and Plosser [1984], endogenous responses of money supply were neglected until recently (Ohkusa [1993]). They are to be included in a more comprehensive description of the way the financial sector works, along the line initiated by Diaz-Gimenez, Prescott, Fitzgerald and Alvarez [1992] and Fuerst [1992], as to account for the role of term structure (Donaldson, Johnsen and Mehra [1990]), liquidity effects (Christiano and Eichenbaum [1991]) and equity premium. Until now, the business cycle dynamics associated to credit mechanisms has been developed in specific models (Greenwald and Stiglitz [1987]), it remains a priority to include that dynamics in computable, comprehensive business cycle models.

One advantage in using computable models is that it allows for a quantitative assessment of the cost of business cycle and the trade off between those costs and the cost of stabilization policies. The initial Lucas [1987] message is consistent with the view of Pareto optimal responses associated to walrasian models. Imrohoroglu [1989] shown that limited departures from the basic model (indivisibilities, liquidity constraints) results in non negligible loss of welfare. Greenwood and Huffman [1991] provide interesting analytics but retain standard assumptions. Clark, Leslie and Symons [1994] try to identify welfare costs associated to persistent unemployment, while not in a fully specified general equilibrium model. We think that the consideration of non trivial welfare costs associated to recessions will allows to a relevant normative analysis of stabilization policy, including the long run consequences in an endogenous growth, non stationary model.

While interesting, recent attempts at reformulating in a *RBC* framework the issue of the role of government as providing automatic stabilizers suffer from disregarding some of the main sources of welfare costs of actual business cycles (Gali [1994]). Progresses in estimation and testing of general equilibrium business models are still possible by GMM methods. However, the maximum likelihood methods which were difficult to apply to such dynamic non linear models may now beneficiate from the development of simulated methods. Pathbreaking work in this direction (Smith [1990] and Feve and Guay [1993]) looks promising and pave the way for the diffusion of structural estimation methods of *ARBC* or *KRBC* models.

Bibliography

D. ANDOLFATO. *Business Cycles and Labor Market Search.* Working paper, University of Waterloo, October 1991.

J.P. BENASSY. Imperfect competition, unemployment and policy. *European Economic Review*, 31(1/2):417–426, Février-Mars 1987.

O. BLANCHARD AND N. KIYOTAKI. Monopolistic Competition and the Effect of Aggregate Demand. *American Economic Review*, 77(4):647–666, September 1987.

C. BURNSIDE, M. EICHENBAUM AND S. REBELO. Labor Hoarding and the Business Cycle. *Journal of Political Economy*, 101(2):245–273, 1993.

L. CHRISTIANO AND M. EICHENBAUM. *Liquidity Effects, Monetary Policy and the Business Cycle.* Mimeo, Northwestern University, June 1991.

L. CHRISTIANO AND M. EICHENBAUM. Current Real Business Cycle Theories and Aggregate Labor Market Fluctuations. *American Economic Review*, 82(3):430–450, June 1992.

K. CLARK, D. LESLIE AND E. SYMONS. The Cost of Recession. *Economic Journal*, 104:20–36, 1994.

J. COCHRANE. Permanent and Transitory Components of G.N.P. and Stock Prices. *Quarterly Journal of Economics*, CIX(1):241–266, February 1994.

T. COGLEY AND J. NASON. *Impulse Dynamics and Propagation Mechanisms in Real Business Cycle Models.* Working paper, Federal Reserve Bank of San Francisco, February 1993.

T. COOLEY AND G. HANSEN. The Inflation Tax in a Real Business Cycle Model. *American Economic Review*, 79(4):733–748, September 1989.

J.P. DANTHINE AND J. DONALDSON. Efficiency Wages and the Business Cycles Puzzle. *European Economic Review*, 34(7):1275–301, November 1990.

J.P. DANTHINE AND J. DONALDSON. Methodological and Empirical Issues in Real Business Cycle Theory. *European Economic Review*, 37(1):1–36, January 1993.

J.P. DANTHINE AND J. DONALDSON. Non-Walrasian Economies. In T. Cooley, editor, *Frontiers of Business Cycle Research*, 1994. Forthcoming.

J.P. DANTHINE. Modélisation des fluctuations conjoncturelles: survol de quelques récents développements. *Recherches Economiques de Louvain*, 55(3):213–244, 1989.

M. DEVEUREUX, A. HEAD AND B. LAPHAM. *Exit and Entry, Increasing Returns to Specialization and Business Cycles.* Working paper, University of British Columbia and Queen's University, June 1993.

J. DIAZ-GIMENEZ, E. PRESCOTT, T. FITZGERALD AND F. ALVAREZ. Banking in Computable General Equilibrium Economies. *Journal of Economic Dynamics and Control*, 16:533–559, 1992.

J. DONALDSON, T. JOHNSEN AND R. MEHRA. On the Term Structure of Interest Rates. *Journal of Economic Dynamics and Control*, 14:571–596, 1990.

M. EICHENBAUM. Real Business Cycle Theory: Wisdom or Whimsy? *Journal of Economic Dynamics and Control*, 15:607–626, 1991.

P. FEVE AND A. GUAY. *Calibration and Moment Matching in Macroeconomics.* Working paper, MAD, Université de Paris I, December 1993.

T. FUERST. Liquidity, Loanable Funds, and Real Activity. *Journal of Monetary Economics*, 29(1):3–25, February 1992.

J. GALI. Government Size and Macroeconomic Stability. *European Economic Review*, 38:117–132, 1994.

B. GREENWALD AND J. STIGLITZ. Keynesian, New Keynesian and New Classical Economics. *Oxford Economic Papers*, 39:119–132, 1987.

J. GREENWOOD AND G. HUFFMAN. Tax Analysis in a Real Business Cycle Model : on Measuring Harberger Triangles and Okun Gaps. *Journal of Monetary Economics*, 27:167–190, 1991.

J. GREENWOOD, Z. HERCOWITZ AND G. HUFFMAN. Investment, Capacity Utilisation, and the Real Business Cycle. *American Economic Review*, 78:402–417, 1988.

G. HANSEN AND A. IMROHOROGLU. The Role of Unemployment Insurance in an Economy with Liquidity Constraints and Moral Hazard. *Journal of Political Economy*, 100:118–142, 1992.

G. HANSEN. Indivisible Labor and the Business Cycles. *Journal of Monetary Economics*, 16(3):309–327, November 1985.

A. HORNSTEIN. Monopolistic Competition, Increasing Returns to Scale, and the Importance of Productivity Shocks. *Journal of Monetary Economics*, 31(3):299–316, June 1993.

P.Y. HÉNIN. Une macroéconomie sans monnaie: revue critique des travaux théoriques et empiriques sur les cycles réels. *Revue d'Economie Politique*, 99(4):531–596, July-August 1989.

A. IMROHOROGLU. Cost of Business Cycles with Indivisibilities and Liquidity Constraints. *Journal of Political Economy*, 97:1364–1383, December 1989.

R. KING AND C. PLOSSER. Money, Credit and Prices in a Real Business Cycle. *American Economic Review*, 74(3):363–380, June 1984.

R. KING, C. PLOSSER AND S. REBELO. Production, Growth and Business Cycles I. *Journal of Monetary Economics*, 21(2/3):196–232, March-May 1988.

F. LANGOT AND M. PUCCI. *Qualifications et subventions à l'emploi différentiées dans un modèle intertemporel d'équilibre général.* Working paper, MAD, Université de Paris I, April 1994.

A. LINDBECK AND D. SNOWER. How are Product Demand Changes Transmitted to the Labour Market. *Economic Journal*, 104(423):386–398, March 1994.

R. LUCAS. *Models of Business Cycles.* Basil Blackwell, Oxford, 1987.

I. MINTZ. *Dating Postwar Business Cycles. Methods and their Application to Western Germany, 1950-1967.* NBER (Distributed by Columbia University Press), New-York, 1969.

D. MORTENSEN. *Search Equilibrium and Real Business Cycles.* Working paper , Northwestern University, August 1990.

H. NAISH. Real Business Cycles in a Keynesian Macro Model. *Oxford Economic Papers*, 45:618–638, 1993.

Y. OHKUSA. Money Creation in the Real Business Cycle Theory. *Economic Letters*, 42:367–371, 1993.

F. PORTIER. *Business Formation and Cyclical Markup in the French Business Cycle.* Working paper, MAD, Université de Paris I, January 1994. Forthcoming in Annales d'Economie et de Statistique.

E. PRESCOTT. Theory Ahead of Business Cycle Measurement. *Carnegie Rochester Conference Series on Public Policy*, 25:11–44, Autumn 1986.

A. SMITH. *Three Essays on the Solution and Estimation of Dynamic Macroeconomic Models.* Ph. D. Thesis, Duke University, 1990.

G. STADLER. Business Cycle Models with Endogenous Growth. *American Economic Review*, 80(4):763–778, September 1990.

Part I

Advances into RBC Framework

Chapter 1

Presentation and Evaluation of the Real Business Cycles Approach

Jean-Olivier Hairault

Abstract

The model of King, Plosser and Rebelo [1988] allows us to shed light on the *RBC* approach: indeed, this model relies on the fundamental mechanisms of this approach and illustrates its methods of resolution and validation. The evaluation on French economy reveals its inability to reproduce stylized facts relative to the labor market.

Introduction

Macroeconomics in the eighties was deeply influenced by the development of Real Business Cycles models. Following Lucas [1987], the first *RBC* models are cast in the neoclassical growth model affected by stochastic shocks on global productivity factors only. This is the explanation of the expression "*real* business cycle" in so far as these models intend to show that this framework is rich enough to reproduce economic fluctuations, without introducing monetary shocks. Kydland and Prescott [1982] and Long and Plosser [1983] represent the first models[1] of this approach whose goal is to establish that the *optimal* responses of

[1]The expression *Real Business Cycles* is first used in Long and Plosser [1983].

economic agents confronted to real shocks can generate cyclical features close to observed ones without taking into account *monetary* shocks. Different points at the heart of *RBC* models can be underlined.

- The purpose of *RBC* models is to provide an explanation for business cycle. This one is defined as an aggregate phenomenon characterized by persistent and recurrent variations of macroeconomic activity. It is not a cycle in a narrow sense.

> "My own preference is to use the term "fluctuations" since "business cycle" frequently carries the connotation that there is true periodicity present in economic activity.". (Plosser [1989],p.54)

As for the phenomenon under study, the real business cycle theory is in the line of monetary cycles *à la Lucas.*

> "The cyclical movements do not exhibit uniformity of either period or amplitude, which is to say, they do not resemble the deterministic wave motions which sometimes arise in the natural science. Those regularities which are observed are in the co-movements among different aggregative times series.".
> (Lucas [1987],p.217)

Business cycles are considered all alike whatever the country considered. The project is then to propose a general explanation of economic fluctuations. The *RBC* approach is concerned not only with qualitative features, but also with quantitative features of business cycles. *RBC* models consider then three essential characteristics: relative volatility, high conformity and persistence which can be approached by variances, correlations and autocorrelations on cyclical components of macroeconomic series.

- The objective of *RBC* models is to elaborate a simple representation of an economic system in order to systematically analyze its ability to reproduce quantitatively observed cyclical features. It corresponds to the view described in Lucas [1987]:

> "a fully articulated artificial economy which behaves through time so as to imitate closely the time series behavior of actual economics.".(Lucas [1987],p.219)

- The *RBC* theory is cast within the neoclassical growth model. One may then present this approach as an integrated analysis of fluctuations and growth. A same framework is used to study these two phenomena. However, the core of *RBC* models is centered on the business cycle, and often in a theoretical framework without growth. One may then prefer to refer to the capital accumulation neoclassical model.

> "While many readers may be familiar with some versions of this framework as a model of optimal economic growth, it is better viewed as a framework for economic dynamics (see Hicks [1965], p.4). As such it is natural to consider it as the benchmark model for our understanding of economic fluctuations as well as growth. What is somewhat remarkable is that the implications for fluctuations of this neoclassical approach have not been seriously explored until recently." (Plosser [1989],p.54)

RBC models give theoretical grounds to an old project, particularly Hayek's one: to explain economic fluctuations in the neoclassical framework.

> "The incorporation of cyclical phenomena into the system of economic equilibrium theory, with which they are in apparent contradiction, remains the crucial problem of Trade Cycle Theory ". (Hayek [1933],p.33)

They are consistent with the requirements of Lucas [1987] again:

> "one would like a theory which accounts for the observed movements in quantities (employment, consumption, investment) as an optimizing response to observed movements in prices". (Lucas [1987],p.222)

RBC theory considers economic fluctuations as the result of the optimal response of economic agents to stochastic shocks on global productivity. Indeed, optimum and equilibrium are equivalent at each period. The business cycle may not be viewed as recurrent deviations relative to a natural rate, but rather as the result of the interaction of real factors only, namely preferences and the production technology. The welfare implications of these models are then well-known: all external interventions which would imply a different path lead to welfare losses:

> "Business cycle characteristics exhibited by this economy are chosen in preference to outcomes that exhibit no business cycles". (Plosser [1989],p.56)
>
> "Costly efforts at stabilization are likely to be counterproductive". (Prescott [1986], p.39)

One may then recognize one advantage to *RBC* models: to propose an explanation of economic fluctuations in an idealized framework without imperfections which can be used as a benchmark:

> "Progress towards understanding this idealized state is essential because it is logically impossible to attribute an important portion of fluctuations to market failure without an understanding of the sorts of fluctuations that would be observed in the absence of the hypothesized market failure." (Plosser [1989],p.53)

- *RBC* theory is developed in the impulsion-propagation framework. The neoclassical growth model is used in its stochastic version : the only shocks are the ones that hit total factor productivity. These exogenous shocks are interpreted as technological ones. It is the interaction of the model structure and of these shocks which generates cyclical properties close to the observed ones according to a Slutsky effect.

- The *RBC* approach can also be defined by its specific resolution and validation methods. As there is no closed form solution, approximate economies are considered. Furthermore, stochastic simulations are performed after model calibration. These simulations allow to compute second order moments on generated series in order to compare them with the observed ones.

Hence evaluating the scope of *RBC* models requires a preliminary detailed presentation of these ones. It is meaningful to consider the canonical model of King, Plosser and Rebelo [1988] which is a benchmark model in so far as it contains all the mechanisms which are at the heart of these models. The objective in this chapter is not to present an exhaustive survey of *RBC* literature[2], but rather to expose its specificity.

As the *RBC* theory is to propose a general explanation of economic fluctuations, it is necessary to examine its ability to reproduce the business cycles of different countries. We propose then the first validation of *RBC* models on French economy[3] on the basis of a specific calibration.

It then appears that the success of the *RBC* approach lies more on methodological improvements than on its economic contribution. The evaluation of the *RBC* canonical model both on United States and France reveals its inability to reproduce some important stylized facts, more particularly on the labor market. The introduction of labor indivisibility in the line of Hansen [1985] does not lead one to temper this negative conclusion.

1.1 Presentation of the Canonical *RBC* Model

The presentation of the canonical *RBC* model of King, Plosser and Rebelo [1988] allows to reveal in an unified framework the specificities of the *RBC* models. The dynamics of the economy is the result of the decisions of many agents that maximize their utility with respect to technological and resources constraints. The project of *RBC* models is to use the neoclassical growth model for reproducing the dynamics of the economy. However, this purpose implies the use of par-

[2]See Hénin [1991].

[3]Danthine and Donaldson [1991] in their comparison of stylised facts among developped countries show that the French economy is representative of European ones.

ticular resolution and validation methods: contrary to King, Plosser and Rebelo [1988], we take into account explicitly rational expectations, which leads us to refer to the method proposed by Blanchard and Kahn [1980]. At last, the dynamics of the models lies on economic mechanisms which are relative to their intertemporal framework: numerical simulations of the model are proposed in order to underline these mechanisms.

1.1.1 Exposition of the Model

Let us consider a perfectly competitive economy with a representative household and a representative firm. The preferences of the household are given by:

$$u = u(C_t, L_t)$$

C_t is the amount of consumption and L_t the amount of leisure at period t. The function u is assumed to be strictly increasing, concave, twice continuously differentiable and to satisfy Inada-type conditions.

At each period, the total amount of time, normalized to one, is allocated between leisure and labor. Consumption and investment can not exceed total income.

$$L_t + H_t \leq 1$$

$$C_t + I_t \leq Y_t$$

The accumulation process of capital is given by:

$$K_{t+1} = (1 - \delta)K_t + I_t$$

where δ is the rate of depreciation.

The representative firm ensures the production Y_t of the good according to a constant returns to scale production function which is concave, twice continuously differentiable, and satisfies the Inada conditions:

$$Y_t = A_t F\left(K_t, X_{H,t} H_t\right)$$

where K_t is the predetermined capital stock and H_t the quantity of labor input. X_H represents labor augmenting technical progress at the constant rate γ_{XH}. A_t is a temporary stochastic shock to the total factor productivity, which can be interpreted as a technological shock. In this economy, it can be measured by the Solow residual. Taken in logarithm, it is assumed to follow a stationary autoregessive process of order one:

$$\log(A_t) = \rho_A \log(A_{t-1}) + (1-\rho_A)\log(A) + \varepsilon_{A,t}$$

where $\log(A)$ is the mean of the process, $|\rho_A| < 1$ and $\varepsilon_{A,t}$ its innovation which variance is σ_A^2.

The competitive equilibrium corresponds to the social planner one. This latter can be computed by solving the following problem:

$$\begin{array}{ll} \max\limits_{C_t,L_t} & E_0 \sum\limits_{t=0}^{\infty} \beta^t u(C_t, L_t) \\ \text{s.t.} & C_t + I_t \leq A_t F(K_t, X_{H,t} H_t) \end{array}$$

β represents the discount factor, E_0 the expectation conditional to the information at the period 0. This information is given by K_0 and by the vector $\chi_0 = (A_0, X_{H,0})$. At period t, the state variables are K_t and χ_t, while the control variables are C_t and H_t.

Restrictions on individual preferences are necessary to ensure steady state growth[4]. The utility function must be of the following form:

$$u(C,L) = \frac{C^{1-\sigma}}{1-\sigma} v(L) \quad \text{for} \quad \sigma \in]0,1[\cup]1,+\infty[$$

$$u(C,L) = \log(C) + v(L) \quad \text{for} \quad \sigma = 1$$

The rate of growth of output, consumption, capital and investment are then constant and determined by the rate of growth specific to labor[5].

$$\gamma_Y = \gamma_C = \gamma_K = \gamma_I = \gamma_{XH}$$

Given the time constraint, labor can not grow: $\gamma_H = 1$. The production function is generally chosen as a Cobb-Douglas type.

$$Y_t = A_t K_t^{\alpha} (X_{H,t} H_t)^{1-\alpha}$$

[4]See King, Plosser and Rebelo [1988].

[5]See King, Plosser and Rebelo [1988].

1.1.2 The Resolution Method

The resolution strategy is to approximate the Euler conditions linearly around the steady state and to solve the resulting linear dynamic system.

By deflating all variables by $X_{H,t}$, the model can be expressed in terms of variables that will be constant along the steady state path. These variables are: $c_t = C_t/X_{H,t}$, $k_t = K_t/X_{H,t}$, $y_t = Y_t/X_{H,t}$ and $i_t = I_t/X_{H,t}$. So, the objective function becomes:

$$U = (X_{H,0}^{1-\sigma})E_0 \sum_{t=0}^{+\infty} (\beta^\star)^t \frac{c_t^{1-\sigma}}{1-\sigma} v(L_t) \quad \text{for} \quad \sigma \in]0,1[\cup]1,+\infty[$$

$$U = E_0 \sum_{t=0}^{+\infty} (\beta^\star)^t (\log(c_t) + v(L_t) + \log(X_{H,t})) \quad \text{for} \quad \sigma = 1$$

where $\beta^\star = \beta(\gamma_{XH})^{1-\sigma}$. To ensure that lifetime utility is finite, it is assumed that:

$$\beta^\star < 1 \Longleftrightarrow \beta < \gamma_{XH}^{\sigma-1}$$

The terms $X_{H,0}^{1-\sigma}$ and $\log(X_{H,t})$ will be neglected further. The evolution capital becomes:

$$\gamma_{XH} k_{t+1} = (1-\delta)k_t + A_t k_t^\alpha H_t^{1-\alpha} - c_t$$

The problem is solved in closed loop by writing it in a recursive form. Its solution verifies the Bellman equation for an optimal path of the capital:

$$\begin{aligned} V(k_t, A_t) &= \max_{c_t, H_t} \{u(c_t, L_t) + \beta^\star E_t [V(k_{t+1}, A_{t+1})]\} \\ \text{with} \quad \gamma_{XH} k_{t+1} &= (1-\delta)k_t + A_t k_t^\alpha H_t^{1-\alpha} - c_t \end{aligned}$$

The optimality conditions are:

$$\begin{aligned} \frac{\partial u}{\partial c_t} + \frac{\partial k_{t+1}}{\partial c_t}\lambda_t &= 0 \\ \frac{\partial u}{\partial H_t} + \frac{\partial k_{t+1}}{\partial H_t}\lambda_t &= 0 \\ \frac{\partial V(k_t, A_t)}{\partial k_t} - \frac{\partial k_{t+1}}{\partial k_t}\lambda_t &= 0 \\ \gamma_{XH} k_{t+1} - (1-\delta)\, k_t - A_t F(k_t, H_t) + c_t &= 0 \\ \lim_{\tau\to\infty} \left[\beta^{\star t+\tau} \lambda_{t+\tau} k_{t+1+\tau}\right] &= 0 \end{aligned}$$

with the notation:

$$\lambda_t = \beta^\star E_t \left[\frac{\partial V(k_{t+1}, A_{t+1})}{\partial k_{t+1}} \right].$$

The optimality conditions imply three kinds of trade-off : a trade-off between current and future leisure, a trade-off between current and future consumption and a trade-off between current consumption and leisure. The first two trade-off involve the expected discounted marginal value (in utility terms) of next period capital, while the third one relies on the present value of labor marginal productivity only. So, each increase in λ makes current consumption and leisure more expensive relative to future consumption and leisure; each increase in the marginal productivity of labor leads to an increase in the price of current leisure relative to consumption. At last, a transversality condition implies that at the infinity, the actualized value of the capital in terms of marginal utility of consumption is null.

The optimality conditions can be written:

$$\begin{aligned}
c_t^{-\sigma} v(1-H_t) - \frac{1}{\gamma_{XH}} \lambda_t &= 0 && (1.1)\\
\frac{c_t^{1-\sigma}}{1-\sigma} v'(1-H_t) - \frac{1}{\gamma_{XH}} (1-\alpha) A_t k_t^\alpha H_t^{-\alpha} \lambda_t &= 0 && (1.2)\\
\frac{\beta^\star}{\gamma_{XH}} E_t \left[\left(1 - \delta + \alpha A_{t+1} k_{t+1}^{\alpha-1} H_{t+1}^{1-\alpha}\right) \lambda_{t+1} \right] - \lambda_t &= 0 && (1.3)\\
\gamma_{XH} k_{t+1} - (1-\delta) k_t - A_t k_t^\alpha H_t^{1-\alpha} + c_t &= 0 && (1.4)\\
\lim_{\tau \to \infty} E_t \left[\beta^{\star t+\tau} \lambda_{t+\tau} k_{t+1+\tau} \right] &= 0 && (1.5)
\end{aligned}$$

Approximation around the steady state yields the following conditions:

$$\zeta_{cc} \widehat{c}_t - \zeta_{cl} \frac{H}{1-H} \widehat{H}_t - \widehat{\lambda}_t = 0 \qquad (1.6)$$

$$\zeta_{lc} \widehat{c}_t - \zeta_{ll} \frac{H}{1-H} \widehat{H}_t - \widehat{\lambda}_t - \widehat{A}_t - \alpha \widehat{k}_t + \alpha \widehat{H}_t = 0 \qquad (1.7)$$

$$E_t \widehat{\lambda}_{t+1} + \eta_A E_t \widehat{A}_{t+1} + \eta_k \widehat{k}_{t+1} + \eta_H E_t \widehat{H}_{t+1} = \widehat{\lambda}_t \qquad (1.8)$$

with $\zeta_{cc} = -\sigma$, $\zeta_{cl} = \frac{LDv(L)}{v(L)}$, $\zeta_{lc} = 1-\sigma$ et $\zeta_{ll} = \frac{LD^2v(L)}{Dv(L)}$. The "$\eta$" are the elasticities of the marginal productivity of the capital relative to the variables $(\widehat{A}_t, \widehat{k}_t, \widehat{H}_t)$, taken at the steady state:

$$\begin{aligned}\eta_A &= \frac{[\gamma_{XH} - \beta^*(1-\delta)]}{\gamma_{XH}} \\ \eta_k &= (1-\alpha)\frac{[\gamma_{XH} - \beta^*(1-\delta)]}{\gamma_{XH}} \\ \eta_H &= (1-\alpha)\frac{[\gamma_{XH} - \beta^*(1-\delta)]}{\gamma_{XH}}\end{aligned}$$

Log-linearization of the production function and the resource constraint leads to:

$$\widehat{y}_t = \widehat{A}_t + \alpha\widehat{k}_t + (1-\alpha)\widehat{H}_t \tag{1.9}$$

$$\widehat{y}_t = s_c\widehat{c}_t + \phi s_i\widehat{k}_{t+1} - (\phi-1)s_i\widehat{k}_t \tag{1.10}$$

where s_c and s_i represent the relative shares of consumption and investment to total output:

$$\begin{aligned}s_i &= \frac{(\gamma_{XH} - (1-\delta))\beta^*\alpha}{\gamma_{XH} - \beta^*(1-\delta)} \\ s_c &= 1 - s_i\end{aligned}$$

and $\phi = \gamma_{XH}/[\gamma_{XH} - (1-\delta)] > 1$. It is then easy to compute labor productivity $\widehat{p}$, investment $\widehat{i}$ and the real interest rate $\widehat{r}$.

$$\widehat{p}_t = \widehat{y}_t - \widehat{H}_t = \widehat{A}_t + \alpha\widehat{k}_t - \alpha\widehat{H}_t \tag{1.11}$$

$$\widehat{i}_t = \frac{1}{s_i}\widehat{y}_t - \frac{s_c}{s_i}\widehat{c}_t \tag{1.12}$$

Let be z_t the capital marginal productivity:

$$\widehat{z}_t = \widehat{y}_t - \widehat{k}_t = \widehat{A}_t + (\alpha-1)\widehat{k}_t + (1-\alpha)\widehat{H}_t \tag{1.13}$$

So,

$$\widehat{r}_t = \frac{z}{z-\delta}\widehat{z}_t \tag{1.14}$$

The equations constitute a system of linear difference equations of order one. The appendix shows that this problem is analogous to Blanchard and Kahn [1980]. Finally, it is possible to give the evolution of the capital according to its own past and the exogenous shock:

$$\begin{pmatrix}\widehat{k}_{t+1} \\ \widehat{A}_{t+1}\end{pmatrix} = \begin{pmatrix}\mu_1 & \pi_{kA} \\ 0 & \rho_A\end{pmatrix}\begin{pmatrix}\widehat{k}_t \\ \widehat{A}_t\end{pmatrix} + \begin{pmatrix}0 \\ \epsilon_{A,t+1}\end{pmatrix}$$

which can be noted as:

$$\widehat{s}_{t+1} = M\widehat{s}_t + \epsilon_{t+1} \tag{1.15}$$

$\widehat{d}_t$ is the vector of the deviations of consumptions, hours worked, output, investment, labor productivity, and real interest rate:

$$\widehat{d}_t = \Pi\widehat{s}_t \tag{1.16}$$

with

$$\Pi = \begin{pmatrix} \Pi_{ck} & \Pi_{cA} \\ \Pi_{Hk} & \Pi_{HA} \\ \Pi_{yk} & \Pi_{yA} \\ \Pi_{ik} & \Pi_{iA} \\ \Pi_{pk} & \Pi_{pA} \\ \Pi_{rk} & \Pi_{rA} \end{pmatrix}$$

The equations (1.15) and (1.16) represent the state-space form of the model. The matrices Π and M depend on the parameters specifying utility and production functions. These two equations allow to compute the cyclical properties of the model.

1.1.3 The Economic Mechanisms at the Heart of *RBC* Models

At each period, the agents determine their optimal decisions according to the value of the endogenous and exogenous state variables: the matrix Π contains these decision rules. When the model is submitted to a shock ε_A at period t, one can distinguish two propagation channels of this shock on the variables: a direct effect measured by the second column of the matrix Π and an indirect effect due to the deviation of capital from its stationary value, measured by the first column of Π. The dynamic properties of the model result then on the one hand from the specific effect of the shock, in particular on investment and so on capital at the next period, and on the other hand from the responses of the variables when capital is not at its steady state level.

The sensibility of the coefficients of M and of Π to the deep parameters of the model can reveal quantitatively the economic mechanisms at the heart of the *RBC* models. This numerical analysis implies to calibrate the model. The benchmark calibration[6] is reported in the table 1.1. The specification retained corresponds to the case $\sigma = 1$ among the class of admissible utility functions: the cross elasticity ζ_{cl} is then equal to zero.

Table 1.1: Benchmark Calibration

ζ_{cc}	ζ_{ll}	H	α	δ	β^*	γ_{XH}	ρ_A	σ_A
-1	-1	.2	.42	.025	.988	1.004	.95	.9

The Optimal Responses to a Deviation of Capital from the Steady State

Let us consider an initial positive deviation of capital in an economy without stochastic shocks. The dynamics considered here is given by:

$$\widehat{k}_{t+1} = \mu_1 \widehat{k}_t$$

and one considers only the first column of the matrix Π:

$$\Pi = \begin{pmatrix} \Pi_{ck} \\ \Pi_{Hk} \\ \Pi_{yk} \\ \Pi_{ik} \\ \Pi_{pk} \\ \Pi_{rk} \end{pmatrix}$$

The coefficients of Π can be interpreted as the instantaneous elasticities of model's variables relative to capital deviations from steady state. The dynamics of the economy will converge slowly towards the steady state when μ_1 is close to 1. The benchmark calibration leads to the values presented in table 1.2.

When the capital stock is initially above its steady state level, the financial income of the household is high, the marginal labor productivity is high, while the marginal capital productivity is low. The first and

[6]This calibration is a benchmark one that has been chosen for a sensibility analysis. We come further to the problem of country-specific calibration.

Table 1.2: Elasticities $\Pi_{.k}$ (Benchmark Calibration)

μ_1	Π_{ck}	Π_{Hk}	Π_{yk}	Π_{ik}	Π_{pk}	Π_{rk}
.953	.617	-.294	.249	-.629	.544	-.715

the third factor imply a transitory decrease of worked hours by a wealth effect and an intertemporal substitution effect. The second factor plays in the opposite direction due to a trade-off between leisure and consumption. For the chosen specification, the first two effects dominate. The response of output results from the interaction between the response of hours and the deviation of the capital stock. The responses of consumption and investment are due to the effect of the capital stock deviation: the positive wealth effect decreases the value of consumption in the future, so investment is below its steady state level. Intertemporal substitution mechanisms reinforce this effect. The dynamics of consumption can be explained by taking into account the dynamics of interest rate. Interest rate is instantaneously below its steady state level and then increases to its stationary value. The consumption path displays an opposite shape. All these responses are reported in the figures 1.1 et 1.2.

As these responses result from the resolution of the model, they depend on the parameters which specify the preferences and the production, and more particularly on the intertemporal substitution elasticity of leisure, which is given by:

$$\epsilon_l = \frac{\zeta_{cc}}{\zeta_{cc}\zeta_{ll} - \zeta_{cl}\zeta_{lc}}$$

These ζ parameters correspond to the different elasticities of the marginal utility. The intertemporal substitution elasticity of labor can be deduced from the following equality:

$$\epsilon_n = -\frac{1 - H_t}{H_t}\epsilon_l \tag{1.17}$$

Let us consider different values for this intertemporal substitution elasticity of labor: this allows to shed light on both the effect of intertempo-

Figure 1.1: Transitory Dynamics (Shock of 1% on Capital)

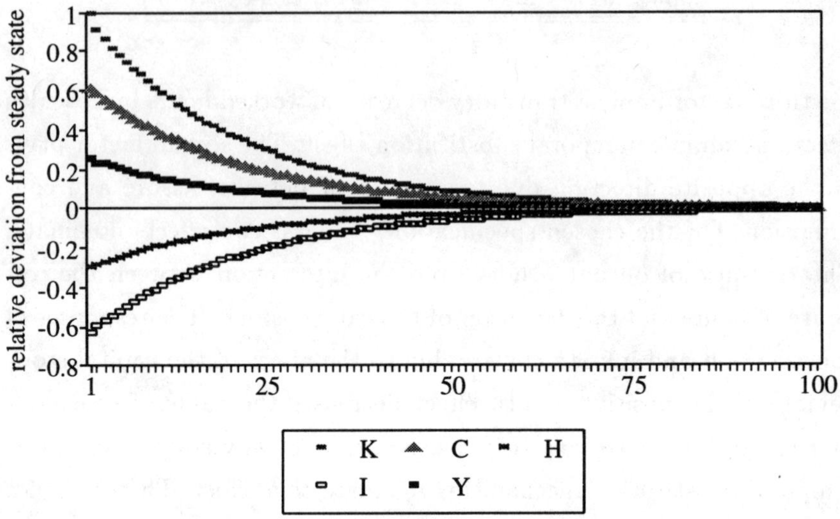

Figure 1.2: Transitory Dynamics (Shock of 1% on Capital)

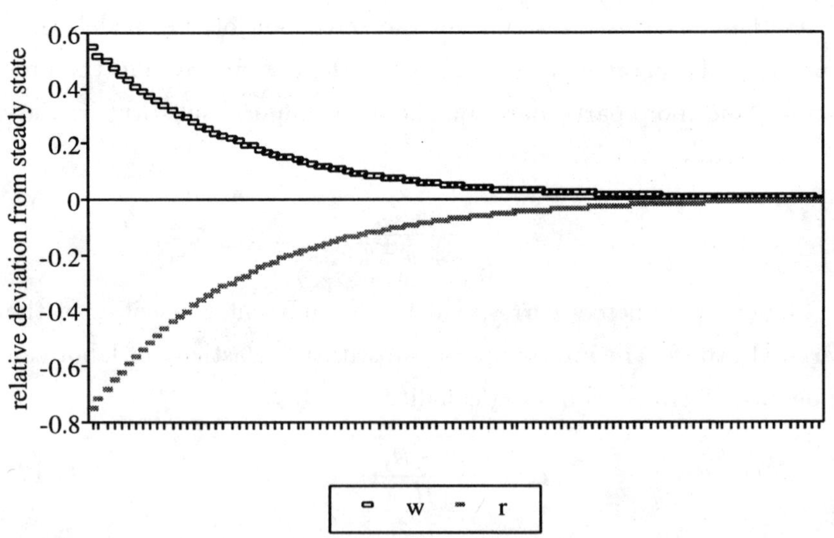

ral substitution and the sensibility of the transitory dynamics to this parameter (table 1.3).

Table 1.3: Sensibility of $\Pi_{.k}$ Elasticities to ϵ_n

ϵ_n	.04	.1	.4	2	10	∞
μ_1	.966	.965	.963	.956	.950	.947
Π_{ck}	.667	.664	.654	.627	.606	.598
Π_{Hk}	-.009	-.023	-.080	-.225	-.359	-.424
Π_{yk}	.414	.406	.374	.289	.212	.174
Π_{ik}	-.189	-.210	-.296	-.519	-.732	-.838
Π_{pk}	.424	.430	.454	.514	.571	.598
Π_{rk}	-.565	-.572	-.603	-.680	-.749	-.782

To increase the intertemporal substitution elasticity has for consequence to reinforce the effect of intertemporal substitution. When capital is above its stationary level, the negative response of hours is stronger. Therefore, the response of output decreases and the adjustment speed is higher.

The Instantaneous Responses to a Productivity Shock

Let us consider a positive 1% deviation of $\widehat{A}$ from its steady state level. Such a shock leads to the instantaneous responses described in the second column of the matrix Π:

$$\widehat{k}_{t+1} = \Pi_{kA}\widehat{A}_t$$

$$\Pi = \begin{pmatrix} \Pi_{cA} \\ \Pi_{HA} \\ \Pi_{yA} \\ \Pi_{iA} \\ \Pi_{pA} \\ \Pi_{rA} \end{pmatrix}$$

Following a purely transitory productivity shock, the household could totally consume this increase of output at the first period without changing its investment or its labor supply. In such a case, the shock will induce no persistent effect as capital will at its stationary value. However, the household may decide to invest a part of this output increase, and then to consume more in the future. Such a behavior relies on the agent's desire to smooth its consumption. The technological shock induces then two opposite effects on the intertemporal trade-off: a wealth effect that reduces worked hours and investment and an intertemporal substitution effect that induces an opposite behavior. Moreover, the agent increases its labor supply as the result of a trade-off between current consumption and current leisure.

Being given our model calibration, the responses of hours and investment are strongly positive. The benchmark calibration leads to the values reported in the table 1.4.

Table 1.4: Elasticities $\Pi_{.A}$ (Benchmark Calibration)

Π_{cA}	Π_{HA}	Π_{yA}	Π_{iA}	Π_{pA}	Π_{rA}
.398	.898	1.52	4.19	.622	1.35

The positive correlations between variables result then from their common response to the technological shock.

The influence of the intertemporal substitution can be underlined by studying the sensitivity of the responses to the productivity shock with respect to the value of the intertemporal substitution elasticity of labor.

Table 1.5: Sensitivity of $\Pi_{.A}$ Elasticities to ϵ_n

ϵ_n	.04	.1	.4	2	10	∞
Π_{cA}	.302	.306	.326	.375	.418	.439
Π_{HA}	.037	.067	.230	.678	1.18	1.33
Π_{yA}	1.01	1.04	1.33	1.39	1.64	1.77
Π_{iA}	2.71	2.78	3.05	3.81	4.57	4.95
Π_{pA}	.988	.972	.90	.714	.511	.439
Π_{rA}	.919	.939	1.02	1.245	1.46	1.56

When the intertemporal substitution elasticity of labor increases, the response of hours to productivity shock is higher, as the response of output, consumption and investment. At the opposite, the response of the marginal productivity of labor decreases.

One may study the effect of the degree of autocorrelation of the productivity shock (table 1.6).

Table 1.6: Sensitivity of $\Pi_{.A}$ Elasticities to ρ_A

ρ_A	0	.1	.25	.50	.75
Π_{cA}	.107	.110	.117	.137	.189
Π_{HA}	1.33	1.32	1.31	1.28	1.20
Π_{yA}	1.77	1.76	1.76	1.74	1.70
Π_{iA}	5.73	5.72	5.68	5.57	5.30
Π_{pA}	.440	.442	.447	.459	.492
Π_{rA}	-.124	.052	.317	.752	1.16

The more persistent the shocks are, the higher is the wealth effect, while the intertemporal substitution effect is weaker: the responses of hours and investment are then weaker too.

The Dynamics Generated by a Productivity Shock

The dynamics induced by a productivity shock results from the optimal responses both to the shock and to the deviation of the capital stock relative to its stationary level. The dynamics is then given by the following equations:

$$\begin{aligned}\widehat{k}_{t+1} &= \Pi_{kA}\widehat{A}_t + \mu_1\widehat{k}_t \\ \widehat{A}_{t+1} &= \rho_A\widehat{A}_t\end{aligned}$$

and the responses of the other variables are computed from equation (1.16).

Responses of the different variables, for the benchmark calibration, are displayed on figures 1.3 and 1.4. Following a technological shock, all the variables first increase, and then converge after 100 periods to their stationary level.

The high level of the autocorrelation coefficient ρ_A explains that, during the first periods, these dynamics are close to the instantaneous responses to the productivity shock. At longer horizons, the difference of behavior in the transitory dynamics explains the particular shape of labor, interest rate and investment.

Figure 1.3: Responses to a Technological Shock (Shock of 1%)

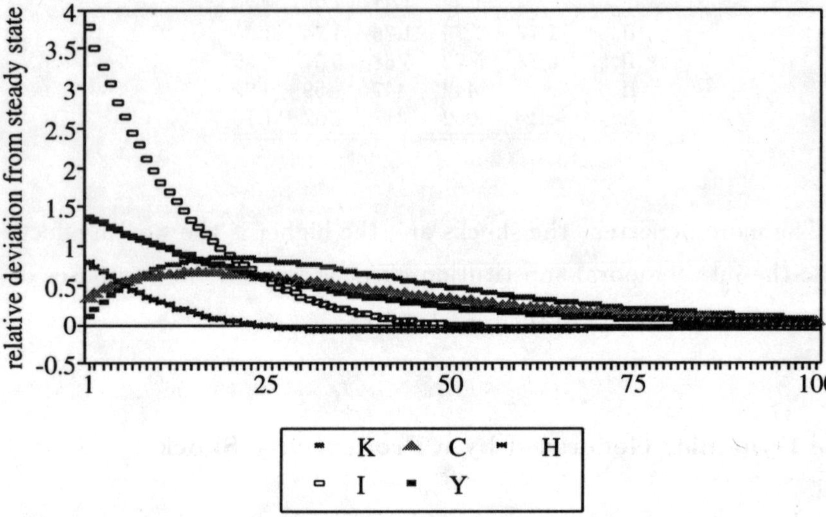

Figure 1.4: Responses to a Technological Shock (Shock of 1%)

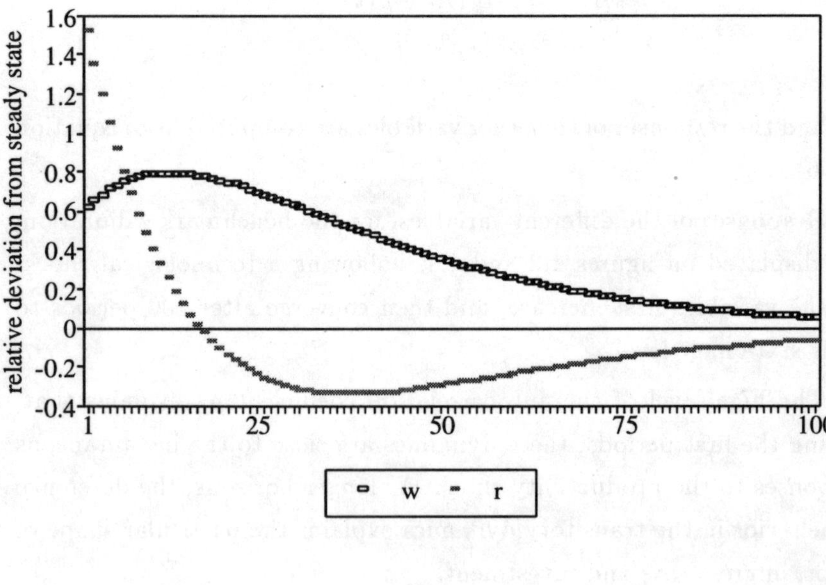

1.2 The Evaluation of *RBC* Approach

The *RBC* approach has innovated by the validation method retained: the comparison of moments generated by the model with the observed ones.

The resolution method gives us the theoretical moments of relative deviations from the steady-state and the impulse responses functions to one shock.

The model response at period $t+j$ to one shock ε at period $t+1$ on k, A and g is given by

$$\widehat{s}_{t+j} - E_t(\widehat{s}_{t+j}) = M^{j-1}\varepsilon_{t+1} \tag{1.18}$$

$$\widehat{d}_{t+j} - E_t(\widehat{d}_{t+j}) = \Pi M^{j-1}\varepsilon_{t+1} \tag{1.19}$$

Furthermore, with $\Sigma_{\widehat{s}\widehat{s}} = E(\widehat{s}_t\widehat{s}_t')$ the covariance matrix of $\widehat{s}$ (this matrix is computed from equation (1.16)), the order j autocovariance matrix of $\widehat{d}$ is given by:

$$E(\widehat{d}_t\widehat{d}_{t+j}') = \Pi M^j \Sigma_{\widehat{s}\widehat{s}}\Pi'$$

King, Plosser and Rebelo [1988] compare these moments to the ones of actual series, which are assumed Trend-Stationary. These trend-stationarized moments have no particular economic meaning with respect to the business cycle literature[7]. By *Business Cycle*, one must understand high-frequency movements of macroeconomic series. King and Rebelo [1993] have shown that the Hodrick-Prescott filter eliminates all low-frequency cycles in a series (more than five years), and can therefore gives a measure to the Business Cycle. Hodrick and Prescott [1980] solve the problem of the decomposition of a series x_t between a trend component τ_t and a cycle component c_t by using a smoothing algorithm:

$$\min_{\tau_t} \sum_{t=1}^{T} c_t^2 + \lambda \sum_{t=2}^{T-1} [d\tau_t - d\tau_{t-1}]^2$$

where $c_t = x_t - \tau_t$. The case $\lambda = \infty$ corresponds to a linear trend component. On the opposite, low values of λ give to this component

[7] The business cycle is not here the stationary component of a series, in a statistical sense.

the majority of the variance of the series. Our aim is therefore to extract from the model the moments of the Hodrick-Prescott cyclical components of the variables.

To do so, we simulate the model with samples of technological and monetary innovations, compute the macro series and filter them with the HP filter.

We draw for each simulation 124 [8] ε_A from a pseudo-random number generator, with respect to a normal distribution with zero mean, and where the variances are the one estimated over the period. With these shocks, we compute series of 124 relative deviations from the steady-state path $\widehat{x}$ for each x variable of the model. From the initial value K_0, we build for each x variable the level series x^T. This variable grows at rate γ except for hours (rate 0). Raw series x^B (trend+cycle) are therefore given by:

$$x_t^B = x_t^T(1 + \widehat{x}_t)$$

for $t = 1, 124$. These raw series are logged and filtered with Hodrick-Prescott to compute a trend x^{HP}. The filtered cycle is then given by:

$$\widehat{x}^{HP} = x_t^B - x_t^{HP}$$

This is done for each x variable and for 100 different pseudo-samples of ε_A. Order two moments of the HP cycle (variances, covariances, autocorrelations and cross-correlations) are given as the empirical mean over the 100 simulations.

1.2.1 The Stylized Facts of the French and US Fluctuations

The cyclical components of actual series are computed with $\lambda = 1600$ for the Hodrick-Prescott filter. The series are taken from the INSEE TRAC database for France and the Citibase for the United States.

In the United States, the variability of consumption appears weaker than output and investment ones. The variability of worked hours is similar to the output one and greater than labor productivity one.

[8]This is the length of the actual data.

Table 1.7: Cyclical Properties on U.S. Data (1959-1990)

Variable	$\widehat{y}$	$\widehat{c}$	$\widehat{i}$	$\widehat{h}$	$\widehat{p}$
S.D.	1.76	1.28	8.47	1.42	.89
S.D./S.D.($\widehat{y}$)	1	.72	4.81	.80	.50
Autocor. order 1	.85	.86	.81	.84	.52
Cor. with $\widehat{y}$	1	.81	.90	.86	.59
Cor. with $\widehat{H}$					.10

The procyclicality of the variables appears clearly, the correlation of labor productivity being the weakest. Moreover, the correlation between labor and its productivity is close to 0. Persistence, measured by autocorrelation of order 1, is rather high, except for labor productivity.

Table 1.8: Cyclical Properties on French Data (1970-1990)

Variable	$\widehat{y}$	$\widehat{c}$	$\widehat{i}$	$\widehat{h}$	$\widehat{p}$
S.D.	.91	.81	3.64	.83	.65
S.D./S.D.($\widehat{y}$)	1	.9	4.01	.92	.72
Autocor. order 1	.76	.67	.82	.89	.63
Cor. with $\widehat{y}$	1	.63	.80	.71	.45
Cor. with $\widehat{h}$					-.35

One finds the same relative variability of the aggregate demand components on French data, as for most of the industrialized countries[9]. However, the correlations with output and the autocorrelations are weaker than in the U.S. Moreover, the correlation between hours and productivity is negative on French data. Danthine and Donaldson [1991] underline the potential influence of differentiated institutional aspects on the cyclical features of different countries, specially for the labor market.

One may note that the standard-deviation of output is about .90%, weaker than in the United States. This low relative volatility of France with respect to the U.S. is true for all variables.

[9]See Danthine and Donaldson [1991].

1.2.2 Calibration

The calibration lies on independent informations of the cyclical features which are analyzed: parameters estimated on panel data and ratios computed from National Accounts. In particular, the intertemporal substitution elasticity of leisure is taken from Pencavel [1986]. The parameters of the autoregressive process followed by the exogenous shock are obtained by estimating an AR(1) on the Solow residual.

Table 1.9: Calibration on US Economy

H	ζ_{cc}	ζ_{ll}	α	δ	β^*	γ_{XH}	ρ_A	σ_A
.2	-1	-10	.42	.025	.988	1.004	.95	.9

The values reported in the table 1.9 are the ones chosen by King, Plosser and Rebelo [1988], except ρ and σ_A which are estimated. The values related to the technological shock are similar to KPR's ones, although the standard-deviation of the technological innovation is higher than the one generally retained for the United States.

Table 1.10: Calibration on French Economy

N	ζ_{cc}	ζ_{ll}	α	δ	β^*	γ_{XH}	ρ_A	σ_{ϵ_A}
.2	-1	-5	.46	.0125	.99	1.0067	.98	.9

The calibration on French economy (table 1.10) is based on the recent works of Laffargue, Malgrange and Pujol [1990] and Letournel and Schubert [1991], however, in a different framework. The third value in table 1.10 corresponds to an intertemporal substitution elasticity of labor of 0.8, which is a mean value. We retain a value of .2 for the mean value of hours for the period considered here. The share of wages is equal to 54% (see Laffargue, Malgrange and Pujol [1990]). The rate of capital depreciation is set to 5% per year, the rate of growth at 1.067 (*cf.* Laffargue, Malgrange and Pujol [1990]), the discount factor at .99 which corresponds to a quarterly value of 1% for the interest rate.

1.2.3 Cyclical Properties of the Model

The model allows to reproduce the relative variability of consumption, income, and investment: the volatility of these variables are correctly ranked. An intertemporal substitution mechanism explains the smoothness of consumption. Moreover, the sign of the cross correlations with output well mimics the data. The dynamics of the technological shocks explains such positive correlations. The persistence in the cyclical dynamics is mainly the consequence of the high autocorrelation coefficient ρ_A of the exogenous shock.

Table 1.11: King-Plosser-Rebelo Model Calibrated on the United States

Variable	$\widehat{y}$	$\widehat{c}$	$\widehat{i}$	$\widehat{h}$	$\widehat{p}$
S.D.	1.29	.43	3.50	.26	1.03
S.D./S.D.($\widehat{y}$)	1	.33	2.71	.20	.80
Autocor. order 1	.69	.78	.68	.68	.70
Cor. with $\widehat{y}$	1	.90	.99	.97	.99
Cor. with $\widehat{h}$					.96

Table 1.12: King-Plosser-Rebelo Model Calibrated on France

Variable	$\widehat{y}$	$\widehat{c}$	$\widehat{i}$	$\widehat{h}$	$\widehat{p}$
S.D.	1.42	.48	3.71	.43	.99
S.D./S.D.($\widehat{y}$)	1	.33	2.60	.30	.69
Autocor. order 1	.68	.72	.67	.67	.69
Cor. with $\widehat{y}$	1	.95	.99	.98	.99
Cor. with $\widehat{h}$					.97

At the opposite, the neoclassical growth model fails to reproduce some key features of the business cycle. The relative volatility of consumption and investment are too weak. Moreover, the cross-correlation coefficient are too high, while autocorrelations coefficient are too low.

For the United States, the canonical model does not generate enough volatility. This statement is reversed for the French case. However, the limits of this canonical model are to be found on the labor market:

The Problem of the Relative Volatility of Labor and its Productivity

The first limit is the relative volatility between hours and labor productivity. The introduction of labor indivisibility in the lines of Hansen [1985] and Rogerson [1988] allows to reproduce the observed features.

It is assumed in *RBC* models that the sub-utility of leisure $v(L_t)$ is concave, with a constant elasticity of its derivative:

$$\frac{L_t v"(L_t)}{v'(L_t)} = \zeta_{ll} \quad \forall L_t \tag{1.20}$$

This elasticity ζ_{ll} is the inverse of the intertemporal elasticity of substitution of leisure, which happens to be determinant in the cyclical behavior of the model. Let ϵ_l be the intertemporal elasticity of substitution of labor, one have:

$$\epsilon_L = -\left(\frac{L_t}{1-L_t}\right)\frac{1}{\zeta}$$

Following Hansen [1985] and Rogerson [1988], one can assume that jobs are indivisible in our economy: each household works H_0 hours or does not work. This is linked to the fact that a large part of worked hours fluctuations are in the extensive margin (jobs fluctuations) and not in the intensive one (fluctuations in the average hour length of a job). Under this assumption, the household problem is convexified using Rogerson [1988] lotteries. We assume that each household sells at each period a contract, specifying that he will work H_0 with probability $\pi_{i,t}$ and 0 with probability 1-$\pi_{i,t}$. Its wage is given by the price of this contract; whether it works or not, it will get that wage. As households are identical, they all choose the same $\pi_{i,t} = \pi_t$ and only π_t% of them will work; 1-π_t is then the unemployment rate of the economy.

One can easily show that, at the symmetrical equilibrium, the representative agent utility function is linear in labor, and that the elasticity of the marginal disutility of labor ζ is null, which means that the intertemporal elasticity of substitution of leisure is infinite.

The average level of worked hours is therefore given by

$$H_{i,t} = \pi_t H_0$$

and the expected utility of the representative household at period t can be written:

$$\begin{aligned} U(C_t, H_t) &= \log(C_t) + \pi_t A_l \log(1 - H_0) + (1 - \pi_t) A_l \log(1) \\ &= \log(C_t) - B H_t \end{aligned} \tag{1.21}$$

with

$$B = -\frac{A_l \log(1 - H_0)}{H_0}$$

An important feature of this model lies on the difference between the intertemporal substitution elasticity of leisure at the individual level (finite) and at the aggregate one (infinite). With this hypothesis, the neoclassical growth model reproduces better the observed variability of productivity and hours. Indeed, the increase of the intertemporal substitution elasticity of labor induces a higher (weaker) response of hours (productivity) to a technological shock[10].

Table 1.13: Model with Labor Indivisibility Calibrated on the United States

Variable	$\widehat{y}$	$\widehat{c}$	$\widehat{i}$	$\widehat{h}$	$\widehat{p}$
S.D.	2.11	.64	5.93	1.59	.64
S.D./S.D.($\widehat{y}$)	1	.30	2.81	.75	.30
Autocor. order 1	.70	.80	.69	.69	.80
Cor. with $\widehat{y}$	1	.86	.98	.98	.86
Cor. with $\widehat{h}$					.74

Table 1.14: Model with Labor Indivisibility Calibrated on France

Variable	$\widehat{y}$	$\widehat{c}$	$\widehat{i}$	$\widehat{h}$	$\widehat{p}$
S.D.	1.85	.57	5.00	1.32	.57
S.D./S.D.($\widehat{y}$)	1	.30	2.69	.71	.30
Autocor. order 1	.68	.73	.67	.67	.73
Cor. with $\widehat{y}$	1	.93	.99	.98	.93
Cor. with $\widehat{h}$					.87

With labor indivisibility, there is still a difference between France and the United States in reproducing the variability of the business

[10]See the table 1.5.

cycle . In the former the volatility of the model is too high when the shock is calibrated according to the estimation. We then try to set the variance of $\widehat{A}$ in order to reproduce the variance of output[11].

Table 1.15: Model with Labor Indivisibility Calibrated on France (Process of $\widehat{A}$ "Fixed")

Variable	$\widehat{y}$	$\widehat{c}$	$\widehat{i}$	$\widehat{h}$	$\widehat{p}$
S.D.	.95	.34	3.37	.64	.34
S.D./S.D.($\widehat{y}$)	1	.35	3.54	.67	.36
Autocor. order 1	.70	.75	.69	.69	.75
Cor. with $\widehat{y}$	1	.94	.99	.98	.94
Cor. with $\widehat{h}$					.85

With a standard-deviation of $\widehat{A}$ reduced of one half, the model is more accurate. However, nothing in the specification allows to reduce this variance, as for instance imperfect competition or labor hoarding hypothesis.

The Problem of the Correlation Between Hours and Productivity

The correlation between hours and productivity generated by the model is highly positive, in so far as the adjustment in the labor market after a technological shock corresponds to a shift of the demand curve along the supply curve. However, this correlation is null and negative respectively in the United States and in France. This limit is then due to the uniqueness and to the nature of the perturbation in the *RBC* approach: a shock on the total factor productivity.

The Real Wage Behavior

An other limit relative to the labor market, generally forgotten in this literature[12], is the identity between the real wage and the marginal productivity of labor: the cyclical behavior of the average productivity

[11] We keep the value of ρ and modify σ_{ϵ_A}.

[12] Except Christiano and Eichenbaum [1988].

$\widehat{p}$ and of the real wage $\widehat{w}$ are then the same in the model. However, the observation is in contradiction with this feature (table 1.16).

Table 1.16: Behaviour of the Real Wage

Correlations with $\widehat{w}$	$\widehat{h}$	$\widehat{p}$
United States	.20	.35
France	-.37	.43

An interesting correlation is the one relative to the interrelation between real wage and labor. It is an old debate in applied macroeconomics since the works of Dunlop [1938] and Tarshis [1939]. As the *RBC* approach retains only productivity shocks, the correlation generated is highly positive, while it is weakly positive in the United States and negative in France (table 1.16).

Finally, the simulation of the King, Plosser and Rebelo [1988] model and of the Hansen [1985] model underlines the difficulties of the *RBC* approach to generate cyclical properties in conformity with the observed dynamics in the labor market. Calibrating the model on the French economy reinforces this statement.

1.3 Concluding Comments

The objective of this chapter was not to present a survey on the *RBC* literature. It was rather to present the methods and the main problems of the *RBC* approach in the canonical framework of King, Plosser and Rebelo [1988]. It is then not surprising that the extensions of the *RBC* approach are now numerous in order to eliminate the limits of the neoclassical growth model. It appears finally that the remaining message of the *RBC* approach is the methodological one suggested by Lucas: to build fully articulated artificial economy which behaves through time so as to imitate closely the time series behavior of actual economics.

1.4 Appendix : Solving the Linear System

Equations (1.6) and (1.7) give the controls $\widehat{c}_t$ and $\widehat{H}_t$ as a function of the state variables $\widehat{k}_t$ and $\widehat{A}_t$, and of the co-state variable $\widehat{\lambda}_t$. In matricial form, this sub-system can be written:

$$M_1 \begin{pmatrix} \widehat{c}_t \\ \widehat{H}_t \end{pmatrix} = M_2 \begin{pmatrix} \widehat{k}_t \\ \widehat{\lambda}_t \end{pmatrix} + M_3 \widehat{A}_t \tag{1.22}$$

Equations (1.8) and (1.10) describe the state $\widehat{k}_t$ and co-state $\widehat{\lambda}_t$ variables evolution as a function of the control and exogenous state variables $\widehat{A}_t$ (after elimination of $\widehat{y}_t$ by substitution of (1.9) into (1.10)):

$$E_t M_4(L) \begin{pmatrix} \widehat{k}_{t+1} \\ \widehat{\lambda}_{t+1} \end{pmatrix} = E_t M_5(L) \begin{pmatrix} \widehat{c}_{t+1} \\ \widehat{H}_{t+1} \end{pmatrix} + E_t M_6(L) \widehat{A}_{t+1} \tag{1.23}$$

where the matrices M_1, M_2, M_3 have real coefficients, and where $M_4(L)$, $M_5(L)$, $M_6(L)$ are polynomial matrices of order one and with real coefficients.

It is possible to write the evolution of state and co-state variables as a function of their own past and of the exogenous state variable by sustituting (1.22) in (1.23). The system can be then written as:

$$\begin{pmatrix} \widehat{c}_{t+1} \\ \widehat{H}_{t+1} \end{pmatrix} = M_1^{-1} M_2 \begin{pmatrix} \widehat{k}_{t+1} \\ \widehat{\lambda}_{t+1} \end{pmatrix} + M_1^{-1} M_3 \quad \widehat{A}_{t+1}$$

and

$$\begin{pmatrix} \widehat{k}_{t+1} \\ E_t \widehat{\lambda}_{t+1} \end{pmatrix} = W \begin{pmatrix} \widehat{k}_t \\ \widehat{\lambda}_t \end{pmatrix} + R E_t \widehat{A}_{t+1} + Q \widehat{A}_t \tag{1.24}$$

where

$$\begin{aligned} W &= [M_4(0) - M_5(0) M_1^{-1} M_2]^{-1} [M_5(1) M_1^{-1} M_2 - M_4(1)] \\ R &= [M_4(0) - M_5(0) M_1^{-1} M_2]^{-1} [M_5(0) M_1^{-1} M_3 + M_6(0)] \\ Q &= [M_4(0) - M_5(0) M_1^{-1} M_2]^{-1} [M_5(1) M_1^{-1} M_3 + M_6(1)] \end{aligned}$$

The resolution method of this linear system is analogous to the one proposed by Blanchard and Kahn [1980]. The existence and the uniqueness of the solution depend on position of the eigenvalues of W with respect to the unit circle. The model has a predetermined variable k and a forward one λ: there must be one eigenvalue of modulus less than one and one of modulus greater than one. The resolution lies then on the diagonalization of W. Let us call μ_1 and μ_2 the two eigenvalues of W, with $|\mu_1| < |\mu_2|$, and P the matrix of eigenvectors. A first result shows that the output of the two characteristic roots is constant[13]:

$$\mu_1 \mu_2 = \frac{1}{\beta^\star}$$

Moreover, one have [14]:

$$\mu_1 < 1 \quad \text{et} \quad \mu_2 > 1$$

It then exists a saddle path $\{\widehat{k}_t\}_{t=0}^{\infty}$, $\{\widehat{\lambda}_t\}_{t=0}^{\infty}$ solution of the problem. There will be a single choice of the initial shadow price $\widehat{\lambda}_0$ which makes the solution $\{\widehat{k}_t\}_{t=0}^{\infty}$ and $\{\widehat{\lambda}_t\}_{t=0}^{\infty}$ consistent with the transversality condition. To determine this initial value, one write the system in a diagonal form. Let us define the variables $\widetilde{k}$ et $\widetilde{\lambda}$ as:

$$\begin{pmatrix} \widetilde{k}_t \\ \widetilde{\lambda}_t \end{pmatrix} = P^{-1} \begin{pmatrix} \widehat{k}_t \\ \widehat{\lambda}_t \end{pmatrix} \tag{1.25}$$

By noting

$$P = \begin{pmatrix} P_{11} & P_{12} \\ P_{21} & P_{22} \end{pmatrix}, \; P^{-1} = \begin{pmatrix} P_{11}^\star & P_{12}^\star \\ P_{21}^\star & P_{22}^\star \end{pmatrix}, \; R = \begin{pmatrix} R_{ka} \\ R_{\lambda a} \end{pmatrix}, \; Q = \begin{pmatrix} Q_{ka} \\ Q_{\lambda a} \end{pmatrix}$$

the evolution of $\widetilde{k}$ and $\widetilde{\lambda}$ is then given by:

$$\widetilde{k}_{t+1} = \mu_1 \widetilde{k}_t + [P_{11}^\star R_{ka} + P_{12}^\star R_{\lambda a}] E_t \widehat{A}_{t+1} + [P_{11}^\star Q_{ka} + P_{12}^\star Q_{\lambda a}] \widehat{A}_t \tag{1.26}$$

$$E_t \widetilde{\lambda}_{t+1} = \mu_2 \widetilde{\lambda}_t + [P_{21}^\star R_{ka} + P_{22}^\star R_{\lambda a}] E_t \widehat{A}_{t+1} + [P_{21}^\star Q_{ka} + P_{22}^\star Q_{\lambda a}] \widehat{A}_t \tag{1.27}$$

One solves this last equation forward as $\mu_2 > 1$:

$$\widetilde{\lambda}_t = \mu_2^{-1} E_t \widetilde{\lambda}_{t+1} - \mu_2^{-1} [P_{21}^\star R_{ka} + P_{22}^\star R_{\lambda a}] E_t \widehat{A}_{t+1} - \mu_2^{-1} [P_{21}^\star Q_{ka} + P_{22}^\star Q_{\lambda a}] \widehat{A}_t$$

[13] See Fairise, Hairault, Langot and Portier [1991].

[14] See Fairise, Hairault, Langot and Portier [1991] for a proof of this proposition.

By successive substitution:

$$\begin{aligned}\widetilde{\lambda}_t &= \lim_{\tau\to+\infty}\left(-\sum_{j=0}^{\tau}\mu_2^{-j-1}[P_{21}^{\star}R_{ka}+P_{22}^{\star}R_{\lambda a}]E_t\widehat{A}_{t+j+1}\right.\\ &\left. - \sum_{j=0}^{\tau}\mu_2^{-j-1}[P_{21}^{\star}Q_{ka}+P_{22}^{\star}Q_{\lambda a}]E_t\widehat{A}_{t+j}+\mu_2^{-\tau}E_t\widetilde{\lambda}_{t+\tau}\right) \quad (1.28)\end{aligned}$$

$$\widetilde{\lambda}_t = \lim_{\tau\to\infty}\left(h_{t+\tau}+\mu_2^{-\tau}E_t\widetilde{\lambda}_{t+\tau}\right) \quad (1.29)$$

with

$$\begin{aligned}h_{t+\tau} &= -\sum_{j=0}^{\tau}\mu_2^{-j-1}[P_{21}^{\star}R_{ka}+P_{22}^{\star}R_{\lambda a}]E_t\widehat{A}_{t+j+1}\\ &- \sum_{j=0}^{\tau}\mu_2^{-j-1}[P_{21}^{\star}Q_{ka}+P_{22}^{\star}Q_{\lambda a}]E_t\widehat{A}_{t+j}\end{aligned}$$

μ_2 being of modulus greater than one, the coefficients of the matrices P, P^{-1}, R and Q being real and the process followed by A_t being stationary, $h_{t+\tau}$ converges to a finite value when τ goes to infinity. Indeed, for process of $\{\widehat{A}\}_{t=0}^{\infty}$ corresponding to ARMA models, the calculus of $\lim_{\tau\to\infty}h_{t+\tau}$ is given by Hansen and Sargent [1980]. If one considers an $AR(1)$, this limit is given by:

$$\lim_{\tau\to\infty}h_{t+\tau} = (Z_1\rho_A+Z_0)(1-\mu_2^{-1}\rho_A)^{-1}\widehat{A}_t$$

with $Z_0=\mu_2^{-1}(P_{21}^{\star}Q_{ka}+P_{22}^{\star}Q_{\lambda a})$ et $Z_1=\mu_2^{-1}(P_{21}^{\star}R_{ka}+P_{22}^{\star}R_{\lambda a})$.

$\widetilde{\lambda}_t$ will take a finite value if the limit of $\mu_2^{-\tau}E_t\widehat{\lambda}_{t+\tau}$ is finite when τ goes to infinity. By the transversality condition (1.5), one has[15]:

$$\lim_{\tau\to\infty}\mu_2^{-\tau}\widetilde{\lambda}_{t+\tau}=0$$

One may write the equation (1.28) as:

$$\widetilde{\lambda}_t = (Z_1\rho_A+Z_0)(1-\mu_2^{-1}\rho_A)^{-1}\widehat{A}_t \quad (1.30)$$

The equations (1.26) et (1.28) can be written as:

$$\begin{aligned}\begin{pmatrix}\widetilde{k}_{t+1}\\ E_t\widetilde{\lambda}_{t+1}\end{pmatrix} &= \begin{pmatrix}\mu_1 & 0\\ 0 & 0\end{pmatrix}\begin{pmatrix}\widetilde{k}_t\\ \widetilde{\lambda}_t\end{pmatrix}+\begin{pmatrix}P_{11}^{\star}R_{ka}+P_{12}^{\star}R_{\lambda a}\\ 0\end{pmatrix}E_t\widehat{A}_{t+1}\\ &+\begin{pmatrix}P_{11}^{\star}Q_{ka}+P_{12}^{\star}Q_{\lambda a}\\ 0\end{pmatrix}\widehat{A}_t+\begin{pmatrix}0\\ 1\end{pmatrix}E_t\widetilde{\lambda}_{t+1} \quad (1.31)\end{aligned}$$

[15] See Fairise, Hairault, Langot and Portier [1991] for a proof.

By multiplying this system by P, one gets the relative deviations to the steady state:

$$\begin{aligned}
\begin{pmatrix} \widehat{k}_{t+1} \\ E_t\widehat{\lambda}_{t+1} \end{pmatrix} &= \begin{pmatrix} P_{11}\mu_1 P^\star_{11} & P_{11}\mu_1 P^\star_{12} \\ P_{21}\mu_1 P^\star_{11} & P_{21}\mu_1 P^\star_{12} \end{pmatrix} \begin{pmatrix} \widehat{k}_t \\ \widehat{\lambda}_t \end{pmatrix} \\
&+ \begin{pmatrix} P_{11}(P^\star_{11}R_{ka} + P^\star_{12}R_{\lambda a}) \\ P_{21}(P^\star_{11}R_{ka} + P^\star_{12}R_{\lambda a}) \end{pmatrix} E_t\widehat{A}_{t+1} \qquad (1.32) \\
&+ \begin{pmatrix} P_{11}(P^\star_{11}Q_{ka} + P^\star_{12}Q_{\lambda a}) \\ P_{21}(P^\star_{11}Q_{ka} + P^\star_{12}Q_{\lambda a}) \end{pmatrix} \widehat{A}_t + \begin{pmatrix} P_{12} \\ P_{22} \end{pmatrix} E_t\widetilde{\lambda}_{t+1}
\end{aligned}$$

By introducing the equations (1.25) and (1.27) in the system, one obtains the evolution equation of $\widehat{k}_t$:

$$\widehat{k}_{t+1} = P_{11}\mu_1 P^{-1}_{11}\widehat{k}_t + (P_{11}\mu_1 P^\star_{12} + P_{12}\mu_2 P^\star_{22})P^{\star-1}_{22}\widetilde{\lambda}_t + R_{ka}E_t\widehat{A}_{t+1} + Q_{ka}\widehat{A}_t$$

By using this last equation and by substituting $\widetilde{\lambda}_t$ by its value given in equation (1.30), it is possible to give the capital evolution as a function of its own past and of the exogenous shock:

$$\begin{pmatrix} \widehat{k}_{t+1} \\ \widehat{A}_{t+1} \end{pmatrix} = \begin{pmatrix} \mu_1 & \pi_{kA} \\ 0 & \rho_A \end{pmatrix} \begin{pmatrix} \widehat{k}_t \\ \widehat{A}_t \end{pmatrix} + \begin{pmatrix} 0 \\ \epsilon_{A,t+1} \end{pmatrix}$$

which can be noted as:

$$\widehat{s}_{t+1} = M\widehat{s}_t + \epsilon_{t+1}$$

$\widehat{d}_t$ being the vector of deviations of consumptions, hours worked, output, investment, labor productivity, and real interest rate, one can write the evolution of these last ones in the following way, from the equations (1.6), (1.7), (1.9), (1.11), (1.12) et (1.14):

$$\widehat{d}_t = \Pi\widehat{s}_t$$

Bibliography

O. Blanchard and C. Kahn. The Solution of Linear Difference Models under Rational Expectations. *Econometrica*, 48(5):1305–1311, July 1980.

L. Christiano and M. Eichenbaum. *Is Theory Really Ahead of Measurement? Current Real Business Cycle Theory and Aggregate Market Fluctuations.* Working paper 2700, NBER, 1988.

J.P. Danthine and J. Donaldson. *Methodological and Empirical Issues in Real Business Cycle Theory.* Cahiers de Recherche Économique 9102, Université de Lausanne, 1991.

J. Dunlop. The Movements of Real and Money Wages Rates. *Economic Journal*, 48:413–434, September 1938.

X. Fairise, J.O. Hairault, F. Langot and F. Portier. *Ecriture et résolution du modèle canonique des cycles réels.* Cahiers ECO & MATHS 92.30, MAD, Université de Paris I, 1991.

L. Hansen and T. Sargent. Formulating and Estimating Dynamic Linear Rational Expectations Models. *Journal of Economics Dynamic and Control*, 2:7–46, February 1980.

G. Hansen. Indivisible Labor and the Business Cycles. *Journal of Monetary Economics*, 16(3):309–327, November 1985.

F. Hayek. *Monetary Theory and the Trade Cycle.* Jonathan Cape, Londres, 1933.

P.Y. Henin. *Développements de la théorie des cycles réels.* Working paper 9113, CEPREMAP, Paris, 1991.

J. Hicks. *Capital and Growth.* New York: Oxford University Press, 1965.

R. Hodrick and E. Prescott. *Post-War U.S. Business Cycles: an Empirical Investigation.* Mimeo , Carnegie-Mellon University, November 1980.

R. King and S. Rebelo. Low Frequency Filtering and the Real Business Cycles. *Journal of Economic Dynamics and Control*, 17(1/2):207–232, January-March 1993.

R. King, C. Plosser and S. Rebelo. Production, Growth and Business Cycles I. *Journal of Monetary Economics*, 21(2/3):196–232, March-May 1988.

F. Kydland and E. Prescott. Time to Build and Aggregate Fluctuations. *Econometrica*, 50(6):1345–1370, November 1982.

J.P. Laffargue, P. Malgrange and T. Pujol. *Une maquette trimestrielle de l'économie française avec anticipations rationnelles et concurrence monopolistique.* Working paper, CEPREMAP, April 1990. Rapport de contrat pour le Commissariat Général au Plan.

P.Y. Letournel and K. Schubert. *Un modèle d'équilibre général appliqué à l'étude de la fiscalité française: résultats de long terme.* Working paper, Direction de la Prévision, Paris, 1991.

J. Long and C. Plosser. Real Business Cycle. *Journal of Political Economy*, 91(1):39–69, February 1983.

R. Lucas. *Models of Business Cycles.* Basil Blackwell, Oxford, 1987.

J. Pencavel. Labor Supply of Men : a survey. In O. Ashenfelter and R. Layard, editor, *Handbook of Labor Economics*, chapter 1, pages 3–102, North-Holland, Amsterdam, 1986.

C. Plosser. Understanding Real Business Cycles. *Journal of Economic Perspectives*, 3(3):51–57, Summer 1989.

E. Prescott. Theory Ahead of Business Cycle Measurement. *Carnegie Rochester Conference Series on Public Policy*, 25:11–44, Autumn 1986.

R. Rogerson. Indivisible Labor, Lotteries and Equilibrium. *Journal of Monetary Economics*, 21(1):3–16, January 1988.

L. Tarshis. Changes in Real and Money Wages. *Economic Journal*, 49:150–154, March 1939.

Chapter 2

A RBC Model for Explaining Cyclical Labor Market Features

Xavier Fairise & François Langot

Abstract

Standard *RBC* models do not enable one to reproduce main labor market stylized facts : employment is more variable than productivity and labor productivity leads employment fluctuations. Moreover, these models rely on an exogenous Solow residual which is necessary to reproduce economic fluctuations. In order to match cyclical labor market features of French and US economies, we consider a model with indivisible labor, labor hoarding and adjustment costs. The model also explains how the naive Solow residual is affected by government spending shocks.

Introduction

Since Kydland and Prescott [1982] and Long and Plosser [1983] papers, the stochastic version of neoclassical growth model is extended in order to explain macroeconomic fluctuations. In a walrasian world, these fluctuations merely correspond to the representative agent's optimal responses to exogenous technological shocks (see chapter 1).

The first criticism addressed to this approach is the assumption of uniqueness and exogeneity of the key impulses to business cycle. *RBC* analysts use the Solow residual to measure the technological shocks, and the quantitative validation of these models depends on the variability of this shock alone[1]. Summers [1986] and Hall [1989] have shown that most movements of the Solow residual are endogenous. Hence, another class of exogenous perturbations should be identified.

The second failure of the standard *RBC* approach lies in its inability to explain the labor market stylized facts. To reproduce a greater variability for employment than for labor productivity, Hansen [1985] has built a model with indivisibility in labor. With this assumption, employment is more variable than productivity, but this model does not reproduce the other labor market stylized facts. Christiano and Eichenbaum [1992].introduced a government spending shock which reduces the instantaneous correlation between employment and labor productivity. However, the stylized facts suggest that labor productivity should be considered as an advanced indicator of employment fluctuations: this stylized fact is referred to the *labor productivity cycle*[2]. The model of Burnside, Eichenbaum and Rebelo [1993] suggests how to introduce a lag between employment and labor productivity adjustments. However their model does not reproduce the right length of the US labor productivity cycle.

The aim of this chapter is to determine the main mechanisms of the joint dynamics of employment and labor productivity.

Then, in a first step, we can remark that all *RBC* models assume that employment is a "flexible" input, contrarily to the traditional theory of labor demand:

> "The concept of labor as a quasi-fixed factor is, in my opinion, the relevant one for a short-run theory of employment."(Oi [1962], p.538)

In the same direction, the impact of the utilization rate fluctuations in the employment dynamic explanation is traditionally analyzed, contrarily to the usual practice in *RBC* literature. More precisely,

[1] See Prescott [1986] for a justification of this methodology.

[2] See Gordon [1979] or McCallum [1989] for further details or empirical supports.

> "It must be emphasized that the degree to which employees are utilized consists not only of the average number of hours worked per man, but also of the intensity and continuity of his effort"(Brechling [1965], p.188)

These first remarks suggest to introduce, in *RBC* model, labor adjustment costs and a distinction between hours, effort and number of men at work in labor input. These firsts assumptions allows us to give the traditional interpretation of the *labor hoarding* phenomenon. Nevertheless, an other assumption is usually considered in the seminal papers of short run fluctuations of employment: Brechling [1965], Kennan [1979] and Gordon [1979] assume that employment is chosen before the observation of the macroeconomic shocks realizations. With this last assumption, *labor hoarding* comes from the fact that there exist a delay between hiring and production decisions[3]

In order to evaluate the relative contribution of these different assumptions on the labor demand, we propose to introduce them in a *RBC* model. So, with labor adjustment costs, the employment decisions are smoothed over time. These inertia on the labor market can explain the length of the labor productivity cycle. Indeed, more than the instantaneous correlation between labor productivity and employment, we want to explain the correlation between labor productivity and past and advanced employment. Moreover, this labor hoarding model shows that the measurement error is pro-cyclical: the variability of the Solow residual systematically overestimates the technological shocks. Following Burnside, Eichenbaum and Rebelo [1993], by introducing a government spending shock, we show that this model can explain the correlation between the Solow residual and the government policy instruments, as it is showed in several empirical studies.

Then, we extend the standard indivisible labor model of Hansen [1985] by introducing effort in production and utility functions, as well as government spending shocks. We analyze qualitatively and quantitatively the implications of the two types of labor hoarding previously presented. Indeed, as our model encompasses the Hansen [1985], Christiano

[3]This assumption is retained by Burnside, Eichenbaum and Rebelo [1993].

and Eichenbaum [1992] and Burnside, Eichenbaum and Rebelo [1993] models, it allows us to test if the introduction of labor adjustment costs improves the performance of these *RBC* models.

Danthine and Donaldson [1993] showed how different are the stylized facts of the labor market from the USA to European countries. Then, we try to reproduce the labor market cyclical properties of US and a representative European country, France. In the two countries studied here, we can measure the amplitude of the overshooting of the naive Solow residual in response to structural shocks.

The simulation results show that the introduction of government spending shocks and labor hoarding leads the model to reproduce a productivity cycle. For the US economy, the model gives us the good length of the labor productivity cycle, with a relative variance hours/labor productivity close to one. In the case of France, the length of the labor productivity cycle needs a calibration such that the relative variance of hours and labor productivity is less than one. Then, the calibration of the adjustment cost parameter displays the limits of this model.

This chapter proceeds as follows. In a first section, we present the debate on the Solow residual and on the labor productivity cycle. Section 2 provides a description of the economy. In section 3, we discuss the solution method and the model parameterizations for the USA and France. In section 4, we analyze the impulse response functions of the model which give the dynamic properties of the model. Section 5 contains the simulation results, respectively for the US and French economies. The last section is devoted to concluding remarks.

2.1 Productivity, Labor Productivity and Business Cycle

First, we briefly review the debate about exogeneity assumption for the Solow residual. Second, we describe our strategy for mimicking the observed labor productivity cycle.

2.1.1 The Solow Residual in *RBC* Models

Traditionally, the total factor productivity is calculated by the methodology introduced by Solow [1957]: productivity is the part of the product growth unexplained by the growth of the factors. With perfect competition in all markets, constant returns to scale, and measurability of all inputs, the Solow residual is a measure of technological innovations. This technical progress is usually considered as exogenous. In the standard *RBC* models, all these assumptions are maintained, and Prescott [1986] provides support to this methodology by estimating that 75% of macroeconomic fluctuations are due to technological innovations.

Nevertheless, many empirical studies give some evidence about the endogeneity of the Solow residual on US data. Hall [1989] tests the orthogonality of the Solow residual relative to different variables. He rejects this assumption, and in particular, he shows that the Solow residual is correlated with per capita military expenditures. Evans [1992] finds that money supply and government expenditures explain a significant part of the Solow residual variance. The invariance property of the Solow residual (Hall [1989], proposition 1 p.5) is rejected by empirical tests on US data.

As we want to compare the cyclical features of the US and French economies, it seems relevant to test the exogeneity of the Solow residual on French data. We test Granger causality in a bivariate system,including government expenditures and Solow residual[4].

Granger causality test : ΔRS (France)

Variables	$F - Stat$	Signif. level
ΔG	3.2189	.0768769
ΔRS	.16092	.689469

The two series are taken in difference, and the B.I.C. statistics indicates that the optimal V.A.R. model has one lag. We accept the Gran-

[4]We use quaterly data from the I.N.S.E.E. data base. The sample of the estimation is 1970:3- 1989:4.

ger causality from the government expenditures to the Solow residual at 10%.

The results seem to be similar for the two countries: the fluctuations of the naive Solow residual are correlated with demand shocks. This result can be extended to the five majors countries of O.E.C.D. Using panel data, Langot [1992] shows that 25% of the Solow residual variance is explained by demand shocks.

Burnside, Eichenbaum and Rebelo [1993] estimate, by the Generalized Method of Moments, a *RBC* model with labor hoarding and government expenditures shocks. Their estimated variance of the real technological shock is reduced by 50% relatively to the standard *RBC* model calibrations. Their model gives an explanation of the Solow residual contamination by government spending shocks: after a government spending innovation, firms adjust labor input through effort because employment is decided before observing this shock. The effort is thus pro-cyclical, and the naive Solow residual increases in boom: the measurement error is pro-cyclical too. This gives theoretical grounds to Summers [1986]'s argument that Prescott [1986]'s measure of the Solow residual variance is overestimated. Furthermore, the estimation of Burnside, Eichenbaum and Rebelo [1993] answers to Hall [1989]'s criticism according to which the effort fluctuations cannot explain the overstated variance of the Solow residual.

Thus, our model reproduces this process of contamination of the naive Solow residual by effort.

2.1.2 Labor Productivity Cycle : a Stylized Fact

In standard *RBC* models, the hours / labor productivity correlation is strongly positive. But, the US and French stylized facts show that this correlation is close to zero or negative.

The US and French Business Cycles

Different cyclical indicators of main macroeconomic series are reported in tables (2.1) and (2.3) for the US economy and in tables (2.2) and

(2.4) for the French economy[5].

The analysis of the productivity cycle is our main purpose. Thus, we are concerned with the correlations between productivity and past, instantaneous, and advanced employment. These moments are reported in tables (2.1) and (2.2).

Table 2.1: US Productivity Employment Correlations $(\widehat{p}_t, \widehat{N}_{t+i})$

5	-4	-3	-2	-1	0	1	2	3	4	5
-0.21	-0.26	-0.17	-0.08	0.06	0.11	0.37	0.47	0.47	0.34	0.29

Table 2.2: French Productivity Employment Correlations $(\widehat{p}_t, \widehat{N}_{t+i})$

-5	-4	-3	-2	-1	0	1	2	3	4	5
-0.23	-0.34	-0.44	-0.45	-0.40	-0.30	-0.14	0.02	0.14	0.22	0.23

Our objective is to explain the observed labor productivity cycle, with a model able to reproduce the main cyclical indicators. We report in tables (2.3) and (2.4) the moments usually taken into account in the literature[6].

Table 2.3:US Economic Fluctuations

Va	*S.D.*	*S.D./S.D.*$_{\widehat{y}}$	*AR*(1)	Cross-correlations with y						
				4	2	1	0	-1	-2	-4
$\widehat{y}$	1.76	1	0.85	0.15	0.67	0.85	1	0.85	0.67	0.15
$\widehat{c}$	1.28	0.72	0.86	0.02	0.46	0.65	0.81	0.82	0.75	0.49
$\widehat{i}$	8.47	4.81	0.81	0.02	0.52	0.75	0.90	0.78	0.61	0.23
$\widehat{N}$	1.42	0.80	0.84	0.44	0.76	0.86	0.86	0.71	0.49	0.12
$\widehat{p}$	0.89	0.50	0.52	-0.20	0.09	0.31	0.59	0.55	0.52	0.25

[5] The series used are those of the CitiBase for the USA and of the Base Trimestrielle de l'I.N.S.E.E. for France. The series are logged and filtered by Hoddrick-Prescott method. Then, the moments of the observed series are calculated from these filtered series.

[6] Namely, the standard deviation of the product $\widehat{y}$, consumption $\widehat{c}$, investment $\widehat{i}$, employment $\widehat{N}$, and apparent productivity of labor $\widehat{p}$, the autocorrelations and cross-correlations with the product.

Table 2.4:French Economic Fluctuations

Va	*S.D.*	*S.D./S.D.*$_{\widehat{y}}$	*AR*(1)	Cross-correlations with *y*							
			1	4	2	1	0	-1	-2	-4	
$\widehat{y}$	0.91	1	0.76	0.11	0.54	0.76	1	0.76	0.54	0.11	
$\widehat{c}$	0.81	0.9	0.67	0.39	0.71	0.72	0.63	0.32	0.11	-0.24	
$\widehat{i}$	3.64	4.01	0.82	0.24	0.55	0.72	0.80	0.62	0.43	0.05	
$\widehat{N}$	0.83	0.92	0.89	0.01	0.34	0.54	0.71	0.73	0.68	0.43	
$\widehat{p}$	0.65	0.72	0.63	-0.38	0.30	0.34	0.45	0.1	0.14	-0.13	

Main Characteristics of Correlations and Interpretation: In the USA, the instantaneous correlations between productivity and employment are 0, or weakly positive. The lagged correlations are negative or close to 0. The advanced correlations are positive. In France, the instantaneous correlation between productivity and employment is unambiguously negative (it takes the value -0.3). All the lagged correlations are negative. The advanced correlation between productivity and employment at lead 1 is negative, -0.14, at lead 2 is 0, then these correlations are unambiguously positive.

As a whole, the past correlations are negative and the advanced correlations are positive. That is the case for the USA as well as for France. The maximum positive correlation between productivity and employment occurs at lead 2 or 3 for the USA and at lead 5 for France. The interpretation is the following : the labor productivity leads the employment cycle. The aim of this chapter is to account for this productivity cycle.

Labor Productivity Cycle and *RBC* Models

The observed labor productivity cycle is not generated by *RBC* models. The main reason for this failure is that the technological shock leads the labor demand curve to move along the labor supply curve.

To solve the puzzle of the correlation between employment and labor productivity, Christiano and Eichenbaum [1992] introduce a government expenditure shock shifting the labor demand curve. They just reduce the instantaneous correlation but their model fail to generate the labor productivity cycle observed on US data[7].

Economic theory suggests a simple explanation of the labor productivity lead on employment fluctuations. During the booms, the firms increase their output but do not have sufficiently variable input factors. The first explanation of this phenomenon is suggested by Oi [1962]: employment is a quasi-fixed factor. This can be explained by training costs traditionally modelled by labor adjustment costs. Another possibility is to suppose that the organization of the labor market requires the firm to follow a sequence of employment decisions where hirings are done before the observation of the shocks. This modification of the standard model captures the constraint for firms to choose employment with a partial information — *i.e.* before the beginning of the production — and leads to labor hoarding.

With these two labor hoarding behaviors, we can explain the advance of output on employment fluctuations and thus explain that labor productivity is a leading indicator of employment fluctuations.

In order to evaluate the relative contribution of these theoretical explanations of labor productivity cycle, we introduce in an intertemporal general equilibrium framework, government expenditures shocks, labor adjustment costs, labor utilization rate (modelled by effort) and imperfect information on labor market.

2.2 The Model

The equilibrium model considered here remains the features familiar in the *RBC* literature. More specifically it extends the the model of Burnside, Eichenbaum and Rebelo [1993] by introducing labor adjustment costs.

[7]This is showed section 2.4 of this chapter.

2.2.1 The Firms

All firms have access to the same constant returns to scale production function to produce an homogeneous good:

$$Y_t = A_t K_t^{1-\alpha} (N_t^p)^\alpha$$

where A_t, K_t and N_t^p denote respectively the level of the technology, the beginning of period capital stock and the productive employment used by firms. The productive labor input is defined as a percentage of efficient employment:

$$N_t^p = e_t N_t H \gamma_x^t (1 - \phi(Z_t))$$

where e_t is the level of effort and N_t the total number of workers, *i.e.* the total employment. Labor efficiency grows with the technical progress index γ_x. The number of worked hours is exogenously fixed at the level H. Nevertheless, a fraction of the efficient employment is devoted to cover adjustment costs on the number of workers. This is modelled by the following function[8] $\phi(Z_t)$:

$$\phi(Z_t) = \frac{\gamma}{2}(\log Z_t)^2 = \frac{\gamma}{2}\left(\log \frac{N_t}{N_{t-1}}\right)^2$$

The production function is then given by:

$$\begin{aligned} Y_t &= A_t \gamma_x^{\alpha t} K_t^{1-\alpha} \left[(e_t N_{t-1} Z_t H) \left(1 - \frac{\gamma}{2}(\log Z_t)^2\right)\right]^\alpha \\ &= A_t F(K_t, N_t^p) \end{aligned}$$

Thus, the production function have constant returns to scale relatively to the productive factors.

The technological factor evolves according to the following process:

$$\log(A_t) = \rho_a \log(A_{t-1}) + (1 - \rho_a) \log(A) + \epsilon_{at}$$

where $\log(A)$ is the unconditional mean of the process, $|\rho_a| < 1$ and ϵ_{at} the innovation with standard deviation $\sigma_{\epsilon a}$.

[8]This adjustment cost function satisfies the following property:

$$\phi' > 0 \quad \text{et} \quad \phi'' > 0$$

Thus, the adjustment cost is symetrical.

We assume that firms accumulate capital. The accumulation technology is given by:

$$K^\star_{t+1} = (1-\delta)K^\star_t + I_t$$

where I_t is the total investment of the period used to produce at the next period. The existing capital stock depreciates at the constant rate δ. The firms pay the productive work N^p_t which corresponds to workers doing piecework. Hence workers bear their training costs.

2.2.2 The Households

Following Burnside, Eichenbaum and Rebelo [1993], the instantaneous utility of the representative individual is, provided that at each time t he can go to work ($s=1$) with the probability π_t or not ($s=0$) with the probability $1-\pi_t$:

$$u(C_t(s), e_t(s), \pi_t) = \begin{cases} \log(C_t(1)) & + \quad \theta\log(T-\xi-e_t(1)H) \\ \log(C_t(0)) & + \quad \theta\log(T) \end{cases}$$

where $C_t(s)$ denotes household consumption and $e_t(1)$ the level of effort if the individual goes to work. T represents the individual's time endowment, and H the fixed shift length of worked hours. When the individual is employed, he must support a fixed utility cost ξ: this ensures that even if the optimal effort is zero, the instantaneous utility is lower for employed worker. θ is a positive scalar.

As Hansen [1985] and Rogerson [1988] do, we suppose that all the households supply H hours of work. But only a percentage of this supply can be satisfied and the firms pay only their labor force. Thus, each household chooses its probability π_t of working H hours, and a complete insurance. As all households are identical, they choose the same probability of working and the same insurance contract: the individuals who are not working are fired at random, by a lottery, among the suppliers. At each time t, there is some unemployment in this economy.

The complete insurance contract is chosen in order to allow the same consumptions for employed and unemployed households. Thus, the unemployment compensation is equal to the labor income.

So, if the population is normalized to one, $\pi_t = N_t$, where N_t denotes the number of employees. The instantaneous objective of the representative household can be written as:

$$u(C_t, e_t, N_t) = \log(C_t) + N_t\theta\log(T - \xi - e_t H) + (1 - N_t)\theta\log(T)$$

Households pay at each time a lump-sum tax, denoted τ_t, to the government in order to finance its consumption.

2.2.3 The Government

The government consumption X_t evolves according to a deterministic component which grows at the rate of labor augmenting technical progress γ_x, and to a exogenous stochastic component:

$$X_t = \gamma_x^t G_t$$

where G_t is the stochastic component following a stationary process defined by:

$$\log(G_t) = \rho_g \log(G_{t-1}) + (1 - \rho_g)\log(G) + \epsilon_{gt}$$

$\log(G)$ is the unconditional mean of the process, $|\rho_g| < 1$ and ϵ_{gt} denotes the innovation of the process with $\sigma_{\epsilon g}$ as standard deviation.

In this problem, the ricardian equivalence holds. Then, the timing of the tax has no incidence of the household behaviors. The simplest constraint of the government results have thus the following form:

$$X_t = \tau_t \quad \forall\, t$$

2.2.4 The Planner's Decision Rules

In the model, the labor market is in equilibrium. The adjustment occurs through variation in effort that households are asked to supply. The effort fluctuations will be costly for the firms because workers do piecework. On the other hand, the labor utilization rate, effort, reduces the utility of households. So, this utilization rate depends on the worker choices.

Thus, as in standard *RBC* models, the employment fluctuations are Pareto-optimal responses to aggregate shocks.

The aggregate resource constraint is given by:

$$K_{t+1} = A_t F(K_t, N_t^p) + (1-\delta)K_t - X_t - C_t$$

This problem verifies the necessary conditions of the neoclassical growth. Then, it is possible and convenient to transform the economy into a stationary one. This transformation involves dividing all variables by their common trend. Thus we define:

$$c_t = C_t/\gamma_x^t, \quad k_t = K_t/\gamma_x^t, \quad y_t = Y_t/\gamma_x^t, \quad i_t = I_t/\gamma_x^t, \quad x_t = G_t = X_t/\gamma_x^t$$

Using this transformation, the intertemporal utility function and the aggregate resource constraint can be written as:

$$U = \mu + E_0 \left[\sum_{t=0}^{+\infty} \beta^t \left\{ \log(c_t) + \theta N_t \log\left(\frac{T - \xi - e_t H}{T} \right) \right\} \right]$$

$$\gamma_x k_{t+1} = (1-\delta)k_t + A_t F(k_t, N_t^p) - c_t - G_t$$

where we note $\mu = \sum_{t=0}^{+\infty} \beta^t [\log(\gamma_x^t) + \theta \log(T)]$.

The first decision of the planner is to choose the hiring level, without knowledge of current shocks A_t and G_t. The hiring decision rule is relative to the state vector $(k_t, N_{t-1}, A_{t-1}, G_{t-1})$, whereas the consumption and effort decision rules are relative to the state vector (k_t, N_t, A_t, G_t). The decision rules are then solution to the following value functions:

$$V_0(k_t, N_{t-1}, A_{t-1}, G_{t-1}) = \max_{\{Z_t\}} E\left[V_1(k_t, N_t, A_t, G_t) | \Omega_t^\star\right]$$

$$\text{with } N_t = Z_t N_{t-1}$$

with the notation $V_1(t) = V_1(k_t, N_t, A_t, G_t)$,

$$V_1(t) = \max_{\{c_t, e_t, k_{t+1}\}} \left\{ \log(c_t) + N_t \theta \log\left(\frac{T - \xi - e_t H}{T} \right) \beta E\left[V_1(t+1) | \Omega_t\right] \right\}$$

$$\text{s.t. } \gamma_x k_{t+1} = (1-\delta)k_t + A_t F(k_t, N_t^p) - G_t - c_t$$

The first order conditions are:

$$\frac{1}{c_t} = \lambda_t$$

$$-\frac{\partial u}{\partial e_t} = A_t \frac{\partial F}{\partial N_t^p} \frac{N_t^p}{\partial e_t} \lambda_t$$

$$E\left[-\frac{\partial u}{\partial N_t}\frac{\partial N_t}{\partial Z_t}|\Omega_t^\star\right] = E\left[A_t \frac{\partial F}{\partial N_t^p}\frac{\partial N_t^p}{\partial Z_t}\lambda_t + N_{t-1}\mu_t|\Omega_t^\star\right]$$

$$\text{where}\lambda_t = E\left[\frac{\beta}{\gamma_x}\frac{\partial V(t+1)}{\partial k_{t+1}}|\Omega_t\right] \quad \text{and} \quad \mu_t = E\left[\beta\frac{\partial V(t+1)}{\partial N_t}|\Omega_t\right]$$

The envelope conditions are given by:

$$\frac{\gamma_x}{\beta}\lambda_t = E\left[\left(1-\delta+A_{t+1}\frac{\partial F}{\partial k_{t+1}}\right)\lambda_{t+1}|\Omega_t\right]$$

$$\frac{\mu_t}{\beta} = E\left[\frac{\partial u}{\partial N_{t+1}}\frac{N_{t+1}}{\partial N_t} + A_{t+1}\frac{\partial F}{\partial N_{t+1}^p}\frac{\partial N_{t+1}^p}{\partial N_t}\lambda_{t+1} + Z_{t+1}\mu_{t+1}|\Omega_t^\star\right]$$

We impose the following transversality conditions:

$$\lim_{t\to+\infty} E_0\left[\beta^t\lambda_t k_{t+1}\right] = 0$$

$$\lim_{t\to+\infty} E_0\left[\beta^t\mu_t N_t\right] = 0$$

This dynamic programming problem has no analytical solution. It is thus necessary to use approximation methods. Following King, Plosser and Rebelo [1988] we log-linearize the efficiency conditions around the stationary deterministic steady state of the economy[9].

2.3 Solution Method and Calibration

The log-linearized system of the efficiency conditions (where $\widehat{x}_t$ is the percentage of deviation of X_t from its stationary value X:

$$\widehat{x}_t = \log(X_t/X)$$

constitutes a rational expectations equations system that is solved by using Blanchard and Kahn [1980] and King, Plosser and Rebelo [1988] methods.

[9]The computation of the steady state is presented in appendix 2.7.

The State-Space Form

The hiring decisions are taken without knowledge of current shocks $\widehat{A}_t$ and $\widehat{G}_t$. They are conditional on an information set $\Omega_t^\star$ excluding the current shocks $\widehat{A}_t$ and $\widehat{G}_t$. Once these shocks are known, the decisions of consumption, effort, and investment are taken and are conditional on $\Omega_t = \Omega_t^\star \bigcup \{\widehat{A}_t, \widehat{G}_t\}$.

In the equation of employment determination, the expectations are conditional on the information set $\Omega_t^\star$, whereas in the other equations, the expectations are conditional on Ω_t.

To solve our model[10], we proceed in two stages[11]. First, all the optimality conditions are projected on the information set $\Omega_t^\star$. We then determine the hiring variable z_t as a function of $\Omega_t^\star$.

$$\widehat{z}_t = \eta_{zk}\widehat{k}_t + \eta_{zN}\widehat{N}_{t-1} + \eta_{zA}\widehat{A}_{t-1} + \eta_{zg}\widehat{G}_{t-1} \qquad (2.1)$$

Second, coming back to the initial system, we replace the employment first order condition by (2.1). This implies that the decisions of consumption, effort and employment — *i.e.* $(\widehat{c}_t, \widehat{e}_t, \widehat{i}_t)$ — are taken after the hiring one.

Let M be the matrix linking the current state vector with the lagged one, and Π the matrix linking the other variables with the state variables. The π_{ij} element denotes the elasticity of the variable i with respect to the variable j. We finally obtain :

$$\begin{bmatrix} \widehat{k}_{t+1} \\ \widehat{N}_{t+1} \\ \widehat{A}_{t+1} \\ \widehat{G}_{t+1} \end{bmatrix} = M \begin{bmatrix} \widehat{k}_t \\ \widehat{N}_t \\ \widehat{A}_t \\ \widehat{G}_t \end{bmatrix} + \begin{bmatrix} 0 \\ 0 \\ \epsilon_{At+1} \\ \epsilon_{gt+1} \end{bmatrix}$$

[10]In this section, we present the method employed to solve our model in the case of labor hoarding. The method to solve without labor hoarding is the same and requires only one stage, the information set being Ω_t: see appendix 2.7

[11]The complete resolution of the model is presented in appendix 2.7

and

$$\begin{bmatrix} \hat{y}_t \\ \hat{c}_t \\ \hat{e}_t \\ \hat{i}_t \\ \hat{p}_t \\ \widehat{RS}_t \end{bmatrix} = \Pi \begin{bmatrix} \hat{k}_t \\ \widehat{N}_t \\ \hat{A}_t \\ \hat{G}_t \end{bmatrix}$$

- p_t is the apparent labor productivity.
- RS_t is the naive Solow residual — *i.e.* $RS_t = A_t e_t^{\alpha}$ —.

Calibration

In order to simulate the model and to compute different moments of interest, it is necessary to give a value to the parameters of the model.

Preferences: Due to the lack of comparative evidence on this point, we assume that preferences of US and French agents are similar. Thus, the discount factor, β is chosen equal to 0.99, which corresponds to a discount rate of 1% per quarter. Following Burnside, Eichenbaum and Rebelo [1993] the individual's time endowment T is taken equal to 1369 and corresponds to the time available per quarter. The hours spent at work H are chosen equal to 1369/2 : half of the available time is devoted to work. The parameter ξ, expressed in hours, is fixed at 60[12]. The parameter θ is chosen such as the term $BE = \theta \log\left(\frac{T-\xi-eH}{T}\right)$ always be equal to -2. We thus obtain a stationary level of employment of about 0.42 (without government spending)[13].

Preferences

β	T	H	ξ	N
0.99	1369	684.5	60	0.42

The two countries differ by their technology and by the processes followed by the shocks which affect the economy.

[12]See Burnside, Eichenbaum and Rebelo [1993]
[13]See Hansen [1985]

The USA:

The depreciation rate δ is set at 0.025, and is equivalent to an annual rate of 10%. The labor share $\alpha = 0.58$ is the average ratio of total employee compensation to G.N.P. for the period 1948-1986. The growth rate γ_x is, following King, Plosser and Rebelo [1988] equal to 1.004 per quarter. It corresponds to the common trend rate of growth of output, consumption and investment which is 1.6% per year in the post-war era. The stationary level of government spending is chosen such that it represents 21% of the stationary output and corresponds to the mean of the government spending share in the US G.N.P. during the post-war era. The parameters ρ_g and $\sigma_{\epsilon g}$ of the process followed by the government spending were estimated by Christiano and Eichenbaum [1992] on US data at $\rho_g = 0.97$ and $\sigma_{\epsilon g} = 0.02$. The persistence parameter ρ_a is set at 0.95. The parameter $\sigma_{\epsilon A}$ which is the standard deviation of the technological shock innovation, is fixed such that the standard deviation of the cyclical component of the output is equal to 1.76 (See above). Its values will evolve between 0.006 and 0.01. The parameter γ of the adjustment cost is not easy to determine as it lacks empirical counterpart. The value taken by γ should not be too high as to avoid an excessive smoothing of the variables of the model. Thus, we set γ equal to 1.

US Parameters

α	δ	γ_x	γ	ρ_g	$\sigma_{\epsilon g}$	s_g	ρ_a
0.58	0.025	1.004	1	0.97	0.02	0.21	0.95

France:

According to Laffargue and Malgrange [1991] and Hairault in chapter 1 of this book, the parameters take the following values. The depreciation rate δ is set at 0.0125. The labor share is chosen equal to 0.545. The growth rate was estimated at 1.0067, which correspond to a common trend rate of growth of output, consumption and investment of 2.68% per year the post-war era. The government spending share corresponds in France to 18.5% of the output. The parameters of the process followed by the government spending were estimated at $\rho_g = 0.985$ and $\sigma_{\epsilon g} = 0.0083$. The term ρ_a of persistence of the technological shock is set at 0.975. The standard deviation of the innovation of the technological shock is fixed such that the standard deviation of the cyclical component of the output is equal to 0.91 (See above)

French Parameters

α	δ	γ_x	γ	ρ_g	$\sigma_{\epsilon g}$	s_g	ρ_a
0.545	0.0125	1.0067	1	0.985	0.0083	0.185	0.975

The model is then simulated, each simulation consisting of $T = 120$ quarters.

With different combinations of assumptions we can directly compare our models to the following contributions:

The Different Models

Adjust. Costs	$\gamma = 0$	$\gamma = 1$
N.L.H. / N.G.	Hansen [1985]	Model I
N.L.H. / G.	Christiano and Eichenbaum [1992]	Model II
L.H. / N.G.	Hansen [1985] with L.H.	Model III
L.H. / G.	Burnside, Eichenbaum and Rebelo [1993]	Model IV

N.L.H.: without labor hoarding
N.G.: without government expenditures shocks
L.H.: with labor hoarding
G: with government expenditures shocks

Our model encompasses the actual *RBC* literature focussing on labor market fluctuations. Then, it is easy to analyze the introduction of government spending shocks, labor hoarding or labor adjustments cost.

2.4 Impulse Response Functions for Technological and Government Spending Shocks

The study of the responses to shocks helps us to highlight the propagation of a technological shock or a government spending shock. It is then possible to evaluate the dynamical properties of the model. We present the results of four models to disentangle the effects of different assumptions, in particular the assumption of labor hoarding.

The responses to shocks figures are reported in appendix 2.7. We comment the models without labor hoarding (models I and II) and with labor hoarding (models III and IV), calibrated for the USA and France, and shed light on their fundamental mechanisms[14].

2.4.1 Technological Shocks

The technological shocks are interpreted as supply shocks because they alters the aggregate production function.

I.R.F. of Employment

A positive technological shock increases capital and employment. The more the employment response is favorable, the weaker is the adjustment cost. We note that the employment begins to respond positively to a technological shock. Afterwards, during the adjustment, it falls under its stationary value. Around the 25th period, the effect of the technological shock vanishes. The transitory dynamics governed by π_{Nk} and π_{NN} is predominant in the employment evolution.

Without labor hoarding (models I and II), the wealth effect induces instantaneously less saving and less labor supply — less factors accumu-

[14]As a whole, the profiles of the different variables responses to a productivity or a government spending shock are the same as in the model without labor hoarding. Moreover, the eigenvalues of the labor hoarding model are the same as in the model without labor hoarding. This means that the mean adjustment speeds are unchanged. Figures confirm this observation, thus, the trajectories of the different variables taken with or without labor hoarding converge in the long run (after ten periods). Labor hoarding have only a short run effect.

lation — since it allows to produce the same quantity of output with less production factors. The substitution effect operates instantaneously in the opposite way. A positive technological shock increases the marginal productivity of factors, capital and labor. Then, the agents are lead to increase their labor supply.

The employment comes back to its stationary value faster than the capital. This strong capital inertia leads to a high level around the 30th period. This high capital level, combined with a negative instantaneous employment response to capital, induces then the fall the employment over its stationary state value at this time. Indeed, an increase of the capital stock under its stationary value will increase the capital returns level[15]. This increase of the capital returns will reduce the labor supply. A high capital stock level has two other effects. It reduces the marginal productivity of capital and increases the marginal productivity of work — *i.e.* the real interest rate is low and the real wage is high —. The second effect tends to reduce the labor supply whereas the third tends to increase it. In our model, the negative effects dominate the positive ones, such that a high level of capital leads the employment under its stationary value.

Effect of Labor Hoarding: Wealth and substitution effects are approximately identical to the ones of the model without labor hoarding. The difference between the initial responses in the two cases are due to a high inertia affecting the employment (models III and IV). Firstly, the level of employment is thus predetermined. Secondly, when we introduce adjustment costs, employment does not allow to instantaneously set at its desired value. Thus, the adjustment is done with the effort variable. Employment will then gradually adjust and effort will come back to its stationary value.

[15]The interest rate falls under its stationary value, the difference between it and its stationary value will be very low.

I.R.F. of Effort

The effort responds positively to a technological shock. The effort response is due to the existence of the adjustment cost (models I and II). Facing a productivity shock, the firms increase the efficient work. Then, they can choose between an increase of employment and an increase of effort. The adjustment cost does not allow the firms to completely adjust the employment. It will be adjusted only partially. The adjustment will be carried out by mean of effort. Note that in absence of adjustment costs — *i.e.* $\gamma = 0$ — the effort will always be at its stationary value. The adjustment will only be made through employment because the effort disutility is higher than the employment one.

Effect of Labor Hoarding: On the labor market, effort adjustments in response to information that was not available when employment decisions were taken. This suggests that the response of effort to a shock will be more important in a labor hoarding framework. This idea is confirmed by figures where the effort responses to a technological shock are represented (models III and IV).

I.R.F. of Solow Residual

Here, the computed Solow residual is the naive one, that is $RS_t = A_t e_t^{\alpha}$. This residual does not correspond to the technological shock. RS_t depends on the whole state vector. We note that the elasticity of the Solow residual with respect to the technological shock is higher than 1 [16]. The response of the naive residual overshoots the technological shock $\widehat{A}_t$. We have $\pi_{RSA} = 1 + \alpha\pi_{eA}$. The elasticity of the naive Solow residual can be decomposed in two effects, a direct effect due to the technological shock and an indirect one working through effort.

Effect of Labor Hoarding: As it was previously underlined, a technological shock $\widehat{A}_t$ alters the naive Solow residual through two effects. It has a direct effect and an indirect one working through the

[16] The elasticity of naive Solow residual π_{RSA} is equal to 1.2604 without government spending and 1.2057 with government spending in the US case.

effort variable. The effort responds more greatly to a technological shock in presence of labor hoarding. Thus, the sensitivity of the naive Solow residual to shocks will be greater in case of labor hoarding.

2.4.2 Government Spending Shock

This shock is interpreted as a tax shock because it alters the aggregate labor supply *via* the budget constraint.

I.R.F. of Employment

Without labor hoarding, the response of employment to a government spending shock is instantaneously positive (model II). An increase in government spending reduces agents' wealth. They are thus lead to work more to (or to try to) maintain their income level. The effect of adjustment costs on work is easily seen on figures: the employment gradually increases and after 4 quarters decreases to its stationary value.

Effect of Labor Hoarding: The consequences of the introduction of a labor hoarding behavior clearly appear on impulse response function figures (model IV). The employment response is logically lagged.

I.R.F. of Effort

The effort positively responds to a government spending shock. The higher the adjustment cost is, the larger is the effort response. The effect of adjustment costs on effort is easily seen on figures: effort instantaneously jumps and then gradually comes back to its stationary value.

Effect of Labor Hoarding: Instantaneously, the effort increase is not sufficient to reach the level of output obtained without labor hoarding. The effort response is insufficient because the marginal disutility of effort increases with it whereas the marginal disutility of work is constant. The labor supply elasticity is infinite whereas the one of effort is not.

I.R.F. of Solow Residual

The naive Solow residual responds positively to a government spending shock through effort. This makes clear that naive Solow residual changes can be caused by government spending shocks, such as the government spending shock, and not only by technological shocks. Thus, the adjustment costs make the government spending shock persistent in the dynamic of naive Solow residual. The effect of government spending vanishes around the 8th quarter.

Effect of Labor Hoarding: The response of the naive Solow residual to a government spending shock is higher in the case of labor hoarding. A government spending shock will also contaminate the Solow residual through effort. The effort responds more greatly to government spending shock in presence of labor hoarding. Thus, the sensitivity of the naive Solow residual to shocks will be greater in case of labor hoarding. With labor adjustment costs, the persistence of the government spending shock in the dynamic of the naive Solow residual is also explained.

I.R.F. of Labor Productivity

The government spending shock induces the fall of labor productivity. Here, the elasticity of product with respect to government spending is less than the one of employment. This is due to low adjustment costs. With higher adjustment costs, the response of employment to a government spending shock would be lower. In this case, the adjustment would be realized through a more important change in effort. Thus, with sufficiently high adjustment costs, the labor productivity will positively respond to a government spending shock.

High adjustment costs should allow to reproduce characteristics of productivity cycle, that is, the labor productivity increases in case of a government spending shock and the labor productivity increase leads the increase in employment. The problem of too high an adjustment cost is that it excessively smooths the employment, that is to say, the variability of employment is too low with respect to the stylized facts we try to reproduce.

The introduction of labor hoarding behavior, combined with a low adjustment cost will allow to reproduce the characteristics of the productivity cycle without excessively smoothing employment.

Effect of Labor Hoarding: The labor hoarding allows to reproduce a productivity cycle even with low adjustment costs. This still is true without adjustment cost. The employment being a predetermined variable, a shock involving an output increase will lead at first to an apparent labor productivity increase. With labor hoarding, the labor adjustment costs act after the observation of the shocks, —*i.e.* the employment response is lagged because, on the one hand, the employment is predetermined, and on the other hand, employment adjustment are partial after the observation of shocks—. This labor productivity can then be taken as an advanced cycle indicator, as suggested by analysts of business cycle before the eighties and actual observations.

2.5 Simulation Results

The characteristics of the business cycle are summarized in section 2.1.2 by different moments of order 2 : namely the variances, correlations and cross-correlations. We compare the moments generated by Monte-Carlo simulations with those of the US and French series filtered by Hodrick-Prescott method. We are then able to evaluate quantitatively our models.

The standard deviation σ_ϵ of the innovation of the technological shock is chosen to make the standard deviation of the G.N.P. equal to 1.76 for the USA and to 0.91 for France — *i.e.* the standard deviations of the observed G.N.P. series filtered by Hodrick-Prescott method —.

2.5.1 The USA

Before studying the correlation between productivity and employment, we note that the standard deviation of the different variables — *i.e.*

consumption, investment, employment and productivity — have the order of magnitude of those obtained by simulation of standard *RBC* models. The results are reported in tables (2.5),(2.6),(2.7) and (2.8).

Table 2.5: USA : Model I

Va	*S.D.*	$S.D./S.D._{\widehat{y}}$	$AR(1)$	Cross-correlations with y							
$\sigma_{\epsilon A} = 0.81$			1	4	2	1	0	-1	-2	-4
$\widehat{y}$	1.77	1	0.72	0.09	0.47	0.72	1	0.72	0.47	0.09
$\widehat{c}$	0.52	0.30	0.79	-0.15	0.24	0.53	0.88	0.76	0.63	0.39
$\widehat{i}$	4.76	2.68	0.71	0.15	0.50	0.74	0.99	0.68	0.41	0.02
$\widehat{N}$	1.03	0.58	0.86	0.11	0.46	0.69	0.95	0.85	0.62	0.15
$\widehat{p}$	0.84	0.48	0.48	0.07	0.42	0.66	0.93	0.46	0.21	0.01

Table 2.6: USA : Model II

Va	*S.D.*	$S.D./S.D._{\widehat{y}}$	$AR(1)$	Cross-correlations with y						
$\sigma_{\epsilon A} = 0.86$			1	4	2	1	0	-1	-2	-4
$\widehat{y}$	1.77	1	0.72	0.09	0.47	0.72	1	0.72	0.47	0.09
$\widehat{c}$	0.77	0.44	0.74	-0.13	0.17	0.40	0.67	0.56	0.46	0.28
$\widehat{i}$	4.58	2.59	0.71	0.14	0.48	0.71	0.97	0.68	0.41	0.04
$\widehat{N}$	1.08	0.61	0.86	0.13	0.44	0.64	0.87	0.77	0.56	0.13
$\widehat{p}$	0.97	0.55	0.56	0.04	0.35	0.58	0.84	0.44	0.22	0.02

Table 2.7: USA : Model III

Va	*S.D.*	$S.D./S.D._{\widehat{y}}$	$AR(1)$	Cross-correlations with y						
$\sigma_{\epsilon A} = 0.86$			1	4	2	1	0	-1	-2	-4
$\widehat{y}$	1.76	1	0.73	0.13	0.49	0.73	1	0.73	0.49	0.13
$\widehat{c}$	0.54	0.31	0.79	-0.10	0.28	0.56	0.89	0.75	0.62	0.40
$\widehat{i}$	4.69	2.66	0.73	0.17	0.52	0.75	0.99	0.70	0.43	0.06
$\widehat{N}$	0.98	0.55	0.85	0.06	0.32	0.50	0.73	0.95	0.83	0.35
$\widehat{p}$	1.22	0.70	0.39	0.15	0.44	0.65	0.85	0.30	0.04	-0.09

Table 2.8: USA : Model IV

Va	*S.D.*	*S.D./S.D.*$_{\hat{y}}$	*AR*(1)	Cross-correlations with *y*						
$\sigma_{\epsilon A} = 0.91$			14	2	1	0	-1	-2	-4	
$\widehat{y}$	1.75	1	0.74	0.12	0.49	0.74	1	0.74	0.49	0.12
$\widehat{c}$	0.80	0.46	0.75	-0.09	0.21	0.43	0.70	0.58	0.47	0.29
$\widehat{i}$	4.56	2.60	0.73	0.17	0.50	0.73	0.97	0.70	0.44	0.06
$\widehat{N}$	1.00	0.57	0.86	0.05	0.30	0.47	0.66	0.85	0.74	0.30
$\widehat{p}$	1.30	0.75	0.47	0.12	0.42	0.61	0.82	0.33	0.09	-0.07

For the different models, the standard deviation of consumption evolves between 0.52 and 0.80, and is clearly below the value of 1.28 given by the series. We remark that the variability of consumption is higher with government consumption in the model. The standard deviation of investment is under the value of 8.47 given by the series. The variability reproduced for employment is below the value obtained by Hansen [1985], in spite of the presence of an indivisible labor. This smoothness effect is due to the adjustment cost, which mechanically reduces the employment variability. The productivity variability obtained by our different models is more satisfactory than the one obtained by Hansen [1985] which takes the value of 0.5. With our different specifications, we obtain, in absence of labor hoarding, a standard deviation of productivity evolving between 0.84 and 0.92. The introduction of the hypothesis of labor hoarding leads to an increase of this standard deviation to 1.20 to 1.30.

The models do not always reproduce an employment variability larger than the productivity one. It is worth noting that labor hoarding tends to increase the variability of productivity whereas the variability of employment is not significantly altered.

Now, we will center our attention on the correlations between productivity and employment which are reported in table (2.9), (2.10), (2.11) and (2.12).

Table 2.9: USA : Model I corr($\widehat{p}_t, \widehat{N}_{t+i}$)

-4	-3	-2	-1	0	1	2	3	4
.03	0.10	0.20	0.40	0.77	0.74	0.55	0.33	0.12
(0.14)	(0.14)	(0.12)	(0.10)	(0.03)	(0.05)	(0.07)	(0.07)	(0.09)

Table 2.10: USA : Model II corr($\widehat{p}_t, \widehat{N}_{t+i}$)

-4	-3	-2	-1	0	1	2	3	4
02	0.04	0.09	0.21	0.47	0.44	0.31	0.16	0.03
(0.18)	(0.18)	(0.17)	(0.15)	(0.12)	(0.13)	(0.14)	(0.14)	(0.14)

Effects of Labor Hoarding

First, we note that a weak adjustment cost is not sufficient to reproduce a productivity cycle. This intuition is supported by the examination of the correlation between productivity and employment in absence of labor hoarding. With or without government expenditures, the higher correlation between productivity and employment is the actual one : it clearly shows that productivity is not an advanced indicator of the economic cycle.

A higher adjustment cost would probably give a productivity cycle. However, it would excessively smooth the other variables of the model, which is not acceptable since our aim is to reproduce in an acceptable way the major stylized facts of the economy.

The labor hoarding enables us to reproduce a productivity cycle without smoothing the employment. It even increases the variability of productivity and makes the variability of productivity larger than the employment one. Our results about the correlation between productivity and employment are satisfactory and our model is clearly able to exhibit a productivity cycle.

Without government spending, the instantaneous correlation is positive and equal to 0.25. The higher correlation between productivity and employment occurs at lead 2 and is equal to 0.7. The past correlations are approximately equal to 0. With government spending, the instanta-

Table 2.11 :USA : Model III corr($\widehat{p}_t, \widehat{N}_{t+i}$)

-4	-3	-2	-1	0	1	2	3	4
-0.06	-0.06	-0.03	0.05	0.26	0.68	0.70	0.55	0.36
(0.12)	(0.12)	(0.13)	(0.14)	(0.10)	(0.03)	(0.04)	(0.07)	(0.09)

Table 2.12: USA : Model IV corr($\widehat{p}_t, \widehat{N}_{t+i}$)

-4	-3	-2	-1	0	1	2	3	4
-0.08	-0.09	-0.08	-0.02	0.13	0.47	0.50	0.39	0.26
(0.16)	(0.15)	(0.14)	(0.14)	(0.14)	(0.10)	(0.12)	(0.13)	(0.13)

neous correlation between productivity and employment falls from 0.25 to 0.13, which is very close to the value given by the series. The lagged correlations are all negative, but close to 0, while the advanced correlations are significantly positive and the correlation between productivity and employment is maximum at lead 2.

To sum up, the model with labor hoarding and government spending reproduces the US productivity cycle. Note that our results are coherent with those of Burnside, Eichenbaum and Rebelo [1993]. Nevertheless, the government spendings play a crucial role to obtain such results.

Role of the Government Spending

Burnside, Eichenbaum and Rebelo [1993] assert that their good results are due to the labor hoarding without asking about the role of government spending. The simulation results of the model with labor hoarding and with or without government spending allows us to precise the following fact : if the productivity cycle comes with labor hoarding, the government spendings play an important role because they reduce the instantaneous correlation between productivity and employment and thus contribute to give it a more realistic value. The negative impact of public spending induces households to work more through a wealth effect. The result is a negative effect on the instantaneous correlation between productivity and employment. The productivity / employment correlation is lowered by the government spending.

Role of Adjustment Costs

The characteristics of our model, compared to Burnside, Eichenbaum and Rebelo [1993], is the introduction of adjustment costs on employment in addition to labor hoarding. To highlight the contribution of adjustment costs, we simulated the model without adjustment costs.

The productivity / employment correlations are reported in table (2.13) (The model includes labor hoarding and government spending).

Table 2.13: USA Model IV without Adjustment Costs

	-4	-3	-2	-1	0	1	2	3	4
corr($\widehat{p}_t, \widehat{N}_{t+i}$)	0.03	0.03	0.03	0.02	-0.009	0.51	0.31	0.16	0.05
(0.10)	(0.11)	(0.10)	(0.10)	(0.10)	(0.10)	(0.10)	(0.10)	(0.10)	

The productivity cycle is reproduced : the higher productivity / employment correlation occurs for productivity at date t and employment at date $t+1$. The actual and past correlations are weakly negative, in fact non significantly different from 0. The adjustment cost that we introduce in the model is low in the sense that it does not involve by itself a productivity cycle. Nevertheless, it makes the correlation between productivity and lagged employment negative. The maximum correlation between productivity and employment occurs at lead 2. Moreover, the instantaneous correlation becomes positive. To sum up, adjustment costs lengthen the productivity cycle. This is not surprising since adjustment costs strengthen the inertia of employment. With and without adjustment costs, it is always possible to change largely the volume of employment even if it is done with one period of lag. With adjustment costs, current employment depends on its past values. The productivity cycle is then lengthened compared to the model without adjustment costs and the peak of the productivity / employment correlation occurs at lead 2, which is in accordance with the stylized facts.

We note that the results obtained without adjustment costs are close to those of Burnside, Eichenbaum and Rebelo [1993]. They find that the correlation between productivity and employment is maximum at lead 1. To conclude, we have shown that the labor hoarding mechanically advances only of one period the maximum correlation between productivity and employment. Adjustment costs, even if low, permit to lengthen the productivity cycle: the maximum correlation between productivity and employment occurs at lead 2 instead of lead 1.

2.5.2 France

The standard deviation of the innovation of the technological shock is chosen to make the standard deviation of the product equal to 0.91. The results of the simulations are reported in tables (2.14) to (2.21).

Table 2.14: France : Model I

Va	*S.D.*	*S.D./S.D.*$_{\widehat{y}}$	*AR*(1)	Cross-correlations with *y*						
$\sigma_{\epsilon A} = 0.44$			1	4	2	1	0	-1	-2	-4
$\widehat{y}$	0.88	1	0.72	0.09	0.47	0.72	1	0.72	0.47	0.09
$\widehat{c}$	0.26	0.29	0.75	-0.09	0.32	0.60	0.94	0.75	0.58	0.29
$\widehat{i}$	2.39	2.73	0.72	0.14	0.50	0.73	0.99	0.69	0.43	-0.04
$\widehat{N}$	0.52	0.59	0.86	0.09	0.44	0.68	0.95	0.86	0.65	0.19
$\widehat{p}$	0.41	0.47	0.46	0.09	0.44	0.66	0.92	0.43	0.18	-0.04

Table 2.15: France : Model II

Va	*S.D.*	*S.D./S.D.*$_{\widehat{y}}$	*AR*(1)	Cross-correlations with *y*						
$\sigma_{\epsilon A} = 0.49$			1	4	2	1	0	-1	-2	-4
$\widehat{y}$	0.90	1	0.70	0.11	0.45	0.70	1	0.70	0.45	0.11
$\widehat{c}$	0.41	0.46	0.72	-0.03	0.27	0.52	0.81	0.62	0.47	0.25
$\widehat{i}$	2.40	2.65	0.70	0.15	0.47	0.70	0.99	0.68	0.42	0.07
$\widehat{N}$	0.50	0.55	0.85	0.14	0.42	0.63	0.88	0.72	0.57	0.16
$\widehat{p}$	0.52	0.58	0.55	0.06	0.38	0.61	0.89	0.46	0.23	0.05

As for US economy, the variability of consumption is too low relatively to the variability of product. The model reproduces a variability of employment higher than the one of productivity only in simplest cases. — *i.e.* labor hoarding without government spending —. The variability of productivity is well reproduced by the models with labor hoarding. In all cases, the variability of employment is too low, always close to 0.5, whereas the series give 0.83.

The data give for France an instantaneous correlation between productivity and employment close to -0.3. Moreover, the correlation between productivity and employment occurs at lead 5 (whereas for the

Table 2.16: France : Model III

Va	$S.D.$	$S.D./S.D._{\widehat{y}}$	$AR(1)$	Cross-correlations with y						
$\sigma_{\epsilon A} = 0.48$			1	4	2	1	0	-1	-2	-4
$\widehat{y}$	0.94	1	0.74	0.13	0.50	0.74	1	0.74	0.50	0.13
$\widehat{c}$	0.28	0.30	0.75	-0.04	0.35	0.63	0.94	0.75	0.58	0.31
$\widehat{i}$	2.54	2.71	0.75	0.17	0.52	0.76	0.99	0.73	0.46	0.07
$\widehat{N}$	0.55	0.58	0.86	0.01	0.30	0.49	0.72	0.95	0.85	0.39
$\widehat{p}$	0.65	0.70	0.40	0.18	0.46	0.65	0.82	0.27	0.00	-0.14

Table 2.17: France : Model IV

Va	$S.D.$	$S.D./S.D._{\widehat{y}}$	$AR(1)$	Cross-correlations with y						
$\sigma_{\epsilon A} = 0.49$			1	4	2	1	0	-1	-2	-4
$\widehat{y}$	0.90	1	0.74	0.11	0.49	0.74	1	0.74	0.49	0.11
$\widehat{c}$	0.40	0.45	0.72	-0.06	0.29	0.53	0.82	0.64	0.49	0.23
$\widehat{i}$	2.36	2.62	0.74	0.14	0.51	0.74	0.99	0.73	0.47	0.07
$\widehat{N}$	0.50	0.55	0.87	0.02	0.30	0.48	0.69	0.88	0.78	0.34
$\widehat{p}$	0.65	0.74	0.46	0.13	0.45	0.64	0.84	0.35	0.09	-0.11

USA it occurs at lead 2). This shows a larger inertia of employment in France than in the USA. The productivity cycle is longer in France.

Table 2.18: France : Model I corr($\widehat{p}_t, \widehat{N}_{t+i}$)

-4	-3	-2	-1	0	1	2	3	4
-0.03	0.04	0.15	0.36	0.76	0.75	0.59	0.38	0.18
(0.13)	(0.13)	(0.11)	(0.08)	(0.02)	(0.04)	(0.06)	(0.07)	(0.08)

Table 2.19: France : Model II corr($\widehat{p}_t, \widehat{N}_{t+i}$)

-4	-3	-2	-1	0	1	2	3	4
04	0.07	0.13	0.28	0.57	0.54	0.40	0.23	0.08
(0.15)	(0.16)	(0.16)	(0.14)	(0.11)	(0.12)	(0.14)	(0.15)	(0.15)

Table 2.20 France : Model III corr($\widehat{p}_t, \widehat{N}_{t+i}$)

-4	-3	-2	-1	0	1	2	3	4
-0.15	-0.13	-0.10	-0.01	0.21	0.64	0.69	0.58	0.41
(0.12)	(0.10)	(0.10)	(0.10)	(0.09)	(0.02)	(0.05)	(0.08)	(0.09)

The model with labor hoarding and government spending reproduces a productivity cycle. But the maximum correlation between productivity and employment is at lead 2 as in the USA. Compared to the stylized facts, this result is not satisfactory. It would be possible to lengthen the productivity cycle by increasing the adjustment cost parameter γ. Such a possibility cannot be kept because too high adjustment costs would excessively smooth the other variables of the model. Moreover, the instantaneous correlation between productivity and employment is in the best case —*i.e.* labor hoarding and adjustment costs — equal to 0.19, which is far from -0.3 given by the series.

Clearly, the different specifications of the model simulated with French calibration fail to reproduce the stylized facts of the French economy, especially the labor market ones. We obtain a variability of employment too low, even smaller than the variability of productivity. The results are also disappointing concerning the productivity cycle generated by the model: it is too short.

2.5.3 Conclusion of the Quantitative Analysis

The simulations carried out on the USA give satisfactory results, whereas those obtained with French calibration do not match the stylized

Table 2.21: France : Model IV corr($\widehat{p}_t, \widehat{N}_{t+i}$)

-4	-3	-2	-1	0	1	2	3	4
-0.12	-0.11	-0.08	-0.01	0.19	0.55	0.59	0.48	0.33
(0.14)	(0.15)	(0.14)	(0.14)	(0.12)	(0.08)	(0.09)	(0.11)	(0.12)

Table 2.22: France Model IV without Adjustment Costs corr($\widehat{p}_t, \widehat{N}_{t+i}$)

-4	-3	-2	-1	0	1	2	3	4
02	0.05	0.06	0.07	0.09	0.63	0.4	0.21	0.07
(0.12)	(0.12)	(0.13)	(0.12)	(0.12)	(0.07)	(0.09)	(0.10)	(0.11)

facts. The chapter 1 has already underlined the failure to mimic French stylized facts.

The main difficulty is to reproduce the labor market stylized facts. The model of King, Plosser and Rebelo [1988] appears unable to reproduce, even approximately, the variability of productivity and employment as well as the productivity cycle. The model of indivisible labor proposed by Hansen [1985] leads to better results compared to the initial canonical model. If the model of Hansen [1985] can reproduce the variability of employment and productivity, it fails to reproduce accurately the correlation between productivity and employment. More generally, this model is unable to reproduce the lagged, instantaneous and advanced correlations between productivity and employment: it fails to exhibit a productivity cycle. The aim of the paper of Burnside, Eichenbaum and Rebelo [1993] is to build a model displaying a productivity cycle. This model gives encouraging results without exhibiting in a statistically significative way, a productivity cycle. The maximum correlation between productivity and employment occurs at lead 1. Labor hoarding allows to display mechanically a productivity cycle. The introduction of adjustment costs, even low, allows us to lengthen the duration of the productivity cycle : the maximum correlation is then obtained at lead 2. We are then closer to the stylized fact, at least for the USA. Nevertheless, the adjustment costs reduce the performances of the model, concerning the relative variability of employment to labor productivity, whereas it would be necessary to increase them, particularly in France, to reproduce the productivity cycle.

2.6 Concluding Comments

The aim of our model was to account for the economic mechanisms able to answer the two main criticisms faced by the standard *RBC* models : first, the exogeneity and the unicity of the impulse source, second, the inability to reproduce the labor market stylized facts.

In the neoclassical growth model framework, on the one hand we have introduced a labor hoarding behavior and an adjustment cost, on the other hand, a government spending shock to evaluate quantitatively and qualitatively if it allows to overcome the failures of this theory.

We show how the government spending shock alters the naive Solow residual fluctuations. The hypothesis of adjustment costs permits to increase the persistence of the pro-cyclical measurement error on the Solow residual. With labor hoarding but no adjustment costs, the effort is not at its stationary value only at the period of the shock, and returns to it the next period without adjustment delay. Thus, if the measurement error is due to effort variations, it is controlled by economic agent and depends on government spending disturbances.

On the one hand, under the hypothesis of perfect competition, we exhibit a productivity cycle which is a stylized fact of most developed economies. Adjustment costs on employment permit to control the length of the productivity cycle whereas the hypothesis of labor hoarding involves a mechanical gap between productivity and employment without smoothing employment. On the other hand, we show that without government spending shocks, the model is unable to exhibit a productivity cycle.

The simulations of the US economy shows that the model with labor hoarding seems to reproduce the relative variability of productivity and employment, and the productivity cycle. Nevertheless, that cycle does not have the right length : adjustment costs allow to correct this failure, nonetheless it leads to a degradation of the relative variability of productivity and employment.

In France, the productivity cycle is longer than in the USA. The adjustment cost necessary to reproduce this stylized fact greatly alters the relative variability of productivity and employment.

At this stage, we can perceive the limits of the model proposed by Hansen [1985]. With a particular assumption — *i.e.* a model with indivisible labor inducing an infinite elasticity of labor supply — it reproduces in a satisfactory way, the variability of employment relatively to the productivity one. The extension of the basic model proposed in this chapter, in spite of encouraging results, does not correctly mimic all the data concerning the characteristics of labor market, particularly with French parameterization.

2.7 Appendix

A. Computation of the Steady State

Here, we compute the steady state of the deterministic model: we take the terms A_t and G_t as being constant over time. That is $A_t = 1$ and $G_t = G\ \forall t$. The stationary state ($\bar{c}$, $\bar{k}$, $\bar{N}$, $\bar{z}$, $\bar{e}$, $\bar{\lambda}$, $\bar{\mu}$) will be the solution of the system formed by the optimality conditions and the budget constraint. All the variables are taken at the same date. To begin with, it is obvious that at the stationary state $z = 1$. The other variables verify the following system:

$$\frac{1}{\bar{c}} = \bar{\lambda} \tag{2.2}$$

$$-\theta \log\left(\frac{T-\xi-\bar{e}H}{T}\right) = \alpha\lambda(\bar{e}H)^{\alpha}k^{1-\alpha}N^{\alpha-1}+\bar{\mu} \tag{2.3}$$

$$\frac{\theta}{T-\xi-\bar{e}H} = \alpha\lambda k^{1-\alpha}N^{\alpha-1}(\bar{e}H)^{\alpha-1} \tag{2.4}$$

$$\frac{\gamma_x}{\beta} = (1-\alpha)\bar{k}^{-\alpha}(\bar{N}\bar{e}H)^{\alpha}+1-\delta \tag{2.5}$$

$$\begin{aligned}\bar{\mu}(1-\beta) &= \beta\theta\log\left(\frac{T-\xi-\bar{e}H}{T}\right)\\ &\quad +\beta\alpha\bar{k}^{1-\alpha}(\bar{e}H)^{\alpha}\bar{N}^{\alpha-1}\lambda\end{aligned} \tag{2.6}$$

$$\bar{k}^{1-\alpha}(\bar{e}H)^{\alpha}\bar{N}^{\alpha} = \bar{c}+G+(\gamma_x-1+\delta)\bar{k} \tag{2.7}$$

From (2.3) and (2.6) it is clear that $\bar{\mu} = 0$. Taking (2.3) and (2.4), we eliminate $\bar{k}$, $\bar{N}$ and $\bar{\lambda}$ to obtain the following equation giving $\bar{e}$. That is :

$$\bar{e} = -\left(\frac{T-\xi-\bar{e}H}{H}\right)\log(T-\xi-\bar{e}H)$$

This equation has no analytical solution, but, for particular values of parameters, it is easy to compute numerically an approximated solution $\bar{e}$.

Once $\bar{e}$ determined, it is possible to express the per capita capital $\frac{\bar{k}}{\bar{N}}$ as a function of the parameters and $\bar{e}$. From (2.6) we obtain:

$$\frac{\bar{k}}{\bar{N}} = \left\{ \frac{\frac{\gamma_x}{\beta} - 1 + \delta}{(1-\alpha)(\bar{e}H)} \right\}^{-\frac{1}{\alpha}}$$

The value of the other variables is then determined as a function of the parameters, $\frac{\bar{k}}{\bar{N}}$ and $\bar{e}$. $\bar{\lambda}$ is computed using (2.3).

$$\bar{\lambda} = -\theta \frac{\log\left(\frac{T-\xi-\bar{e}H}{T}\right)}{\alpha(\bar{e}H)^{\alpha}\left(\frac{\bar{k}}{\bar{N}}\right)^{1-\alpha}}$$

and $\bar{c} = \frac{1}{\bar{\lambda}}$. We note that the stationary level of consumption is independent of the government spending. The equation (2.7) enables us to determine $\bar{k}$.

$$\bar{k} = \frac{\bar{c} + G}{(\bar{e}H)^{\alpha}\left(\frac{\bar{k}}{\bar{N}}\right)^{-\alpha} - \gamma_x + 1 - \delta}$$

We finally deduce that: $\bar{N} = \left(\frac{\bar{k}}{\bar{N}}\right)^{-1}\bar{k}$. We can then linearize the model around this steady state.

B. Solving the Labor Hoarding Model

The method employed to solve our model is taken from King, Plosser and Rebelo [1988]. It is based on the log-linearization of the first order condition of the optimization problem. The linearized optimality conditions are :

$$\widehat{c}_t = -\widehat{\lambda}_t \qquad (2.8)$$

$$\begin{aligned}[\alpha - 1 - \gamma]\widehat{z}_t + (\alpha-1)E(\widehat{e}_t|\Omega_t^{\star}) &= \\ -(1-\alpha)\widehat{k}_t + (1-\alpha)\widehat{N}_{t-1} - E(\widehat{\lambda}_t|\Omega_t^{\star}) - \frac{N s_c}{\alpha}E(\mu_t|\Omega_t^{\star}) - E(\widehat{A}_t|\Omega_t^{\star}) & \qquad (2.9)\end{aligned}$$

$$(\alpha-1)\widehat{z}_t + \left[\alpha - 1 - \frac{\alpha}{N\theta s_c}\right]\widehat{e}_t = -(1-\alpha)\widehat{k}_t - (\alpha-1)\widehat{N}_{t-1} - \widehat{\lambda}_t - \widehat{A}_t \qquad (2.10)$$

$$\begin{aligned}\alpha\widehat{k}_{t+1} - \alpha\widehat{N}_t - \frac{s_i\phi}{\beta(1-\alpha)}E(\widehat{\lambda}_{t+1}|\Omega_t) + \frac{s_i\phi}{\beta(1-\alpha)}\widehat{\lambda}_t &= \\ \alpha E(\widehat{z}_{t+1}|\Omega_t) + \alpha E(\widehat{e}_{t+1}|\Omega_t) + E(\widehat{A}_{t+1}|\Omega_t) & \qquad (2.11)\end{aligned}$$

$$(1-\alpha)\widehat{k}_{t+1} + (\alpha-1)\widehat{N}_t + E(\widehat{\lambda}_{t+1}|\Omega_t) + \frac{N s_c}{\alpha}E(\mu_{t+1}|\Omega_t) - \frac{N s_c}{\beta\alpha}\mu_t \quad =$$

$$-(\alpha-1)E(\widehat{z}_{t+1}|\Omega_t)-(\alpha-1)E(\widehat{e}_{t+1}|\Omega_t)-E(\widehat{A}_{t+1}|\Omega_t) \quad (2.12)$$

$$\begin{aligned}\phi s_i\widehat{k}_{t+1}-[s_i(\phi-1)+(1-\alpha)]\widehat{k}_t-\alpha\widehat{N}_{t-1} &= \\ -s_c\widehat{c}_t+\alpha\widehat{z}_t+\alpha\widehat{e}_t+\widehat{A}_t-s_g\widehat{G}_t & \end{aligned} \quad (2.13)$$

$$\widehat{N}_t-\widehat{N}_{t-1}=\widehat{z}_t \quad (2.14)$$

Equations (2.8) to (2.10) express the decision variables as a function of the state variables. Equations (2.11) to (2.14) are the motion equations of the state variables. In equation (2.9) that serves to determine employment, the effort variable $\widehat{e}_t$ was replaced by its prediction conditional on $\Omega_t^\star$. The hiring decision is taken conditionally on the prediction of the other variables of the model.

Computation of Employment

We project the optimality conditions on the information set $\Omega_t^\star$. Then, equations (2.8) to (2.10) and (2.11) to (2.14) take the following matricial form :

$$M_{cc}\begin{bmatrix} E(\widehat{c}_t|\Omega_t^\star) \\ \widehat{z}_t \\ E(\widehat{e}_t|\Omega_t^\star)\end{bmatrix} = M_{cs}\begin{bmatrix}\widehat{k}_t \\ \widehat{N}_{t-1} \\ E(\widehat{\lambda}_t|\Omega_t^\star) \\ E(\mu_t|\Omega_t^\star)\end{bmatrix} + M_{ce}\begin{bmatrix} E(\widehat{A}_t|\Omega_t^\star) \\ E(\widehat{G}_t|\Omega_t^\star)\end{bmatrix} \quad (2.15)$$

and

$$M_{ss0}\begin{bmatrix}\widehat{k}_{t+1} \\ \widehat{N}_t \\ E(\widehat{\lambda}_{t+1}|\Omega_t^\star) \\ E(\mu_{t+1}|\Omega_t^\star)\end{bmatrix} + M_{ss1}\begin{bmatrix}\widehat{k}_t \\ \widehat{N}_{t-1} \\ E(\widehat{\lambda}_t|\Omega_t^\star) \\ E(\mu_t|\Omega_t^\star)\end{bmatrix} = M_{sc0}\begin{bmatrix} E(\widehat{c}_{t+1}|\Omega_t^\star) \\ E(\widehat{z}_{t+1}|\Omega_t^\star) \\ E(\widehat{e}_{t+1}|\Omega_t^\star)\end{bmatrix} +$$

$$M_{sc1}\begin{bmatrix} E(\widehat{c}_t|\Omega_t^\star) \\ \widehat{z}_t \\ E(\widehat{e}_t|\Omega_t^\star)\end{bmatrix} + M_{se0}\begin{bmatrix} E(\widehat{A}_{t+1}|\Omega_t^\star) \\ E(\widehat{G}_{t+1}|\Omega_t^\star)\end{bmatrix} + M_{se1}\begin{bmatrix} E(\widehat{A}_t|\Omega_t^\star) \\ E(\widehat{G}_t|\Omega_t^\star)\end{bmatrix} \quad (2.16)$$

We finally deduce :

$$\begin{bmatrix} E(\widehat{k}_{t+1}|\Omega_t^\star) \\ \widehat{N}_t \\ E(\widehat{\lambda}_{t+1}|\Omega_t^\star) \\ E(\mu_{t+1}|\Omega_t^\star)\end{bmatrix} = W\begin{bmatrix}\widehat{k}_t \\ \widehat{N}_{t-1} \\ E(\widehat{\lambda}_t|\Omega_t^\star) \\ E(\mu_t|\Omega_t^\star)\end{bmatrix} + R\begin{bmatrix} E(\widehat{A}_{t+1}|\Omega_t^\star) \\ E(\widehat{G}_{t+1}|\Omega_t^\star)\end{bmatrix} + Q\begin{bmatrix} E(\widehat{A}_t|\Omega_t^\star) \\ E(\widehat{G}_t|\Omega_t^\star)\end{bmatrix} \quad (2.17)$$

The matrix W has two eigenvalues greater than one and two eigenvalues less than one[17]. The system (2.17) has two predetermined variables and two forward variables. Thus, this rational expectation equation has a unique solution[18], the transversality conditions being verified. The diagonalization and the application of the Hansen-Sargent formula[19] allow us to determine the $\widehat{N}_t$ solution which take the form :

$$\widehat{N}_t = \eta_{Nk}\widehat{k}_t + \eta_{NN}\widehat{N}_{t-1} + \eta_{NA}\widehat{A}_{t-1} + \eta_{Ng}\widehat{G}_{t-1} \tag{2.18}$$

or :

$$\widehat{z}_t = \eta_{zk}\widehat{k}_t + \eta_{zN}\widehat{N}_{t-1} + \eta_{zA}\widehat{A}_{t-1} + \eta_{zg}\widehat{G}_{t-1} \tag{2.19}$$

Complete Resolution of the Model

We then consider the system (2.8) to (2.14). The equation (2.9) is replaced by (2.18). To eliminate $\widehat{z}_t$, we substitute (2.14) in the other equations. Then, μ_t is only an argument of (2.12), the system to solve is finally consists of the following equations :

$$\widehat{c}_t = -\widehat{\lambda}_t \tag{2.20}$$

$$[\alpha - \frac{1}{N\theta c}\alpha y]\widehat{e}_t = -(1-\alpha)\widehat{k}_t + (1-\alpha)\widehat{N}_t - \widehat{\lambda}_t - \widehat{A}_t \tag{2.21}$$

$$\begin{aligned}\alpha\widehat{k}_{t+1} - \alpha\widehat{N}_{t+1} - \frac{\gamma_x}{\beta}\frac{k}{(1-\alpha)y}E(\widehat{\lambda}_{t+1}|\Omega_t) + \frac{\gamma_x}{\beta}\frac{k}{(1-\alpha)y}\widehat{\lambda}_t \; &= \\ \alpha E(\widehat{e}_{t+1}|\Omega_t) + E(\widehat{A}_{t+1}|\Omega_t)&\end{aligned} \tag{2.22}$$

$$\phi s_i\widehat{k}_{t+1} - [s_i(\phi-1) + (1-\alpha)]\widehat{k}_t - \alpha\widehat{N}_t = -s_c\widehat{c}_t + \alpha\widehat{e}_t + \widehat{A}_t - s_g\widehat{G}_t \tag{2.23}$$

$$-\eta_{Nk}\widehat{k}_{t+1} + \widehat{N}_{t+1} - \eta_{NN}\widehat{N}_t = \eta_{NA}\widehat{A}_t + \eta_{Ng}\widehat{G}_t \tag{2.24}$$

[17] The eigenvalues are ordered as follows:

$$\mu_1 < \mu_2 < 1 < \mu_3 < \mu_4$$

These eigenvalues satisfy: $\mu_1\mu_4 = \mu_2\mu_3 = \beta^{-1}$. See Levhari and Liviatan [1972] for a demonstration.

[18] See Blanchard and Kahn [1980] proposition 1.

[19] For more details, see King, Plosser and Rebelo [1988] technical appendix or Fairise, Hairault, Langot and Portier [1991]

At this stage, $\widehat{c}_t$ and $\widehat{e}_t$ appear as control variables and $\widehat{k}_t$, $\widehat{N}_t$ and $\widehat{\lambda}_t$ as state variables. (2.20) and (2.21) express each decision variable as a function of the state variables. (2.22) to (2.24) are the motion equations of the state variables.

The system (2.20) to (2.24) take the form :

$$N_{cc}\begin{bmatrix}\widehat{c}_t\\ \widehat{e}_t\end{bmatrix} = N_{cs}\begin{bmatrix}\widehat{k}_t\\ \widehat{N}_{t-1}\\ \widehat{\lambda}_t\end{bmatrix} + N_{ce}\begin{bmatrix}\widehat{A}_t\\ \widehat{G}_t\end{bmatrix} \tag{2.25}$$

and

$$N_{ss0}\begin{bmatrix}\widehat{k}_{t+1}\\ \widehat{N}_t\\ E(\widehat{\lambda}_{t+1}|\Omega_t)\end{bmatrix} + N_{ss1}\begin{bmatrix}\widehat{k}_t\\ \widehat{N}_{t-1}\\ \widehat{\lambda}_t\end{bmatrix} = N_{sc0}\begin{bmatrix}E(\widehat{c}_{t+1}|\Omega_t)\\ E(\widehat{e}_{t+1}|\Omega_t)\end{bmatrix} + N_{sc1}\begin{bmatrix}\widehat{c}_t\\ \widehat{e}_t\end{bmatrix} +$$

$$N_{se0}\begin{bmatrix}E(\widehat{A}_{t+1}|\Omega_t)\\ E(\widehat{G}_{t+1}|\Omega_t)\end{bmatrix} + N_{se1}\begin{bmatrix}\widehat{A}_t\\ \widehat{G}_t\end{bmatrix} \tag{2.26}$$

Then, substituting (2.25) in (2.26) and eliminating the controls, we get :

$$\begin{bmatrix}\widehat{k}_{t+1}\\ \widehat{N}_t\\ E(\widehat{\lambda}_{t+1}|\Omega_t)\end{bmatrix} = W_{II}\begin{bmatrix}\widehat{k}_t\\ \widehat{N}_{t-1}\\ \widehat{\lambda}_t\\ \mu_t\end{bmatrix} + R_{II}\begin{bmatrix}E(\widehat{A}_{t+1}|\Omega_t)\\ E(\widehat{G}_{t+1}|\Omega_t)\end{bmatrix} + Q_{II}\begin{bmatrix}\widehat{A}_t\\ \widehat{G}_t\end{bmatrix} \tag{2.27}$$

$$\begin{aligned}
W_{II} &= -(N_{ss0} - N_{sc0}N_{cc}^{-1}N_{cs})^{-1}(N_{ss1} - N_{sc1}N_{cc}^{-1}N_{cs})\\
R_{II} &= (N_{ss0} - N_{sc0}N_{cc}^{-1}N_{cs})^{-1}(N_{se0} - N_{sc0}N_{cc}^{-1}N_{ce})\\
Q_{II} &= (N_{ss0} - N_{sc0}N_{cc}^{-1}N_{cs})^{-1}(N_{se1} - N_{sc1}N_{cc}^{-1}N_{ce})
\end{aligned}$$

In (2.27), $\widehat{k}_{t+1}$ and $\widehat{N}_t$ are predetermined and $\widehat{\lambda}_t$ is forward. W_{II} has two eigenvalues less than 1 and one eigenvalue greater than 1. The rational expectation equation has then a unique solution (the transversality conditions being verified). The diagonalization of the system and the application of the Hansen-Sargent formula lead to a $\widehat{k}_t$ solution of the form :

$$\widehat{k}_{t+1} = \pi_{kk}\widehat{k}_t + \pi_{kN}\widehat{N}_t + \pi_{kA}\widehat{A}_t + \pi_{kg}\widehat{G}_t$$

The equation of determination of employment (2.18) can be rewritten as follows :

$$\widehat{N}_{t+1} = \pi_{Nk}\widehat{k}_t + \pi_{NN}\widehat{N}_t + \pi_{NA}\widehat{A}_t + \pi_{Ng}\widehat{G}_t \tag{2.28}$$

We denote by M the matrix linking the current state vector on the lagged state vector, and Π the matrix linking the interest variables with the states variables. We finally obtain :

$$\begin{bmatrix} \widehat{k}_{t+1} \\ \widehat{N}_{t+1} \\ \widehat{A}_{t+1} \\ \widehat{G}_{t+1} \end{bmatrix} = M \begin{bmatrix} \widehat{k}_t \\ \widehat{N}_t \\ \widehat{A}_t \\ \widehat{G}_t \end{bmatrix} + \begin{bmatrix} 0 \\ 0 \\ \epsilon_{At+1} \\ \epsilon_{gt+1} \end{bmatrix}$$

with

$$M = \begin{bmatrix} \pi_{kk} & \pi_{kN} & \pi_{kA} & \pi_{kg} \\ \pi_{Nk} & \pi_{NN} & \pi_{NA} & \pi_{Ng} \\ 0 & 0 & \rho_a & 0 \\ 0 & 0 & 0 & \rho_g \end{bmatrix}$$

and

$$\begin{bmatrix} \widehat{y}_t \\ \widehat{c}_t \\ \widehat{e}_t \\ \widehat{i}_t \\ \widehat{p}_t \\ \widehat{RS}_t \end{bmatrix} = \Pi \begin{bmatrix} \widehat{k}_t \\ \widehat{N}_t \\ \widehat{A}_t \\ \widehat{G}_t \end{bmatrix}$$

- p_t is the apparent mean productivity of work.
- RS_t is the naive Solow residual — *i.e.* $RS_t = A_t e_t^{\alpha}$ —.

C. Solution of the Model without Labor Hoarding

The same method leads to the following solution :

$$\begin{bmatrix} \widehat{k}_{t+1} \\ \widehat{N}_t \\ \widehat{A}_{t+1} \\ \widehat{G}_{t+1} \end{bmatrix} = M_1 \begin{bmatrix} \widehat{k}_t \\ \widehat{N}_{t-1} \\ \widehat{A}_t \\ \widehat{G}_t \end{bmatrix} + \begin{bmatrix} 0 \\ 0 \\ \epsilon_{At+1} \\ \epsilon_{gt+1} \end{bmatrix} \tag{2.29}$$

where

$$M_1 = \begin{bmatrix} \omega_{kk} & \omega_{kN} & \omega_{kA} & \omega_{kg} \\ \omega_{Nk} & \omega_{NN} & \omega_{NA} & \omega_{Ng} \\ 0 & 0 & \rho_a & 0 \\ 0 & 0 & 0 & \rho_g \end{bmatrix}$$

Denote by Π_1 the matrix relying the interest variables on the state variables. Then, we have :

$$\begin{bmatrix} \widehat{y}_t \\ \widehat{c}_t \\ \widehat{e}_t \\ \widehat{i}_t \\ \widehat{p}_t \\ \widehat{RS}_t \end{bmatrix} = \Pi_1 \begin{bmatrix} \widehat{k}_t \\ \widehat{N}_{t-1} \\ \widehat{A}_t \\ \widehat{G}_t \end{bmatrix} \tag{2.30}$$

We note that the state vector is formed by $\widehat{k}_t$, $\widehat{N}_{t-1}$, $\widehat{A}_t$ and $\widehat{G}_t$ whereas in the case of labor hoarding, it was formed by $\widehat{k}_t$, $\widehat{N}_t$, $\widehat{A}_t$ and $\widehat{G}_t$, more precisely, here the employment appears at date t. This is due to labor hoarding, employment is then a function of $\Omega_t^\star = \Omega_{t-1}$. At the beginning of period t, employment is predetermined like the capital stock.

D. Figures

The solid lines represent the responses to shocks of the model without labor hoarding and the dashed lines the responses to shocks of the model with labor hoarding.

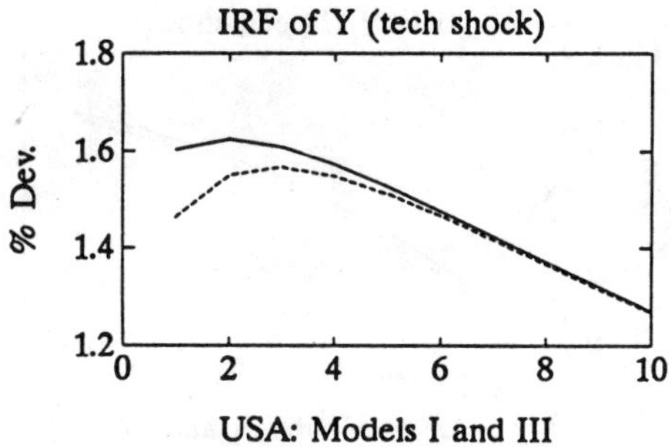
IRF of Y (tech shock)
% Dev.
USA: Models I and III

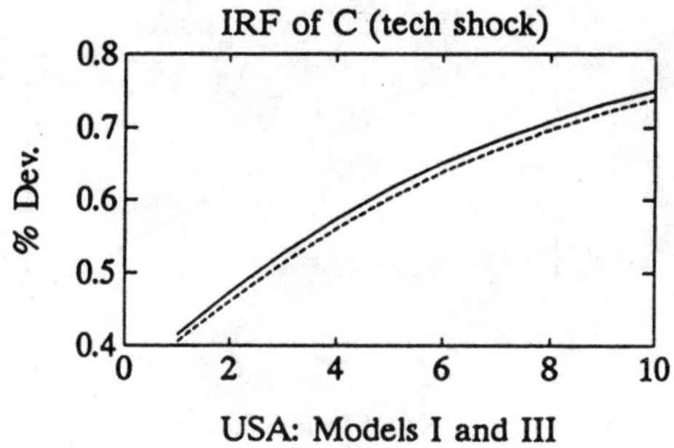
IRF of C (tech shock)
% Dev.
USA: Models I and III

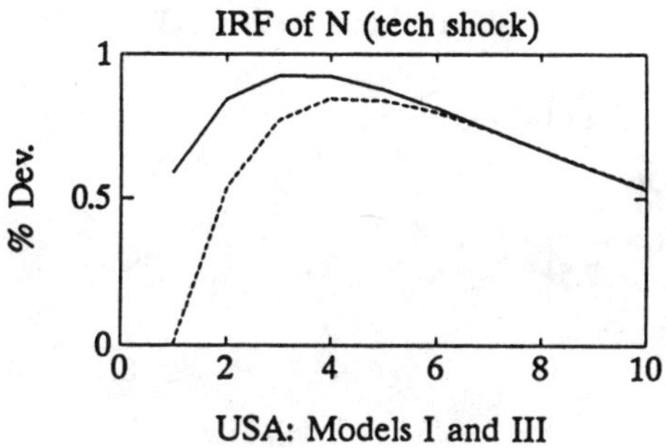
IRF of N (tech shock)
% Dev.
USA: Models I and III

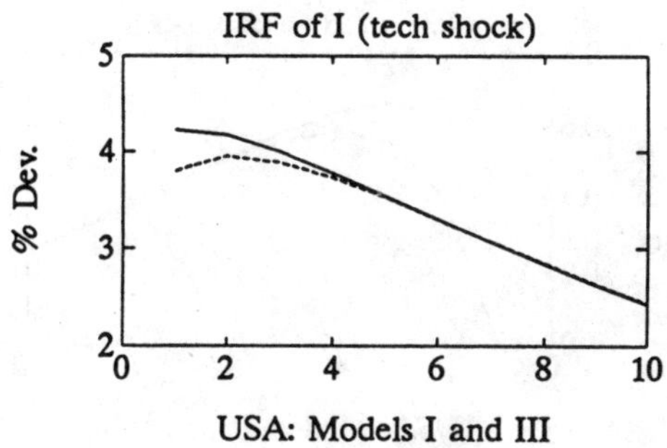
IRF of I (tech shock)
% Dev.
USA: Models I and III

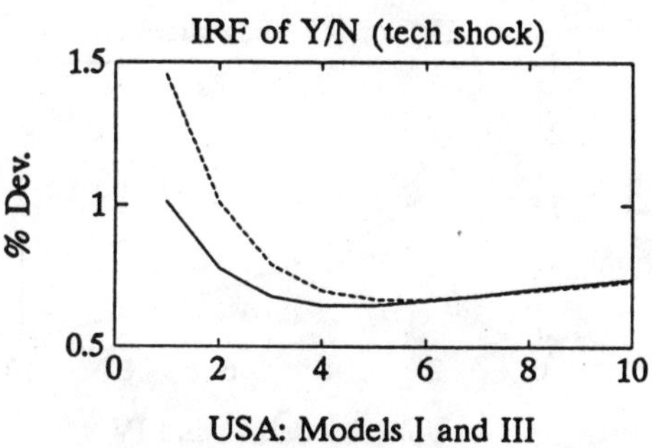
IRF of Y/N (tech shock)
% Dev.
USA: Models I and III

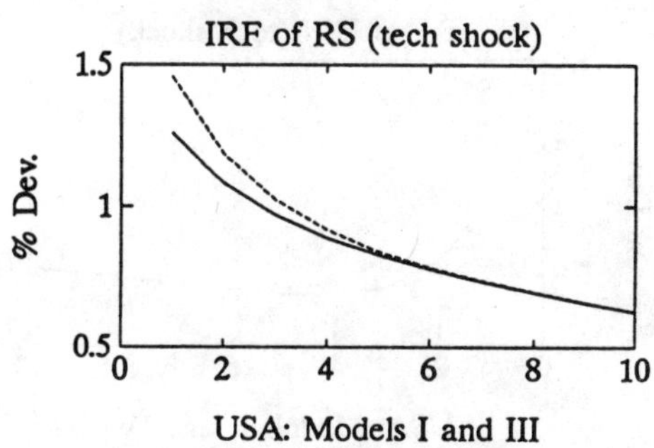
IRF of RS (tech shock)
% Dev.
USA: Models I and III

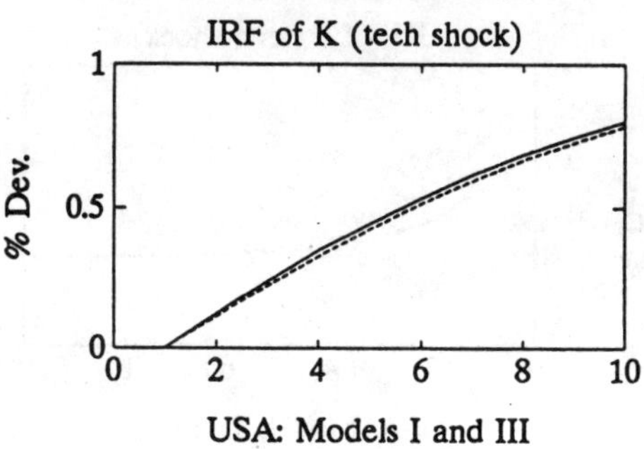
IRF of K (tech shock)
% Dev.
USA: Models I and III

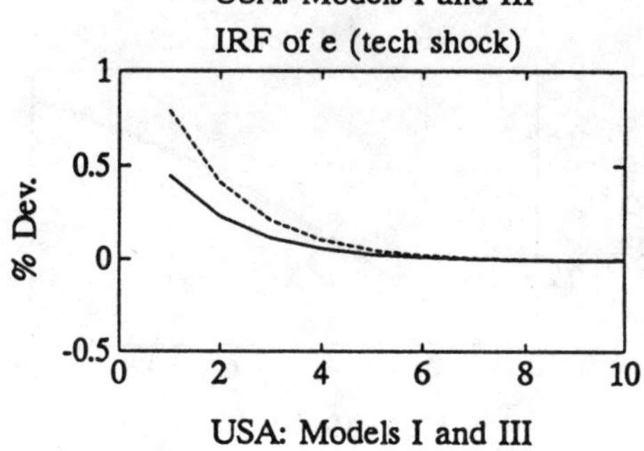
IRF of e (tech shock)
% Dev.
USA: Models I and III

IRF of Y (tech shock)

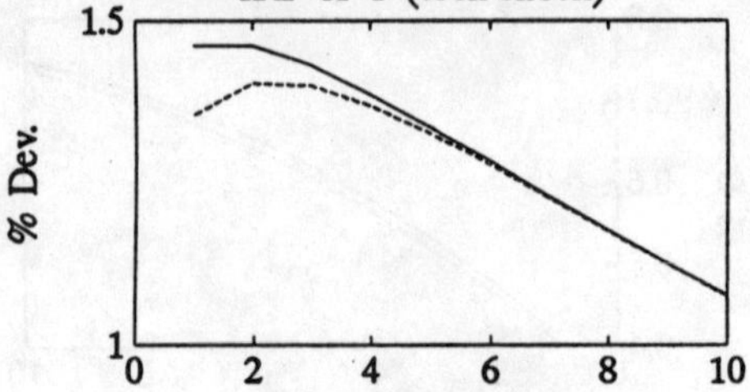

USA: Models II and IV

IRF of C (tech shock)

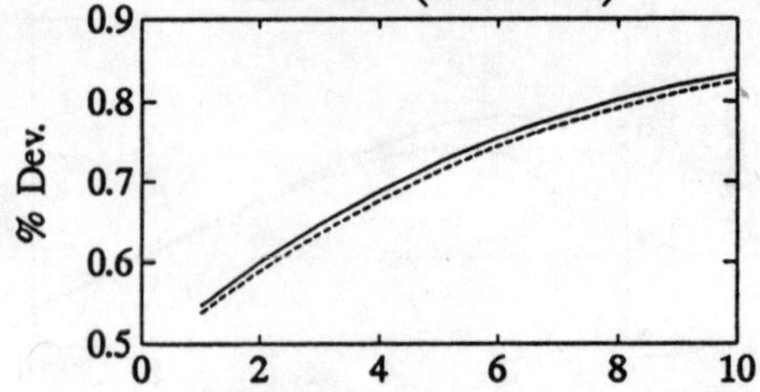

USA: Models II and IV

IRF of N (tech shock)

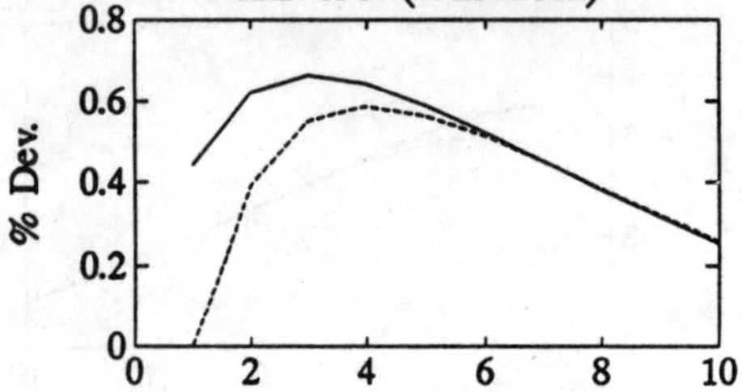

USA: Models II and IV

IRF of I (tech shock)

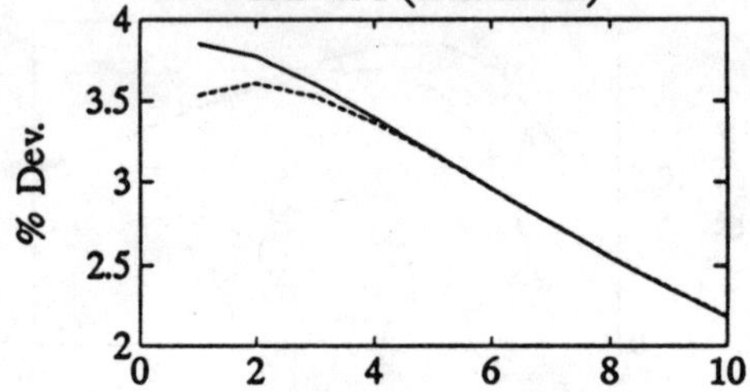

USA: Models II and IV

IRF of Y/N (tech shock)

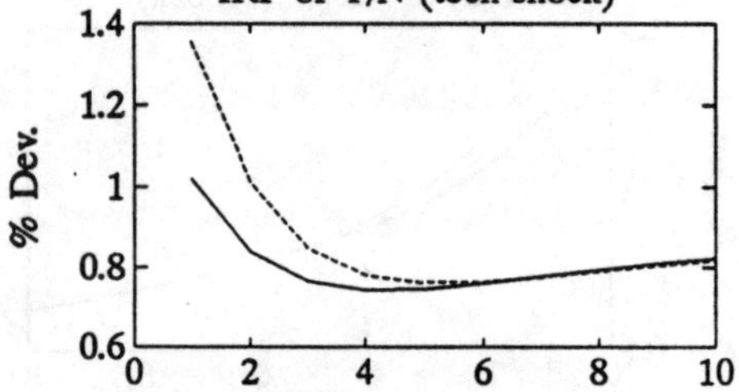

USA: Models II and IV

IRF of RS (tech shock)

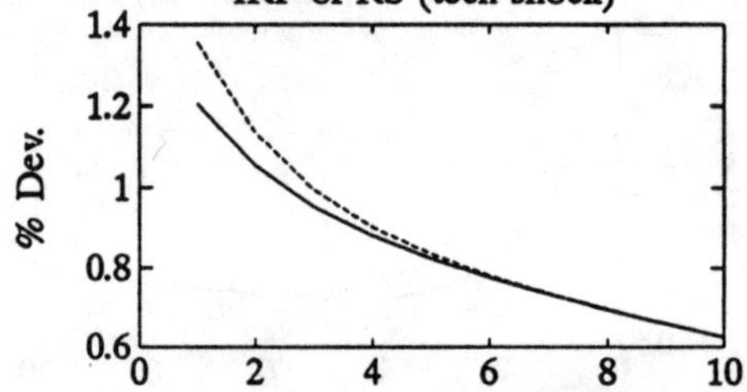

USA: Models II and IV

IRF of K (tech shock)

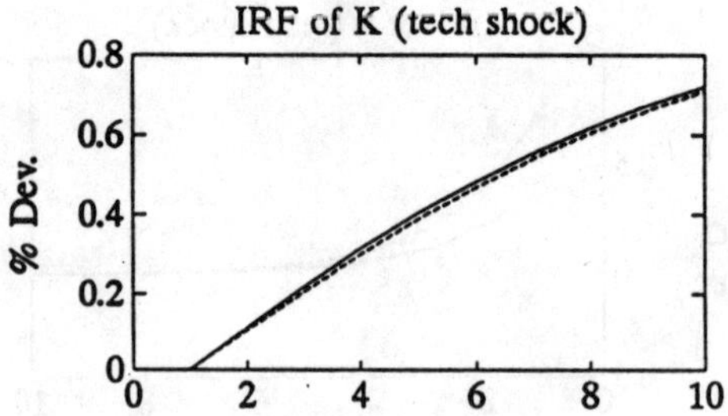

USA: Models II and IV

IRF of e (tech shock)

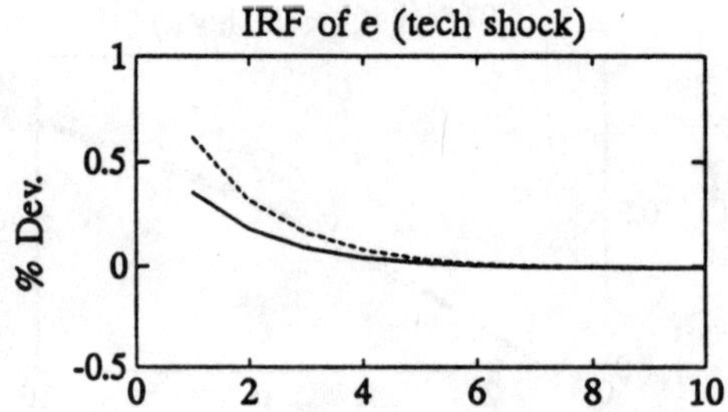

USA: Models II and IV

IRF of Y (gov shock)

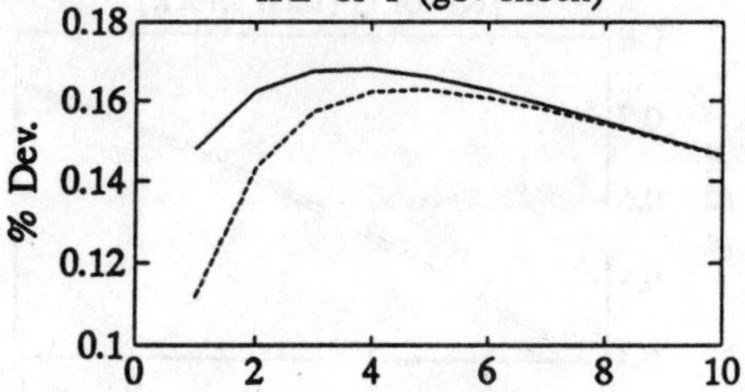

USA: Models II and IV

IRF of C (gov shock)

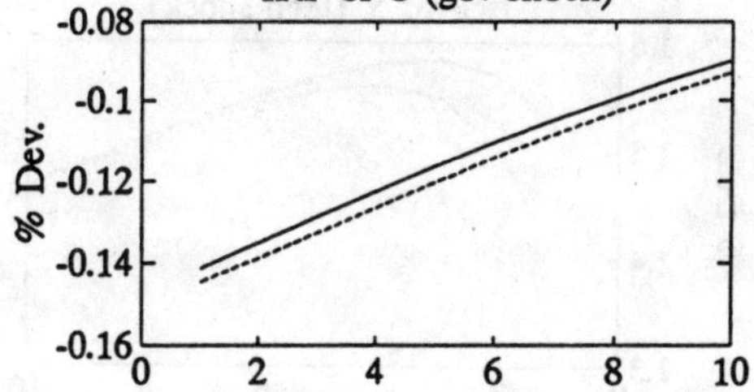

USA: Models II and IV

IRF of N (gov shock)

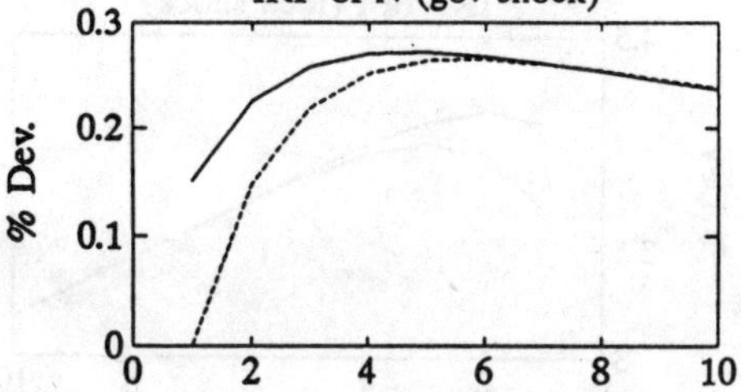

USA: Models II and IV

IRF of I (gov shock)

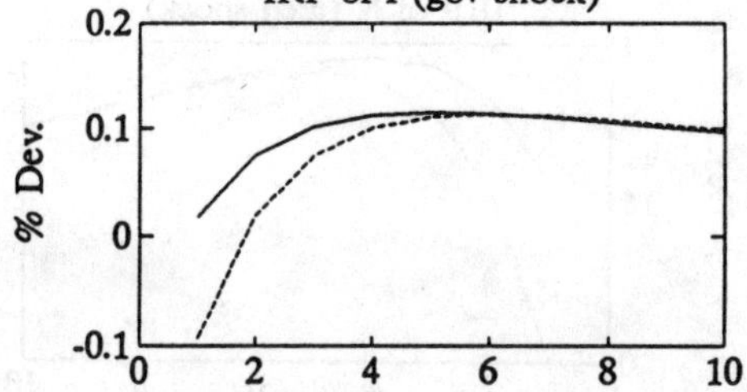

USA: Models II and IV

IRF of Y/N (gov shock)

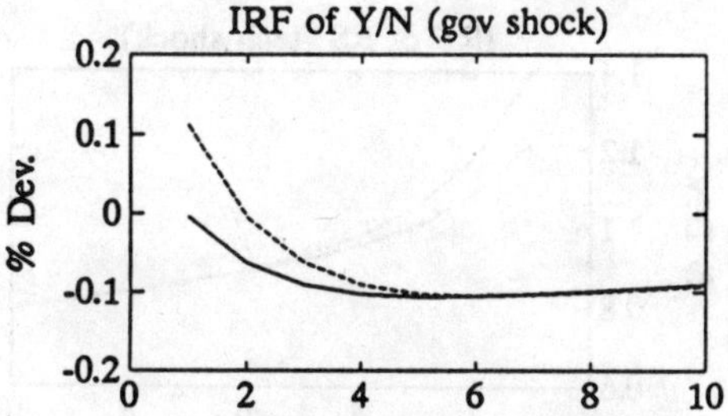

USA: Models II and IV

IRF of RS (gov shock)

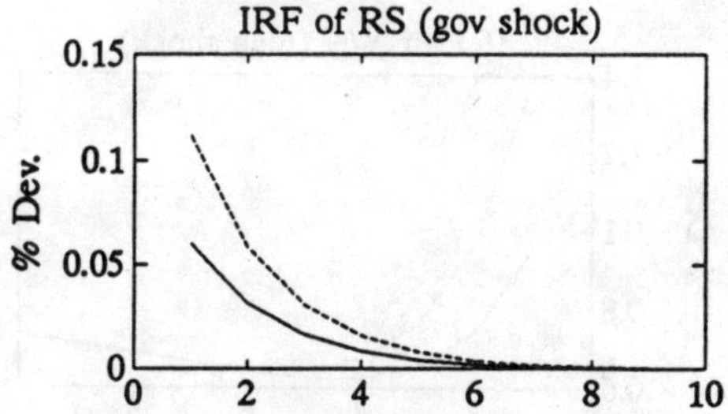

USA: Models II and IV

IRF of K (gov shock)

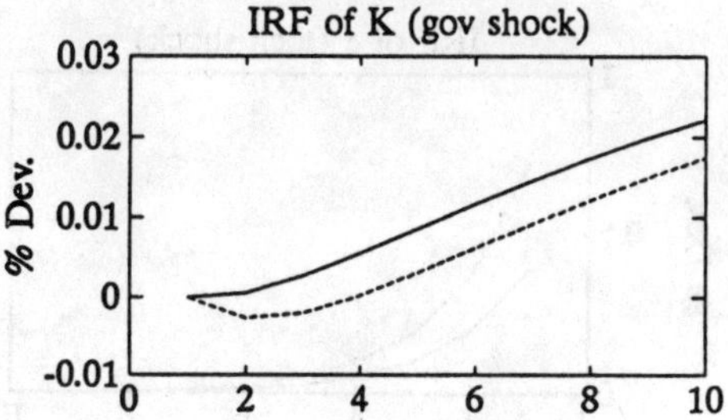

USA: Models II and IV

IRF of e (gov shock)

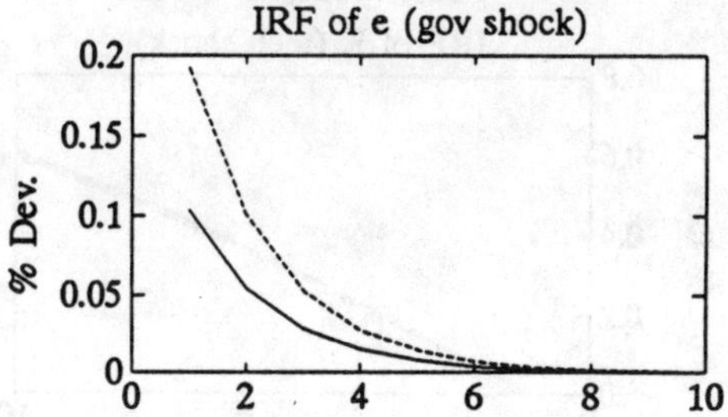

USA: Models II and IV

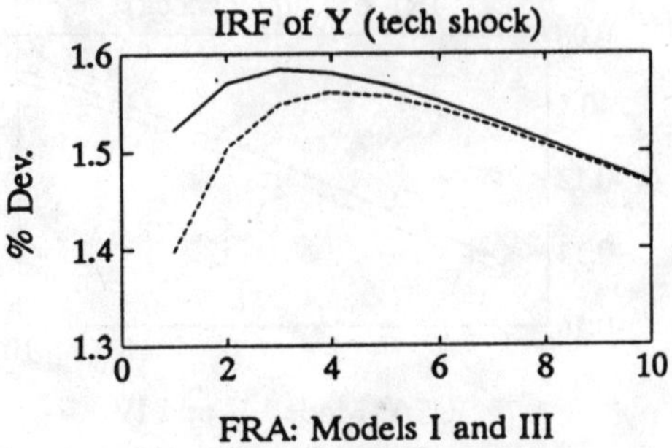
IRF of Y (tech shock)
% Dev.
FRA: Models I and III

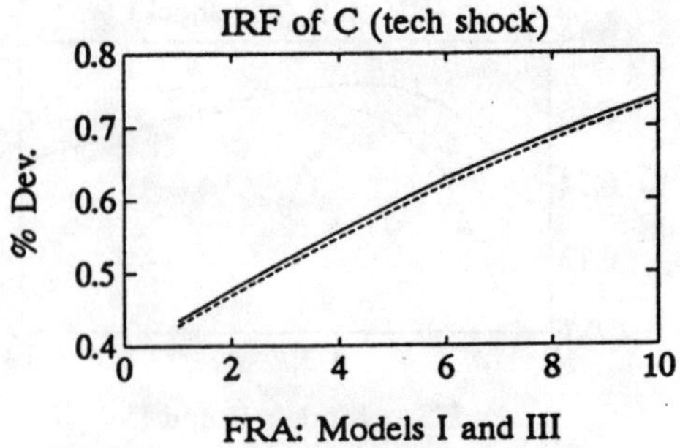
IRF of C (tech shock)
% Dev.
FRA: Models I and III

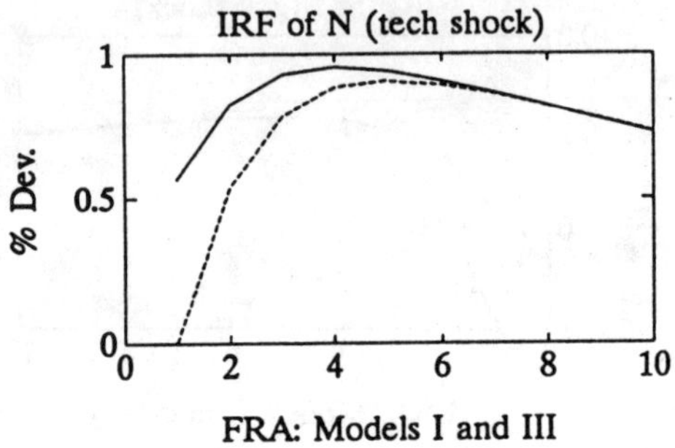
IRF of N (tech shock)
% Dev.
FRA: Models I and III

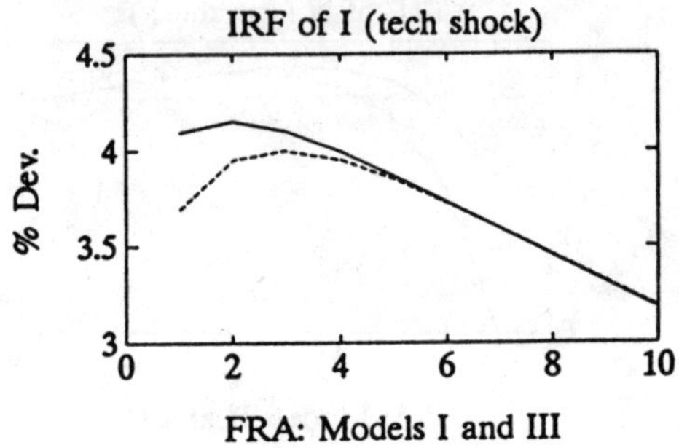
IRF of I (tech shock)
% Dev.
FRA: Models I and III

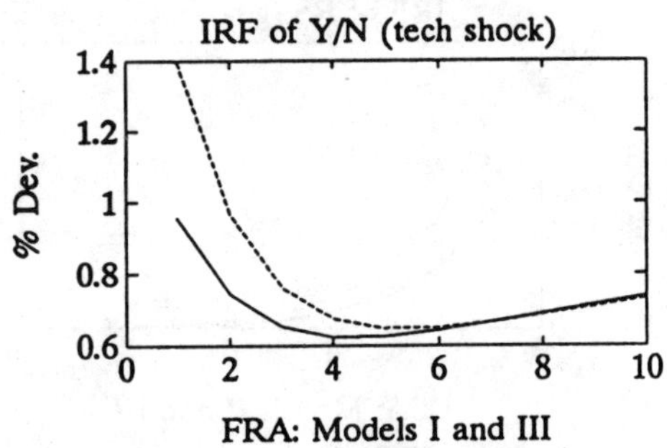
IRF of Y/N (tech shock)
% Dev.
FRA: Models I and III

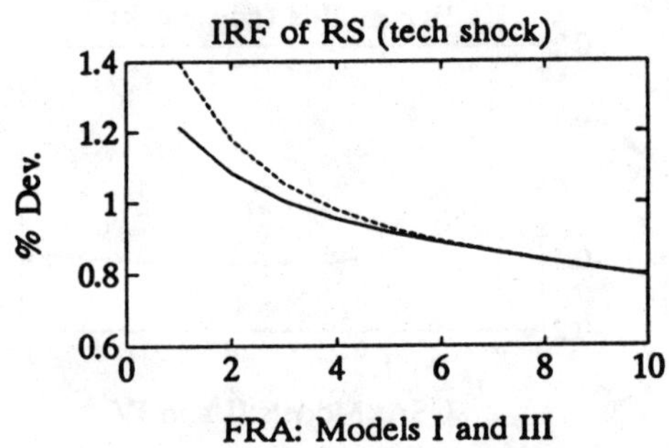
IRF of RS (tech shock)
% Dev.
FRA: Models I and III

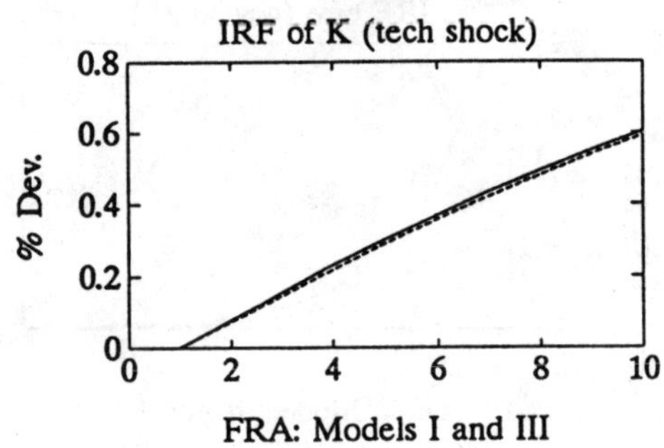
IRF of K (tech shock)
% Dev.
FRA: Models I and III

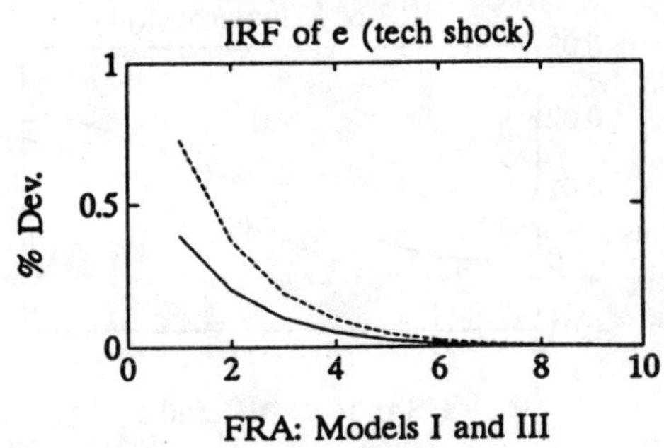
IRF of e (tech shock)
% Dev.
FRA: Models I and III

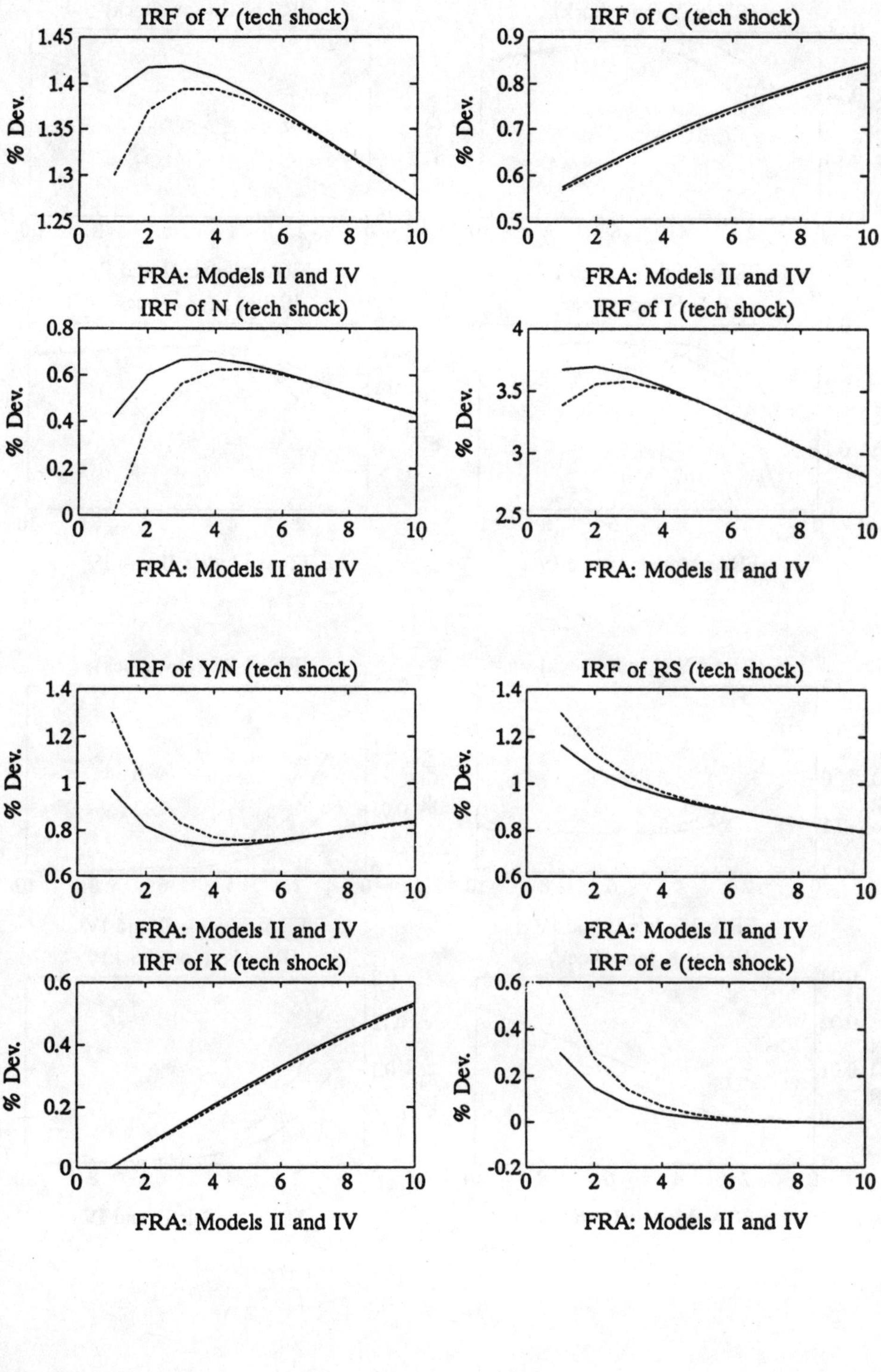
IRF of Y (tech shock)
% Dev.
FRA: Models II and IV
IRF of C (tech shock)
% Dev.
FRA: Models II and IV
IRF of N (tech shock)
% Dev.
FRA: Models II and IV
IRF of I (tech shock)
% Dev.
FRA: Models II and IV
IRF of Y/N (tech shock)
% Dev.
FRA: Models II and IV
IRF of RS (tech shock)
% Dev.
FRA: Models II and IV
IRF of K (tech shock)
% Dev.
FRA: Models II and IV
IRF of e (tech shock)
% Dev.
FRA: Models II and IV

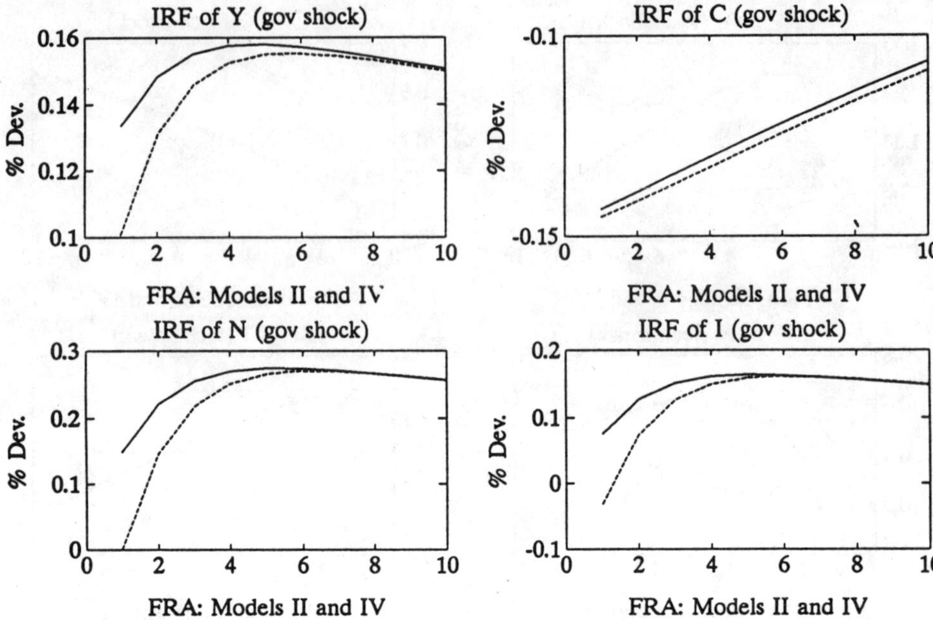
IRF of Y (gov shock)
% Dev.
FRA: Models II and IV
IRF of C (gov shock)
% Dev.
FRA: Models II and IV
IRF of N (gov shock)
% Dev.
FRA: Models II and IV
IRF of I (gov shock)
% Dev.
FRA: Models II and IV

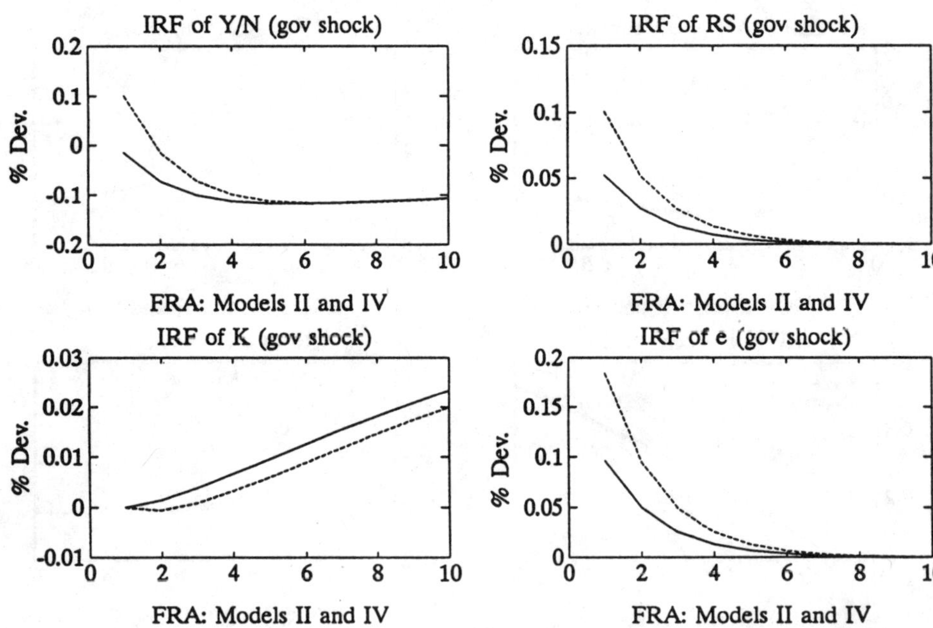
IRF of Y/N (gov shock)
% Dev.
FRA: Models II and IV
IRF of RS (gov shock)
% Dev.
FRA: Models II and IV
IRF of K (gov shock)
% Dev.
FRA: Models II and IV
IRF of e (gov shock)
% Dev.
FRA: Models II and IV

Figure 2.1: US Labor Productivity Cycle
Productivity Employment Cross-Correlations

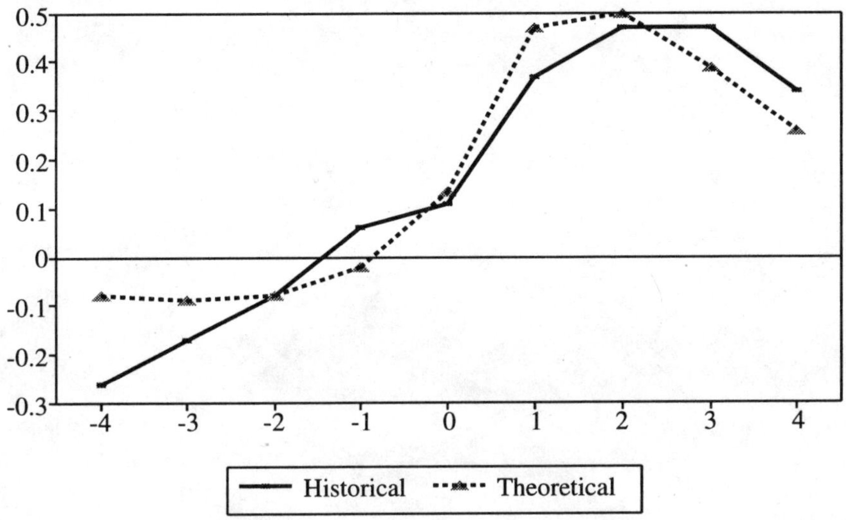

Figure 2.2: French Labor Productivity Cycle
Productivity Employment Cross-Correlations

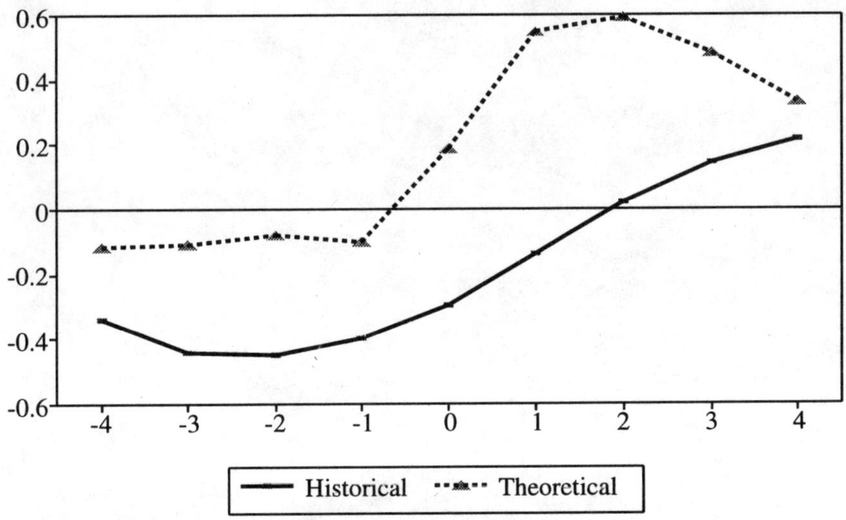

Bibliography

O. Blanchard and C. Kahn. The Solution of Linear Difference Models under Rational Expectations. *Econometrica*, 48:1305–1311, July 1980.

F. Brechling. The Relationship between Output and Employment in British Manufacturing Industries. *Review of Economic Studies*, 32(3):187–216, 1965.

C. Burnside, M. Eichenbaum and S. Rebelo. Labor Hoarding and the Business Cycle. *Journal of Political Economy*, 101(2):245–273, 1993.

L. Christiano and M. Eichenbaum. Current Real Business Cycle Theories and Aggregate Labor-Market Fluctuations. *American Economic Review*, 82(3):430–450, June 1992.

J.P. Danthine and J. Donaldson. Methodological and Empirical Issues in Real Business Cycle Theory. *European Economic Review*, 37(1):1–36, January 1993.

C. Evans. Productivity Shocks and Real Business Cycles. *Journal of Monetary Economics*, 29(2):191–208, April 1992.

X. Fairise, J.O. Hairault, F. Langot and F. Portier. *Ecriture et résolution du modèle canonique des cycles réels.* Cahiers ECO & MATHS 92.30, MAD, Université de Paris I, 1991.

R. Gordon. The End-of-Expansion Phenomenon in Short-Run Productivity Behaviour. *Brookings Papers on Economic Activity*, 2:447–461, 1979.

R. Hall. *Invariance Properties of Solow's Productivity Residual.* Working paper 3034, NBER, July 1989.

L. Hansen. Indivisible Labor and the Business Cycles. *Journal of Monetary Economics*, 309–327, 1985.

J. Kennan. The Estimation of Partial Adjustment Models with Rational Expectations. *Econometrica*, 47(6):1441–1455, 1979.

R. King, C. Plosser and J Rebelo. Production, Growth and Business Cycles I. *Journal of Monetary Economics*, 21:196–232, 1988.

F. Kydland and E. Prescott. Time to Build and Aggregate Fluctuations. *Econometrica*, 50:1345–1370, 1982.

J.P. Laffargue and P. Malgrange. *Une maquette trimestrielle de l'économie française avec anticipations rationnelles et concurrence monopolistique.* Working paper , CEPREMAP, 1991.

F. Langot. Composantes sectorielles et nationales dans l'évolution du résidus de Solow. *Annales d'Economie et de Statistique*, 24:134–154, 1992.

D. Levhari and N. Liviatan. On Stability in the Saddle-Point Sense. *Journal of Economic Theory*, 4:88–93, 1972.

J. Long and C. Plosser. Real Business Cycle. *Journal of Political Economy*, 39–69, 1983.

B. McCallum. Real Business Cycles Models. In *Handbook of Modern Business Cycle Theory*, Barro, R., 1989.

W. Oi. Labor as a Quasi Fixed Factor. *Journal of Political Economy*, 70:538–555, 1962.

E. Prescott. Theory Ahead of Business Cycle Measurement. *Federal Reserve Bank of Minneapolis Quaterly Review*, 10:9–22, 1986.

R. Rogerson. Indivisible Labor, Lotteries and Equilibrium. *Journal of Monetary Economics*, 21:3–16, 1988.

R. Solow. Technical Change and the Aggregate Production Function. *Review of Economics and Statistics*, 312–320, 1957.

L. Summers. Some Skeptical Observations on Real Business Cycles Theory. *Federal Reserve Bank of Minneapolis, Quaterly Review*, 23–27, 1986.

Chapter 3

Cash-In-Advance Constraint and the Business Cycle

J.O. Hairault & F. Portier

Abstract

We propose in this chapter a theoretical and empirical study of the effects of monetary shocks through a cash in advance constraint on the French and American business cycle, in an intertemporal general equilibrium setting. The cash in advance model of Cooley and Hansen [1989] is extended to include current investment in the cash constraint. This last specification gives a role to monetary disturbances in short run dynamics of the model.
The stochastic simulation of the model and its comparison with French and American data show that the model is able to mimic the real dimension of the business cycle. Nevertheless, the nominal dimension is not correctly reproduced in such a monetarized neoclassical model.

Introduction

Macroeconomic fluctuations analysis has been deeply renewed by the Real Business Cycle literature: on a theoretical side, fluctuations are optimal responses to exogenous shocks, and therefore any stabilizing policy is undesirable; on an empirical side, and to follow the line drawn by Lucas [1977], *RBC* models are small and simplified representation of reality, which allow for simulation and quantitative validation. The frontiers of the *RBC* literature, whose main goal was in the early eighties to mimic business cycle with a standard neoclassical growth model and with only one technological shock, are becoming more fuzzy nowadays.

On can distinguish two main lines of improvement of the standard model: the first one enriches the seminal model without denying the essential role of the technological disturbance; the second one adds nominal disturbances to account for the role of monetary shocks in the business cycle. This second line of research deals with *outside money*, and does not intersect with the literature on financial intermediation and the role of *inside money* (King and Plosser [1984] et Williamson [1987]).

We follow that second line in this paper, and we add a monetary shock to the standard neoclassical growth model. To give a role to money, we try to depart as less as possible from the neoclassical "idea of the world", and we do not assume any non-walrasian features as nominal rigidities, quantity rationing or non-rational expectations. Following Lucas [1985], we assume that money is valuable because of a cash-in-advance constraint. This assumption has already being done by Cooley and Hansen [1989], in the framework of the Hansen [1985] model, where consumption was constrained by cash-in-advance. In our model, we extend this assumption, and assume that consumption or consumption *and* investment can be constrained.

In such a model, the optimum-equilibrium equivalence is no longer valid, and one must *explicitly* solve for a competitive equilibrium. Furthermore, money may have a real impact on business cycle through anticipated inflation.

We study the consequences of such a constraint on the business cycle in the King, Plosser and Rebelo [1988] model. The model is solved by log linearization of the Euler conditions, and not by quadratic-approximation of the objective function, as in Cooley and Hansen [1989] or Kydland and Prescott [1982]).

We show that monetary shocks do not significantly modify order two moments of the simulated model, except when investment is also constrained by cash-in-advance. Nevertheless, even in that case, the nominal features of the business cycle, in France and the US, are badly reproduced. Money-output correlation is null and inflation-output correlation is negative. Furthermore, the effect of a monetary shock on output does not display the typical *hump shape* shown in empirical works (Barro [1981] or Blanchard [1989]). Therefore, our model shows that inflationary tax cannot be considered as the main transmission channel of monetary shock to economic activity.

3.1 The Model

The model is an extension of King, Plosser and Rebelo [1988]. We first present the fundamentals of the model, then the competitive equilibrium and its approximated solution.

3.1.1 The Neoclassical Growth Model with Cash-In-Advance

Technology and Preferences

The economy is composed of a continuum of identical households and a continuum of identical firms. Firms have access to the same constant returns to scale technology and act competitively. Firm j produces the final good with respect to the production function:

$$Y_{j,t} \leq A_t K_{j,t}^{\alpha} (X_t H_{j,t})^{1-\alpha} \tag{3.1}$$

where $K_{j,t}$ is the stock of capital, $H_{j,t}$ the level of employment and X_t a scale parameter of labor productivity.

A_t is given by the following stochastic process:

$$\log(A_t) = \rho_A \log(A_{t-1}) + (1 - \rho_A) \log(A) + \varepsilon_{A,t} \tag{3.2}$$

where $\varepsilon_{A,t}$ are *i.i.d.* with respect to a normal distribution with zero mean and variance σ_A^2, and where $\rho_A < 1$. The variable A_t is a temporary technological shock common to all firms, and we assume that A_t is known at the beginning of period t.

X_t grows at constant rate $\gamma > 1$, and stands for a labor-augmenting technical progress (Harrod-neutral). The growth-side of the model is therefore exogenous.

Households preferences are given by the utility function U, which represents the expected discounted sum of utility flows u, conditionally to the information set of date $t = 0$:

$$U = E_0 \sum_{t=0}^{\infty} \beta^t u(C_{i,t}, L_{i,t}) = E_0 \sum_{t=0}^{\infty} \beta^t (\log(C_{i,t}) + v(L_{i,t})) \tag{3.3}$$

where $\beta \in]0,1[$, $C_{i,t}$ [1] is consumption and $L_{i,t}$ leisure at period t. Households are endowed at each period with one unit of time that they allocate between work and leisure. They supply work to firms, they accumulate capital and rent it to firms. The accumulation technology is given by:

$$K_{i,t+1} = (1-\delta)K_{i,t} + I_{i,t}$$

where $I_{i,t}$ is the flow of investment at period t and $\delta \in [0,1]$ is the depreciation rate.

Each household is constrained by cash-in-advance in the following way:

$$C_{i,t} + \nu(K_{i,t+1} - (1-\delta)K_{i,t}) \leq \frac{M_{i,t}}{P_t} \tag{3.4}$$

where $\nu \in \{0,1\}$. This general form of the cash-in-advance constraint has constraint on consumption solely or on consumption and investment as particular cases. When $\nu = 0$, equation (3.4) means that the payment of consumption goods must be done with money transferred from the last period. When $\nu = 1$, consumption and investment payment must be done with money transferred from the last period. Capital revenues and wage income of period t cannot be used for consumption ($\nu = 0$) or for consumption and investment ($\nu = 1$) of the period.

Each household enters period t with some nominal balances $M_{i,t}$ which correspond to its demand for money at the end of period $t-1$. It also gets a monetary lump-sum transfer $N_{i,t}$ that cannot be used for current consumption (or consumption and investment), wage income and

[1] i indexes individual variables, by opposition to aggregate ones.

capital revenues. z_t is the real cost of gross capital[2]. At period t, household i decides of its consumption level, labor supply, money demand $M_{i,t+1}$ and the capital level $K_{i,t+1}$ it will intertemporally transfer. With w_t the real wage and P_t the general price level, household i budgetary constraint at period t is given by:

$$\begin{aligned} P_t K_{i,t+1} + M_{i,t+1} &\leq P_t(1-\delta)K_{i,t} + M_{i,t} + N_{i,t} \\ &\quad + P_t z_t K_{i,t} + P_t W_t H_{i,t} - P_t C_{i,t} \end{aligned} \tag{3.5}$$

Household i maximizes, for given $K_{i,0}$, $M_{i,0}$,g_0 and A_0, in ($C_{i,t}$, $H_{i,t}$, $M_{i,t+1}$, $K_{i,t+1}$), $t \in [0, +\infty[$, the objective U, with respect with the budgetary constraint (3.5) at each period. This program can be written in a recursive way, and its solution verifies the Bellman equation:

$$\begin{aligned} V_i\left(K_{i,t}, M_{i,t}, \mathcal{I}_{i,t}\right) &= \max_{C_{i,t}, L_{i,t}, K_{i,t+1}, M_{i,t+1}} \Big\{ u\left(C_{i,t}, L_{i,t}\right) \\ &+ \beta E_t \left[V_i\left(K_{i,t+1}, M_{i,t+1}, \mathcal{I}_{i,t+1}\right)\right] \Big\} \end{aligned}$$

with respect to (3.5):

$$\begin{aligned} P_t K_{i,t+1} + M_{i,t+1} &\leq P_t(1-\delta)K_{i,t} + M_{i,t} + N_{i,t} \\ &+ P_t z_t K_{i,t} + P_t W_t H_{i,t} - P_t C_{i,t} \qquad (\lambda_{i,t}) \end{aligned}$$

and to the cash-in-advance constraint (3.4):

$$C_{i,t} + \nu(K_{i,t+1} - (1-\delta)K_{i,t}) \leq \frac{M_{i,t}}{P_t} \qquad (\mu_{i,t})$$

$\lambda_{i,t}$ and $\mu_{i,t}$ are respectively the Lagrange multipliers of the budgetary constraint and the cash-in-advance constraint, $\mathcal{I}_{i,t}$ is the informational set of household i at period t: $\mathcal{I}_{i,t} = \{g_t, A_t, P_t, w_t, z_t\}$. We also impose the transversality conditions:

$$\lim_{\tau \to +\infty} E_t \left(\beta^{t+\tau} \frac{\partial V_{i,t+1+\tau}}{\partial M_{i,t+1+\tau}} M_{i,t+\tau} \right) = 0 \tag{3.6}$$

and

$$\lim_{\tau \to +\infty} E_t \left(\beta^{t+\tau} \frac{\partial V_{i,t+1+\tau}}{\partial K_{i,t+1+\tau}} K_{i,t+\tau} \right) = 0 \tag{3.7}$$

[2]Real interest rate of period t is given by $r_t = z_t - \delta$.

Money Supply

The aggregate stock of money M_t grows at rate $(g_t - 1)$:

$$M_{t+1} = g_t M_t \tag{3.8}$$

This rate g_t has a mean $\overline{g}$ and follows a random process:

$$\log(g_t) = \rho_g \log(g_{t-1}) + (1 - \rho_g) \log(\overline{g}) + \varepsilon_{g,t} \tag{3.9}$$

Monetary shocks $\varepsilon_{g,t}$ are *i.i.d.* and normally distributed with zero mean and variance σ_g^2, and $\rho_g < 1$. We assume that g_t is known at the beginning of period t, and that all the money created at period t is distributed to households:

$$(g_t - 1)M_t = \sum_i N_{i,t}$$

Labor Indivisibility

We assume that $v(L_{i,t})$ is concave, with a constant elasticity of its derivative:

$$\frac{L_{i,t} v''(L_{i,t})}{v'(L_{i,t})} = \zeta \quad \forall L_{i,t} \tag{3.10}$$

This elasticity ζ is the inverse of the intertemporal elasticity of substitution of leisure, which happens to be determinant in the cyclical behavior of the model. Let ϵ_N be the intertemporal elasticity of substitution of labor, one have:

$$\epsilon_N = -\left(\frac{1-H}{H}\right)\frac{1}{\zeta}$$

Following Hansen [1985] and Rogerson [1988], we will assume that jobs are indivisible in our economy: each household works H_0 hours or does not work. One can easily show[3] that, at the symmetrical equilibrium, the representative agent utility function is linear in labor, and that the elasticity of the marginal disutility of labor ζ is null, which means that the intertemporal elasticity of substitution of leisure is infinite.

[3]See chapter 1.

Existence of a Steady Growth Path

The model verifies the standard existence condition of a steady growth path[4] at rate γ. All aggregate variables $Y_t, K_t, C_t, X_t, M_t/P_{t-1}, W_t$, individual variables $Y_{i,t}, K_{i,t}, C_{i,t}, M_{i,t}/P_{t-1}$, investment levels I_t and $I_{i,t}$ grow at rate γ. Worked hours H_t are bounded by the total amount of time at each period (which is constant), and the only admissible growth rate of worked hours is therefore null.

The model can therefore be written as a stationary model, by deflating all real variables (except H) by the exogenous growth component X_t. We will then work with the following deflated variables $y_t = Y_t/X_t$, $k_t = K_t/X_t$, $c_t = C_t/Xt$, $m_t = M_t/(P_{t-1}X_t)$, $i_t = I_t/$, $y_{i,t} = Y_{i,t}/X_t$, $w_t = W_t/X_t$, $k_{i,t} = K_{i,t}/X_t$, $c_{i,t} = C_{i,t}/X_t$, $i_{i,t} = I_{i,t}/X_t$ and $m_{i,t} = M_{i,t}/(P_{t-1}X_t)$.

This deflated economy is similar to the initial one except for two points. First, capital accumulation equations must be written:

$$\gamma k_{t+1} = (1-\delta)k_t + i_t$$

and

$$\gamma k_{i,t+1} = (1-\delta)k_{i,t} + i_{i,t}$$

Second, the utility function must be written:

$$u(c_{i,t}, H_{i,t}) = \log(c_{i,t}) - BH_{i,t} + \log(X_t)$$

where $\log(X_t)$ is at each period an additive constant independent of the optimal choice of households. household i objective is therefore given by:

$$U = E_0 \sum_{t=0}^{\infty} \beta^t (\log(c_{i,t}) - BH_{i,t})$$

The Bellman equation of the stationarized model is:

$$\begin{aligned} V_i\left(k_{i,t}, m_{i,t}, \mathcal{I}_{i,t}\right) &= \max_{c_{i,t}, L_{i,t}, k_{i,t+1}, m_{i,t+1}} \Big\{ u\left(c_{i,t}, L_{i,t}\right) \\ &\quad + \beta E\left[V_i\left(k_{i,t+1}, m_{i,t+1}, \mathcal{I}_{i,t+1}\right)\right] \Big\} \end{aligned}$$

[4]See King, Plosser and Rebelo [1987] and Fairise, Hairault, Langot and Portier [1991] for an extensive treatment.

with respect to

$$\gamma k_{i,t+1} + m_{i,t+1} \leq (1-\delta)k_{i,t} + m_{i,t}\frac{P_{t-1}}{P_t} + n_{i,t} + z_t k_{i,t} + w_t H_{i,t} - c_{i,t}$$

$$c_{i,t} + \nu(\gamma k_{i,t+1} - (1-\delta)k_{i,t}) \leq m_{i,t}\frac{P_{t-1}}{P_t}$$

Competitive Equilibrium of the Economy

A *Competitive Equilibrium of the Economy* is given by a set of decision rules of households $c_{i,t}(s_t)$, $k_{i,t+1}(s_{i,t})$, $m_{i,t+1}(s_{i,t})$ and $H_{i,t}(s_{i,t})$ (where $s_{i,t} = (K_{i,t}, m_{i,t}, \mathcal{I}_{i,t})$ is the state variables vector of household i), a capital demand $k_{j,t}(s_{j,t})$ and a labor demand $H_{j,t}(s_{j,t})$ of firms (where $s_{j,t} = (g_t, A_t, P_t, w_t, z_t)$ is the state variables vector of firm j), a price vector $(P_t(s_t), w_t(s_t), z_t(s_t))$ (where $s_t = (g_t, A_t, k_t, m_t)$ such that:

- $c_{i,t}(s_{i,t})$, $H_{i,t}(s_{i,t})$, $k_{i,t+1}(s_{i,t})$ and $m_{i,t+1}(s_{i,t})$ maximize :

  $$V_{i,t}\left(k_{i,t}, m_{i,t}, \mathcal{I}_{i,t}\right)$$

  with respect to (3.4) and (3.5) for prices $(P_t(s_t), w_t(s_t), z_t(s_t))$,

- $k_{j,t}(s_{j,t})$ and $H_{j,t}(s_{j,t})$ maximize firm j profit at each period with respect to (3.1) and for prices $(P_t(s_t), w_t(s_t), z_t(s_t))$,

- $(P_t(s_t), w_t(s_t), z_t(s_t))$ clear consumption good market, capital market, labor market and money market (the numéraire of the economy); which is respectively $\sum_i (c_{i,t}(s_t) + i_{i,t}(s_t)) = \sum_j y_{j,t}$, $\sum_i k_{i,t}(s_{t-1}) = \sum_j k_{j,t}(s_t)$, $\sum_i H_{i,t}(s_t) = \sum_j H_{j,t}(s_t)$ and $\sum_i m_{i,t+1}(s_t) = g_t \sum_i m_{i,t} P_{t-1}$.

3.1.2 How to Solve the Model?

We cannot give an analytical solution to this model, and we must adopt an approximation method to solve it. We choose a first-order approximation (around the steady-state equilibrium) of the competitive equilibrium equations. Danthine, Donaldson and Mehra [1989] have shown that such an approximation introduces a relatively small bias. By neglecting second-order terms, one must notice that decision rules will be independent of the variance of exogenous disturbances.

We first compute the steady-state, then log-linearized the set of equations defining the competitive equilibrium around that steady-state, and at last solve the linear system we get.

Extensive Definition of the Competitive Equilibrium

First-order conditions of household i are given by, $\forall t \in [0, +\infty[$:

$$\begin{aligned}
\frac{\partial u}{\partial c_{i,t}} - \lambda_{i,t} - \mu_{i,t} &= 0 \\
\frac{\partial u}{\partial H_{i,t}} + w_t \lambda_{i,t} &= 0 \\
\beta E_t \left[\frac{\partial V(i,t+1)}{\partial k_{i,t+1}} \right] - \gamma \lambda_{i,t} - \nu \gamma \mu_{i,t} &= 0 \\
\beta E_t \left[\frac{\partial V(i,t+1)}{\partial m_{i,t+1}} \right] - \lambda_{i,t} &= 0 \\
\frac{\partial V(i,t)}{\partial k_{i,t}} - \lambda_{i,t}(1-\delta+z_t) - \nu(1-\delta)\mu_{i,t} &= 0 \\
\frac{\partial V(i,t)}{\partial m_{i,t}} - \frac{P_{t-1}}{P_t}\lambda_{i,t} - \frac{P_{t-1}}{P_t}\mu_{i,t} &= 0 \\
\lambda_{i,t} &\geq 0 \\
\lambda_{i,t}\Big(\gamma k_{i,t+1} + m_{i,t+1} - (1-\delta)k_{i,t} - \frac{P_{t-1}}{P_t} m_{i,t} & \\
- n_{i,t} - z_t k_{i,t} - w_t H_{i,t} + c_{i,t} \Big) &= 0 \\
\mu_{i,t} &\geq 0 \\
\mu_{i,t}(c_{i,t} + \nu(\gamma k_{i,t+1} - (1-\delta)k_{i,t}) - m_{i,t}) &= 0 \\
\lim_{\tau \to \infty} \left[\beta^{t+\tau} \frac{\partial V(t+1+\tau)}{\partial k_{t+1+\tau}} k_{t+\tau} \right] &= 0 \\
\lim_{\tau \to \infty} \left[\beta^{t+\tau} \frac{\partial V(t+1+\tau)}{\partial m_{t+1+\tau}} m_{t+\tau} \right] &= 0
\end{aligned}$$

These conditions can be written:

$$\frac{1}{c_{i,t}} = \lambda_{i,t} + \mu_{i,t} \tag{3.11}$$

$$\lambda_{i,t} w_t = B \tag{3.12}$$

$$\gamma(\lambda_{i,t} + \nu \mu_{i,t}) = \beta E_t \left[\lambda_{i,t+1}(1-\delta+z_{t+1}) + \nu \mu_{i,t+1}(1-\delta) \right] \tag{3.13}$$

$$\lambda_{i,t} = \beta E_t \left[\frac{P_t}{P_{t+1}} (\lambda_{i,t+1} + \mu_{i,t+1}) \right] \tag{3.14}$$

with the two transversality conditions.

First order conditions of firm j program are given by:

$$z_t = \alpha A_t k_{j,t}^{\alpha-1} H_{j,t}^{1-\alpha} \tag{3.15}$$

$$w_t = (1-\alpha) A_t k_{j,t}^{\alpha} H_{j,t}^{-\alpha} \tag{3.16}$$

The competitive equilibrium is also defined by the following equilibrium and definition equations:

$$f_t \sum_i m_{i,t+1} = g_t m_t \tag{3.17}$$

$$f_t \sum_i m_{i,t+1} = m_t + \sum_{i=1}^{h} n_{i,t} \tag{3.18}$$

$$y_{j,t} = A_t (k_{j,t})^{\alpha} (H_{j,t})^{1-\alpha} \tag{3.19}$$

$$\sum_j k_{j,t} = \sum_i k_{i,t} \tag{3.20}$$

$$\sum_j H_{j,t} = \sum_i H_{i,t} \tag{3.21}$$

$$\sum_j y_{j,t} = \sum_i (c_{i,t} + i_{i,t}) \tag{3.22}$$

Equations (3.11) to (3.22) give the extensive definition of the competitive equilibrium.

Stationary Equilibrium

With the normalization $i = j = 1$, the resolution of the former system at the steady-state allow us to compute the stationary competitive equilibrium for the model with cash-in-advance constraint on consumption (Model I) and cash-in-advance constraint on consumption and investment (Model II).

Model I: The solution of the model at the steady-state is given by the following ratios:

$$z = \frac{\gamma}{\beta} - 1 + \delta \tag{3.23}$$

$$\frac{k}{y} = \frac{\alpha\beta}{(\gamma - \beta(1-\delta))} \tag{3.24}$$

$$\frac{c}{y} = 1 - (\gamma + 1 - \delta)\frac{k}{y} \tag{3.25}$$

$$\frac{i}{y} = (\gamma + 1 - \delta)\frac{k}{y} \tag{3.26}$$

$$H = \frac{(1-\alpha)\beta}{B\overline{g}}\frac{y}{c} \tag{3.27}$$

The cash-in-advance constraint has no effect on the ratios $c/y, k/y$ and i/y. Nevertheless, consumption is more expensive, because of the inflationary tax, and the cash-in-advance constraint leads to a substitution consumption-leisure towards leisure. Equation (3.27) shows that worked hours depend negatively on the growth rate of money supply $\overline{g}$. Differing from models without any labor supply behavior (Abel [1985] and Stockman [1981]), money is not super-neutral.

Model II: The solution of the model at the steady-state is given by the following ratios: :

$$\frac{k}{y} = \frac{\alpha\beta^2\gamma}{\overline{g}(\gamma - \beta(1-\delta))} \tag{3.28}$$

$$\frac{c}{y} = 1 - (\gamma + 1 - \delta)\frac{k}{y} \tag{3.29}$$

$$\frac{i}{y} = (\gamma + 1 - \delta)\frac{k}{y} \tag{3.30}$$

$$H = \frac{(1-\alpha)\beta}{B\overline{g}}\frac{y}{c} \tag{3.31}$$

At the competitive stationary equilibrium, the ratios $c/y, k/y, i/y$ are now functions of the money supply growth rate. As investment is more expensive because of the inflationary tax, the capital-output ratio is now weaker, as it is shown in equation (3.28). Again, leisure price is not affected by the inflationary tax, and its steady-state value is therefore an increasing function of $\overline{g}$ (equation (3.31)).

In both models, one must notice that the cash-in-advance constraint will be binding if and only if $\overline{g} > \beta$, as the multiplier μ is given by

$$\mu = \max\left\{\lambda(\frac{g}{\beta} - 1), 0\right\}$$

In the following, we will then choose $\overline{g}$ and the support of ϵ_g such that the approximation that this constraint is always binding can be made.

Linearization and Resolution

We log-linearized the system defining the equilibrium to obtain the following system (where $\widehat{x}_t$ is the percentage of deviation of X_t from its stationary value X). To solve the model for any value of ν, one must adopt a resolution method which differs from King, Plosser and Rebelo. We assume that decisions rules for $\widehat{m}_{t+1}$ and $\widehat{\mu}_{t+1}$ are given by:

$$\begin{pmatrix} \widehat{m}_{t+1} \\ \widehat{\mu}_t \end{pmatrix} = \Psi \begin{pmatrix} \widehat{k}_t \\ \widehat{m}_t \\ \widehat{A}_t \\ \widehat{g}_t \end{pmatrix} \tag{3.32}$$

where Ψ is a (2×3) matrix of undetermined coefficients.

With that assumption, the log-linearized system defining the stochastic competitive equilibrium can be written:

$$\begin{aligned} M_1(\Psi)\widehat{\Omega}_t &= M_2(\Psi)\widehat{\Theta}_t + M_3(\Psi)\widehat{e}_t & (3.33) \\ M_4(\Psi, L)E_t\left[\widehat{\Theta}_{t+1}\right] &= M_5(\Psi, L)E_t\left[\widehat{\Omega}_{t+1}\right] + M_6(\Psi, L)E_t\left[\widehat{e}_{t+1}\right] & (3.34) \end{aligned}$$

where $M_j(\Psi)$ are real coefficients matrix and $M_j(\Psi, L)$ are polynomial matrix of L, with order less or equal to one, and:

$$\widehat{\Theta}_t = \begin{pmatrix} \widehat{k}_t \\ \widehat{m}_t \\ \widehat{\lambda}_t \end{pmatrix}, \quad \widehat{\Omega}_t = \begin{pmatrix} \widehat{c}_t \\ \widehat{H}_t \\ \widehat{w}_t \\ \widehat{z}_t \\ \widehat{y}_t \\ \widehat{f}_t \\ \widehat{i}_t \\ \widehat{\mu}_t \end{pmatrix}, \quad \widehat{e}_t = \begin{pmatrix} \widehat{A}_t \\ \widehat{g}_t \end{pmatrix}$$

Equations (3.33) and (3.34) give a dynamic relation between $\widehat{\Theta}$ and $\widehat{e}$:

$$\widehat{\Theta}_{t+1} = W(\Psi)\widehat{\Theta}_t + Q(\Psi)\widehat{e}_t + R(\Psi)\widehat{e}_{t+1} \tag{3.35}$$

where $W(\Psi)$, $R(\Psi)$ and $Q(\Psi)$ are real matrix.

The system (3.35) is then solved following Blanchard and Kahn [1980]. $W(\Psi)$ has two eigenvalues; one with modulus less than one and one with modulus more than one. The solution is therefore a saddle-path, and the transversality condition (3.7) is used to get the initial value of the forward variable (λ)[5].

The model is linear and Markovian, and one can use formulas from Hansen and Sargent [1980] to get, from equations (3.2) and (3.9)), the new formulation of equation (3.35):

$$\widehat{s}_{t+1} = M(\Psi)\widehat{s}_t + \varepsilon_t \tag{3.36}$$

$$\widehat{d}_t = \Pi(\Psi)\widehat{s}_t \tag{3.37}$$

where $\widehat{s}_t$ is the state variables vector (predetermined or exogenous) and $\widehat{d}_t$ the control variables vector:

$$\widehat{s}_t = \begin{pmatrix} \widehat{k}_t \\ \widehat{m}_t \\ \widehat{A}_t \\ \widehat{g}_t \end{pmatrix}, \quad \widehat{d}_t = \begin{pmatrix} \widehat{c}_t \\ \widehat{h}_t \\ \widehat{w}_t \\ \widehat{z}_t \\ \widehat{y}_t \\ \widehat{\lambda}_t \\ \widehat{\mu}_t \\ \widehat{f}_t \\ \widehat{i}_t \end{pmatrix}, \quad \widehat{\varepsilon}_t = \begin{pmatrix} 0 \\ 0 \\ \varepsilon_{A,t} \\ \varepsilon_{g,t} \end{pmatrix}$$

and

$$M = \begin{pmatrix} \pi_{kk} & \pi_{km} & \pi_{kA} & \pi_{kg} \\ \pi_{mk} & \pi_{mm} & \pi_{mA} & \pi_{mg} \\ 0 & 0 & \rho_A & 0 \\ 0 & 0 & 0 & \rho_g \end{pmatrix}, \quad \Pi = \begin{pmatrix} \pi_{ck} & \pi_{cm} & \pi_{cA} & \pi_{cg} \\ \pi_{Hk} & \pi_{Hm} & \pi_{HA} & \pi_{Hg} \\ \pi_{wk} & \pi_{wm} & \pi_{wA} & \pi_{wg} \\ \pi_{rk} & \pi_{rm} & \pi_{rA} & \pi_{rg} \\ \pi_{yk} & \pi_{ym} & \pi_{yA} & \pi_{yg} \\ \pi_{\mu k} & \pi_{\mu m} & \pi_{\mu A} & \pi_{\mu g} \\ \pi_{\lambda k} & \pi_{\lambda m} & \pi_{\lambda A} & \pi_{\lambda g} \\ \pi_{fk} & \pi_{fm} & \pi_{fA} & \pi_{fg} \\ \pi_{ik} & \pi_{im} & \pi_{iA} & \pi_{ig} \end{pmatrix}$$

We then have from (3.36) and (3.37)

$$\begin{pmatrix} \widehat{m}_{t+1} \\ \widehat{\mu}_t \end{pmatrix} = \Phi(\Psi) \begin{pmatrix} \widehat{k}_t \\ \widehat{m}_t \\ \widehat{A}_t \\ \widehat{g}_t \end{pmatrix} \tag{3.38}$$

[5]The transversality condition (3.6) is necessary for the existence of decision rules Ψ.

where $\Phi(\Psi)$ is a (2×3) matrix.

Equation (3.38) allows the identification of the undetermined coefficients matrix $\overline{\Psi}$, and the solution of the model is given by the triple $(M(\overline{\Psi}), \Pi(\overline{\Psi}), \overline{\Psi})$, where $\overline{\Psi}$ is the solution of:

$$\overline{\Psi} = \Phi(\overline{\Psi})$$

3.2 Dynamic Features of the Cash-In-Advance Constraint Model

Before performing stochastic simulations and impulse response functions analysis, we study the model sensibility to various calibration parameters, and analyze its dynamic properties.

When the economy is shocked by a technological or monetary shock, one can distinguish two different channel of transmission of these shocks: a direct effect measured by the second and third column of the Π matrix and a indirect effect which relies on the deviation of capital, and which is measured by the first column of matrix Π. One must notice that a deviation of $\widehat{m}_t$ will only generate more inflation[6]. The dynamical properties of the model therefore depend, on the one hand on the specific effects of the two shocks, and more precisely on the response of investment, and on the other hand on the dynamics of the model when capital is not at its steady-state (transitional dynamics).

To study the parameter sensibility of the model, we will use the US calibration as the benchmark one[7]:

γ	δ	α	β	ζ
1.004	.025	.42	.988	-1

$\overline{g}$	ρ_g	σ_g	ρ_A	σ_A
1.014	.377	.9	.95	.9

[6]Let us recall that this variable is not the monetary shock, but the level of real balances.

[7]We will comment these elasticity values in section 2.2.

3.2.1 Transitional Dynamics

We assume an initial deviation of capital from its steady-state value in an economy without any shocks. The model will converge back to its steady-state. The closer to one will be the autoregressive coefficient μ_1 of the capital law of motion equation ($\mu_1 = \pi_{kk}$), the smaller will be the speed of convergence of the economy.

Coefficients Π_{jk} are instantaneous elasticities with respect to the deviation of capital. The benchmark calibration gives the following values (table 3.1):

Table 3.1

	μ_1	Π_{ck}	Π_{Hk}	Π_{mk}	Π_{yk}	Π_{ik}	Π_{wk}	Π_{rk}
Model *I*	.953	.617	-.294	.617	.249	-.626	.543	-.715
Model *II*	.954	.610	-.261	.268	.268	-.571	.529	-.698

These responses can be interpreted as in a model without cash-in-advance constraint, except for real balances. For a given level of money supply, real balances are negatively dependant on the price level fluctuations caused by variations of the money demand. These variations of the money demand are the consequences of the cash-in-advance constraint, through consumption variations in Model *I* and output (consumption + investment) variations in model *II*.

When capital is initially below its steady-state level, all variables monotonically converge towards their steady-state level. Consumption and output are always below, which implies an price increase and a real balances decrease. Investment and worked hours are always above their stationary level.

These transitional paths can be understood with respect to three effects that are consequences of the low level of capital. Financial income of households is lower, marginal productivity of capital is higher and marginal productivity of labor is lower. The two first factors lead to an increase of labor supply, as the third one has an opposite effect. With the technology and preferences chosen, the two first effects always dominate the third: worked hours are counter-cyclical.

The speed of convergence depends on the labor-leisure intertemporal substitution. The higher is that intertemporal elasticity of substitution –*i.e.* the lower is ζ –, the faster is the adjustment (tables 3.2 and 3.3).

Table 3.2: Model *I*

ζ	-100	-40	-10	-2	-.4
μ_1	.966	.965	.963	.956	.950
Π_{ck}	.667	.664	.654	.627	.606
Π_{Hk}	-.009	-.023	-.080	-.225	-.359
Π_{mk}	.667	.664	.654	.627	.606
Π_{yk}	.414	.406	.374	.289	.212
Π_{ik}	-.189	-.210	-.296	-.519	-.732
Π_{wk}	.424	.430	.454	.514	.571
Π_{rk}	-.565	-.572	-.603	-.680	-.749

Table 3.3: Model *II*

ζ	-100	-40	-10	-2	-.4
μ_1	.965	.965	.962	.957	.952
Π_{ck}	.659	.656	.645	.620	.601
Π_{Hk}	-.009	-.022	-.07	-.203	-.314
Π_{mk}	.414	.407	.377	.302	.237
Π_{yk}	.414	.407	.377	.302	.237
Π_{ik}	-.186	-.205	-.282	-.481	-.656
Π_{wk}	.423	.429	.451	.505	.552
Π_{rk}	-.565	-.592	-.599	-.668	-.726

One must notice that, in Model *I*, the Π elasticities with respect to capital are strictly identical to those of the canonical *RBC* model[8]. On the contrary, speed of convergence is smaller in Model *II*, as the response of investment is smaller.

This point can also be seen when one study the influence of the growth rate of money supply $\overline{g}$. According to Abel [1985], there is no effect of $\overline{g}$ on μ_1 in Model *I*, but $\overline{g}$ matters in Model *II*.

[8]See chapter 1 of this book.

Table 3.4: Model *I*

$\overline{g}$	1.001	1.14	1.40	1.90
μ_1	.9547	.954	.9531	.9518
Π_{ck}	.613	.589	.558	.522
Π_{Hk}	-.264	-.231	-.188	-.139
Π_{mk}	.266	.285	.310	.338
Π_{yk}	.266	.285	.310	.338
Π_{ik}	-.568	-.591	-.624	-.667
Π_{wk}	.531	.517	.499	.478
Π_{rk}	-.70	-.681	-.657	-.629

An increase in $\overline{g}$ leads to a higher speed of convergence, because the elasticity of investment increases. These numerical simulations extend the results of Abel [1985], who study the particular cases $\delta = 0$ and $\delta = 1$.

3.2.2 Instantaneous Responses to a Technological Shock

Following a once-for-all productivity shock, a representative household with infinite preference for present will instantaneously consume the surplus of production, and will not modify its investment. One will therefore observe no dynamical effect of such a temporary shock. As soon as the preference for present is not infinite, the household will not consume the all surplus of output and will transfer consumption to the future through capital accumulation: part of the output surplus will be invested. This arbitrage between consumption today and consumption tomorrow depends on the intertemporal elasticity of consumption, which value is one in our model with log-utility function. The household can also respond to a technological shock through labor supply behavior, with respect to a double arbitrage: leisure today-leisure tomorrow and consumption today-leisure today. If productivity of labor is higher today, a substitution effect leads to more labor supply and a income effect to less labor supply. In our specification, the substitution effect dominates. Therefore, even a once-for-all productivity shock will have persistent effects. In a model with only technological shocks, real variables respond pro-cyclically (table 3.5).

These elasticities are not different from a model without cash-in-advance constraint except for the price level adjustment, because money demand varies. A technological shock increases good supply, reduces prices and lowers the inflationary tax.

Table 3.5

	Π_{kA}	Π_{cA}	Π_{HA}	Π_{mA}	Π_{yA}	Π_{iA}	Π_{wA}	Π_{rA}
Model *I*	.121	.398	.898	.398	1.52	4.19	.622	1.35
Model *II*	.113	.415	.738	1.42	1.42	3.91	.689	1.27

With a lower intertemporal elasticity of leisure, worked hours, output, consumption and investment responses are weaker and the labor productivity one is higher.

Table 3.6: Model *I*

ζ	-100	-40	-10	-2	-.4
Π_{cA}	.302	.306	.326	.375	.418
Π_{HA}	.037	.067	.230	.678	1.18
Π_{mA}	.302	.306	.326	.375	.418
Π_{yA}	1.01	1.04	1.33	1.39	1.64
Π_{iA}	2.71	2.78	3.05	3.81	4.57
Π_{wA}	.988	.972	.90	.714	.511
Π_{rA}	.91	.939	1.02	1.24	1.46

Table 3.7: Model *II*

ζ	-100	40	-10	-2	-.4
Π_{cA}	.326	.331	.349	.395	.433
Π_{HA}	.024	.058	.201	.569	.899
Π_{mA}	1.01	1.03	1.11	1.33	1.52
Π_{yA}	1.01	1.03	1.11	1.33	1.52
Π_{iA}	2.70	2.76	3.0	3.62	4.19
Π_{wA}	.989	.975	.915	.760	.622
Π_{rA}	.917	.935	1.0	1.19	1.35

The Π matrix is also affected by the persistence of the technological shock. In Model *I*, these effects are the same than in a model without a cash-in-advance constraint, except for the reduction of the inflationary tax. The responses of hours and investment are lower; Π_{yA} and Π_{kA} are therefore smaller. The increase of households financial income is higher, which explains the lower response of hours and investment (table 3.8).

Table 3.8: Model *I*

ρ_A	0	.1	.25	.50	.75
Π_{cA}	.107	.110	.117	.137	.189
Π_{HA}	1.33	1.32	1.31	1.28	1.20
Π_{yA}	1.77	1.76	1.76	1.74	1.70
Π_{iA}	5.73	5.72	5.68	5.57	5.30
Π_{wA}	.440	.442	.447	.459	.492
Π_{rA}	-.124	.052	.317	.752	1.16

In Model *II*, an increase in the persistence of the technological shock has an effect on worked hours which is opposite to the canonical *RBC* model one. The anticipation of a lower inflationary tax in the future when ρ_A increases leads to an increase of hours elasticity (table 3.9).

Table 3.9: Model *II*

ρ_A	0	.10	.25	.50	.75
Π_{cA}	.060	.068	.084	.121	.193
Π_{HA}	-.025	.050	.174	.416	.688
Π_{mA}	.985	1.03	1.10	1.24	1.39
Π_{yA}	.985	1.03	1.10	1.24	1.39
Π_{iA}	3.25	3.38	3.60	3.99	4.36
Π_{wA}	1.01	.979	.926	.825	.710
Π_{rA}	-.068	.031	.199	.536	.957

3.2.3 Instantaneous Responses to a Monetary Shock

In these cash-in-advance models, only the anticipated component of inflation has an effect on real variables. The effects of these shocks are therefore very different from those of a model with imperfect information or with price rigidities.

A change in the average growth rate of money supply, the money supply being deterministic or stochastic, does not modify the cyclical properties of Model *I*, but matters in Model *II*.

Instantaneous responses to a monetary shock and for the benchmark calibration are given in table 3.10.

Table 3.10

	Π_{kg}	Π_{cg}	Π_{Hg}	Π_{mg}	Π_{yg}	Π_{ig}	Π_{wg}	Π_{rg}
Model *I*	.059	-.937	-.093	-.937	-.054	2.04	.039	-.064
Model *II*	-.052	-.024	-.943	-.547	-.547	-1.83	.396	-.167

In both models, a monetary shock at the beginning of period t decreases the demand for money, as households anticipate an increase of prices next period. Therefore, this shock decreases consumption in Model I and output in Model II. Leisure increases in both models, as this good is not taxed by inflation. The key differences between the two models is the responses of hours and investment. In Model I, consumption is reduced and investment increases. Investment is here the only way of transferring wealth into the future to avoid the increase of the inflationary tax due to the monetary shock: there is therefore a Tobin-effect in Model I. In model II, investment is also reduced, as it is now taxed by inflation. The only *credit-good* (by opposition to *cash-good*) is now leisure, and worked hours decrease. In Model I, when the persistence of the monetary shock is low, the elasticity of hours is weakly negative (table 3.11).

Table 3.11: Model I

ρ_g	0	.1	.5	.75	.95
Π_{cg}	-.959	-.955	-.923	-.862	-.615
Π_{hg}	-.060	-.066	-.114	-.205	-.573
Π_{mg}	-.959	-.955	-.923	-.862	-.615
Π_{yg}	-.035	-.038	-.066	-.119	-.332
Π_{ig}	2.16	2.14	1.97	1.64	.342
Π_{wg}	.025	.028	.048	.086	.240
Π_{rg}	-.047	-.050	-.076	-.125	-.323

In model II, this elasticity is strongly negative when the monetary shock is persistent (table 3.12).

Table 3.12: Model *II*

ρ_g	0	.1	.5	.75	.95
Π_{cg}	-.027	-.027	-.020	.003	.129
Π_{hg}	-.788	-.823	-1.01	-1.20	-1.55
Π_{mg}	-.457	-.477	-.586	-.696	-.903
Π_{yg}	-.457	-.477	-.586	-.696	.903
Π_{ig}	-1.51	-1.58	-1.97	-2.41	-3.44
Π_{wg}	.331	.345	.424	.504	.654
Π_{rg}	.031	-.014	-.251	-.471	-.785

3.3 Can a Cash-In-Advance Constraint Account for the Role of Monetary Shocks in the Business Cycle?

The theoretical model we presented in the two first sections can explain why money matters in the business cycle. Money has an effect through the inflationary tax households must pay when they transfer money from one period to another. Our aim is now to judge of the empirical relevance of this mechanism for the French and American business cycle. Can a cash-in-advance constraint explain the role of monetary shocks? Do the responses of key macro-variables to a monetary shock mimic empirical studies? To answer these questions, we first develop the stochastic simulation method and the calibration of the model.

3.3.1 Simulation Method and Calibration Issues

We follow here the traditional validation method of the *RBC* models by computing second order moments of the model variables[9]. The results of these stochastic simulations depend on the choice of parameters. We use estimated values to calibrate the model.

For the US, we use the calibration chosen in King, Plosser and Rebelo [1988] for a first panel of parameters, and assume labor indivisibility (ζ is null):

[9]See chapter 1.

Table 3.13

γ	δ	α	β	ζ	H
1.004	.025	.42	.988	0	.2

We estimated on quarterly US data over 1959-1990 the processes of technological and monetary shock. We estimate an $AR(1)$ on the relative deviation of total factor productivity to its mean value, and on the relative deviation of the growth rate of $M1$ to its mean value. The results are given in table 3.12:

Table 3.14

$\overline{g}$	ρ_g	σ_g	ρ_A	σ_A
1.014	.377	.9	.95	.9

We follow the same method for France, using previous calibration of Laffargue, Malgrange and Pujol [1990] and estimating the shock processes.

Table 3.13 bis

γ	α	δ	β	ζ	H
1.0067	.46	.0125	.988	0	.2

Table 3.14 bis

$\overline{g}$	ρ_g	σ_g	ρ_A	σ_A
1.028	.50	.98	.98	.9

3.3.2 The Specific Role of Monetary Shocks in Cash-In-Advance Models

We simulate Model I and Model II with and without monetary shocks, using the US calibration. The results are given in tables 3.15, 3.16, 3.17 and 3.18[10].

[10]These moments are means over 100 simulations of 124 points each. The figures between parenthesis are empirical standard-deviation of these moments over the 100 simulations.

Table 3.15. Model I without Monetary Shocks (US Calibration)

Variable	$\widehat{y}$	$\widehat{c}$	$\widehat{i}$	$\widehat{h}$	$\widehat{w}$	$\widehat{inf}$
S.D.	1.98	.60	5.61	1.49	.60	.37
	(.002)	(.006)	(.008)	(.002)	(.001)	(.000)
S.D./S.D.($\widehat{y}$)	1	.30	2.81	.75	.30	.19
	(0)	(.02)	(.06)	(.02)	(.02)	(.02)
Autocor. order 1	.68	.79	.67	.67	.79	-.01
	(.07)	(.06)	(.07)	(.07)	(.06)	(.09)
Cor. with $\widehat{y}$	1	.86	.98	.97	.86	-.58
	(0)	(.02)	(.00)	(.01)	(.02)	(.02)
Cor. with $\widehat{H}$					.74	
					(.04)	

Table 3.16. Model I with Monetary Shocks (US Calibration)

Variable	$\widehat{y}$	$\widehat{c}$	$\widehat{i}$	$\widehat{h}$	$\widehat{w}$	$\widehat{M}$	$\widehat{inf}$
S.D.	2.06	1.05	6.13	1.55	.62	1.60	.92
	(.003)	(.001)	(.008)	(.001)	(.002)	(.001)	(.001)
S.D./S.D.($\widehat{y}$)	1	.51	2.97	.75	.30	.78	.45
	(0)	(.02)	(.07)	(.02)	(.02)	(.07)	(.12)
Autocor. order 1	.68	.43	.66	.67	.79	.82	.23
	(.07)	(.08)	(.07)	(.07)	(.06)	(.08)	(.07)
Cor. with $\widehat{y}$	1	.52	.93	.98	.87	.01	-.28
	(0)	(.04)	(.00)	(.01)	(.02)	(.01)	(.06)
Cor. with $\widehat{H}$	-	-	-	-	.73	-	-
					(.04)		

The model with a cash-in-advance constraint on consumption has already been studied by Cooley and Hansen [1989]. In that model I, monetary shocks do not modify greatly order two moments, except for consumption and inflation. Consumption is more volatile, less autocorrelated and less pro-cyclical. Inflation is also more volatile and less counter-cyclical. The money-output correlation is null.

Model II gives more interesting results:

Table 3.17. Model *II* without Monetary Shocks (US Calibration)

Variable	$\widehat{y}$	$\widehat{c}$	$\widehat{i}$	$\widehat{h}$	$\widehat{w}$	$\widehat{inf}$
S.D.	1.95	.63	5.46	1.28	.74	.14
	(.003)	(.001)	(.008)	(.002)	(.001)	(.001)
S.D./S.D.($\widehat{y}$)	1	.33	2.79	.65	.38	.78
	(0)	(.02)	(.06)	(.02)	(.02)	(.02)
Autocor. order 1	.67	.77	.67	.67	.75	-.05
	(.07)	(.06)	(.07)	(.07)	(.06)	(.09)
Cor. with $\widehat{y}$	1	.89	.99	.98	.93	-.37
	(0)	(.02)	(.00)	(.01)	(.01)	(.04)
Cor. with $\widehat{H}$	-	-	-	-	.84	-
					(.04)	

Table 3.18. Model *II* with Monetary Shocks (US Calibration)

Variable	$\widehat{y}$	$\widehat{c}$	$\widehat{i}$	$\widehat{h}$	$\widehat{w}$	$\widehat{M}$	$\widehat{inf}$
S.D.	1.97	.62	5.66	1.64	.86	1.60	1.61
	(.003)	(.001)	(.008)	(.002)	(.001)	(.001)	(.001)
S.D./S.D.($\widehat{y}$)	1	.31	2.86	.83	.43	.80	.82
	(0)	(.02)	(.06)	(.03)	(.02)	(.08)	(.16)
Autocor. order 1	.64	.78	.61	.48	.59	.82	.04
	(.08)	(.07)	(.08)	(.09)	(.07)	(.09)	(.09)
Cor. with $\widehat{y}$	1	.85	.98	.90	.55	-.10	-.46
	(0)	(.02)	(.00)	(.01)	(.02)	(.09)	(.04)
Cor. with $\widehat{H}$	-	-	-	-	.13	-	-
					(.05)		

A cash-in-advance constraint on consumption and investment reduces the variance of the model without monetary shocks. With monetary shocks, these variances increase, specially hours and labor productivity ones. There is no more distortion between consumption, investment and output and the relative standard-deviations are similar to the one of the canonical *RBC* model.

In Model *II*, the output-productivity and hours-productivity correlations are strongly reduced, because of the monetary shocks. Relatively to Model *I*, the money-output correlation is more negative.

Therefore, a model with a cash-in-advance constraint on consumption does not depart strongly from a pure real Hansen [1985] type model. On the contrary, Model *II* gives a more important role to monetary shocks in the business cycle. We then need to know if the model allow for a better reproduction of the French and American business cycle.

3.3.3 Monetary Shocks and Cash-In-Advance Constraint: a Counter-Factual Impulsion-Propagation Scheme

Quantitative Validation

Simulations for the US economy are given in tables 3.16 and 3.18, simulations for the French one are given in tables 3.16 bis and 3.18 bis.

Table 3.16 bis. Model *I* with Monetary Shocks (French Calibration)

Variable	$\widehat{y}$	$\widehat{c}$	$\widehat{i}$	$\widehat{h}$	$\widehat{w}$	$\widehat{M}$	$\widehat{inf}$
S.D.	1.87	1.07	5.70	1.32	.59	1.84	.96
	(.002)	(.001)	(.007)	(.001)	(.002)	(.001)	(.001)
S.D./S.D.($\widehat{y}$)	1	.57	3.05	.70	.31	1.0	.52
	(0)	(.02)	(.13)	(.03)	(.01)	(.08)	(.15)
Autocor. order 1	.68	.48	.63	.67	.73	.85	.3
	(.07)	(.08)	(.07)	(.07)	(.06)	(.08)	(.07)
Cor. with $\widehat{y}$	1	.56	.90	.98	.93	.00	-.26
	(0)	(.06)	(.01)	(.01)	(.01)	(.01)	(.06)
Cor. with $\widehat{H}$	-	-	-	-	.86	-	-
					(.03)		

Table 3.18 bis. Model *II* with Monetary Shocks (French Calibration)

Variable	$\widehat{y}$	$\widehat{c}$	$\widehat{i}$	$\widehat{h}$	$\widehat{w}$	$\widehat{M}$	$\widehat{inf}$
S.D.	1.91	.62	5.69	1.68	.89	1.83	1.55
	(.003)	(.001)	(.006)	(.001)	(.001)	(.001)	(.001)
S.D./S.D.($\widehat{y}$)	1	.32	2.98	.88	.47	.98	.82
	(0)	(.01)	(.08)	(.04)	(.03)	(.08)	(.17)
Autocor. order 1	.66	.74	.61	.51	.58	.85	.10
	(.08)	(.07)	(.08)	(.09)	(.07)	(.07)	(.09)
Cor. with $\widehat{y}$	1	.88	.98	.87	.45	-.11	-.46
	(0)	(.01)	(.002)	(.01)	(.06)	(.1)	(.04)
Cor. with $\widehat{H}$	-	-	-	-	-.01	-	-
					(.10)		

The actual moments for the two economies are given in tables 3.19 and 3.20:

Table 3.19. Business Cycle on US Data

Variable	$\widehat{y}$	$\widehat{c}$	$\widehat{i}$	$\widehat{h}$	$\widehat{w}$	$\widehat{M}$	$\widehat{inf}$
S.D.	1.76	1.28	8.47	1.42	.89	1.27	.39
S.D./S.D.($\widehat{y}$)	1	.72	4.81	.80	.50	.72	.22
Autocor. order 1	.85	.86	.81	.84	.52	.72	.24
Cor. with $\widehat{y}$	1	.81	.90	.86	.59	.36	.18
Cor. with $\widehat{H}$					.06		

Table 3.20. Business Cycle on French Data

Variable	$\widehat{y}$	$\widehat{c}$	$\widehat{i}$	$\widehat{h}$	$\widehat{w}$	$\widehat{M}$	$\widehat{inf}$
S.D.	.91	.81	3.64	.83	.65	5.4	.52
S.D./S.D.($\widehat{y}$)	1	.9	4.01	.92	.72	6	.57
Autocor. order 1	.76	.67	.82	.89	.63	.63	.20
Cor. with $\widehat{y}$	1	.63	.80	.71	.45	.18	.15
Cor. with $\widehat{h}$	-	-	-	-	-.35	-	-

Models *I* and *II* well mimic the relative variances of real variables, as in the canonical *RBC* model. Furthermore, the worked hours-labor productivity variance ratio is well reproduced. This fact is essentially due to the indivisibility hypothesis[11]. Model *I* allows for a higher variance of consumption. Autocorrelations are too weak, particularly those of inflation and worked hours.

The model cannot reproduce the money-output and inflation-output correlations. Model *II* produces a negative money-output correlation, in contradiction with the data. This point is a serious shortcoming of the model, as one of its aim was the reproduction of the nominal features of the business cycle.

Model *II* better mimics the productivity-hours correlation, but this fact is due to the introduction of a demand shock (the monetary shock), and not to the specific propagation mechanism of the model (the inflationary tax). This shows that this empirical puzzle for standard *RBC* models can be answered by adding a demand shock to the model.

[11]Without indivisibility, the canonical *RBC* model gives standard-deviations of 1.50, .67 and .91 for output, productivity and hours. (See chapter 1).

Both models overestimate the variance of the French economy, which may be an explained by the fact the Solow residual is not an accurate measure of the technological shock.

The introduction of money through a cash-in-advance constraint does not allow a better comprehension of the business cycle. Model I has the same limits than the Hansen's model (low persistence, low variance of consumption, positive productivity-hours correlation), and money does not have a significant effect. This effect is more important in model II: the productivity-hours correlation is lower, but the money-output and inflation-output correlations are negative.

Qualitative Validation

The impulse response functions are generated from a unit shock on total factor productivity and money growth rate.

IRF **to a Positive Technological Shock** : These *IRF* are similar to the ones of the canonical *RBC* model[12].

Real balances increases, as prices decreases with the increase of money demand (due to an increase in consumption for model I and an increase in consumption and investment for model II), and with constant money supply. Worked hours are above their steady-state value for 20 quarters, capital and investment are always above.

IRF **to a Positive Monetary Shock:** Real balances decrease instantaneously in both models, because of the increase in the inflationary tax. This response is opposite to the one of a model with price rigidities. Capital response is dramatically different in the two models, as investment responds positively in Model I and negatively in Model II. Consumption response is negative in both models. Hours response is always negative, and stronger in Model II, where investment is no longer a credit-good. The response of output derives from the ones of consumption and investment: negative and positive in Model I, always negative in Model II.

[12] The figures are displayed in appendix.

3.4 Concluding Comments

Our aim was to understand the economic mechanism in an intertemporal stochastic general equilibrium model with cash-in-advance constraint on consumption or consumption and investment.

The main mechanism for the money shock is a relative price effect that we referred as an inflationary tax effect: prices of cash-goods increase relatively to prices of credit goods when money increases. This effect can be important when labor supply is modelled, which is not generally done in the literature on inflationary tax.

Nevertheless, the effect of money appeared to be very small (Model *I*) or counter-factual (Model *II*). If the cash-in-advance constraint is an appropriate theoretical way of introducing money in general equilibrium, it is not a mechanism that can account for the role of monetary shocks in the business cycle.

3.5 Appendix

Figure 3.1: *IRF* to a Technological Shock (Model *I*)

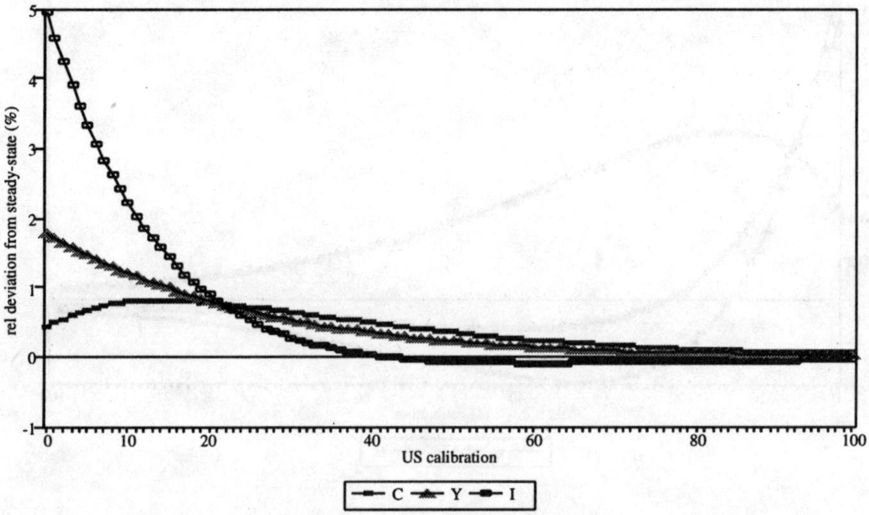

Figure 3.2: *IRF* to a Technological Shock (Model *II*)

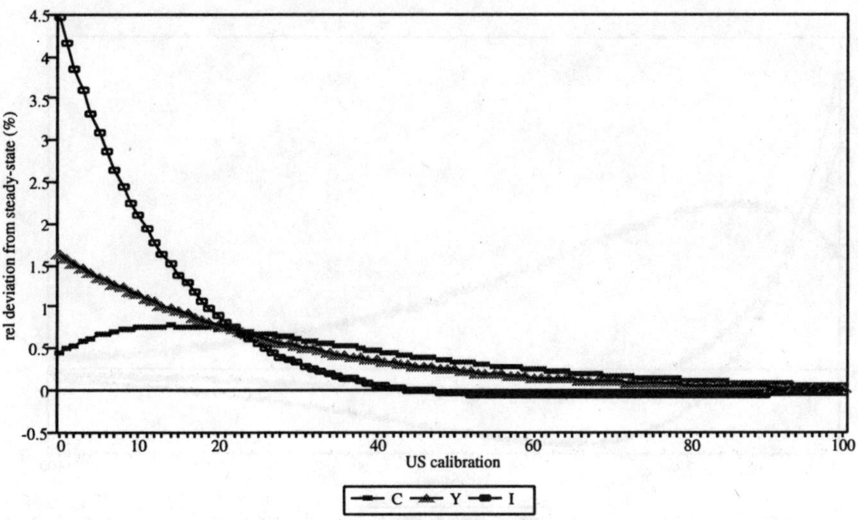

Figure 3.3: *IRF* to a Technological Shock (Model *I*)

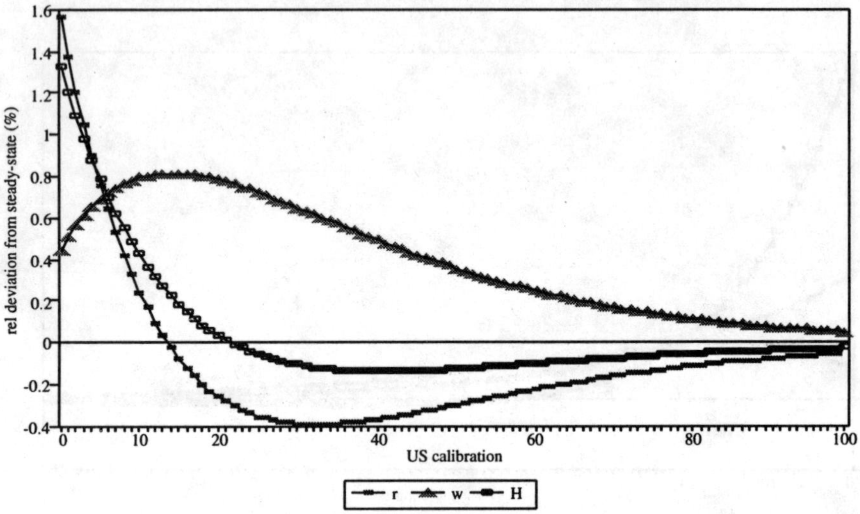

Figure 3.4: *IRF* to a Technological Shock(Model *II*)

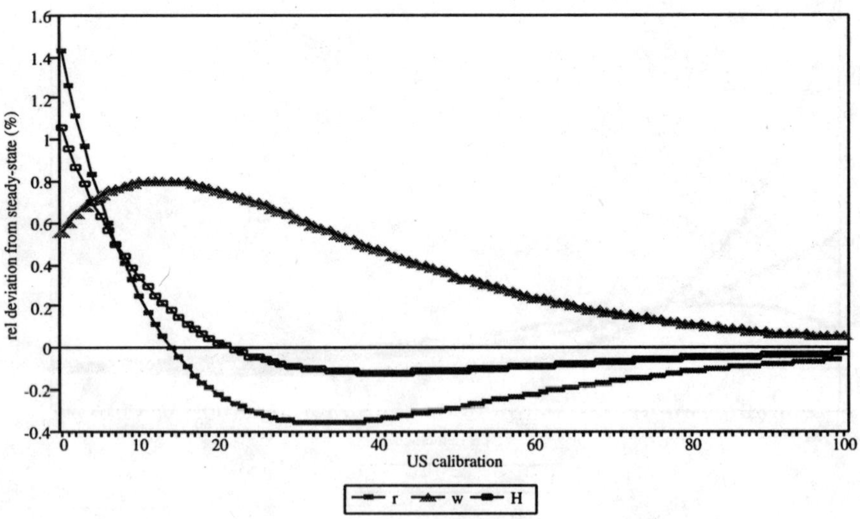

Figure 3.5: *IRF* to a Monetary Shock (Model *I*)

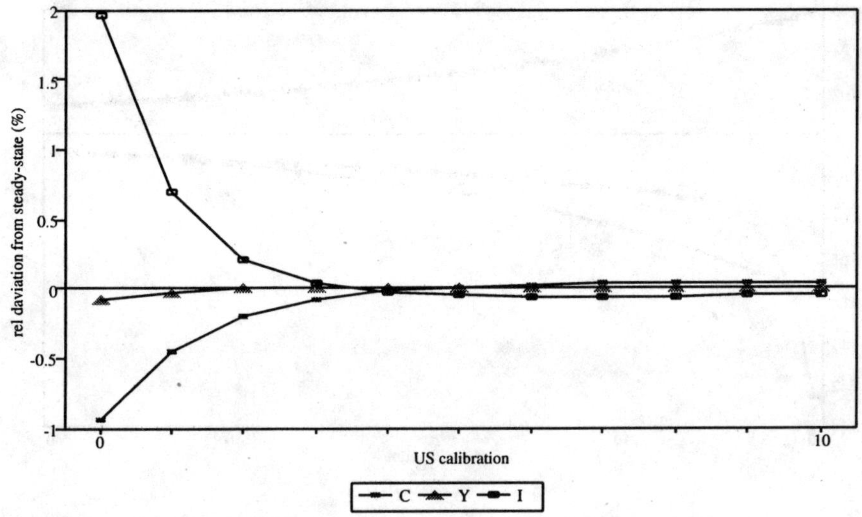

Figure 3.6: *IRF* to a Monetary Shock (Model *II*)

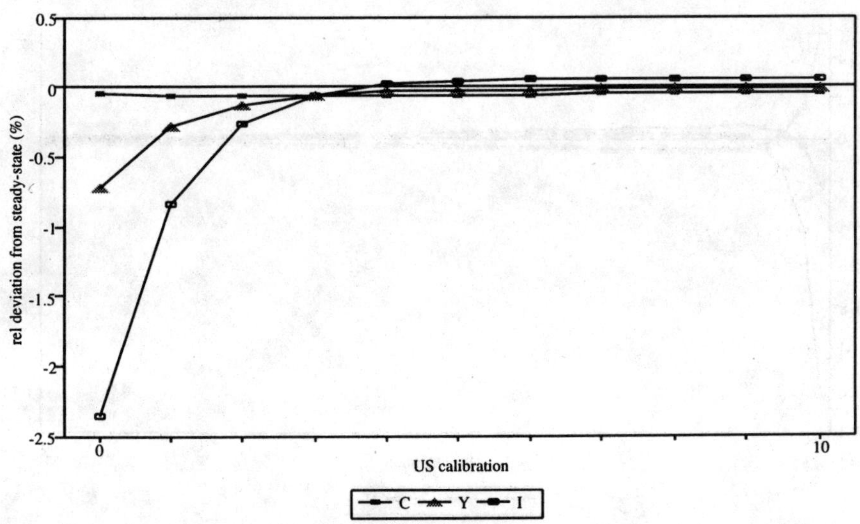

Figure 3.7: *IRF* to a Monetary Shock (Model *I*)

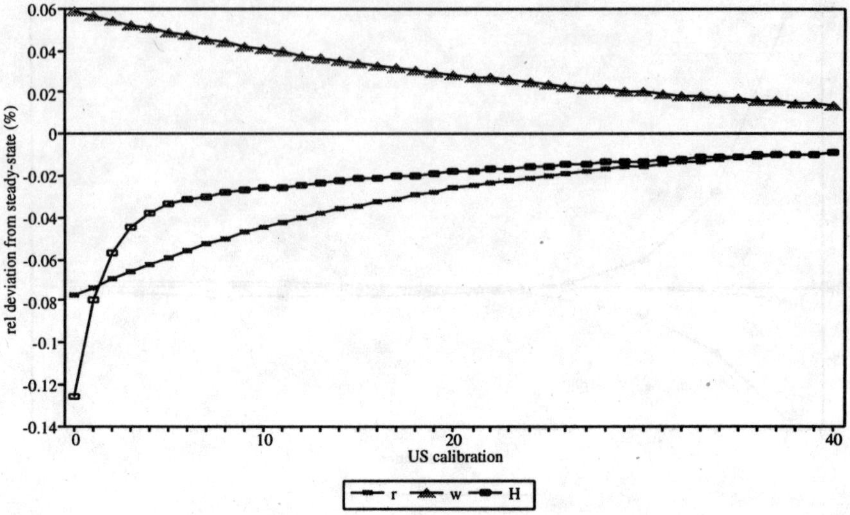

Figure 3.8: *IRF* to a Monetary Shock (Model *II*)

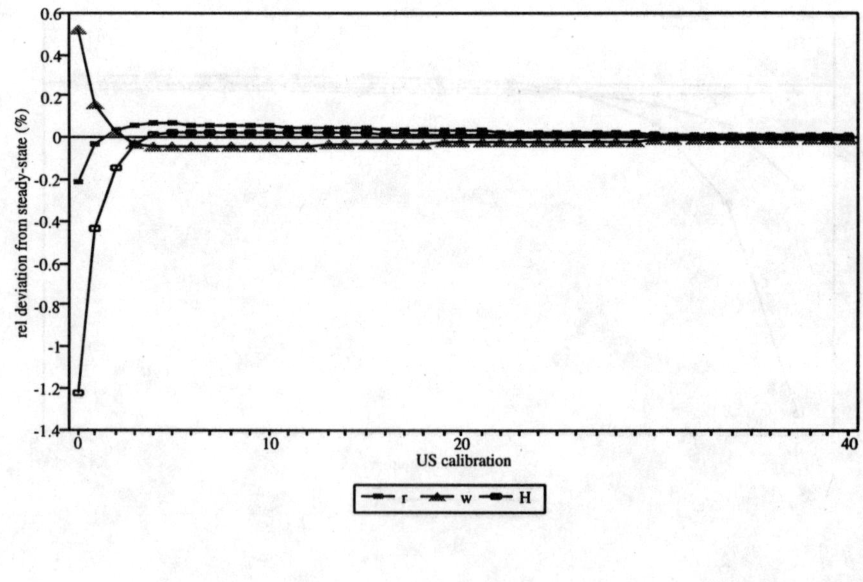

Figure 3.9: *IRF* of Inflation (Model *I*)

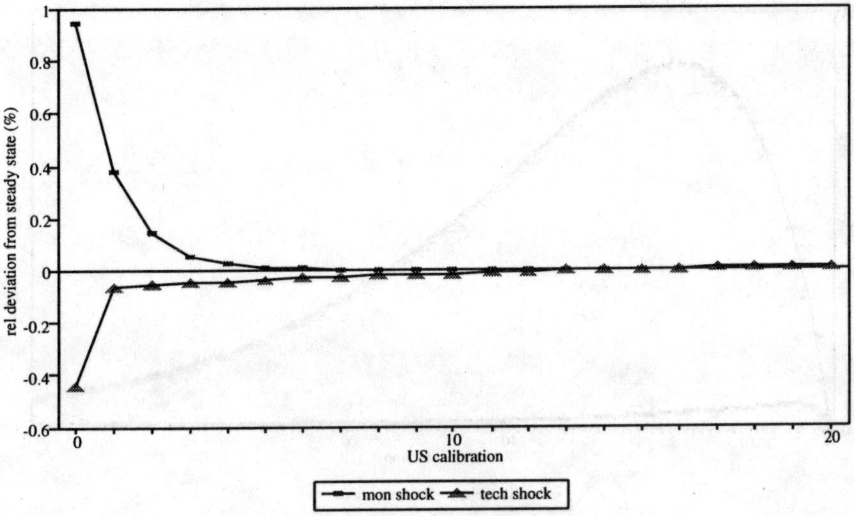

Figure 3.10: *IRF* of Inflation (Model *II*)

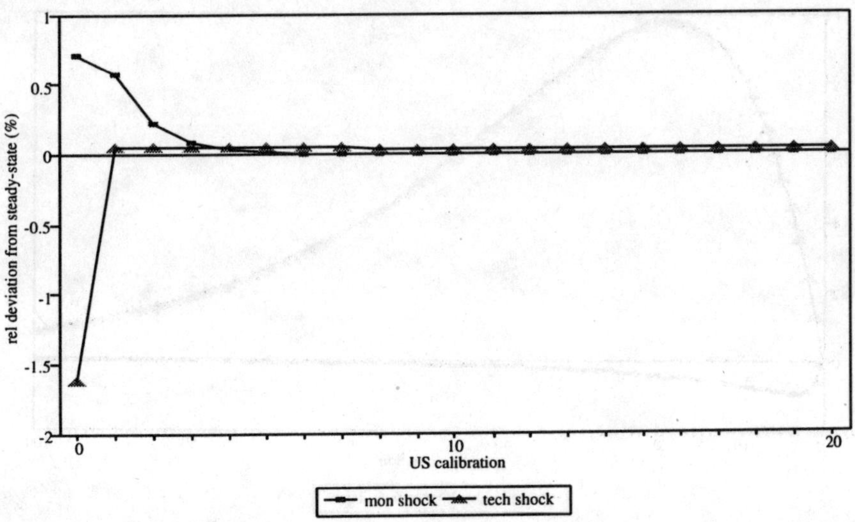

Figure 3.11: *IRF* of Capital (Model *I*)

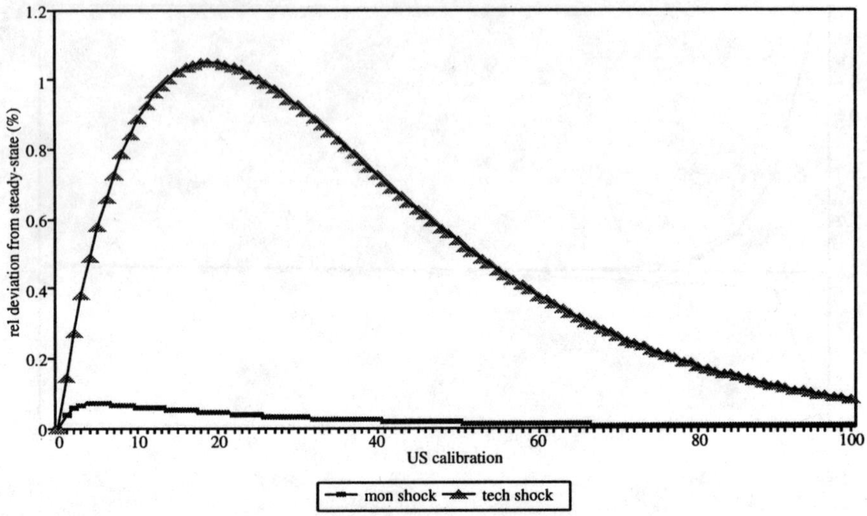

Figure 3.12: *IRF* of Capital (Model *II*)

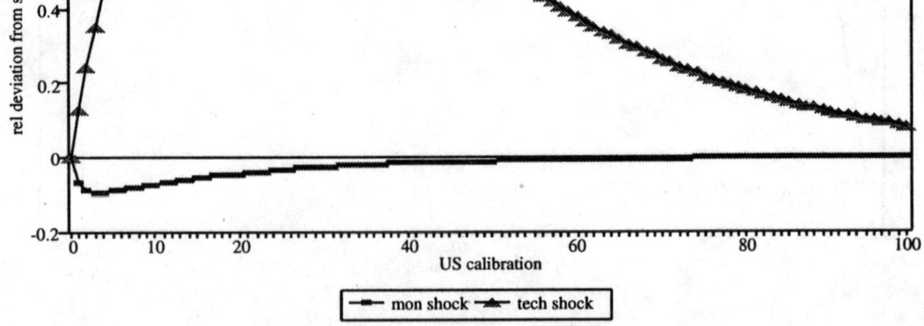

Bibliography

A. ABEL. Dynamic Behavior of Capital Accumulation in a Cash-in-Advance Model. *Journal of Monetary Economics*, 16(1):55–71, January 1985.

R. BARRO. Unanticipated Money Growth and Economic Activity. In R. Barro, editor, *Money, Expectations and Business Cycles*, chapter 5, Academic Press, New-York, 1981.

O. BLANCHARD AND C. KAHN. The Solution of Linear Difference Models under Rational Expectations. *Econometrica*, 48(5):1305–1311, July 1980.

O. BLANCHARD. A Traditional Interpretation of Economic Fluctuations. *American Economic Review*, 79(5):1146–1164, December 1989.

T. COOLEY AND G. HANSEN. The Inflation Tax in a Real Business Cycle Model. *American Economic Review*, 79(4):733–748, September 1989.

J.P. DANTHINE, J. DONALDSON AND R. MEHRA. On some Computational Aspect of Equilibrium Business Cycle Theory. *Journal of Economic Dynamics and Control*, 13(3):449–470, July 1989.

X. FAIRISE, J.O. HAIRAULT, F. LANGOT AND F. PORTIER. *Ecriture et résolution du modèle canonique des cycles réels.* Cahiers ECO & MATHS 92.30, MAD, Université de Paris I, 1991.

L. HANSEN AND T. SARGENT. Formulating and Estimating Dynamic Linear Rational Expectations Models. *Journal of Economics Dynamics and Control*, 2:7–46, February 1980.

G. HANSEN. Indivisible Labor and the Business Cycles. *Journal of Monetary Economics*, 16(3):309–327, November 1985.

R. KING AND C. PLOSSER. Money, Credit and Prices in a Real Business Cycle. *American Economic Review*, 74(3):363–380, June 1984.

R. KING, C. PLOSSER AND S. REBELO. *Production Growth and Business Cycles: Technical Appendix.* Working paper, University of Rochester, 1987. Revised May 1990.

R. KING, C. PLOSSER AND S. REBELO. Production, Growth and Business Cycles I. *Journal of Monetary Economics*, 21(2/3):196–232, March-May 1988.

F. Kydland and E. Prescott. Time to Build and Aggregate Fluctuations. *Econometrica*, 50(6):1345–1370, November 1982.

J.P. Laffargue, P. Malgrange and T. Pujol. *Une maquette trimestrielle de l'économie française avec anticipations rationnelles et concurrence monopolistique.* Working paper, CEPREMAP, April 1990. Rapport de contrat pour le Commissariat Général au Plan.

R. Lucas. Understanding Business Cycles. In K. Brunner and A. Meltzer, editor, *Stabilization of the Domestic and International Economy*, Carnegie Rochester Conference Series on Public Policy, North-Holland, Amsterdam, 1977.

R. Lucas. *Models of Business Cycles.* miméo , The Yrjo Jahnson Lectures, Helsinki, 1985.

R. Rogerson. Indivisible Labor, Lotteries and Equilibrium. *Journal of Monetary Economics*, 21(1):3–16, January 1988.

A. Stockman. Anticipated Inflation and the Capital Stock in a Cash-in-Advance Economy. *Journal of Monetary Economics*, 8(2):387–393, September 1981.

S. Williamson. Financial Intermediation, Business Failures and Real Business Cycles. *Journal of Political Economy*, 95(6):1196–1216, December 1987.

Chapter 4

The International Transmission of Real Business Cycles

Frédérique Bec

Abstract

This paper develops a simple one-sector, two-country equilibrium model which accounts for the relatively low cross-country consumption correlations without damaging the areas of success of existing models. This improvement arises from the modification of the consumption index in order to add public consumption to private consumption in the preferences of the agents, which allows shocks to government purchases to alter the marginal utility of consumption. This model explains quite well both the high correlation between saving and investment and the counter-cyclicality of net exports. However, only a strong cross-correlation of home and foreign technology shocks enables the model to mimic the cross-country correlation of output.

Introduction

Real business cycle models were quite rapidly extended to two-country models[1] in order to evaluate their ability to mimic some open-economy aspects of the business cycle pointed out by a growing bulk of empirical studies.

[1]Dellas [1986] and Cantor and Mark [1988] were the pioneers of this line of research.

Indeed, there are several open-economy features in the data that a model which describes the international transmission of business cycle should account for. The studies of, e.g. Backus and Kehoe [1992], Gerlach [1988], Baxter and Stockman [1988] and more recently Blackburn and Ravn [1991], underline some international regularities such as the counter-cyclical behavior of the trade balance, or the high correlation between saving and investment in the main industrialized countries. Moreover, many co-movements are exhibited among international data : the cross-country output correlation is positive and the cross-country consumption correlation is also positive, but less than the output one.

The two-country real business cycle models pay particular attention to the statistics directly related to the allocative role of international markets. While Baxter and Crucini [1993] provide a quantitative analysis of an equilibrium model, with perfect mobility of financial capital and a very high degree of physical capital mobility, which suggests that simulated and observed correlation between saving and investment are close to each other, the other aspects of the business cycle in an open-economy setting seem much more difficult to reproduce.

First, due to the too high volatility of investment generated by this kind of model, the counter-cyclicity of the trade balance and its variability relative to output raises an issue for, e.g. Backus, Kehoe and Kydland [1992] or Baxter and Crucini [1993]. Then, there is an endogenous tendency of the two-country neoclassical model to generate outputs that move in opposite directions. This is due to resources that shift to the more productive location.

Finally, the most striking failure of these models with complete markets, whether they are one-sector or two-sector models, as in Stockman and Tesar [1990], is that they find that consumption is perfectly (or nearly perfectly) correlated across countries. The kind of preferences widely adopted in this literature, jointly with the optimal risk-sharing allowed by frictionless international financial markets, explain this discrepancy between data and theory. The two-sector, two-country model developed by Stockman and Tesar [1990], which includes non-traded goods, requires both shocks to technology and tastes to break the link between home and foreign consumption. Another way to obtain more realistic cross-country consumption correlation is suggested by Devereux, Gregory and Smith [1992]. They adopt preferences which exhibit a particular non-separability between consumption and labor supply. This setting allows domestic hours of work, and so domestic consumption, to respond directly to the domestic productivity shock. Since Devereux, Gregory and Smith [1992] assume that productivity shocks are independent across countries, the foreign consumption does not respond immediately to the domestic productivity shock. However, productivity shocks are found to be positively correlated across countries by both Backus, Kehoe and Kydland [1992] and Stockman and Tesar [1990]. Thus, one may think that correlated productivity shocks will reinforce the cross-country consumption correlation. Besides this problem, one may expect that this model, with independent productivity shocks, produces a negative correlation between domestic and foreign outputs.

This chapter develops a simple one-sector, two-country equilibrium model which accounts for the relatively low cross-country consumption correlation without damaging the areas of success of existing models. This improvement arises from the modification of the index consumption so as to include public consumption beside private consumption in the preferences along the lines suggested by Barro [1981]. Section 2 describes the theoretical grounds of the two-country model and characterize equilibrium. Section 3 discusses the transmission mechanisms it involves. Section 4 reports the model predictions along a number of dimensions, and provides an informal comparison of these predictions with the data.

First, our model can easily be compared with the standard two-country real business cycle model as developed by Baxter and Crucini [1993]. It appears that our representation of preferences notably improves the model predictions concerning the correlation between domestic and foreign consumption. Then, it explains quite well both the high correlation between saving and investment and the countercyclicity of the net exports. These three features are surprisingly robust to the choice of the parameters governing the process of productivity shocks. However, it appears that only a strong cross-country technology shocks correlation enables the model to mimic the cross-country output correlation. In this sense, our model reaches the same limits as those of existing models.

Section 5 concludes the chapter with a brief summary of our results, and discusses extensions and modifications which would improve the model predictions.

4.1 A One-Sector, Two-Country Model

The one-sector, two-country general equilibrium model developed in this section builds on the international real business cycle area (Cantor and Mark [1988], Backus, Kehoe and Kydland [1992], Baxter and Crucini [1993]). The main departure from these models is the choice of a momentary utility function similar to that of Christiano and Eichenbaum [1992], which allows shocks to government purchases to alter the marginal utility of consumption. This helps to account for the relatively low cross-country correlations of consumption.

In our setting, we assume that the theoretical world economy consists of two identical countries. Financial capital is perfectly mobile and there is a very high degree of physical capital mobility. Labor is immobile across countries. In competitive equilibrium, international markets fully pool risks.

Since this is a one-sector model, international trade takes place only to smooth consumption and to ensure that capital is located in the most productive country.

Finally, it can be shown that the world competitive equilibrium with complete markets is Pareto efficient.

We begin with a description of the preferences, production opportunities and constraints[2].

[2]Throughout, stars ' $\star$ ' are used to denote foreign country variables. Where no star is attached in the case of the foreign country, the variable, parameter, or function in question is assumed to be identical accross countries.

4.1.1 Preferences

We assume that each country is inhabited by many identical, infinitely living individuals. Thus, we only consider the behavior of one representative agent in each country. Preferences of home and foreign consumers are assumed to be the same, and are represented by the following additively-separable momentary utility functions with divisible labor :

$$u(c_t, l_t) = \log c_t + \gamma \log l_t, \tag{4.1}$$

in the home country, and

$$u(c_t^\star, l_t^\star) = \log c_t^\star + \gamma \log l_t^\star, \tag{4.2}$$

in the foreign country, $\forall t$. c_t and l_t denote respectively the *per capita* consumption and leisure in home country at date t, and $\gamma > 0$.

This type of utility function is not as standard as it seems, because c_t is the flow of effective consumption at each date, and exceeds the quantity of private *per capita* real expenditures, c_t^p. Indeed, following Barro [1981], effective consumption is defined as follows:

$$c_t = c_t^p + \alpha g_t, \tag{4.3}$$

where g_t denotes the *per capita* government purchases at date t[3]. Here, each unit of *per capita* government purchases is viewed as providing utility services which are equivalent to a fraction α of private consumption, with $0 \leq \alpha \leq 1$. This assumption relies on the existence of government-provided services that may be considered as direct conveyers of utility to consumer, such as libraries, school lunch programs or hospitals. These kinds of public services and private consumption expenditures are thus treated as close substitutes in utility terms.

The distinctive feature of this representation of preferences is that government spending shocks affect the marginal utility of private consumption. Indeed, the derivative of marginal utility of private consumption, c_t^p, with respect to g_t, depends on α. When $\alpha = 1$, c_t^p and g_t have identical effects on the marginal utility of the private consumption.

[3]The effective consumption of the foreign household is analogous.

When $\alpha < 1$, a unit increase in government purchases lowers the marginal utility of private consumption by less than does a unit increase in private consumption. Finally, when $\alpha = 0$, g_t has no effect at all on the marginal utility of private consumption.

Baxter and King [1990], in a closed economy setting, and Stockman and Tesar [1990] in a two-sector, two-country model, introduce shocks on tastes in a similar manner. They adopt a momentary utility function such as $u(c_t + \tau_t, l_t)$, which corresponds to $\alpha = 1$ in (4.3)[4]. Our specification differs from this one in that, contrary to shocks on preferences, government spending shocks are financed by taxes which lower household income. We think that the assumption of the presence of shocks on tastes is less satisfactory, at a theoretical level, than to take into account the fact that some public services are utility conveyers.

The domestic and foreign *per capita* government purchases, financed by lump sum taxes, are assumed to follow an exogenous stochastic process defined respectively by :

$$\log g_t = (1 - \rho_g) \log g + \rho_g \log g_{t-1} + \varepsilon_{g,t}, \tag{4.4}$$

and,

$$\log g_t^\star = (1 - \rho_g^\star) \log g^\star + \rho_g^\star \log g_{t-1}^\star + \varepsilon_{g,t}^\star, \tag{4.5}$$

where g is the average level of *per capita* government purchases, $|\rho_g| < 1$ and the innovations $\varepsilon_{g,t}$ are serially independent with mean zero and variance σ_g^2. Moreover, it is assumed that $\rho_g = \rho_g^\star$ and that $E[\varepsilon_{g,t}\, \varepsilon_{g,t}^{\star'}] = 0$.

4.1.2 Technology

Each country is represented by a production technology, and both countries produce the same good *via* identical constant returns to scale production functions. Although the technologies have the same form, they are subject to exogenous shocks to total factor productivity, which may be partly country-specific. Production in home country uses capital, k_t, and labor n_t. Capital used in the production that takes place in the home (foreign) country is not necessarily owned by residents of the

[4] τ_t is an exogenous stochastic process which represents shocks on preferences.

home (foreign) country. Recall that labor is immobile across countries. Physical capital is mobile, but net investment is subject to adjustment costs.

The home and foreign production functions are respectively given by :

$$y_t = a_t k_t^\theta n_t^{1-\theta} - \left(\frac{\phi}{2}\right)(k_{t+1} - k_t)^2, \tag{4.6}$$

$$y_t^\star = a_t^\star k_t^{\star\theta} n_t^{\star\ 1-\theta} - \left(\frac{\phi}{2}\right)(k_{t+1}^\star - k_t^\star)^2, \tag{4.7}$$

where $0 < \theta < 1$ and $\phi > 0$. y_t is the *per capita* domestic output at date t, n_t is the number of hours worked by the domestic agent, a_t and $a_t^\star$ represent the domestic and foreign total factor productivity, and are assumed to follow an exogenous stationary stochastic multivariate process given by :

$$\begin{aligned}\begin{pmatrix}\log a_t\\ \log a_t^\star\end{pmatrix} &= \begin{pmatrix}\rho & \rho_\star\\ \rho_\star & \rho\end{pmatrix}\begin{pmatrix}\log a_{t-1}\\ \log a_{t-1}^\star\end{pmatrix} + \begin{pmatrix}(1-\rho) & -\rho_\star\\ -\rho_\star & (1-\rho)\end{pmatrix}\begin{pmatrix}\log a\\ \log a^\star\end{pmatrix}\\ &+ \begin{pmatrix}1 & \psi\\ \psi & 1\end{pmatrix}\begin{pmatrix}\varepsilon_{a,t}\\ \varepsilon_{a^\star,t}\end{pmatrix}\end{aligned} \tag{4.8}$$

where a and $a^\star$ are the means of the processes followed by a_t and $a_t^\star$ respectively, $|\rho| < 1$ and $|\rho_\star| < 1$. ψ is a positive parameter which determines the contemporaneous correlation between domestic and foreign technological shocks[5]. $\varepsilon_{a,t}$ and $\varepsilon_{a^\star,t}$, which represent the innovations to productivity variables, are serially independent and such that $E(\varepsilon_{a,t}) = E(\varepsilon_{a^\star,t}) = 0$, $E(\varepsilon_{a,t}\varepsilon'_{a^\star,t}) = 0$, and have the same variance σ_a^2.

Finally, capital accumulates over time according to :

$$k_{t+1} = (1-\delta)k_t + i_t, \quad 0 \leq \delta \leq 1, \tag{4.9}$$

$$k_{t+1}^\star = (1-\delta)k_t^\star + i_t^\star, \quad 0 \leq \delta \leq 1, \tag{4.10}$$

where i_t is gross investment, and δ is the constant depreciation rate.

4.1.3 Constraints

The time endowment of the representative household in each country is normalized at one, so labor constraints are :

$$n_t + l_t \leq 1, \tag{4.11}$$

[5]This statistic is given by $\frac{2\psi}{1+\psi^2}$.

and

$$n_t^\star + l_t^\star \leq 1. \tag{4.12}$$

The government purchases are financed by lump sum taxes, such that $g_t = t_t$ in the home country, the same scenario holding abroad.

Since this theoretical world is a two-country one and since the same good is produced in both the countries, the amount of total exports in a country equals the amount of total imports in the other country. Let π denote the fraction of the world population which lives in the home country, x_t the *per capita* domestic exports, m_t the *per capita* domestic imports and nx_t the domestic net exports. Then, the following relations hold :

$$m_t^\star = \frac{\pi}{(1-\pi)} x_t, \tag{4.13}$$

$$x_t^\star = \frac{\pi}{(1-\pi)} m_t, \tag{4.14}$$

and

$$nx_t^\star = -\frac{\pi}{(1-\pi)} nx_t. \tag{4.15}$$

The resource constraints in each country are given by :

$$\pi(y_t - c_t^p - i_t - g_t - nx_t) = 0, \tag{4.16}$$

$$(1-\pi)(y_t^\star - c_t^{p,\star} - i_t^\star - g_t^\star + \frac{\pi}{(1-\pi)} nx_t) = 0, \tag{4.17}$$

and thus are linked via trade in the single produced good.

4.1.4 Model Resolution

Since a world competitive equilibrium with complete markets is Pareto efficient, competitive equilibrium and social planning optimum are equivalent. So, we solve a social planning problem in which a weighted sum of national utilities is maximized subject to relevant constraints[6].

[6]This approach avoids the detailed specification of trading institutions involved in solving directly for a competitive equilibrium. According to Negishi [1960], one can always find a set of weights such that the allocations which are solution of the planning problem are the same as those corresponding to the competitive equilibrium for a given set of initial endowments. Here, π will be set to 0.5, which corresponds to a same initial wealth in the two countries.

By substituting (4.3), (4.6), (4.7), (4.11), (4.12), (4.9) and (4.10) in (4.1) and (4.2), the following Bellman's equation is obtained, in which $V(k_t, k_t^\star, s_t)$ denotes $V(k_t, k_t^\star, a_t, a_t^\star, g_t, g_t^\star)$:

$$\begin{aligned} V(k_t, k_t^\star, s_t) &= max\left\{\pi \log\left(a_t k_t^\theta n_t^{1-\theta} - \frac{\phi}{2}(i_t - \delta k_t)^2 - i_t - nx_t + (\alpha - 1)g_t\right)\right. \\ &+ \pi\gamma \log(1 - n_t) \\ &+ (1-\pi)\log\left(a_t^\star k_t^{\star\,\theta} n_t^{\star\,1-\theta} - \frac{\phi}{2}(i_t^\star - \delta k_t^\star)^2 - i_t^\star + \frac{\pi}{(1-\pi)}nx_t\right. \\ &+ \left.(\alpha - 1)g_t^\star\right) + (1-\pi)\gamma\log(1 - n_t^\star) \\ &+ \left.\beta E_t V(k_{t+1}, k_{t+1}^\star, s_t)\right\} \end{aligned}$$

over n_t, i_t, nx_t, $n_t^\star$ and $i_t^\star$, subject to :

$$k_{t+1} = (1-\delta)k_t + i_t, \tag{4.18}$$

$$k_{t+1}^\star = (1-\delta)k_t^\star + i_t^\star. \tag{4.19}$$

The home-country's first-order conditions for this maximization problem are given by :

$$\frac{(1-\theta)a_t k_t^\theta n_t^{-\theta}}{a_t k_t^\theta n_t^{1-\theta} - \frac{\phi}{2}(i_t - \delta k_t)^2 - i_t - nx_t + (\alpha-1)g_t} - \frac{\gamma}{1-n_t} = 0 \tag{4.20}$$

$$\frac{\pi(\phi(i_t - \delta k_t) + 1)}{a_t k_t^\theta n_t^{1-\theta} - \frac{\phi}{2}(i_t - \delta k_t)^2 - i_t - nx_t + (\alpha-1)g_t} = \omega_t \tag{4.21}$$

$$\frac{a_t k_t^\theta n_t^{1-\theta} - \frac{\phi}{2}(i_t - \delta k_t)^2 - i_t - nx_t + (\alpha-1)g_t}{a_t^\star k_t^{\star\,\theta} n_t^{\star\,1-\theta} - \frac{\phi}{2}(i_t^\star - \delta k_t^\star)^2 - i_t^\star + \frac{\pi}{(1-\pi)}nx_t + (\alpha-1)g_t^\star} = 1 \tag{4.22}$$

$$\begin{aligned} &\omega_t - \beta(1-\delta)\omega_{t+1} - \\ &\frac{\pi(\theta a_{t+1} k_{t+1}^{\theta-1} n_{t+1}^{1-\theta} + \delta\phi(i_{t+1} - \delta k_{t+1}))}{a_{t+1} k_{t+1}^\theta n_{t+1}^{1-\theta} - \frac{\phi}{2}(i_{t+1} - \delta k_{t+1})^2 - i_{t+1} - nx_{t+1} + (\alpha-1)g_{t+1}} = 0 \end{aligned} \tag{4.23}$$

$$\lim_{t\to\infty} E_0\left(\beta^t \omega_t k_{t+1}\right) = 0 \tag{4.24}$$

where

$$\omega_t = \beta E_t\left(\frac{\partial V(k_{t+1}, k_{t+1}^\star, s_{t+1})}{\partial k_{t+1}}\right).$$

In addition, there are foreign analogues to equations (4.20), (4.21), (4.23) and (4.24).

One may notice, equation (4.22), that an optimal program will entail domestic and foreign marginal utilities of consumption being equalized.

Indeed, this condition implies that, in equilibrium, effective consumptions are the same across countries. Consequently, private consumptions must be the same across countries at each date, and thus will be perfectly correlated across countries, when $\alpha = 0$. The unit correlation between domestic and foreign private consumptions obtained in this case is due to the functional form of utility function adopted here. Indeed, with a non-linear function such as, e.g., a C.E.S. function, the cross-country consumption correlation would be very close to one but not equal to one[7]. As we cannot analytically find the equilibrium, we follow the resolution method adopted by King, Plosser and Rebelo [1988] : the system defining the equilibrium is log-linearized around its steady state. This gives a linear dynamic system describing the path of the deviations of endogenous variables from their steady state value, provided that exogenous shocks hit the system. $\widehat{z}_t = \log\left(\frac{z_t}{z}\right) \simeq \frac{z_t - z}{z}$ will denote the percentage of deviation of z_t from its stationary level z.

In order to characterize the model steady state, the share of government expenditures in total output on the one hand, the percentage of time spent to work on the other hand, and finally the mean of total factor productivity are assumed to be the same across countries, which gives :

$$\frac{g}{y} = \frac{g^\star}{y^\star}, \quad n = n^\star \quad et \quad a = a^\star.$$

Thus, using (4.6), (4.7), (4.9), (4.10), together with the first-order conditions taken in steady state, one gets :

$$\begin{aligned}
c^p &= c^{p\,\star} = \left[\frac{(1-n)(1-\theta)}{\gamma n} - \alpha\frac{g}{y}\right] y \\
k &= k^\star = \left(\frac{\beta\theta}{1-\beta(1-\delta)}\right) y \\
i &= i^\star = \delta k \\
y &= y^\star = a^{1/1-\theta}\left(\frac{k}{y}\right)^{\theta/1-\theta} n \\
nx &= nx^\star = 0
\end{aligned}$$

[7] See for instance Baxter and Crucini [1993], Backus, Kehoe and Kydland [1992] and Devereux, Gregory and Smith [1992] for different kinds of utility function and their consequences on cross-country consumption correlation.

$$g = g^\star$$

Once log-linearized, the first-order conditions can be written as a state-space system :

$$M_{cc}\widehat{C}_t = M_{cs}\widehat{S}_t + M_{ce}\widehat{\epsilon}_t \tag{4.25}$$

$$M_{ss}(L)E_t\widehat{S}_{t+1} = M_{sc}(L)E_t\widehat{C}_{t+1} + M_{se}(L)E_t\widehat{\epsilon}_{t+1} \tag{4.26}$$

where M_{cc}, M_{cs} and M_{se} are real matrices and $M_{ss}(L)$, $M_{sc}(L)$ and $M_{se}(L)$ are polynomial matrices of order one. C_t, S_t and ϵ_t are vectors of variables respectively defined as $C_t = (n_t, i_t, nx_t, n_t^*, i_t^*)'$, $S_t = (k_t, k_t^*, \omega_t, \omega_t^*)'$ and $\epsilon_t = (a_t, a_t^*, g_t, g_t^*)$.

This system is solved along the lines of Blanchard and Kahn [1980] as in King, Plosser and Rebelo [1988]. Letting $e_t = (k_t, k_t^*, a_t, a_t^*, g_t, g_t^*)$ and $\varepsilon_t = (\varepsilon_{a,t}, \varepsilon_{a^*,t}, \varepsilon_{g,t}, \varepsilon_{g^*,t})$, the solution is :

$$\widehat{e}_{t+1} = M\widehat{e}_t + \varepsilon_{t+1} \tag{4.27}$$

Finally, the controls are recovered combining (4.27), (4.25) and (4.26), which gives :

$$\widehat{C}_t = \Pi\widehat{e}_t \tag{4.28}$$

The elements of Π and M, equations (4.27) and (4.28), are non trivial functions of the structural parameters of the model. The Π_{ji}'s are interpreted as the instantaneous elasticity of variable j with respect to variable i.

The simulation of the model and the computation of population moments and impulse response functions are thus based on the system formed by equations (4.27) and (4.28).

Model Parameterization

We follow the widely adopted procedure of *RBC* model evaluation, which consists in the comparison of the statistical properties of quarterly time series, detrended with the Hodrick-Prescott filter, with the artificial ones generated by the model.

The model parameterization is a necessary step toward the confrontation of model predictions with the data. To this end, it is possible to retain parameters values which are either estimated or computed from observed data.

Here, we are interested in the properties of the theoretical world economy when both countries have the same size, structure and parameter values. Thus, we consider the case where $\pi = 0.5$. Then, we follow the same strategy as Baxter and Crucini [1993] and Backus, Kehoe and Kydland [1992] which consists in a parameterization of the model based on previous studies on post-war U.S. economy experience. This seems to be a rather reasonable approximation. So, the two countries are assumed to be identical in all respects except that they are subject to exogenous shocks which are not perfectly (productivity shocks) or not at all (government purchases shocks) correlated across countries.

The values of n, β and δ, reported in Table 4.1 of Section 4.2, are chosen according to King, Plosser and Rebelo [1988], and the value of γ is thus set such that $n = 0.2$. To complete the calibration of preferences, we will analyze the model properties when $\alpha = 0$ and $\alpha = 1$ respectively.

Concerning the technology, the labor's share in output, i.e. $(1-\theta)$, is set to 0.58. This value corresponds to the average ratio of labor income with respect to U.S. output during the period 1948-1986. The adjustment cost parameter, ϕ, is set arbitrarily to 0.05 because this value permits the model to mimic quite well the observed volatility of investment relative to output, and is rather close to the value estimated by Craine [1975] for the United-States.

The share of government expenditures in total output is set to its mean value on post-war U.S. data, i.e. 20%.

Finally, we must specify the parameters governing the processes followed by the exogenous shocks. Concerning the government purchases shocks, we adopt the values estimated by Christiano and Eichenbaum [1992] on U.S. data : $\rho_g = \rho_g^\star = 0.97$ and $\sigma_{\varepsilon,g} = \sigma_{\varepsilon,g}^\star = 0.20$. As already mentioned, these shocks are assumed to be independent across countries. This assumption is rather consistent with the data since the correlation between the US government expenditures and the government expenditures of the six other countries listed in Table 4.3 ranges from $-.17$ for West Germany to .16 for United Kingdom and Canada. In order to define the bivariate process followed by technological shocks, the values of ρ, $\rho_\star$, ψ and σ_a must be specified. Given the lack of quarterly international data on capital stock, we were unable to estimate the autoregressive bivariate system (4.8). Thus, we adopt the values of ρ and σ_a estimated in chapter 6 on US quarterly Solow residual, i.e. 0.95 and 0.009 respectively. Different values will be successively attributed to ψ and $\rho^\star$ in order to measure the model sensitivity to these parameters[8].

Simulation Method

The model is then simulated, each simulation consisting in 138 periods : this corresponds to the length of the sample used by Backus, Kehoe and Kydland [1992] to exhibit the international stylized facts. In order to perform each simulation, four vectors of 138 elements, $\{\varepsilon_a\}_{t=1}^{138}$, $\{\varepsilon_a^*\}_{t=1}^{138}$, $\{\varepsilon_g\}_{t=1}^{138}$ and $\{\varepsilon_g^*\}_{t=1}^{138}$ are drawn in a normal law with zero mean, and a variance equal to σ_a^2 for productivity shocks and σ_g^2 for government spending shocks. The deviation of each variable to its stationary level, $\widehat{z}_t$, may be recovered using the state-space system. The level of these variables, z_t, are then obtained using the following relationship :

$$z_t = z(1 + \widehat{z}_t)$$

where z is the steady state value of z_t. z_t is then taken in logarithms[9] and filtered by Hodrick-Prescott, in order to extract its cyclical component on the basis of which the various moments — variances, correlations, and so on... — are calculated.

Each variable is subjected to this kind of treatment for 50 different series of the four innovations. The various moments reported later correspond to the mean of the moments obtained from these 50 simulations.

[8]Backus, Kehoe and Kydland [1992] estimate the bivariate process of technological shocks under the assumption that the capital stock is constant, and taking the U.S. as the home country while an aggregate of U.K., Germany and France represents the foreign country : these authors find a correlation between innovations which corresponds to $\psi \simeq 0.1$ in our model. The cross-correlation obtained by Stockman and Tesar [1990] on annual data implies $\psi \simeq .2$.

[9]Only net exports are not taken in logarithms.

4.2 Impulse Response to Productivity and Government Spending Shocks

The impulse response functions, hereafter *IRF's*, are performed to emphasize the propagation and transmission mechanisms involved by our theoretical model. They are performed using the following calibration :

Table 4.1

π	β	n	δ	θ	ϕ	ρ	σ_a	$\rho_\star$	ψ	ρ_g	σ_g
.5	.988	.2	.025	.42	.05	.95	.009	.04	.5	.97	.02

Figures 4.1 and 4.2, in Appendix, report the IRF's of the main variables of interest to a positive innovation in domestic productivity, while responses to a positive government spending innovation are plotted in Figures 4.3 and 4.4. Since our economy is entirely symmetric, we do not report IRF's relative to the corresponding foreign shocks. The series plotted are expressed in terms of percentage deviation from their respective steady state level. Finally, we report IRF's for $\alpha = 0$ only, but the case $\alpha = 1$ is also described in what follows.

4.2.1 Effects of Productivity Shock

The impact on the endogenous variables of a one percent shock in $\widehat{a}_t$ is not very sensitive to the value of α which never changes the sign of the responses and does almost not affect their magnitude. Let's begin with the behavior of domestic variables. This shock directly increases domestic output (Fig. 4.1). This leads the household to decrease its labor supply, but the temporary increase in the labor productivity has an opposite effect on the worked hours. The substitution effect seems to prevail since the deviation of worked hours from their steady state level is positive. This induces an increase in the marginal productivity of capital which in turn encourages domestic investment. As a result, both domestic output, consumption, investment and worked hours are above their steady state level. The trade deficit is the necessary counterpart of capital net entries.

Concerning the foreign behavior, foreign capital moves toward the most productive place, i.e. the home country, implying a decrease in

$i^{\star}$, (Fig. 4.2). Moreover, the decrease in the marginal value of capital modifies the intertemporal trade-off of the foreign household in favor of current time : foreign labor supply decreases while foreign consumption increases. All these effects contribute to the decrease in foreign output.

When $\alpha = 1$ — the figures are not reported — all these effects are somewhat larger, may be due to the weaker decrease of the marginal utility of private consumption.

4.2.2 Effects of Government Spending Shock

The main mechanisms involved by a transitory increase in government expenditures are related to the negative income effect induced by this shock. The negative income effect motivates the domestic household to supply more labor : the domestic output (Fig. 4.3) thus raises above its steady state level. As government spending have no direct effect on output, the labor productivity decreases. Moreover, following the temporary increase in marginal productivity of capital, saving today becomes more appealing. So, current consumption decreases while investment raises in the home country. Following these capital entries, net exports are negative.

Due to perfect risk pooling, foreign consumption behaves exactly like domestic consumption. Indeed, domestic demand of capital tends to modify the intertemporal trade-off of the foreign household in favor of the future. This leads to an increase in worked hours and investment, and to a decrease in foreign consumption with the same magnitude as in the home country.

When $\alpha = 1$, the government spending shock leads to a variation in private consumption that exactly offsets the initial shock, letting all other variables unaffected. Thus, only consumption responds to this shock with a decrease.

4.3 Model Predictions and International Business Cycles

In order to evaluate the ability of our model to mimic the features of economic fluctuations, we first report the stylized facts that it must account for. Then, we study to what extent our assumption concerning the form of preferences contributes to improve the model predictions. At this end, we report the results obtained from the model when $\alpha = 0$. This model is comparable to those of Baxter and Crucini [1993] or Backus, Kehoe and Kydland [1992]. Finally, we consider the model performances when government spendings are included in the utility function of the households.

4.3.1 The Stylized Facts

The main stylized facts that closed-economy *RBC* models aim at reproducing are the variances, the relative variances, the autocorrelations and the cross-correlations of real output, consumption, investment, worked hours and labor productivity.

Our goal being mainly to capture features of an open economy, we will focus on the three former dimensions, in what concerns the internal behavior of an economy. The following table reports the empirical moments relative to these variables for the U.S. economy, taken in logarithms and Hodrick-Prescott filtered[10].

Table 4.2

Va.	σ	$\sigma/\sigma_{\widehat{y}}$	$Corr(.,y)$
$\widehat{y}$	1.76	1	1
$\widehat{c}$	1.28	.72	.81
$\widehat{i}$	8.47	4.81	.90

Consumption is around 30% less volatile than output while investment is nearly five times as volatile as output. Both these variables are strongly pro-cyclical. These features seem to be common to many industrialized countries : Blackburn and Ravn [1991] emphasize their international regularity on the basis of a sample of eleven countries.

[10]See chapter 1 for the computation of these statistics.

They find that the volatility of consumption is between 20 and 30% lower and this of investment between 4 and 5.5 times larger than the volatility of output in all countries they consider. Moreover they find that the contemporaneous correlation between consumption and output is between 0.7 and 0.8, and the contemporaneous correlation between investment and output is between 0.7 and 0.9, depending on the country considered.

Concerning the economic fluctuations features that are more specific to open economies, we choose to present the statistics computed by Backus, Kehoe and Kydland [1992] since it seems that these authors dispose of the longer sample of quarterly international data : their sample concerns the period 60:1-90:2 for the United-States, and around 65:1-89:4 for the other countries. These series come from the IFS databank of the International Monetary Fund[11]. The main moments considered in the *RBC* literature in an open-economy setting are the cross-country correlations of output and consumption, the correlation between saving and investment rates on the one hand and between net exports and output on the other hand. The volatility of net exports relative to output is also considered. The statistics presented in the following table thus come from Backus, Kehoe and Kydland [1992].

Table 4.3

		Contemporaneous Cross-Correlations				σ
Country	y/y_{oecd}	y,y_{usa}	c,c_{usa}	s,i	nx,y	nx/y
USA	40 %	1	1	.68	-.36	.42
Japan	17.5 %	.39	.30	.50	-.03	.89
FRG	8.1 %	.42	.39	.42	-.27	.85
France	6.6 %	.22	-.18	-.04	-.17	.83
Italy	5.5 %	.39	.25	.06	-.62	1.41
UK	5.2 %	.48	.43	.07	-.21	1.10
Canada	3.5 %	.77	.65	.06	-.29	.79
Europe	-	.70	.46	-	-	-

The seven countries in Table 4.3 represent nearly 90% of total OECD output[12]. The approximation consisting in calibrating the theo-

[11]The statistics reported in the papers of Blackburn and Ravn [1991] and Baxter and Crucini [1993] are rather close to those of Backus, Kehoe and Kydland [1992].

[12]The percentages given in the table are the mean shares computed from current prices GDP of each country converted in US dollars.

retical model on the basis of US parameter values seems rather justified, provided that this country accounts for 40% of the OECD output.

The cross-country correlation of outputs and consumptions suggest the existence of strong international links between aggregate economic fluctuations. Indeed, the lowest output correlation is obtained between the French and U.S. outputs, while the greatest one is observed between the Canadian and U.S. outputs. Except for the United-States, the average correlation is about .45. Except for France, the cross-country consumption correlation is also high, but far from unity. The average correlation is .30, and so is somewhat lower than cross-country output correlation.

The correlation between saving and investment rates is computed using the definition of saving named "basic saving" by Baxter and Crucini [1993] : this is the most simple way to measure national saving in that it consists in substracting private and public consumptions from national output. This measure is convenient for it is easy to recover from our theoretical model and it is the only one available in a sufficient panel of countries. As can be seen in the table above, the correlation between saving and investment rates is rather high although it tends to be lower in small countries than in big ones (.68 in the United-States vs .06 in Canada and Italy for instance).

Finally, the correlation between net exports and output is negative everywhere, with a maximum of .36 in absolute value. Net exports thus appear to be slightly counter-cyclical.

The end of this section is devoted to the comparison of these statistics with the moments of order two generated by two variants of the theoretical model. This comparison will be rather informal in nature because it is quite difficult to design the empirical equivalent of the two countries constituting our theoretical world.

4.3.2 Model Predictions

In what follows, we present the results for various pairs of the parameters governing the joint evolution of productivity shocks, ρ_* and ψ. The highest eigenvalue of the first matrix of the right-hand side of equation

(4.8) is obtained when $\rho_* = .04$ and equals 0.99 : the cross-country differential of productivity thus vanishes gradually.

We begin with the presentation of the results obtained from the benchmark model in which α is assumed to be zero. We then report the model predictions when $\alpha = 1$.

The Benchmark Model

The results reported below are obtained from the model with $\alpha = 0$. In the following table, the simulated moments consistent with the stylized facts, given their standard deviation, are highlighted with bold characters. Moreover, since the cross-country consumption correlation is perfect due to the functional form of the utility function adopted, this statistics is not mentioned in Table 4.4.

As can be seen, when $\psi = .4$ and $\psi = .5$, i.e. when the cross-country correlation of productivity shocks is very high, this model mimics quite well most of the stylized facts considered[13]. The parameter governing the transmission of technological shocks, ρ_*, seems to have a secondary influence, excepted consumption volatility which is under-stated when it is low.

Three features of international business cycles are well described by this model, for all ρ_* and ψ : the output variability, the slightly counter-cyclical behavior of net exports and the high correlation between saving and investment rates. The latter seems slightly under-estimated compared to the U.S. data, but it is consistent with the international data.

On the contrary, this model seems unable to mimic precisely the volatility of net exports relative to output. This volatility is always over-stated, although the model works better along this dimension when the transmission and the correlation of technology shocks is higher.

The correlation between investment and output is somewhat lower than in U.S. data, although it is always in the interval found by Blackburn and Ravn [1991] for a great number of industrialized countries.

Three statistics depend crucially on the value of ψ : the relative

[13]Note that when the adjustment costs of capital are assumed to be negligible — the results are not reported here — the predictions of this model are counterfactual in almost all dimensions.

Table 4.4

ρ_*	ψ	σ_y	σ_c/σ_y	σ_i/σ_y	$\sigma_{nx/y}$	Contemporaneous Correlations (c,y)	(i,y)	(nx,y)	(s,i)	(y,y^*)
0	.1	**2.32**	.259	7.64	4.49	.391	.653	**-.295**	**.574**	-.385
		(.32)	(.05)	(.62)	(.56)	(.17)	(.06)	(.10)	(.08)	(.16)
0	.2	**2.11**	.305	7.26	3.88	.491	.645	**-.264**	**.561**	-.183
		(.30)	(.05)	(.67)	(.53)	(.14)	(.05)	(.10)	(.06)	(.21)
0	.4	**2.05**	.353	5.98	2.91	**.658**	.682	**-.239**	**.592**	**.245**
		(.23)	(.05)	(.48)	(.24)	(.12)	(.06)	(.11)	(.08)	(.15)
0	.5	**2.00**	.382	**5.33**	2.46	**.698**	.706	**-.217**	**.602**	**.421**
		(.24)	(.05)	(.39)	(.29)	(.10)	(.08)	(.14)	(.09)	(.13)
.03	.1	**2.06**	.340	6.75	3.28	.495	.713	**-.345**	**.647**	-.358
		(.34)	(.05)	(.47)	(.36)	(.15)	(.06)	(.11)	(.04)	(.17)
.03	.2	**1.94**	.413	6.54	2.98	**.532**	.703	**-.306**	**.631**	-.180
		(.23)	(.06)	(.69)	(.35)	(.14)	(.06)	(.12)	(.06)	(.16)
.03	.4	**1.81**	.477	**5.49**	2.26	**.678**	.713	**-.276**	**.636**	**.208**
		(.22)	(.07)	(.53)	(.28)	(.09)	(.07)	(.15)	(.08)	(.18)
.03	.5	**1.76**	.526	**4.74**	1.85	**.756**	.720	**-.216**	**.620**	**.458**
		(.21)	(.05)	(.39)	(.19)	(.07)	(.07)	(.13)	(.09)	(.13)
.04	.1	**1.99**	.459	6.58	2.64	.407	.723	**-.358**	**.665**	-.389
		(.23)	(.08)	(.47)	(.29)	(.15)	(.06)	(.11)	(.04)	(.16)
.04	.2	**1.86**	.526	6.37	2.37	**.547**	.711	**-.317**	**.646**	-.217
		(.22)	(.09)	(.66)	(.29)	(.13)	(.06)	(.11)	(.05)	(.16)
.04	.4	**1.72**	**.673**	**5.37**	1.82	**.672**	.711	**-.284**	**.643**	**.170**
		(.21)	(.09)	(.51)	(.23)	(.08)	(.07)	(.15)	(.07)	(.18)
.04	.5	**1.67**	**.732**	**4.62**	1.49	**.753**	.714	**-.227**	**.621**	**.427**
		(.20)	(.08)	(.39)	(.18)	(.08)	(.07)	(.13)	(.08)	(.13)

volatility of investment, the consumption-output correlation and the cross-country output correlation. Only a high correlation of productivity shocks allows the model to mimic them. Indeed, when $\psi = 0.5$, this correlation is consistent with the observed one between the main OECD countries average output and the U.S. GNP.

It is interesting to compare these model performances with those of the models of Backus, Kehoe and Kydland [1992] and Baxter and Crucini [1993], although remaining aware of the limits of this exercise due the specificity of each model.

The model of Baxter and Crucini [1993] may be compared to the third part of the Table 4.4. It accounts better than our model for the U.S. saving/investment and output/investment correlations, though the latter is slightly over-estimated. However, beyond the fact that domestic and foreign consumptions are nearly perfectly correlated, the relative volatilities of consumption and investment are too low. This suggests that the value of the parameter governing the adjustment costs implies a physical capital less mobile in their model than in ours. Finally, their model seems to work worse in what concerns the cross-country correlation of outputs.

The model with $\rho_\star = .04$ and $\psi = .1$ is probably the most comparable to the benchmark model of Backus, Kehoe and Kydland [1992]. Despite the (four quarters) time-to-build technology adopted by these authors, investment is nearly 11 times more volatile than output, and weakly correlated with it (.27). Furthermore, net exports are slightly pro-cyclical, saving and investment rates are too weakly correlated (.28). Despite its relative simplicity, our model works better along these four dimensions. Only two statistics are somewhat better reproduced by the benchmark model of Backus, Kehoe and Kydland [1992] : the cross-country output correlation is also negative, but more weakly (−0.18), and the cross-country consumption correlation is lower than in our model, but remains too high with .88.

Highly correlated productivity shocks thus enable our model to mimic almost all the stylized facts considered. Its main drawback is that it implies a perfect cross-country consumption correlation.

In order to measure the contribution of government spending shocks to the performance of our model, it was simulated without these shocks. It appears that in this case, the relative volatility of consumption is under-stated, whatever the values of $\rho_\star$ and ψ [14]. Although this seems to be the only sensible difference, it is important enough to justify the presence of government spending shocks.

The Model with $\alpha = 1$

Our intuition according to which the introduction of government spending in the utility function of the households could break the strong link between domestic and foreign consumption is already confirmed by the first order condition (4.22) and the impulse response functions when $\alpha = 1$. Indeed, we noticed that a domestic government purchase shock only affects domestic consumption.

The model predictions when $\alpha = 1$, reported in Table 4.5, also confirm this intuition. As can be seen in this table, the cross-country consumption correlation is now close to what one observes in the data. This correlation is even lower than the output one when productivity shocks are highly correlated. For all pairs of parameters (ρ_*, ψ), this statistics lies in the interval $[.280, .552]$, and is indeed somewhat lower than the output correlation when $\psi = 0.5$.

Beyond the fact that the cross-country consumption correlation is well reproduced by this model, other business cycles features are at least as well reproduced as they were in the former model. Indeed, one may notice a little raise in the saving/investment correlation, which makes this moment more consistent with the data. Furthermore, the relative variability of consumption is better reproduced. Then, the results with $\psi = .4$ are almost as satisfactory as those with $\psi = .5$. However, this level of correlation between productivity shocks still seems unrealistic. It also seems necessary to face the inherent tendency of this model to generate domestic and foreign outputs that move in opposite directions. Finally, one may notice that this version of our model implies a unit cross-country correlation of total consumption. This is partly due to the functional form which represents preferences. Nevertheless, it seems

[14]The results are not reported here, since it suffices to mention that the relative volatility of consumption peaks at .403 for $\rho_\star = .04$ and $\psi = .5$.

Table 4.5

ρ_*	ψ	σ_y	σ_c/σ_y	σ_i/σ_y	$\sigma_{nx/y}$
0	.1	**2.31**	.510	7.60	4.38
		(.28)	(.10)	(.76)	(.43)
0	.2	**2.24**	.541	6.96	3.83
		(.29)	(.10)	(.65)	(.43)
0	.4	**2.10**	**.575**	**5.82**	2.90
		(.28)	(.09)	(.50)	(.35)
0	.5	**2.10**	**.610**	**5.02**	2.35
		(.28)	(.07)	(.53)	(.22)
.03	.1	**2.08**	**.575**	6.79	3.32
		(.26)	(.09)	(.51)	(.32)
.03	.2	**2.09**	**.601**	6.23	3.00
		(.30)	(.10)	(.58)	(.41)
.03	.4	**1.94**	**.684**	**5.16**	2.18
		(.29)	(.10)	(.52)	(.28)
.03	.5	**1.96**	**.721**	**4.36**	1.77
		(.20)	(.09)	(.38)	(.23)
.04	.1	**2.07**	**.655**	6.38	2.65
		(.25)	(.09)	(.50)	(.35)
.04	.2	**2.03**	**.711**	6.04	2.37
		(.29)	(.14)	(.54)	(.35)
.04	.4	**1.86**	**.812**	**4.93**	1.71
		(.24)	(.09)	(.47)	(.23)
.04	.5	**1.87**	**.857**	**4.31**	1.46
		(.24)	(.11)	(.48)	(.22)

Table 4.5 — Continued

ρ_*	ψ	Contemporaneous Correlations					
		(c,y)	(i,y)	(nx,y)	(s,i)	(y,y^*)	(c,c^*)
0	.1	.326	.668	**-.307**	**.590**	-.308	**.280**
		(.17)	(.06)	(.11)	(.07)	(.17)	(.19)
0	.2	.324	.676	**-.288**	**.608**	-.106	**.336**
		(.13)	(.07)	(.14)	(.08)	(.19)	(.15)
0	.4	.428	.680	**-.216**	**.606**	**.297**	**.347**
		(.12)	(.07)	(.13)	(.07)	(.19)	(.16)
0	.5	.507	.707	**-.171**	**.625**	**.530**	**.427**
		(.13)	(.08)	(.17)	(.10)	(.14)	(.14)
.03	.1	.295	.712	**-.335**	**.666**	-.302	**.333**
		(.15)	(.05)	(.11)	(.06)	(.15)	(.17)
.03	.2	.382	.712	**-.303**	**.712**	-.103	**.371**
		(.17)	(.05)	(.10)	(.05)	(.18)	(.15)
.03	.4	.519	.719	**-.238**	**.671**	**.332**	**.441**
		(.14)	(.06)	(.10)	(.06)	(.16)	(.12)
.03	.5	.585	.741	**-.182**	**.680**	**.580**	**.513**
		(.15)	(.07)	(.17)	(.08)	(.14)	(.15)
.04	.1	.329	.704	**-.292**	**.653**	-.332	**.392**
		(.16)	(.05)	(.12)	(.06)	(.16)	(.12)
.04	.2	.423	.725	**-.321**	**.676**	-.120	**.401**
		(.13)	(.06)	(.12)	(.06)	(.17)	(.13)
.04	.4	.556	.715	**-.230**	**.683**	**.338**	**.498**
		(.13)	(.07)	(.16)	(.07)	(.14)	(.11)
.04	.5	.667	.741	**-.190**	**.696**	**.542**	**.552**
		(.09)	(.06)	(.14)	(.07)	(.13)	(.11)

that the introduction of non-traded goods improves the performances of the model along this dimension[15].

4.4 Concluding Comments

This work helps us to evaluate the ability of the two-country, one-sector *RBC* models to reproduce the business cycle features. Mainly three conclusions may be drawn :

- A syncretic explanation of economic fluctuations seems more relevant than an approach relying on the existence of a unique source of impulse, namely technological shocks.
- The introduction of government spending in the agent preferences, as suggested by Barro [1981], succeeds in accounting for the relatively low cross-country consumption correlation, even if it is probably not the only possible explanation. So, this specification of the utility function eliminates one of the main shortcomings of the existing two-country *RBC* models.
- An important drawback of this kind of models still remains : without a high cross-country correlation of productivity shocks, the model fails to reproduce the positive cross-country output correlation. Although we do not know the exact value of the correlation between productivity shocks, we think that the value required by our model is too high to be realistic : Backus, Kehoe and Kydland [1992] find that this correlation is 0.2 on the basis of Solow residuals series computed under the assumption that the stock of capital is constant, while the results reported by Stockman and Tesar [1990] imply that the correlation between technological shocks affecting the traded-good sector is 0.33 from annual data.

Thus, it seems that this kind of model omits some important economic mechanisms. The assumption that government spending shocks are correlated with productivity shocks may perhaps improve our model

[15] See Stockman and Tesar [1990].

predictions for lower degrees of correlation between productivity shocks. However, the problem of this type of model is probably due to their single-good nature. Indeed, Stockman and Tesar [1990] obtain rather promising results by introducing a non-traded good sector in each country.

4.5 Appendix

Figure 4.1: Responses to Technology Shock — Home Country

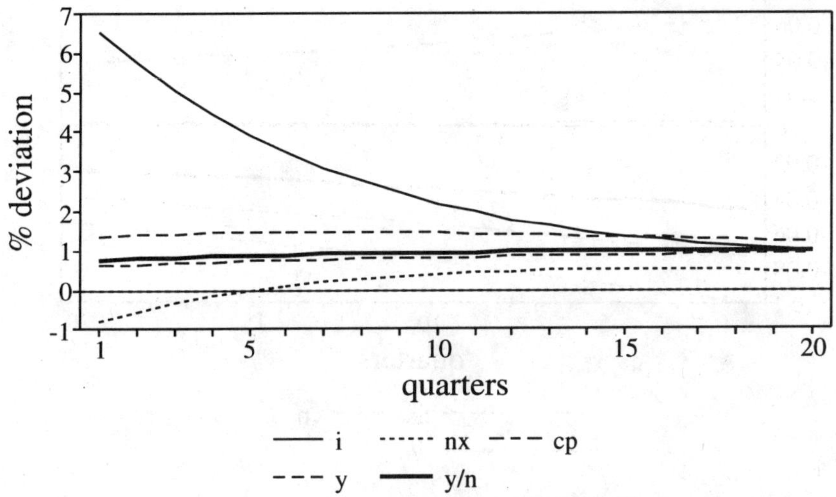

Figure 4.2: Responses to Technology Shock — Foreign Country

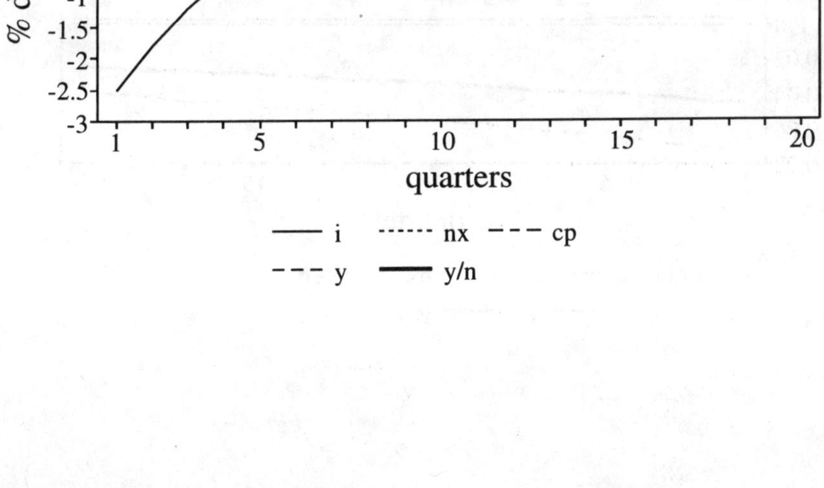

Figure 4.3: Responses to Government Spending Shock — Home Country

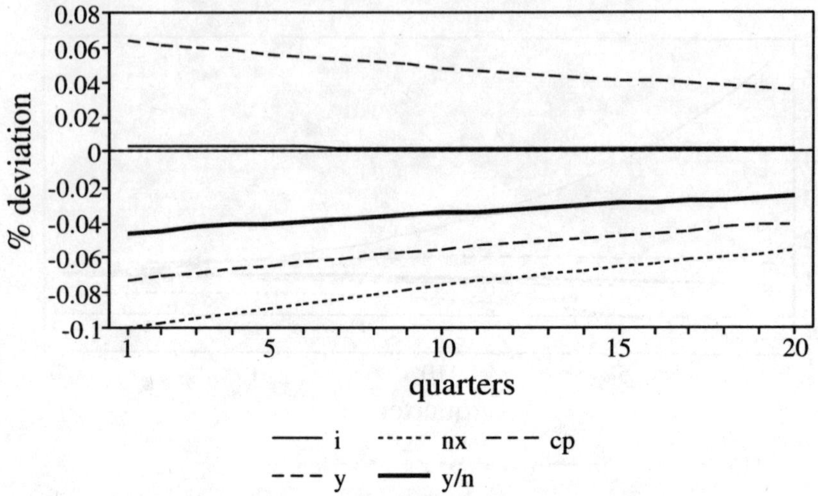

Figure 4.4: Responses to Government Spending Shock — Foreign Country

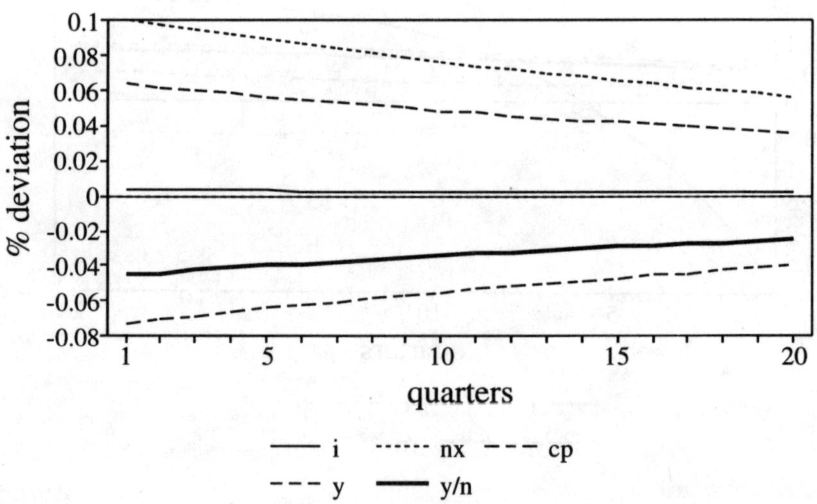

Bibliography

D. Backus and P. Kehoe. International Evidence on the Historical Properties of Business Cycles. *American Economic Review*, 82(4):864–888, September 1992.

D. Backus, P. Kehoe and F. Kydland. International Real Business Cycles. *Journal of Political Economy*, 100(4):745–775, August 1992.

R. Barro. Outputs Effects of Government Purchases. *Journal of Political Economy*, 89(6):1086–1121, 1981.

M. Baxter and M. Crucini. Explaining Saving Investment Correlation. *American Economic Review*, 83(3):416–436, 1993.

M. Baxter and R. King. *Productive Externalities and Cyclical Volatility.* Working paper 245, Rochester Center for Economic Research, 1990.

M. Baxter and A. Stockman. *Business Cycles and the Exchange Rate System: Some International Evidence.* Working paper 2689, NBER, 1988.

K. Blackburn and M. Ravn. *Contemporary Macroeconomic Fluctuations: An International Perspective.* Working Paper 91-12, Centre for International Economics, University of Aarhus, Denmark, 1991.

O. Blanchard and C. Kahn. The Solution of linear Difference Models under Rational Expectations. *Econometrica*, 48:1305–1311, July 1980.

R. Cantor and N. Mark. The International Transmission of Real Business Cycles. *International Economic Review*, 29(3):493–507, 1988.

L. Christiano and M. Eichenbaum. Current Real Business Cycle Theory and Aggregate Labor Market Fluctuations. *American Economic Review*, 82:430–450, June 1992.

R. Craine. Investment, Adjustment Costs, and Uncertainty. *International Economic Review*, 16:648–61, August 1975.

H. Dellas. A Real Model of the World Business Cycle. *Journal of International Money and Finance*, 5:341–394, 1986.

M. Devereux, A. Gregory and G. Smith. Realistic Cross-Country Consumption Correlations in a Two-Country Equilibrium Business Cycle Model. *Journal of International Money and Finance*, 11:3–16, 1992.

S. Gerlach. World Business Cycle Under Fixed and Flexible Exchange Rates. *Journal of Money, Credit and Banking*, 20(4):621–632, November 1988.

R. King, C. Plosser and J Rebelo. Production, Growth and Business Cycles I. *Journal of Monetary Economics*, 21:196–232, 1988.

T Negishi. Welfare Economics and the Existence of an Equilibrium for a Competitive Economy. *Metroeconomica*, 12:92–97, August-December 1960.

A. Stockman and L. Tesar. *Tastes and Technology in a Two-Country Model of the Business Cycle: Explaining International Comovements.* Working Paper 255, Rochester Center for Economic Research, 1990.

Chapter 5

A Small Open Economy RBC Model: the French Economy Case

Catherine Bruno & Franck Portier

Abstract

Two fruitful extensions of the *RBC* paradigm were recently developed. The first one concerns open economy, the second one concerns the introduction of imported inputs in the production function, of energy in particular. In this chapter, we combine these two extensions in order to replicate the French business cycle. So, we stress on the French stylized facts, in particular the Savings-Investment correlation, the imported energy price and the trade balance cyclicity Thus, we develop a theoretical model whose main characteristic is imperfect financial assets substitutability. We use two different validation techniques: firstly, stochastic simulation and second order moment comparison; secondly, computation of *IRF* and comparison with estimated *VAR* ones.

Introduction

The Real Business Cycle (*RBC*) approach of economic fluctuations, following the seminal papers of Kydland and Prescott [1982] and Long and Plosser [1983], proposes a general equilibrium framework to explain some of the key empirical regularities that characterize business cycles. The standard model has been extended to imperfect competition models (see chapter 6), description of the labor market (Burnside, Eichenbaum and Rebelo [1990] and Fairise and Langot [1994] and chapter 2 of this book) and monetary models (Cooley and Hansen [1989], King [1990], Hairault and Portier [1993]) and chapter 3.

Another fruitful extension of the *RBC* paradigm concerns open economies. Some empirical regularities in key international indicators motivate the extension to open-economies *RBC* models. First, there exists a high correlation between savings (S) and investment (I) in all industrialized countries which has first been explained by the imperfect degree of capital mobility (Feldstein and Horioka [1980]) . Thus, some recent theoretical work (Obstfeld [1986]), Finn [1990], Backus, Kehoe and Kydland [1992], Bec [1992]) reinterprets this stylized fact: the $S-I$ correlation depends on the persistence of productivity shocks because these shocks affect simultaneously savings and investment. Second, the current account and the trade balance are counter-cyclical or a-cyclical (Backus, Kehoe and Kydland [1992], Cardia [1991]). According to Mendoza [1991]), "*for the current account or the trade balance be counter-cyclical, the pro-borrowing effect caused by an expected expansion of future output must dominate the pro-saving effect induced by an increase in current output*".

In an other direction, Kim and Loungani [1992] stress on the role of energy in the business cycle, to determine the extent to which the introduction of energy price shocks reduces the reliance of real business cycle models on unobserved technological shock.

Our aim is to combine these two extensions in order to replicate the French business cycle. Basically, France is considered as a *small open economy* because firstly it imports energy and secondly it does not determine the world interest rate. So, our purpose is both theoretical and methodological in its empirical part.

On a theoretical side, we develop an open-economy model in the line of Mendoza [1991], which explicitly includes international assets in the utility function and imported input in the production function. This specification allows us to introduce three specific shocks in the model, namely a technological shock, an imported input price shock and a world real interest rate shock. The model is then solved following King, Plosser and Rebelo [1987].

On an empirical side, our aim is to extend the traditional validation method of *RBC* theorists based on the comparison of theoretical and observed second order moments, to the comparison of the impulse response functions (*IRF* for short) of the *RBC* model with estimated *IRF*. From our point of view, this validation technique must be added to the moment comparison generally used in the literature. These estimated *IRF* must be seen as an other way to read the data, and a Vector AutoRegression *(VAR)* is a good candidate for such an estimation[1].

Firstly , we use standard validation methods by computing model and empirical moments (using the Hodrick-Prescott filter to detrend model and observed variables).

Secondly, we estimate a *VAR* which includes some key macro-economic variables (consumption, investment, output, worked hours, imported input) and the exogenous variables of the *RBC* model as exogenous ones in the *VAR*. Therefore, we compute, with *RBC* and *VAR* models, the impulse response functions of the endogenous variables to three shocks: a technological one (an increase of the Solow residual) , an oil price one (an increase of the price of imported energy) and a world real interest rate one. Using bootstrap techniques, we compute *IRF* confidence bands to evaluate the *RBC* model ability to mimic the estimated *IRF*.

5.1 The *RBC* Model of the French Economy

We present in this section the theoretical model. We describe the model before giving a sketch of its resolution, which follows King, Plosser and Rebelo [1987].

5.1.1 Technology and Preferences

The economy is composed of h identical households indexed by i and n firms indexed by j. All firms have access to the same constant returns

[1]We must notice that Woodford and Rotemberg [1989] used univariate estimations to compute *IRF* to a military expenditure shock and to compare them to their theoretical ones, in an oligopolistic model of business cycle.

to scale production function and produce the domestic good:

$$Y_{j,t} \leq A_t \left(\gamma_1 K_{j,t}^{(\sigma-1)/\sigma} + (1-\gamma_1) E_{j,t}^{(\sigma-1)/\sigma}\right)^{\alpha(\sigma/\sigma-1)} H_{j,t}^{1-\alpha} \tag{5.1}$$

with $\alpha \in]0,1[$, $\gamma_1 \in]0,1[$, $\sigma > 0$.

$K_{j,t}$ is the capital stock used by firm j, $H_{j,t}$ the quantity of labor input and $E_{j,t}$ the quantity of imported energy. A_t is the stationary component of the technical progress, and we assume that it follows the stochastic process:

$$\log(A_t) = \rho_A \log(A_{t-1}) + (1-\rho_A)\log(A) + \varepsilon_{A,t} \tag{5.2}$$

where the $\varepsilon_{A,t}$ are *i.i.d.* stochastic variables following a normal distribution $\mathcal{N}(0, \sigma_A^2)$, A is the steady state value and where $\rho_A < 1$. We assume that A_t and all the other shocks are observed at the beginning of period t.

Households are identical, and their preferences are given by the utility function U_0 which represents the expectation of the discounted sum of instantaneous utility flows u, conditionally to the information available at date $t = 0$:

$$U_0 = E_0 \sum_{t=0}^{\infty} \beta^t \left(\log\left(C_{i,t}\right) + v\left(L_{i,t}\right) - \gamma_2 B_{i,t}^2\right)$$

with $\beta \in]0,1[$ and $\gamma_2 > 0$.

$C_{i,t}$ and $L_{i,t}$ are respectively consumption and leisure levels of household i. Each household is endowed with one unit of time at each period, and allocates it between leisure $L_{i,t}$ and worked hours $H_{i,t}$:

$$H_{i,t} + L_{i,t} \leq 1$$

Each household accumulates capital and rents it to firms. The accumulation technology is given by the following equation:

$$K_{i,t+1} = (1-\delta)K_{i,t} + I_{i,t} - \Phi\left(K_{i,t}, K_{i,t+1}\right)$$

Φ is a capital adjustment cost function, and we assume that it is quadratic:

$$\Phi\left(K_{i,t}, K_{i,t+1}\right) = \frac{\phi}{2}\left(\frac{K_{i,t+1} - K_{i,t}}{K_{i,t}}\right)^2$$

This adjustment cost function reflects the fact that physical capital mobility is imperfect and so that financial capital is more mobile than physical one.

Households have also access to an international financial market. They hold a foreign financial asset $B_{i,t}$ that yields the world real interest rate $r_t^\star$, which is exogenous since perfect international financial integration is assumed. $B_{i,t}$ enters negatively in the utility function. This a convenient way to solve the problem of *small open economy* models with constant rate of time preference. Indeed, these models cannot reproduce well-defined dynamics in some cases. If the world interest rate is different from the rate of time preference, there is no stationary equilibrium: domestic capital is null if the rate of time preference is less than the world interest rate, infinite in the opposite case. If they are preset to be equal, the steady-state is compatible with any level of foreign asset holdings. To avoid such a problem, an endogenous rate of time preference is introduced through stationary cardinal utility functions in Mendoza [1991], and through a finite probability of death (following Yaari [1965] and Blanchard [1985]) in Cardia [1991]. So, the rate of time preference depends on either past consumption (Mendoza [1991]) or financial wealth (Cardia [1991]): the relation between the rate of time preference and domestic variables creates an error correction mechanism toward the stationary equilibrium.

We adopt a more *ad hoc* assumption in that paper. We assume that the international financial asset, which yields a revenue $r^\star$, enters negatively in the utility function. This means that domestic households prefer national assets. So, if both domestic and foreign capital yield the same rate, domestic capital will be preferred. If world interest rate is higher than domestic one, the demand for international financial assets will not be infinite: in effect, domestic households demand international assets until the asset holding disutility does not exceed the asset holding revenue. Such a specification – imperfect asset substitutability – can be seen as a convenient way to model household aversion to foreign specific risks, for instance, due to a lack of information on foreign firms or exchange rate risk .

The steady state value of world interest rate is set exogenously:

$$r^\star = (1+\tau)r$$

where r is the domestic interest rate and τ is the spread of $r^\star$ over r. $r_t^\star$ is exogenous and its stationary component follows the stochastic process:

$$\log(r_t^\star) = \rho_{r^\star}\log(r_{t-1}^\star) + (1-\rho_{p_{r^\star}})\log(r^\star) + \varepsilon_{r^\star,t} \tag{5.3}$$

where the $\varepsilon_{r^\star,t}$ are *i.i.d.* stochastic variables following a normal distribution $\mathcal{N}(0,\sigma_{r^\star}^2)$, $r^\star$ the steady state value and where $\rho_{r^\star} < 1$.

5.1.2 Optimal Behavior of Households and Firms

As households accumulate capital, the intertemporal optimal behavior of the firm can be derived from a sequence of static problems. At period t, each firm j maximizes its profit $\Pi_{j,t}$:

$$\begin{aligned}\Pi_{j,t} &= A_t\left(\gamma_1 K_{j,t}^{(\sigma-1)/\sigma} + (1-\gamma_1)E_{j,t}^{(\sigma-1)/\sigma}\right)^{\alpha\sigma/(\sigma-1)} H_{j,t}^{1-\alpha} \\ &\quad - (z_t K_{j,t} + w_t H_{j,t} + p_t^e E_{j,t})\end{aligned} \tag{5.4}$$

where z_t is the real rental rate of capital, w_t the real wage, p_t^e the real price of imported energy and where the domestic good is chosen as *numeraire*. p_t^e is exogenous and its stationary component follows the stochastic process:

$$\log(p_t^e) = \rho_{p^e}\log(p_{t-1}^e) + (1-\rho_{p_e})\log(p^e) + \varepsilon_{p^e,t} \tag{5.5}$$

where the $\varepsilon_{p^e,t}$ are *i.i.d.* stochastic variables following a normal distribution $\mathcal{N}(0,\sigma_{p^e}^2)$, p^e the steady state value and where $\rho_{p^e} < 1$.

The first order conditions of firm j optimal behavior are:

$$z_t = \alpha\gamma_1 \frac{Y_{j,t}}{K_{j,t}^{1/\sigma}\left(\gamma_1 K_{j,t}^{(\sigma-1)/\sigma} + (1-\gamma_1)E_{j,t}^{(\sigma-1)/\sigma}\right)} \tag{5.6}$$

$$w_t = (1-\alpha)\frac{Y_{j,t}}{H_{j,t}} \tag{5.7}$$

$$p_t^e = \alpha(1-\gamma_1)\frac{Y_{j,t}}{E_{j,t}^{1/\sigma}\left(\gamma_1 K_{j,t}^{(\sigma-1)/\sigma} + (1-\gamma_1)E_{j,t}^{(\sigma-1)/\sigma}\right)} \tag{5.8}$$

Each household maximizes its discounted sum of utility flows with respect to the budget constraint at period t:

$$C_{i,t}+K_{i,t+1}-(1-\delta)K_{i,t}+\Phi\left(K_{i,t+1},K_{i,t}\right)+B_{i,t+1}-B_{i,t}\leq z_tK_{i,t}+w_tH_{i,t}+r_t^{\star}B_{i,t} \tag{5.9}$$

Household i resources are then its capital and labor earnings and the yield of the international asset he owes. The optimization problem can then be written in a recursive way and its optimal solution verifies the Bellman equation:

$$\begin{aligned} V_i\left(K_{i,t},B_{i,t},\mathcal{I}_{i,t}\right) &= \max_{C_{i,t},L_{i,t},K_{i,t+1},B_{i,t+1}}\Big\{u\left(C_{i,t},B_{i,t},L_{i,t}\right) \\ &+ \beta E_t\left[V_i\left(K_{i,t+1},B_{i,t+1},\mathcal{I}_{i,t+1}\right)\right]\Big\} \end{aligned}$$

with respect to the budget constraint (5.9). Let $\lambda_{i,t}$ be the Lagrange multiplier of the budget constraint and $\mathcal{I}_{i,t}$ the informational set of household i at period t: $\mathcal{I}_{i,t}=\{A_t,r_t^{\star},p_t^{e},w_t,z_t\}$. We solve this program to get the first order conditions (with respect to C,L,K and B):

$$u'_{C_{i,t}} = \lambda_{i,t} \tag{5.10}$$

$$u'_{L_{i,t}} = -\lambda_{i,t}w_t \tag{5.11}$$

$$\begin{aligned}\beta E_t\left[\left(1+z_{t+1}-\delta+\phi\frac{1}{K_{i,t+1}}\left(\frac{K_{i,t+2}}{K_{i,t+1}}-1\right)\frac{K_{i,t+2}}{K_{i,t+1}}\right)\lambda_{i,t+1}\right]& \\ -\lambda_{i,t}\left(1+\phi\frac{1}{K_{i,t}}\left(\frac{K_{i,t+1}}{K_{i,t}}-1\right)\right) &= (5012)\end{aligned}$$

$$\beta E_t\left[u'_{B_{i,t+1}}+\lambda_{i,t+1}(1+r_{t+1}^{\star})\right]=\lambda_{i,t} \tag{5.13}$$

We also impose the two following transversality constraints:

$$\lim_{t\to+\infty}E_0\left(\beta^t\lambda_{i,t}K_{i,t}\right) = 0 \tag{5.14}$$

$$\lim_{t\to+\infty}E_0\left(\beta^t\lambda_{i,t}B_{i,t}\right) = 0 \tag{5.15}$$

5.1.3 Competitive Equilibrium of the Economy

With the normalization $h=n=1$, the equilibrium is given by the first order conditions of the firms (equations (5.6) to (5.8)) and households optimal behavior (equations (5.9), (5.10) to (5.13) ,(5.14) and (5.15)) and by the equilibrium conditions (where letters without an i or j subscript denote aggregate values):

$$Y_t + r_t^{\star} B_t = C_t + K_{t+1} - (1-\delta) K_t + B_{t+1} - B_t + \Phi\left(K_{i,t+1}, K_{i,t}\right) \quad (5.16)$$

Equation (5.16) is the aggregate resource constraint of the economy. The trade balance TB evolves according to the following equation:

$$TB_t = B_{t+1} - (1 + r_t^{\star}) B_t \quad (5.17)$$

Exports and imported consumption goods are not modelled, and it is assumed that their evolution is such that (5.17) is always satisfied.

5.1.4 Stationarization and Linearization of the Model

As we cannot find analytically the equilibrium path of the economy, we linearize the system defining the equilibrium around its steady state. We obtain a linear dynamic system which gives the path of the endogenous variables relative deviations from their steady state levels, in presence of exogenous shocks. They are two state (predetermined) variables in the model (K_t and B_t), and two forward variables[2] (λ_t and K_{t+1}). We solve the linear rational expectations model following Blanchard and Kahn [1980] and King, Plosser and Rebelo [1987]. The model respects the Blanchard and Kahn [1980] stability condition, with two eigenvalues with modulus less than one and two with modulus greater than one.

The solution of the linearized model is then given by the following state-space system (where $\widehat{x}_t$ is the relative deviation of any stationarized variable x_t from its steady state value):

$$\begin{pmatrix} \widehat{k}_{t+1} \\ \widehat{b}_{t+1} \\ \widehat{a}_{t+1} \\ \widehat{r^{\star}}_{t+1} \\ \widehat{p^{e}}_{t+1} \end{pmatrix} = V_1 \begin{pmatrix} \widehat{k}_{t} \\ \widehat{b}_{t} \\ \widehat{a}_{t} \\ \widehat{r^{\star}}_{t} \\ \widehat{p^{e}}_{t} \end{pmatrix} + \begin{pmatrix} 0 \\ 0 \\ \varepsilon_{a,t} \\ \varepsilon_{r^{\star},t} \\ \varepsilon_{p^{e},t} \end{pmatrix} \quad (5.18)$$

[2]There is an dynamics of order two in K because of adjustment costs.

$$\begin{pmatrix} \widehat{c}_t \\ \widehat{h}_t \\ \widehat{y}_t \\ \widehat{\imath}_t \\ \widehat{e}_t \\ \widehat{tb}_t \end{pmatrix} = V_2 \begin{pmatrix} \widehat{k}_t \\ \widehat{b}_t \\ \widehat{a}_t \\ \widehat{r^*}_t \\ \widehat{p^e}_t \end{pmatrix} \tag{5.19}$$

V_1 and V_2 are real matrix whose coefficients are complicated and highly non-linear functions of the model parameters (technology, preferences, stochastic processes of the shocks). This state-space system is then used to simulate the theoretical model.

5.2 Two Exercises of Model Validation

We first give the parameter calibration of the theoretical model before comparing empirical and theoretical second order moments (standard deviations) and analyzing estimated and computed *IRF*.

5.2.1 Parameter Calibration of the Benchmark Model

The parameters of the model are calibrated partly according to previous studies on French data and partly according to authors computation. A first group of parameters is set according to Hairault and Portier [1993][3]:

Table 5.1:

α	H	δ	β	ζ
.45	.2	.0125	.9929	0

Labor earnings represent 55% of French output over the sample 1973-1989. The value of H means that households work 20% of their life time. The annual rate of capital depreciation is about 5%. The value

[3] Following Hansen [1985] and Rogerson [1988], we assume that jobs are indivisible in the economy, with lotteries on the labour market. This is equivalent to set the elasticity of the marginal disutility of labour ζ to zero ($\zeta = \frac{Lv''(L)}{v'(L))}$).

of β is such that quarterly French real interest is 0.7 percent, which is exactly the observed average interest rate over the sample.

We estimate the following average ratio on French data (73-89):

$$\frac{TB}{Y} = 0.046\%$$

Trade balance is slightly in excess over the sample. So, at the stationary equilibrium, the domestic household is a debtor *vis à vis* the *Rest of the World*: indeed, balance of payments equilibrium requires that $\frac{TB}{Y} = \frac{-r^{\star}B}{Y}$ and so B is negative. The household behavior is consistent with the fact that over the sample the average interest rate differential is negative: τ is about -4 percents.

The model steady state values are consistent with the estimation of the following set of parameters:

Table 5.2:

$\frac{E}{K}$	σ	ϕ	CA	$\frac{z}{p^e}$	τ
82.10-7	.6	75	.24%	28.10-6	-4%

The scale parameter, ϕ, is determined such that the variability of investment relative to output is well reproduced by the model. CA is the real cost in terms of stationary equilibrium output percents of increasing capital from one percent. The first order conditions of firm optimal behavior on capital and imported energy allow to evaluate the parameter γ_1:

$$\gamma_1 = \frac{\frac{z}{p^e}}{\frac{z}{p^e} + (\frac{E}{K})^{\frac{1}{\sigma}}}$$

where $\frac{E}{K}$ and $\frac{z}{p^e}$ are average values over the sample.

The elasticity of substitution between capital and imported energy, σ, is determined such that these factors are not perfect substitutes (Kim and Loungani [1992]). We can notice that the ratio of imported energy over output is overstated with this calibration (10% in the model *versus* 4.7% in the data).

The $AR1$ stochastic processes of shocks are estimated over the same sample:

Table 5.3:

ρ_A	ε_A	$\rho_{r\star}$	$\varepsilon_{r\star}$	ρ_{p^e}	ε_{p^e}
.57	.01	.93	.002	.98	.096

The computation of Solow residual depends on the value of σ[4]. This Solow residual measure is independent of imported energy price shocks because total factor productivity computation requires the omission of imported energy contribution to output. We compare it to the *traditional* Solow residual[5] issued from a Cobb-Douglas production function in which there are only capital and labor. These two measures[6] are not highly correlated: the correlation value is about 0.5. Moreover, the correlation between our Solow residual and imported energy price is less than the correlation between *traditional* Solow residual and imported energy price (-0.037 *versus* -0.44).

5.2.2 Traditional Validation by Moment Comparison

We present in the following tables the empirical moments of the variables and those calculated from the state-space form of the benchmark model, knowing the exogenous shocks stochastic processes.

A proper filtering of the data and of the model output is required to catch the business cycle, as it was defined by the empirical work of the NBER. King and Rebelo [1989] studied the spectral properties of the Hodrick-Prescott filter (*HP* filter for short) and showed that it eliminates all low frequency components of economic series, even sta-

[4] The Solow residual is obtained as follows. Firstly, we compute total factor productivity by the ratio of output on production factor contribution. So, total factor productivity depends on parameters σ, α and γ_1: the last one also depends on $\frac{E}{K}$ and $\frac{p^e}{z}$. Secondly, we consider total factor productivity logarithm that we regress on a constant and a trend. The residual of this estimation is assimilated to Solow residual.

[5] As it is computed in the *RBC* literature.

[6] Generally speaking, the stochastic processes of these two Solow residual measures are different from each other: the *traditional* Solow residual is more persistent and more variable than our Solow residual, respectively 0.83 *versus* 0.57 for the comparison of the autoregressive parts and 0.03 *versus* 0.02 for the comparison of residual standard deviations.

tionary ones. Then, the relative deviation of a variable from its *HP* growth component is a good approximation of the economic business cycle. *RBC* model output is generally *HP* filtered and compared with the relative variations of macro variables from their *HP* growth components.

This is what is done in the following tables, where are computed the *HP* standard deviations of the French business cycle[7] and the *HP* standard deviations of the benchmark model, computed as mean of 100 stochastic simulations over 100 periods each.

Table 5.4: Cyclical Properties of the Benchmark Model

Variable	$\widehat{y}$	$\widehat{c}$	$\widehat{\imath}$	$\widehat{h}$	$\widehat{e}$	$\widehat{\frac{tb}{y}}$
S.D./S.D.($\widehat{y}$)	S.D.($\widehat{y}$)=2.87	.21	4.64	.87	3.69	.75
Autocor. order 1	.48	.65	.61	.44	.66	.48
Cor. with $\widehat{y}$	1	.67	.64	.98	.67	.36
Cor($\widehat{\imath}, \widehat{s}$)				.71		
Cor($\widehat{y}, \widehat{p^e}$)				-.30		

Table 5.5: Cyclical Properties of French Business Cycle, Quarterly Data (INSEE Database) 1973-1989

Variable	$\widehat{y}$	$\widehat{c}$	$\widehat{\imath}$	$\widehat{h}$	$\widehat{e}$	$\widehat{\frac{tb}{y}}$
S.D./S.D.($\widehat{y}$)	S.D.($\widehat{y}$)=0.99	.85	3.31	.86	6.32	0.66
Autocor. order 1	.77	.67	.77	.87	.38	.66
Cor. with $\widehat{y}$	1	.56	.71	.70	.45	-.36
Cor($\widehat{\imath}, \widehat{s}$)				.60		
Cor($\widehat{y}, \widehat{p^e}$)				-.03		

Firstly, we notice that the *RBC* model overestimates output variability. Two opposite effects explain this result: on one side, the Solow residual variance is small because Solow residual is independent from imported energy price shocks; on the other side, the introduction of imported energy price shocks in the model increases its variability. So, in that case, the second effect dominates. The model well mimics the relative variability of aggregate variables except for consumption. Generally, model variables are less persistent than the data.

[7] Agregate Savings s is computed as Gross National Product - Aggregate Consumption + Trade Balance.

Secondly, the I-S correlation is well reproduced. But, imported energy price is more counter-cyclical than it is in the data: in the model, the increase in imported energy price has a higher recessive impact on output than in the data. Nevertheless, the previously cited overestimation of imported energy to output is responsible for the high counter-cyclicity of imported energy price.

The model does not succeed in reproducing the trade balance counter-cyclicity although this stylized fact is very strong in the data. This empirical regularity is well accounted for by traditional open-economy models which stress on the fact that domestic country imports goods follow an output expansion which *de facto* deteriorates trade balance.

This economic scheme does not always exist in intertemporal models which take into account balance of payments equilibrium. For instance, let us consider the case of a positive technological shock. This shock increases both labor and capital productivity. So, worked hours, output and investment increase. But, there exist two opposite effects: the first one, *a pro-borrowing effect*, means that domestic households borrow to the *Rest of the World* in order to subsidy investment excess. The second one, *a pro-savings effect*, means that domestic households borrow less to the *Rest of the World* because domestic output is larger. If the first effect is larger than the second one, capital balance increases and trade balance decreases in order to warrant balance of payments equilibrium. So, in that case, trade balance is counter-cyclical (Mendoza [1991]).

Two assumptions related to the model specification explain the trade balance pro-cyclicity. Firstly, imperfect asset substitutability increases *the pro-savings effect* and decreases *the pro-borrowing one*. As international asset holdings create disutility for domestic households, *the pro-savings effect* which decreases international debt of domestic households dominates if the domestic country is a net debtor although *the pro-borrowing effect* dominates if the country is a net creditor. So, in our case, *the pro-savings effect* dominates and trade balance is pro-cyclical. Secondly, imperfect substitution between capital and imported energy is responsible for trade balance pro-cyclicity: following an increase in imported energy price, output decreases and trade balance decreases too because of capital-imported energy complementarity.

It appears that trade balance counter-cyclicity is not a solid result of open economy *RBC* models and that the introduction of the real side of international trade *via* imported energy still reduces this strong regularity.

The relative size of the two previously mentioned effects explains the model ability to mimic the cross-correlation between savings and investment. The identity $I = S$ in a closed economy becomes in an open one:

$$S = I + \Delta Cr - \Delta D$$

with Cr and D represent respectively international credit and debt of domestic households.

If *the pro-savings effect* dominates, a technological shock increases investment and reduces more international debt than it increases international credit. So, it contributes to make the S-I correlation higher.

5.2.3 Impulse Response Functions of the *RBC* and *VAR* Models

The estimated *IRF* are stemmed from a Vector Auto-Regressive (*VAR*) model. The Vector Autoregression technique was introduced in macroeconomics theory by Sims [1980]. The *VAR* methods are popular because, on the one hand, they are simple to implement and, on the other hand, they determine imp rtant dynamics characteristics of the economy without imposing restrictions from a particular structural model. A *VAR* model an be seen as the reduced form of an unknown structural model, but its estimation does not require any prior believes on its structural form. Our purpose is not to estimate the state-space form (equations (5.18) and (5.19)) of the *RBC* model, but to extract information from data by the mean of estimated *IRF*.

Our *VAR* model contains five endogenous variables - output, consumption, investment, worked hours, and imported energy - and three exogenous ones - Solow residual as a measure of the technological shock, relative price of imported energy and world real interest rate[8].

[8] All domestic data are from INSEE quarterly data base (1973-1989). World real interest rate is computed from US long term nominal interest rate (OECD *Financial Statistics*) by the Département des Diagnostics of the OFCE. Imported

All variables of the *VAR* are detrended with respect to Hodrick-Prescott filter in order to compare *VAR* results to the *RBC* ones. Nevertheless, it is clear that the estimation of a *VAR* model with *HP* variables corresponds to an over-differentiation of the variables and does not take into account some information about relationships between variables levels, for instance cointegrating relationships.

A good way to solve this problem would consist in integrating explicitly a non-stationary dimension in the *RBC* model, for instance an endogenous technical progress. Such a specification would allow a stationarization method which would be consistent with the theoretical representation of a stochastic trend. Nevertheless, this specification is not developed in recent *RBC* models and the relationship between cycle and trend is to be made[9]. So, we adopt a traditional scheme although we loose information about variables levels : we detrend both variables issued from the *VAR* and *RBC* models with the *HP* filter.

Once all the variables are transformed, we choose the optimal lag length of endogenous variables using likelihood ratio tests, imposing no lag on the exogenous variables. We select one as optimal lag length. Using the coefficient matrix we get by estimating the *VAR*, we shock some of the exogenous variables and compute *IRF*. We perform this technique for the three shocks[10]- Solow residual, world interest rate and price of imported input good. Before the shock, the endogenous and exogenous variables are supposed to be at their steady state level and their deviations are then null. We shock successively each of the three exogenous variables of one percent from its steady state, the other shocks being set to zero. Then, we forecast on fifty periods the endogenous variables in order to obtain their impulse response functions. As the exogenous variables are autoregressive processes, their impacts decrease over time.

Furthermore, we use bootstrap techniques[11] to compute confidence

---

energy, measured by imported fossil energy use, and its price, measured by the average import cost of fossil energy products, are issued from the Observatoire de l'Energie.

[9] Collard [1993] proposes a model in this direction.

[10] As we shock exogenous variables, there is no orthogonalization problem about these shocks.

[11] The bootstrap techniques consist in a finite number of *VAR* model estimations,

bands at 95% . The "theoretical" *IRF* (*i.e.* computed from the model) are performed in the following way. We first simulate the *RBC* on 500 periods. We then get simulated series for output, consumption, investment, worked hours, imported energy and for the three shocks. These series are used to evaluate the "theoretical" *IRF*. In the light of the main economic mechanisms generally evoked, we compare *RBC* and *VAR* impulse response functions. In fact, there is not a good adequation between *RBC* and *VAR* impulse response functions.

IRF to a Technological Shock

We briefly present the main economic mechanisms[12] before comparing the two kinds of *IRF*. When such a shock occurs, domestic output increases *via* the increase in labor supply. Excess output is both consumed and invested. So, consumption, investment and worked hours increase instantaneously: they are pro-cyclical. As imported energy and capital are not perfect substitutes, imported energy use increases with output.

VAR and *RBC* impulse responses of output and investment have the same sign (see figures). Nevertheless, *VAR IRF* of worked hours and consumption are not significantly different from zero. Imported energy impulse responses have opposite signs: a positive one in the *RBC* model, a negative one in the *VAR* model. In general, the theoretical model overestimates the magnitude of technological shocks effects.

IRF to Imported Energy Price and World Real Interest Rate Shocks

Weak capital-imported energy substitution is mainly responsible for the theoretical *IRF* following an imported energy price shock: imported energy use decreases and so output, consumption, worked hours and investment decrease too. Although this recessive impact on real economy is consistent with economic theory, it is not with the *VAR*

---

each estimation corresponding to a specific permutation of the estimated residuals issued from the initial *VAR*.

[12] We refer to Hairault in chapter 1 of this book for an exhaustive development of these effects.

Figure 5.1: Output Response to a Technological Shock

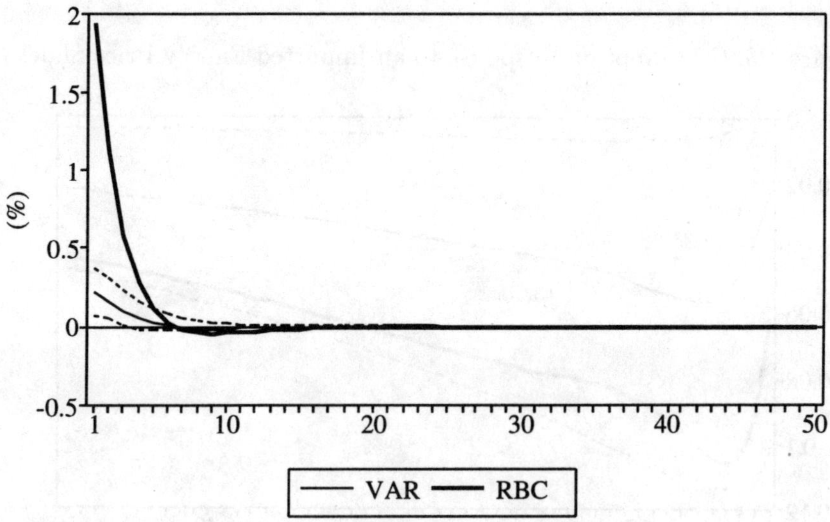

Figure 5.2: Investment Response to a Technological Shock

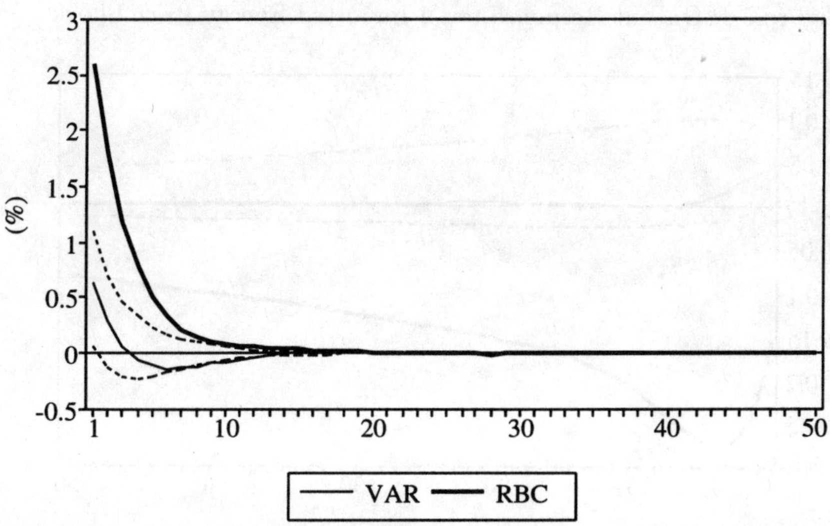

model in which only consumption is significantly reduced (see figure). Other variables impulse responses, as output *IRF* figure shows it, are not significantly different from zero.

Figure 5.3: Consumption Response to an Imported Energy Price Shock

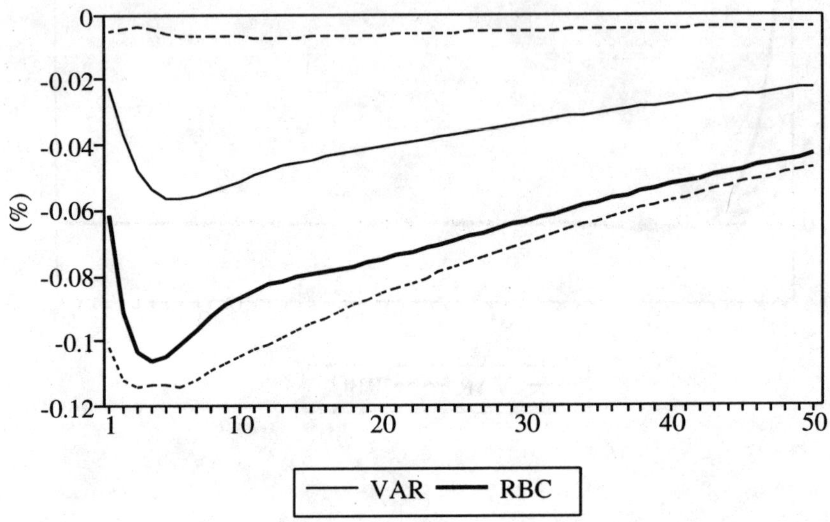

Figure 5.4: Output Response to an Imported Energy Price Shock

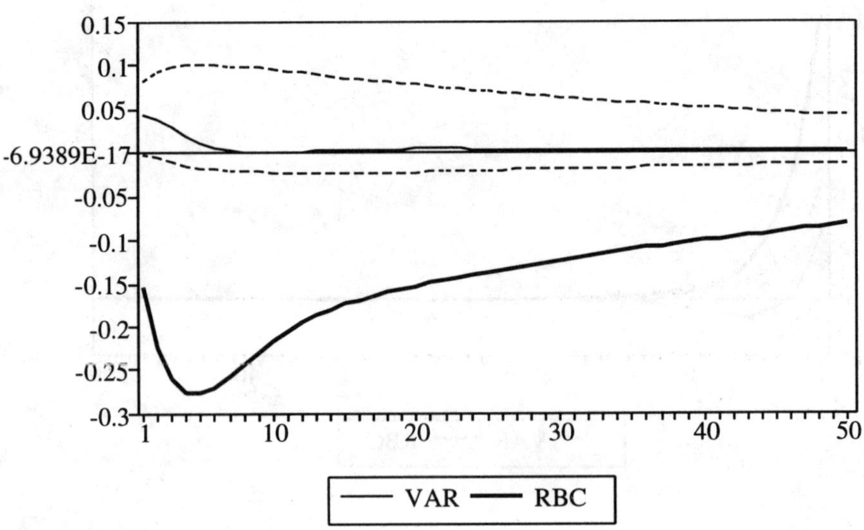

In the case of a positive world real interest rate shock, a substitution of international assets to domestic capital occurs in the model. This effect increases instantaneously worked hours and output. So, domestic households have an income excess which allows them to buy new international assets. Nevertheless, these effects are very negligible in the *RBC* model, world real interest rate shocks have a little impact on cyclical properties of the model. The *VAR* impulse responses of output (see figure), consumption and worked hours are significantly negative. Those of investment and imported energy are not significant. Generally, these *VAR* impulse responses are very different from the *RBC* model ones.

Figure 5.5: Output Response to a World Real Interest Rate Shock

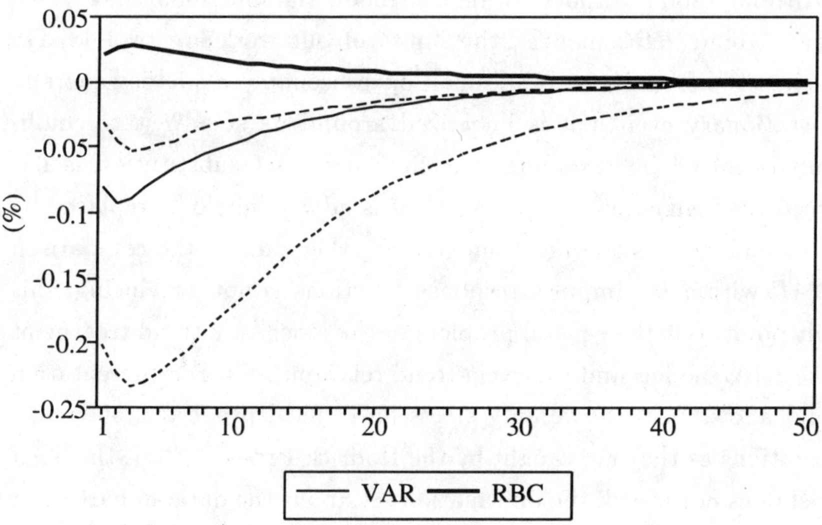

5.3 Concluding Comments

The aim of this hapter is to replicate the French business cycle over the sample 1973-1989 with an open economy *RBC* model. The theoretical model integrates the twofold - real and financial - dimension of the French economy openness. On the real open side, we include imported energy as a production function factor which is an imperfect substitute of capital. On the financial open side, domestic households can choose between international and domestic financial assets although they prefer domestic assets.

Our study refers to recent *RBC* open economy papers. We follow Kim and Loungani [1992] to compute a Solow residual measure whose main characteristics is to be independent from imported energy price changes. However, our research is original according to several points. Firstly, in order to take into account the financial dimension of the French economic openness, we do not follow Mendoza [1991] or Cardia [1991] who assume that the rate of time preference is endogenous. According to us, financial asset substitutability is imperfect. Secondly, we use a new technique, the comparison of estimated and simulated *IRF*, in order to validate the theoretical model.

Although some authors (Summers [1986], Mankiw [1989]) have some caution about *RBC* models, the limits of our work are twofold. On one side, the fact that a *RBC* small open economy model is generally non-stationary even if it is linearized around its steady state equilibrium is solved by assuming that financial asset substitution is not perfect. Such an assumption, because it is *ad hoc* should be replaced by a more endogenous specification. On the other side, as the comparison of *VAR* with *RBC* impulse response functions is not convincing, this result points out the general problem of the stochastic trend treatment in the *RBC* models and the cycle-trend relationship this representation should allow. Because we only stress on cyclical properties of French fluctuations as they are caught by the Hodrick-Prescott filter, the *VAR* model does not use all the information set about the data, in particular about relationships between variables levels. So, further research on a joint representation of cycle and trend in a theoretical model should be fruitful.

Bibliography

D. Backus, P. Kehoe and F. Kydland. International Real Business Cycles. *Journal of Political Economy*, 100(4):745–775, 1992.

F. Bec. *La transmission internationale des fluctuations : une explication de la corrélation croisée des consommations.* Cahiers ECO & MATHS 92.38, MAD, Université de Paris I, 1992.

O. Blanchard and C. Kahn. The Solution of Linear Difference Models under Rational Expectations. *Econometrica*, 48(5):1305–1311, July 1980.

O. Blanchard. Debt, Deficits, and Finite Horizons. *Journal of Political Economy*, 93:223–247, 1985.

C. Burnside, M. Eichenbaum and S. Rebelo. *Labor Hoarding and the Business Cycle.* Working paper 3556, National Bureau of Economic Research, December 1990.

E. Cardia. The Dynamics of a Small Open Economy in Response to Monetary, Fiscal, and Productivity Shocks. *Journal of Monetary Economics*, 28:411–434, 1991.

F. Collard. *La neutralité des chocs conjoncturels sur la dynamique de long terme de la productivité.* Working paper, MAD, Université de Paris I, 1993.

T. Cooley and G. Hansen. The Inflation Tax in a Real Business Cycle Model. *American Economic Review*, 79(4):733–748, September 1989.

X. Fairise and F. Langot. Labor Productivity and Business Cycles: Can RBC Models be Saved? *European Economic Review*, 38, October 1994.

M. Feldstein and C. Horioka. Domestic Savings and International Capital Flows. *Economic Journal*, 90:314–29, 1980.

M. Finn. On Savings and Investment Dynamics in a Small Open Economy. *Journal of International Economics*, 29:1–22, 1990.

J.O. Hairault and F. Portier. Monnaie et inflation dans un modèle de cycles réels. *Recherches Economiques de Louvain*, 59(4):427–461, 1993.

G. HANSEN. Indivisible Labor and the Business Cycles. *Journal of Monetary Economics*, 16(3):309–327, November 1985.

I.M. KIM AND P. LOUNGANI. The Role of Energy in Real Business Cycle Models. *Journal of Monetary Economics*, 29:173–189, April 1992.

R. KING AND S. REBELO. *Low Frequency Filtering and the Real Business Cycles.* Working paper 205, University of Rochester, 1989.

R. KING, C. PLOSSER AND S. REBELO. *Production Growth and Business Cycles: Technical Appendix.* Working paper, University of Rochester, 1987. Revised May 1990.

R. KING. *Money and Business Cycles.* Working paper, University of Rochester, 1990.

F. KYDLAND AND E. PRESCOTT. Time to Build and Aggregate Fluctuations. *Econometrica*, 50(6):1345–1370, November 1982.

J. LONG AND C. PLOSSER. Real Business Cycles. *Journal of Political Economy*, 91(1):39–69, February 1983.

G. MANKIW. Real Busines Cycles: a New Keynesian Perspective. *Journal of Economic Perspectives*, 3(3):79–90, Summer 1989.

E. MENDOZA. Real Business Cycles in a Small Open Economy. *American Economic Review*, 81(4):797–818, September 1991.

M. OBSTFELD. Capital Mobility in the World Economy: Theories and Measurement. *Carnegie Rochester Conference Series on Public Policy*, 42:55–103, 1986.

R. ROGERSON. Indivisible Labor, Lotteries and Equilibrium. *Journal of Monetary Economics*, 21(1):3–16, January 1988.

C. SIMS. Macroeconomics and Reality. *Econometrica*, 48(1):1–48, January 1980.

L. SUMMERS. Some Skeptical Observations on Real Business Cycles Theory. *Federal Reserve Bank of Minneapolis Quaterly Review*, 10:23–27, Autumn 1986.

M. WOODFORD AND J. ROTEMBERG. *Oligopolistic Competition and the Effect of Aggregate Demand on Economic Activity.* Working paper 3206, National Bureau of Economic Research, 1989.

M. YAARI. Uncertain Lifetime, Life Insurance, and the Theory of the Consumer. *Review of Economic Studies*, 32:137–150, 1965.

Part II

Advances beyond RBC Framework

Chapter 6

Nominal Rigidities and Monopolistic Competition: A New-Keynesian View

Jean-Olivier Hairault & Franck Portier

Abstract

We show in this chapter that the business cycle can not be reduced to the real business cycles archetype. A monopolistic competition model with price adjustment costs, affected by technological *and* monetary shocks, better mimics the economic fluctuations in two countries with very different cyclical properties, namely France and the United States. An alternative version of the model with increasing returns to scale is also studied, and is shown to slightly modify the cyclical behavior of the benchmark model. With two independent shocks, one real, more specifically defined than the Solow residual, and one nominal, the benchmark model gives an answer to these empirical puzzles, which were left unexplained by traditional *RBC* models.

Introduction

Two main competing approaches of the business cycle arose in the eighties: the Real Business Cycles theory and the New-Keynesian Macroeconomics. Following the seminal papers of Kydland and Prescott [1982], Long and Plosser [1983] and King, Plosser and Rebelo [1988], *RBC* theorists consider economic fluctuations as the optimal responses of economic agents to exogenous real shocks. The aim of these first models was to explain macroeconomic fluctuations only with technological shocks; demand shocks were unnecessary and nominal shocks were *de facto* absent from these purely real models[1]. Hénin [1989] noticed some attempts to introduce money in such a flex-price competitive framework: the King and Plosser [1984] model introduces financial intermediation and get some insight on the (inside) money-output correlation when technology shocks occur. Nevertheless, the outside money-output link is missing and no quantitative validation of the model is proposed. Outside money shocks are introduced in a cash-in-advance economy by Cooley and Hansen [1989] (constraint on consumption): Hairault and Portier propose in the chapter 4 an extension of this constraint to investment. These models do not provide a good description of the money-output correlation and are not able to reproduce the shape and level of the real variables impulse responses to monetary shocks for a realistic calibration. King [1990] obtains the *triangular shape* of the monetary business cycle in a staggered contracts model where money is introduced *via* a quantitative equation. Nevertheless, this quantitative equation has no microeconomic foundations in the model and no simulated moments are computed. Ambler and Phaneuf [1992] also use staggered contracts in a reduced- form model which provides good approximation of monetary impulse responses, but without explicit microfoundations.

Furthermore, the *RBC* literature initiated a validation method based upon the ability of the model to mimic some macroeconomic stylized facts by stochastic simulations.

On the other hand, the New-Keynesian macroeconomics[2] expanded microfounded macroeconomic models with Keynesian features such as underemployment equilibria, coordination failures, market power, real and nominal rigidities and the importance of nominal shocks in the business cycle.

A first attempt to reconciliate the *RBC* techniques with these new Keynesian developments relies on the introduction of real rigidities on the labor market, *via* efficiency wages (Danthine and Donaldson [1990]), risk sharing contracts (Danthine and Donaldson [1990]b) or labor hoar-

[1]See Part I of this book.

[2]This expression was first used by Parkin [1986], and then popularized by Gordon [1990] and Mankiw and Romer [1991].

ding (Burnside, Eichenbaum and Rebelo [1990], Fairise and Langot [1994], Fairise and Langot in chapter 2 of this book.). Nominal rigidities through wage contracts are introduced by Cho [1990]a, Cho and Cooley [1990] and Fairise in chapter 7 of this book. In an other direction, Rotemberg and Woodford [1989] proposed an oligopolistic competition model with Keynesian features.

Following Kiyotaki [1985], Blanchard and Kiyotaki [1987] and Benassy [1987], the monopolistic competition framework has been widely used to introduce nominal rigidities (staggered contracts or menu costs) and to emphasize the role of demand shocks, and particularly monetary shocks[3].

We propose in this paper a dynamic monopolistic competition model with nominal rigidities and money in the utility function. As Danthine and Donaldson [1991] pointed out the difficulty of a single model to give an accurate description of both US and European fluctuations, we evaluate the ability of our model to mimic two very different business cycles features, namely the French and US ones.

This model allows us to study the effect of monetary shocks in this theoretical framework and with the validation methods of *RBC* theorists[4]. We will show that the presence of monetary shocks sharply modifies the behavior of the model. An alternative version of the model with increasing returns to scale is also studied, and is shown to slightly modify the cyclical behavior of the benchmark model.

With two independent shocks, one real, which cannot be measured by the Solow residual in that framework[5], and one nominal, the model gives an answer to five empirical puzzles, which were unexplained by traditional *RBC* models, on French data as well as on US data.

The first section of this chapter presents the model and its approximated resolution around its stationary steady state. The second section illustrates its qualitative and quantitative cyclical properties on US and

[3]See Blanchard [1990] survey for the Handbook of Monetary Economics: *"Why Does Money Affect Output?"*.

[4]Rotemberg and Woodford [1989] compared their theoretical impulse responses to a military expenditures shock to estimated impulses responses on US data.

[5]Hall [1989] demonstrated that the Solow residual is *contaminated* by demand shocks in imperfectly competitive models and Evans [1992] showed that the Solow residual is Granger-caused by demand shocks on US data.

French data.

6.1 The Model

In that section, we present a dynamic extension of the Blanchard and Kiyotaki [1987]Blanchard and Kiyotaki [1987] model of monopolistic competition with explicit intertemporal household behavior and solve it around its stationary steady state.

6.1.1 A Monopolistic Competition Model with Money in the Utility Function

We describe representative household and firms behavior, and solve the symmetrical monopolistic competition equilibrium of that economy.

Technology et Preferences

The economy is composed of h identical households indexed by i and n firms indexed by j. Firm j is the only firm that produces Y_j units of good j. All firms have access to the same constant returns to scale production function:

$$Y_{j,t} \leq A_t K_{j,t}^{\alpha} H_{j,t}^{1-\alpha} \tag{6.1}$$

where $K_{j,t}$ is the capital stock used by firm j and $H_{j,t}$ the quantity of labor input. A_t follows the stochastic process:

$$\log(A_t) = \rho_A \log(A_{t-1}) + (1-\rho_A)\log(\overline{A}) + \varepsilon_{A,t} \tag{6.2}$$

where the $\varepsilon_{A,t}$ are *i.i.d.* stochastic variables following a normal law $\mathcal{N}(0,\sigma_A^2)$, and where $\rho_A < 1$. The total factor productivity A_t is a technological shock common to all firms of the economy, and we assume that A_t is observed at the beginning of period t.

Households are identical, and their preferences are given by the utility function U_0 which represents the expectation of the discounted sum of instantaneous utility flows u, conditionally to the information available at date $t = 0$:

$$\begin{aligned}U_0 &= E_0\left[\sum_{t=0}^{\infty}\beta^t u(C_{i,t},\frac{M_{i,t}}{P_t},L_{i,t})\right] \qquad (6.3)\\ &= E_0\left[\sum_{t=0}^{\infty}\beta^t\left(\frac{1}{a}\left(C_{i,t}^{\frac{\sigma-1}{\sigma}}+\gamma_2\left(\frac{M_{i,t}}{P_t}\right)^{\frac{\sigma-1}{\sigma}}\right)^{\frac{\sigma}{\sigma-1}a}+\gamma_1 v(L_{i,t})\right)\right]\end{aligned}$$

where $\beta\in]0,1[$, $\gamma_1>0$ and $\gamma_2>0$. $C_{i,t}$ is a *CES* basket of the different goods produced in the economy:

$$C_{i,t}=\left(\sum_{j=1}^{n}C_{i,j,t}^{\frac{1}{1+\gamma}}\right)^{1+\gamma} \qquad (6.4)$$

where $\frac{1+\gamma}{\gamma}$ is the elasticity of substitution between the different goods. We can define a price index P_t:

$$P_t=\left(\frac{1}{n}\sum_{j=1}^{n}P_{j,t}^{\frac{-1}{\gamma}}\right)^{-\gamma} \qquad (6.5)$$

which verifies by construction the equation:

$$P_tC_{i,t}=\sum_{j=1}^{n}P_{j,t}C_{i,j,t} \qquad (6.6)$$

$\frac{M_{i,t}}{P_t}$ represents the real balances of the household at the beginning of period t. The utility of real balances relies on the transaction services allowed by money, as in a *Cash in Advance* model.

Each household is endowed with one unit of time at each period, and allocates it between leisure $L_{i,t}$ and worked hours $H_{i,t}$:

$$H_{i,t}+L_{i,t}\leq 1$$

The constant elasticity of substitution between real balances and the consumption basket is given by σ, and $\frac{1}{1-a}$ is the intertemporal elasticity of substitution of the basket composed of the consumption index and the real balances.

Each household accumulates capital and rents it to firms. Capital is a composite good, given as a *CES* index of the different produced goods. To simplify the computation of the demand function addressed to firm j, we assume that the investment index has the same structure than the consumption one. The accumulation technology is then given by the following equation:

$$\begin{aligned} K_{i,t+1} &= (1-\delta)K_{i,t} + \left(\sum_{j=1}^{n} I_{i,j,t}^{\frac{1}{1+\gamma}} \right)^{1+\gamma} \\ &= (1-\delta)K_{i,t} + I_{i,t} \end{aligned}$$

where $I_{i,t}$ is the investment index. One unit of each consumption good at period t is necessary to get one unit of capital at period $t+1$; the existing capital depreciates at constant rate δ.

The Money Supply

The money supply is specified as in Cooley and Hansen [1989]: the aggregate stock of money M_t grows at rate $(g_t - 1)$:

$$M_{t+1} = g_t M_t \tag{6.7}$$

The rate g_t has a mean $\overline{g}$ and follows the stochastic process:

$$\log(g_t) = \rho_g \log(g_{t-1}) + (1-\rho_g)\log(\overline{g}) + \varepsilon_{g,t} \tag{6.8}$$

Monetary shocks $\varepsilon_{g,t}$ are *i.i.d.* stochastic variables following a $\mathcal{N}(0, \sigma_g^2)$, and where $\rho_g < 1$. We assume that g_t is observed at the beginning of period t, and then all the money created at period t is distributed to households:

$$(g_t - 1)M_t = \sum_{i=1}^{h} N_{i,t} \tag{6.9}$$

The Optimal Composition of the Consumption and Investment Index

The optimal choice of the consumption and investment index composition can be viewed as a static choice. For given levels of consumption and investment $C_{i,t}$ and $I_{i,t}$ [6], household i maximizes respectively these index by choosing $C_{i,j,t}$ et $I_{i,j,t}$ for all j, taking as given prices $P_{j,t}$.

[6] These levels will be chosen later by solving an intertemporal problem.

The solving of these two programs gives the following consumption and investment demands of household i to firm j:

$$\begin{aligned} C_{i,j,t} &= P_{j,t}^{-\frac{1+\gamma}{\gamma}} P_t^{\frac{1+\gamma}{\gamma}} \frac{C_{i,t}}{n} && (6.10) \\ I_{i,j,t} &= P_{j,t}^{-\frac{1+\gamma}{\gamma}} P_t^{\frac{1+\gamma}{\gamma}} \frac{I_{i,t}}{n} && (6.11) \end{aligned}$$

The Intertemporal Behavior of the Household

Each household enters in period t with a predetermined level of capital $K_{i,t}$ and a predetermined level of money $M_{i,t}$. In period t, the household receives a lump sum monetary transfer $N_{i,t}$, its wage income, the remuneration of its capital and a constant share $v_{i,j}$ of real profits $\Pi_{j,t}$ of each firm j. It chooses its level of consumption, its supply of labor and the quantity of capital $K_{i,t+1}$ and money $M_{i,t+1}$ it will transfer next period. If we call w_t the real wage and z_t the capital gross rental rate[7], the budget constraint of household i is given by:

$$\begin{aligned} P_t K_{i,t+1} + M_{i,t+1} \leq\ & P_t(1-\delta+z_t)K_{i,t} + M_{i,t} \\ & + N_{i,t} + P_t w_t H_{i,t} + P_t \sum_{j=1}^{n} (v_{i,j}\Pi_{j,t}) - P_t C_{i,t} \quad (6.12) \end{aligned}$$

Given $K_{i,0}$,$M_{i,0}$,g_0, A_0, household i chooses ($C_{i,t}$, $H_{i,t}$, $M_{i,t+1}$, $K_{i,t+1}$), $t \in [0,+\infty[$ that maximize the expectation of the discounted sum of its utility flows, with respect to the budget constraint (6.12) at each period t. The problem can then be written in a recursive way and its optimal solution verifies the Bellman equation:

$$\begin{aligned} V_i\left(K_{i,t}, M_{i,t}, \mathcal{I}_{i,t}\right) &= \max_{C_{i,t},L_{i,t},K_{i,t+1},M_{i,t+1}} \left\{ u\left(C_{i,t}, \frac{M_{i,t}}{P_t}, L_{i,t}\right) \right. \\ &+ \left. \beta E_t\left[V_i\left(K_{i,t+1}, M_{i,t+1}, \mathcal{I}_{i,t+1}\right)\right]\right\} \end{aligned}$$

with respect to the budget constraint (6.12). Let $\Lambda_{i,t}$ be the Lagrange multiplier of the budget constraint and $\mathcal{I}_{i,t}$ the informational set of household i at period t: $\mathcal{I}_{i,t} = \{g_t, A_t, \{P_{j,t}\}_{j=1}^{n}, w_t, z_t\}$. We solve this

[7] The interest rate is then given by $r_t = z_t - \delta$.

problem to get the first order conditions of the household program. We also impose the transversality conditions:

$$\lim_{\tau \to +\infty} E_t \left[\beta^{t+\tau} K_{i,t+\tau+1} \frac{\partial V_{i,t+\tau+1}}{\partial K_{i,t+\tau+1}} \right] = 0 \tag{6.13}$$

$$\lim_{\tau \to +\infty} E_t \left[\beta^{t+\tau} M_{i,t+\tau+1} \frac{\partial V_{i,t+\tau+1}}{\partial M_{i,t+\tau+1}} \right] = 0 \tag{6.14}$$

Price Adjustment Costs and the Behavior of Firms

We adopt in this model a monopolistic market structure *à la* Blanchard and Kiyotaki [1987][8]. As the elasticity of substitution between the different goods entering in the utility function is not infinite, each firm has a monopoly power on its market. As this elasticity is strictly positive, each firm cares of its price level relatively to the aggregate price level. We assume that the number of firms n is large enough to ensure that each firm has a negligible effect on aggregate variables. Firms play a Nash game on the good market, and each one chooses its price, its labor and capital demands, knowing its good demand function and taking aggregate demand and aggregate price level as given. Without any other assumption, the firm problem is essentially a static one.

We then introduce prices adjustment costs, which refers to different theoretical models (search costs for instance) and are often modelled as menu costs in the *New-Keynesian* literature. To get a simple solution to the firm problem, we assume that these costs are quadratic[9]. We also assume that these costs are null at the steady state. As we will show later that prices grow at rate $\overline{g}$ at the steady state, the real adjustment cost at period t for firm j is given by:

$$\mathcal{CA}_{j,t} = \frac{\phi}{2} \left(\frac{P_{j,t}}{P_{j,t-1}} - \overline{g} \right)^2 \tag{6.15}$$

[8]The separation of the household program in a static and a dynamic one allows us to adopt a very general utility function. As far as we know, only Cho [1990]b introduces an imperfectly competitive assumption in a *RBC* model, but his solution method imposes a very particular utility function (linear in the consumption), which narrows the scope of his results.

[9]If these costs have a lump sum component, the optimal price rule may be very complicated. In some special cases, it can take a (S, s) recursive form but rises tedious aggregation problems (see Bertola and Caballero [1990] for a survey and Portier [1991] for an example.)

where ϕ is the adjustment costs scale parameter. To preserve a simple closing of the model, we assume that these real costs $\mathcal{CA}_{j,t}$ are paid by the firm through the purchase of a *CES* basket of all the produced goods of the economy, with the same elasticity of substitution than the consumption and investment basket. The optimal composition of this basket is identical to (6.10) and (6.11), and the demand of good j' from firm j is given by:

$$\mathcal{CA}_{j,j',t} = P_{j',t}^{-\frac{1+\gamma}{\gamma}} P_t^{\frac{1+\gamma}{\gamma}} \mathcal{CA}_{j,t} \tag{6.16}$$

The problem of firm j is then dynamic, and it maximizes the expectation of the discounted sum $V_{j,0}$ of its profit flows, conditionally to the information available at period $t = 0$:

$$E_0 \left[V_{j,0}\right] = E_0 \left[\sum_{t=0}^{\infty} \rho_t P_t \Pi_{j,t}\right] \tag{6.17}$$

with

$$P_t \Pi_{j,t} = P_{j,t} Y_{j,t} - P_t w_t H_{j,t} - P_t z_t K_{j,t} - P_t \mathcal{CA}_{j,t} \tag{6.18}$$

Following Rotemberg and Woodford [1989], the firm discount factor is given by the stochastic process $\{\rho_t\}$, which represents a pricing kernel for contingent claims.

Let $\nu_{j,t}$ be the Lagrange multiplier of the constraint

$$Y_{j,t} \leq Y_{j,t}^d \tag{6.19}$$

where $Y_{j,t}^d$ is the total demand addressed to firm j. From (6.10),(6.11) and (6.16), the demand is given by:

$$Y_{j,t}^d = P_{j,t}^{-\frac{1+\gamma}{\gamma}} P_t^{\frac{1+\gamma}{\gamma}} \frac{Y_t^d}{n} \tag{6.20}$$

where

$$Y_t^d = \sum_{i=1}^{h} \left(C_{i,t} + I_{i,t}\right) + \sum_{j=1}^{n} \mathcal{CA}_{j,t}$$

is the total demand index.

Knowing its demand function, firm j chooses at period t its price and its labor and capital demands, subject to the constraints (6.1) and (6.19). The firm behavior is then derived from the Bellman equation:

$$V_j\left(P_{j,t-1}, \mathcal{I}_{j,t}\right) = \max_{P_{j,t}, H_{j,t}, K_{j,t}} \left\{ P_t \Pi_{j,t} + E_t \left[\frac{\rho_{t+1}}{\rho_t} V_j\left(P_{j,t}, \mathcal{I}_{j,t+1}\right)\right]\right\}$$

with respect to the constraints (6.1) and (6.19), and where $\mathcal{I}_{j,t}$ is the informational set of firm j at period t: $\mathcal{I}_{j,t} = \{g_t, A_t, P_t, z_t, w_t\}$. We also impose the transversality condition:

$$\lim_{\tau \to +\infty} E_t \left[\frac{\rho_{t+\tau+1}}{\rho_{t+\tau}} \frac{\partial V_{j,t+\tau+1}}{\partial P_{j,t+\tau}} P_{j,t+\tau} \right] = 0 \tag{6.21}$$

Intertemporal Substitution Elasticity of Leisure and Labor Indivisibility

We first assume that $v(L_{i,t})$ is concave and that the elasticity of its derivative with respect to L is constant:

$$\frac{L_{i,t} v''(L_{i,t})}{v'(L_{i,t})} = \zeta \quad \forall L_{i,t} \tag{6.22}$$

This elasticity ζ is inversely related to the intertemporal substitution elasticity of leisure, and will be particularly important when we will calibrate the model.

Following Hansen [1985] and Rogerson [1988], we will assume that jobs are indivisible in our economy: each household works H_0 hours or does not work. This is linked to the fact that a large part of worked hours fluctuations are in the extensive margin (jobs fluctuations) and not in the intensive one (fluctuations in the average hour length of a job). Under this assumption, the household problem is convexified using Rogerson [1988] lotteries. We assume that each household sells at each period a contract, specifying that he will work H_0 with probability $\pi_{i,t}$ and 0 with probability 1-$\pi_{i,t}$. Its wage is given by the price of this contract; whether it works or not, it will get that wage. As households are identical, they all choose the same $\pi_{i,t} = \pi_t$ and only π_t% of them will work; 1-π_t is then the unemployment rate of the economy.

One can easily show that, at the symmetrical equilibrium, the representative agent utility function is linear in labor, and that the elasticity of the marginal disutility of labor ζ is null, which means that the intertemporal elasticity of substitution of leisure is infinite.

6.1.2 Definition and Resolution of the Equilibrium

We first define a symmetrical monopolistic competition equilibrium of the economy, and then briefly describe the resolution method. As we cannot solve analytically for the equilibrium, we linearize the system defining the equilibrium around its steady state. We obtain a linear dynamic system which gives the path of the endogenous variables relative deviations from their steady state level, in presence of exogenous shocks.

Symmetrical Monopolistic Competition Equilibrium of the Economy

A *symmetrical monopolistic competition equilibrium of the economy* is given by a set of decision rules of household i $C_{i,t}(s_{i,t})$, $K_{i,t+1}(s_{i,t})$, $M_{i,t+1}(s_{i,t})$ and $H_{i,t}(s_{i,t})$ (where $s_{i,t} = (K_{i,t}, M_{i,t}, \mathcal{I}_{i,t})$ is the state variables vector of household i), a capital demand rule $K_{j,t}(s_{j,t})$, a labor demand rule $H_{j,t}(s_{j,t})$ and a price rule $P_{j,t}(s_{j,t})$ of firm j (where $s_{j,t}=(P_{j,t-1}, \mathcal{I}_{j,t})$ is the state variables vector of firm j), a price vector $(\{P_{j,t}(s_t)\}_{j=1}^n$, $w(s_t)$, $z(s_t))$ (where $s_t = \left(\{s_{i,t}\}_{i=1}^h, \{s_{j,t}\}_{j=1}^n\right)$ is the aggregate state of the economy) such that:

- $C_{i,t}(s_{i,t})$, $H_{i,t}(s_{i,t})$ $M_{i,t+1}(s_{i,t})$ and $K_{i,t+1}(s_{i,t})$ maximize $V_{i,t}(K_{i,t}, M_{i,t}, \mathcal{I}_{i,t})$ subject to the constraints (6.12), (6.13) and (6.14),
- $K_{j,t}(s_{j,t})$, $H_{j,t}(s_{j,t})$ and $P_{j,t}(s_{j,t})$ maximize $V_{j,t}(P_{j,t-1}, \mathcal{I}_{j,t})$ subject to the constraints (6.1), (6.19) and (6.21),
- $(\{P_{j,t}(s_t)\}_{j=1}^n, w_t(s_t), z_t(s_t))$ clear the goods markets, the capital market, the labor market and the money market (the numéraire of the economy); that is respectively $Y_{j,t}^d(s_t) = Y_{j,t}(s_t)\ \forall j \in \{1, n\}$, $\sum_{i=1}^h K_{i,t}(s_{i,t-1}) = \sum_{j=1}^n K_{j,t}(s_{j,t})$, $\sum_{i=1}^h H_{i,t}(s_{i,t}) = \sum_{j=1}^n H_{j,t}(s_{j,t})$ and $\sum_{i=1}^h M_{i,t+1}(s_t) = g_t M_t$
- $s_{i,t} = s_t^h\ \forall i \in \{1, h\}\ \forall t$ and $s_{j,t} = s_t^f\ \forall j \in \{1, n\}\ \forall t$ (Symmetry of the equilibrium[10]).

Extensive Definition of the Equilibrium

The set of equations defining the equilibrium is given by equations (6.23) to (6.40) (where $u_{x,i,t}$ is the first derivative of the utility function

[10] In the following, we will use the normalization $n = h = 1$.

with respect to $x_{i,t}$ (successively $C_{i,t}$, $M_{i,t}/P$ and $H_{i,t}$), and where $\lambda_{i,t} = \Lambda_{i,t}P_t = \beta E_t\left[\frac{\partial V_{i,t+1}}{\partial K_{i,t+1}}\right] = \beta P_t E_t\left[\frac{\partial V_{i,t+1}}{\partial M_{i,t+1}}\right]$ is the marginal utility of real wealth):

$$u_{C,i,t} = \lambda_{i,t} \tag{6.23}$$

$$u_{H,i,t} = -\lambda_{i,t} w_t \tag{6.24}$$

$$0 = E_t\left[\frac{P_t}{P_{t+1}}\left(\lambda_{i,t+1}\left(\frac{P_{t+1}}{P_t}(1+z_{t+1}-\delta)-1\right) - u_{M/P,i,t+1}\right)\right] \tag{6.25}$$

$$1 = \beta E_t\left[(1+z_{t+1}-\delta)\frac{\lambda_{i,t+1}}{\lambda_{i,t}}\right] \tag{6.26}$$

$$P_t K_{i,t+1} + M_{i,t+1} - P_t(1-\delta)K_{i,t} - M_{i,t} - N_{i,t} - P_t z_t K_{i,t} - P_t w_t H_{i,t} - P_t \sum_{j=1}^{n}(v_{i,j}\Pi_{j,t}) + P_t C_{i,t} = 0 \tag{6.27}$$

$$\lim_{\tau\to+\infty} E\left[\beta^{t+\tau}\lambda_{i,t+\tau}K_{i,t+\tau+1}\right] = 0 \tag{6.28}$$

$$\lim_{\tau\to+\infty} E_t\left[\beta^{t+\tau}\lambda_{i,t+\tau}\frac{M_{i,t+\tau+1}}{P_{t+\tau}}\right] = 0 \tag{6.29}$$

Equation (6.23) equalizes marginal utility and price of current consumption, equation (6.24) marginal disutility and revenue of current labor, equation (6.25) anticipated marginal utility and anticipated price of money balances, where the price of money is the nominal interest rate $\left(\frac{P_{t+1}}{P_t}(1-\delta+z_{t+1})-1\right)$, and illustrates the presence of an inflationary tax. Equation (6.26) corresponds to the optimal intertemporal wealth allocation.

$$P_t w_t = (1-\alpha)\frac{Y_{j,t}}{H_{j,t}}(P_{j,t}-\nu_{j,t}) \tag{6.30}$$

$$P_t z_t = \alpha\frac{Y_{j,t}}{K_{j,t}}(P_{j,t}-\nu_{j,t}) \tag{6.31}$$

$$Y_{j,t} = \frac{1+\gamma}{\gamma}\nu_{j,t}P_{j,t}^{-\frac{1+\gamma}{\gamma}-1}P_t^{\frac{1+\gamma}{\gamma}}\frac{Y_t^d}{n} + \phi\left(\frac{P_t}{P_{j,t-1}}\right)\left(\frac{P_{j,t}}{P_{j,t-1}}-\overline{g}\right) - E_t\left[\phi\frac{\rho_{t+1}}{\rho_t}\left(\frac{P_{j,t+1}}{P_{j,t}}\right)^2\left(\frac{P_{t+1}}{P_{j,t+1}}\right)\left(\frac{P_{j,t+1}}{P_{j,t}}-\overline{g}\right)\right] \tag{6.32}$$

$$Y_{j,t} = Y_{j,t}^d \tag{6.33}$$

$$\begin{aligned} Y_{j,t} &= A_t(K_{j,t})^\alpha (H_{j,t})^{1-\alpha} && (6.34) \\ P_t \Pi_{j,t} &= P_{j,t} Y_{j,t} - P_t w_t H_{j,t} - P_t z_t K_{j,t} \\ &- P_t \frac{\phi}{2} \left(\frac{P_{j,t}}{P_{j,t-1}} - \bar{g} \right)^2 && (6.35) \end{aligned}$$

$$\lim_{\tau \to +\infty} E_t \left[\frac{\rho_{t+\tau+1}}{\rho_{t+\tau}} \frac{\partial V_{j,t+\tau+1}}{\partial P_{j,t+\tau}} P_{t+\tau} \right] = 0 \quad (6.36)$$

Equations (6.30) and (6.31) equalize marginal revenue and marginal cost of capital and labor inputs, and equation (6.32) marginal cost and marginal revenue of production.

$$\begin{aligned} \sum_{i=1}^{h} K_{i,t} &= \sum_{j=1}^{n} K_{j,t} && (6.37) \\ \sum_{i=1}^{h} H_{i,t} &= \sum_{j=1}^{n} H_{j,t} && (6.38) \\ M_t + \sum_{i=1}^{h} N_{i,t} &= \sum_{i=1}^{h} M_{i,t+1} && (6.39) \\ M_{t+1} &= g_t M_t && (6.40) \\ \lambda_{i,t} &= \beta^{-t} \alpha_i \rho_t && (6.41) \end{aligned}$$

Equations (6.37) to (6.40) ensure that capital, labor and money markets clear. Finally, we assume that households and firms have access to a complete set of frictionless securities market, so that (6.41) is verified at all times for some constant α_i.

By symmetry, we have $X_{i,t} = X_t \ \forall i$ and $Z_{j,t} = Z_t \ \forall j$, for all variables (X, Z) of the model.

One can compute the mark-up of the economy from multiplier ν. Equations (6.30) and (6.31) give the condition:

$$C_{m,j,t}(Y_{j,t}) = P_{j,t} - \nu_{j,t}$$

where $C_{m,j,t}(Y_{j,t})$ is the marginal cost of firm i. The mark-up $\mu_{j,t}$ is then given by:

$$P_{j,t} = (1 + \mu_{j,t}) C_{m,j,t} \Longleftrightarrow \mu_{j,t} = \frac{\nu_{j,t}}{P_t - \nu_{j,t}} \quad (6.42)$$

and at the equilibrium steady state:

$$\mu = \gamma$$

With infinite elasticity of substitution between the different consumption goods ($\gamma = 0$), the mark-up μ is null. If this elasticity is finite, μ will measure the market power of the firms. With flexible prices, this value is constant. When a positive technological shock occurs, the marginal cost curve shifts downward, and firms supply more for a lower price[11], according to equation (6.42). When a positive demand shock occurs, prices increase to equalize marginal cost and marginal revenue. If a positive technological shock occurs, the firm will less decrease its price (relatively to the fully flexible case) and the mark-up will increase as the marginal cost curve shifts downward. If a positive demand (monetary) shock occurs, demand shifts along the demand curve, prices increase less than the fully flexible case and output increases, which leads to a cut in the mark-up. Thus, mark-ups are countercyclical when a demand shock occurs and procyclical when a supply shock occurs.

The Equilibrium Steady State

With $m_t = \frac{M_t}{P_{t-1}}$ and $f_t = \frac{P_t}{P_{t-1}}$, one can write equation (6.40) as:

$$\frac{m_t}{m_{t+1}} = \frac{f_t}{g_t} \tag{6.43}$$

Stationarity of m_t means that prices grow at rate $(\overline{g}-1)$. Then, all the nominal variables (M, P, ν) will grow at rate $(\overline{g}-1)$.

With arbitrary values for $\overline{A}$ and P, and for given (calibrated) values of H and $\frac{M}{PY}$ [12], we can calculate the equilibrium steady state, which is given by the following set of equation:

$$\begin{aligned} z &= \left(\frac{1}{\beta}\right) - 1 + \delta \\ \frac{\nu}{P} &= \frac{\gamma}{1+\gamma} \\ \frac{K}{Y} &= \left(\frac{\alpha}{1+\gamma}\right)\frac{1}{z} \end{aligned}$$

[11] These effects are less important than in the competitive case, as the firm profit increases in the monopolistic case.

[12] Imposing specific steady-state values of H and $\frac{M}{PY}$ is equivalent to calibrating the utility function parameters γ_1 and γ_2.

$$
\begin{aligned}
\frac{C}{Y} &= 1-\delta\left(\frac{K}{Y}\right) \\
Y &= A^{1/(1-\alpha)}\left(\frac{K}{Y}\right)^{\alpha/(1-\alpha)} H \\
w &= \left(\frac{1-\alpha}{1+\gamma}\right)\left(\frac{Y}{H}\right) \\
\gamma_2 &= -(1-\overline{g}(1+z-\delta))\left(\frac{M}{P}\right)^{1/\sigma} C^{-1/\sigma}
\end{aligned}
$$

We then log-linearized the system defining the equilibrium to obtain the state space system which is solved following Blanchard and Kahn [1980] and King, Plosser and Rebelo [1987].

6.2 Monetary Disturbances and Business Cycle in France and the United States

The *RBC* literature assesses that technological shocks are sufficient to reproduce the most important stylized facts of the business cycle. This result extends in a more theoretical framework the empirical proposition of Nelson and Plosser [1982]: monetary shocks are not necessary to explain output fluctuations. As it is shown in Hairault and Portier [1993], the cyclical properties of a flex-price competitive model with money in the utility function are very similar to those of a purely real model, and the nominal features of the business cycle are not well reproduced.

Are these results robust to a deviation from such a purely neoclassical framework? As the New-Keynesian literature stressed the importance of non-competitive behavior and price adjustment costs, we ask the question of the necessity of introducing monetary shock in such a theoretical framework.

Using the US case for parameter calibration, we first simulate six different models, each one relative to a particular specification of our model, to evaluate the importance of monopolistic competition, price adjustment costs and monetary shocks. Following the *RBC* literature, we describe the cyclical properties of these models by computing order two moments (standard deviations, correlations, autocorrelations) of the Hodrick-Prescott cyclical components of the macroeconomic series generated by stochastic simulations of the model decision rules. The seven models are:

- a model without monopoly power, without adjustment costs, without monetary shocks and with Solow residual as a measure of technological shock (Model $M1$)
- a model with monopoly power, without adjustment costs, without monetary shocks and with Solow residual as a measure of technological shock (Model $M2$)
- a model with monopoly power, without adjustment costs, with monetary shocks and with Solow residual as a measure of technological shock (Model $M3$)
- a model with monopoly power, with adjustment costs, without monetary shocks and with Solow residual as a measure of technological shock (Model $M4$)
- a model with monopoly power, with adjustment costs, with monetary shocks and with Solow residual as a measure of technological shock (Model $M5$)
- a model with monopoly power, with adjustment costs, with monetary shocks and without technological shocks (Model $M6$)
- a model with monopoly power, with adjustment costs, with monetary shocks, with a purged Solow residual as a measure of technological shock and with increasing returns (Model $M7$)

We then simulate, for French and US parameter calibration, our benchmark model with monopolistic competition, price adjustment costs, monetary shocks, and with a Solow residual *purged* of the monetary shock as a measure of technological shock. The moments of the Hodrick-Prescott cyclical components of the series generated by these models are compared to the sample ones to evaluate the model ability to reproduce the main stylized facts. We also propose a qualitative validation by computing impulse responses to monetary shocks.

6.2.1 Parameter Calibration

The parameter of the model are calibrated partly according to previous studies on US and French data and partly according to our own computations.

In the US case, we follow King, Plosser and Rebelo [1988] for a first group of parameters (H, δ and β). α is set to get a share of labor income in total income of .58, and the measure of money supply is $M1$.

Table 6.1

α	H	δ	β	$\frac{M}{PY}$
.3	.2	.025	.988	.1

We assume indivisibility of labor supply, which is equivalent to $\zeta = 0$. Elasticities σ, $\frac{1}{1-a}$ and γ are set according to previous panel data estimations. The elasticity of substitution between consumption index and real balances σ is small but significantly different from zero on US data (Koenig [1990]); we set it at 1/9. This value can also be interpreted as the interest elasticity of real money balances (which is given by $-\sigma$ in the model). Eichenbaum, Hansen and Singleton [1988] showed that the intertemporal elasticity of substitution is between 1/3 and 2; we choose a value of 3/4 ($a = -1/3$). This value is smaller than the one chosen in most *RBC* models with log utility function ($a = 1$). The value of the parameter γ (which is equal to the mark-up μ at the steady state) relies on Morrison [1990]. This author estimated $\mu = .197$ for the American manufacturing sector (1960-1986). This estimation is based upon a more general model (including increasing returns, imperfect competition and quasi-fixed factors) than Domowitz, Hubbard and Petersen [1987] who obtained .36 for the all US industry 1958-1981 and Hall [1989] who estimated $\mu > 1$. As there are no materials in our model, this mark-up value is very conservative, and if one assumes that material inputs are about half of the total costs (as shown by Domowitz, Hubbard and Petersen [1987]), then Morrisson's estimate suggest a value around $\mu = .5$. Nevertheless, we did not choose such a large mark-up because the pure profit share in total income is already 17% in our artificial economy (with $\mu = .197$), which seems to be higher than any empirical studies for the US economy. The only possible way of increasing μ and decreasing the share of pure profit is to include increasing returns (through a fixed cost of installation), as it is done in Rotemberg and Woodford [1989]. Such an economy is presented and simulated in model $M7$.

We do not dispose of any estimations of the price adjustment costs parameter ϕ and we set it arbitrarily. A small value will be enough to get significative effects, according to the menu cost literature. To measure this cost, we compute the real adjustment cost of an increase of 1 point (.01) of the price growth rate, as a percentage of the steady state output. This ratio is denoted $\frac{CA(.01)}{Y}$. A study of the model sensibility to the parameter ϕ is presented in appendix C.

Table 6.2

a	σ	ζ	γ	ϕ	$\frac{CA(.01)}{Y}$
-1/3	1/9	0	.197	1	.01%

We follow the same method to calibrate French parameters. Labor income share in total income is 54%, as it is computed on Quarterly National Accounts. Laffargue, Malgrange and Pujol [1990] set a mark-up of .41 in their model. For the same reasons than in the US case, and as we do not dispose of any empirical studies on French data, we arbitrarily set it at .225, higher than the US rate, as the French economy is considered less competitive than the US one. We choose the same value of a and σ than in the US, following Charpin [1989]. Price adjustment cost parameter ϕ is also set equal to the US one. We choose the money supply $M2$, because it better explains output on the period.

Table 6.3

α	H	δ	β	$\frac{M}{PY}$
.335	.2	.0125	.988	.25%

Table 6.4

a	σ	ζ	γ	ϕ	$\frac{CA(.01)}{Y}$
-1/3	1/9	0	.225	1	.007%

6.2.2 Estimation of the Exogenous Shocks Processes

We estimated on quarterly US data (1959-1990) an $AR(1)$ process for the technological and monetary shocks. This $AR(1)$ is estimated on the relative deviations of the total factor productivity (Solow residual) from its average level on the period and on the relative deviations of the growth rate of $M1$ from its average level on the period. As the Solow residual is contaminated by demand shocks with imperfect competition (Hall [1989]), it is not a good proxy for the technological shock, and we need to purged it from the demand shocks (monetary shocks in our model). We then estimated a two dimension VAR composed of the relative deviations from their average of the Solow residual and the money growth rate. We identify the technological shock as the share of the Solow residual innovation not explained by the monetary innovation. The *purged* Solow residual $\widehat{A}$ will be the variable generated only by the technological innovation, by opposition to the *naive* (unpurged) Solow residual

From a technical point of view, the process of $\widehat{A}$ has to be generated only by the *true* technological shocks ϵ_A.

Let be ϵ the vector of structural shocks, ϵ_A and ϵ_g. The joint process of the money growth (g) and the *naive* Solow residual (SR), both as relative deviation from their average level, is given by the following Vectorial Moving Average representation:

$$\begin{pmatrix} \widehat{g}_t \\ \widehat{SR}_t \end{pmatrix} = A(L) \begin{pmatrix} \epsilon_{g,t} \\ \epsilon_{A,t} \end{pmatrix} = \begin{pmatrix} A_{(1,1)}(L) A_{(1,2)}(L) \\ A_{(2,1)}(L) A_{(2,2)}(L) \end{pmatrix} \begin{pmatrix} \epsilon_{g,t} \\ \epsilon_{A,t} \end{pmatrix} \tag{6.44}$$

We define the *purged* Solow residual[13] $\widehat{A}$ as the component of the Solow residual generated only by ϵ_A.

[13] Another strategy to recover the *pure* technological innovation is to built a *purged*

$$\widehat{A} = A_{(2,2)}(L)\epsilon_{A,t} \tag{6.45}$$

To recover $A_{22}(L)$ and ϵ_A, we estimate a two dimension VAR with $\widehat{SR}$ and $\widehat{g}$, including four lags. The estimation on US and French data are given in tables 6.5 and 6.6, where the Student statistics are given under each coefficient, and the significance level of the Fisher statistics (global exclusion of the variable in the equation) is given under its value:

Table 6.5. Estimations of the VAR Model

	U.S. data			French data	
	$\widehat{g}_t$	$\widehat{SR}_t$		$\widehat{g}_t$	$\widehat{SR}_t$
$\widehat{g}_{t-1}$	.27	.09	$\widehat{g}_{t-1}$	.006	.01
	(2.76)	(1.07)		(.05)	(1.02)
$\widehat{g}_{t-2}$	.04	.22	$\widehat{g}_{t-2}$	-.04	-.01
	(.43)	(2.4)		(.35)	(.18)
$\widehat{g}_{t-3}$	-.06	-.09	$\widehat{g}_{t-3}$	-.14	.25
	(.59)	(1.02)		(1.1)	(2.49)
$\widehat{g}_{t-4}$	.13	-.008	$\widehat{g}_{t-4}$	-.01	-.2
	(1.26)	(.087)		(.08)	(2.01)
F-stat	2.6	2.24	F-stat	.34	2.84
	(.04%)	(.07%)		(.84%)	(.03%)
$\widehat{SR}_{t-1}$	-.04	1.0	$\widehat{SR}_{t-1}$	-.07	1.22
	(.40)	(9.82)		(.13)	(.07)
$\widehat{SR}_{t-2}$	.14	.12	$\widehat{SR}_{t-2}$	-.03	.01
	(.91)	(.90)		(.13)	(.07)
$\widehat{SRg}_{t-3}$	-.14	-.24	$\widehat{SRg}_{t-3}$	-.05	-.001
	(.95)	(1.79)		(.23)	(.01)
$\widehat{SR}_{t-4}$	.83	.03	$\widehat{SR}_{t-4}$	.05	-.22
	(.82)	(.35)		(.42)	(2.05)
F-stat	.94	342	F-stat	3.69	624
	(.44%)	(.00%)		(.01%)	(.00%)

We invert that VAR representation to get the Wold representation of the bivariate process:

$$\begin{pmatrix} \widehat{g}_t \\ \widehat{SR}_t \end{pmatrix} = C(L) \begin{pmatrix} u_{g,t} \\ u_{A,t} \end{pmatrix} \tag{6.46}$$

Solow residual from data on output and factors, as it is developped in Hall [1989] and illustrated in Rotemberg and Woodford [1991].

where $u = (u_g, u_{SR})'$ is the vector of VAR residuals.

From equation (6.44), there is a rectangular matrix (2,2) A_0 such that $u_t = A_0 \epsilon_t$ and $A(L) = C(L)A_0$. As long as A_0 is identified, $A(L)$ is known and one can recovers the ϵ's from the u's. We assume that the two true exogenous shocks of the model ϵ_g and ϵ_A are uncorrelated. Then one must have:

$$A_0 A_0' = V$$

where V is the variance-covariance matrix of the estimated shocks ε. This equation implies three restrictions on the coefficients of A_0, as V is symmetric. Then, an additional restriction is needed to identify A_0. We assume that $A_{0(1,2)} = 0$, the technological shock has no immediate effect on money growth. With that restriction, we recover the VMA representation (6.44) and compute the *purged* Solow residual $\widehat{A}$ according to (6.45).

The estimated $AR(1)$ coefficients are given in table 6.7 for the U.S.:

Table 6.7

$\overline{g}$	ρ_g	ε_g	ρ_A naive	ε_A naive	ρ_A purged	ε_A purged
1.014	.377	.009	.95	.009	.95	.008

The correction of the Solow residual is more important on French data, which supports the greater monopoly power we retained.

Table 6.8

$\overline{g}$	ρ_g	ε_g	ρ_A naive	ε_A naive	ρ_A purged	ε_A purged
1.028	.50	.0098	.98	.009	.99	.0058

We simulate the model using the linearized state-space form and generate series of shocks according to their estimated process. Each simulated series is 124 points long (which is the size of the data sample), and simulations are repeated 100 times. The resulting moments are the average of these 100 simulations, and we also computed the standard deviation of each moments on these 100 simulations.

6.2.3 The Effect of Monetary Shocks, Monopolistic Competition and Price Stickiness

Models $M1$ and $M2$ are models with money, and real money balances in the utility function, but a constant growth rate of the money supply is assumed.

Model $M1$ is closely related to the canonical *RBC* model of King, Plosser and Rebelo [1988], with a more realistic intertemporal elasticity of substitution of consumption (King, Plosser and Rebelo [1988] used a *log* utility function with unit elasticity). As there is no pure profit in that economy, α is set to 42, to keep a 58% share of labor income in national income. We obtained the following results[14]:

Table 6.9. Model $M1$
(US calibration)

Variable	$\widehat{y}$	$\widehat{c}$	$\widehat{i}$	$\widehat{h}$	$\widehat{x}$	$\widehat{f}$
S.D.	1.86	.50	5.56	1.29	.67	.36
S.D./S.D.($\widehat{y}$)	1	.27	2.98	.69	.35	.19
Autocor. order 1	.67	.75	.66	.66	.75	-.02
Cor. with $\widehat{y}$	1	.89	.99	.97	.89	-.57
Cor. with $\widehat{h}$	-	-	-	-	.77	-

The model exhibits the traditional *RBC* relative variability of consumption, output and investment and a worked hours standard deviation higher than the labor productivity ($\widehat{x}$) one, due to the indivisibility assumption. Autocorrelations are relatively high (.67 for output) and correlations of real variables with output are all positive. The labor productivity-worked hours correlation is large and positive (.77), as the labor market clears by shifts of the labor demand curve along the labor supply curve with technological shocks. The output-inflation correlation is negative, as the cycle is driven by technological shocks.

Model $M2$ includes monopoly power:

[14] As the standard deviation are very similar from a model to another, we only present them for the benchmark model.

Table 6.10.Model $M2$
(US calibration)

Variable	$\widehat{y}$	$\widehat{c}$	$\widehat{i}$	$\widehat{h}$	$\widehat{x}$	$\widehat{f}$
S.D.	2.06	.71	9.36	1.25	.94	.51
S.D./S.D.($\widehat{y}$)	1	.34	4.52	.60	.45	.25
Autocor. order 1	.70	.77	.68	.68	.77	.02
Cor. with $\widehat{y}$	1	.92	.98	.95	.92	-.54
Cor. with $\widehat{h}$	-	-	-	-	.76	-

As prices are fully flexible, mark-up are constants in model $M2$. Absolute levels of standard-errors are slightly higher than in the perfect competitive case. Despite the indivisibility hypothesis, labor productivity standard deviation is close to hours one. Output-inflation correlation is still negative. Globally, monopolistic competition by itself does not provide significant differences, except for the high investment variability (9.36 *vs* 5.56 in model $M1$).

Model $M3$ introduces money as in Hairault and Portier [1993], but in a monopolistic competition framework. As prices are still fully flexible, mark-up are constant. $\widehat{M}$ represents the Hodrick-Prescott cyclical component of the money supply level.

Table 6.11. Model $M3$
(US calibration)

Variable	$\widehat{y}$	$\widehat{c}$	$\widehat{i}$	$\widehat{h}$	$\widehat{x}$	$\widehat{M}$	$\widehat{f}$
S.D.	2.05	.71	9.31	1.24	.94	1.65	1.31
S.D./S.D.($\widehat{y}$)	1	.34	4.54	.60	.45	.81	.64
Autocor. order 1	.69	.77	.67	.68	.77	.83	.01
Cor. with $\widehat{y}$	1	.92	.98	.95	.92	.00	-.22
Cor. with $\widehat{h}$	-	-	-	-	.76	-	-

We obtain the same results than in the competitive case studied by Hairault and Portier [1993]: money has little effect upon the real features of the model; money-output correlation is null and inflation-output correlation is negative in the short run. Inflation variability is nevertheless higher than in model $M2$, because of the growth monetary shocks. We must notice that the effects of money growth shocks are smaller than in Cooley and Hansen [1989] model, as we do not impose a strict cash-in-advance constraint (which will correspond to the case $\sigma = 0$).

There are no monetary shocks in model $M4$, but prices adjustment costs are introduced.

Table 6.12. Model $M4$
(US calibration)

Variable	$\widehat{y}$	$\widehat{c}$	$\widehat{i}$	$\widehat{h}$	$\widehat{x}$	$\widehat{\mu}$	$\widehat{f}$
S.D.	1.78	.65	7.86	.99	.93	.98	.47
S.D./S.D.($\widehat{y}$)	1	.36	4.40	.55	.52	.55	.26
Autocor. order 1	.77	.75	.78	.80	.60	-.11	-.06
Cor. with $\widehat{y}$	1	.92	.98	.92	.91	.30	-.39
Cor. with $\widehat{h}$	-	-	-	-	.70	-	-

Mark-up $\widehat{\mu}$ are procyclical, as technological shocks drive the cycle. Standard deviations of real variables are smaller than in the fully flexible case, but the moments are globally close to the fully flexible model ones, except than hours and labor productivity standard deviations are now almost equal.

Model $M5$ is the theoretical model of the first section: monopolistic competition with sticky prices and monetary shocks. In that model, monetary shocks do modify the simulated business cycle (compared to model $M4$), by opposition to previous studies.

Table 6.13. Model $M5$
(US calibration)

Variable	$\widehat{y}$	$\widehat{c}$	$\widehat{i}$	$\widehat{h}$	$\widehat{x}$	$\widehat{\mu}$	$\widehat{M}$	$\widehat{f}$
S.D.	2.05	.65	9.93	1.71	1.05	2.62	1.67	1.27
S.D./S.D.($\widehat{y}$)	1	.32	4.85	.84	.51	1.29	.82	.62
Autocor. order 1	.61	.75	.51	.27	.49	-.01	.83	.01
Cor. with $\widehat{y}$	1	.82	.97	.85	.53	-.32	.09	.29
Cor. with $\widehat{h}$	-	-	-	-	.03	-	-	-

The standard deviation of output and the wedge between consumption and investment standard deviations are higher. Worked hours are now more volatile than labor productivity and real variables autocorrelation are smaller, in particular for worked hours. Mark-up are countercyclical. As output responses to technological and monetary shocks are always positive and mark-up response is positive for a monetary shock and negative for a technological one, this indicates that the cycle is not only driven by technological shocks.

The worked hours-labor productivity is now negative and close to zero, which is the opposite result than the *RBC* literature. This correlation stresses again the dominance of demand (monetary) shocks in the cycle.

The nominal features of the simulated cycle are now sharply different: money-output and inflation-output correlation are positive. The model clearly exhibits an output-inflation trade-off in the short run.

Model $M6$ allows us to get some insight on the specific effect of monetary growth shocks, as they are the only impulsion source in that model.

Table 6.14. Model $M6$
(US calibration)

Variable	$\widehat{y}$	$\widehat{c}$	$\widehat{i}$	$\widehat{h}$	$\widehat{x}$	$\widehat{\mu}$	$\widehat{M}$	$\widehat{f}$
S.D.	.94	.06	5.51	1.36	.43	2.38	1.58	1.15
S.D./S.D.($\widehat{y}$)	1	.06	5.86	1.45	.46	2.54	1.68	1.23
Autocor. order 1	-.03	.83	-.04	-.04	-.03	-.03	.83	-.00
Cor. with $\widehat{y}$	1	.20	.99	.99	-.98	-.99	.14	.99
Cor. with $\widehat{h}$	-	-	-	-	-.99	-	-	-

These results emphasize the difference between models $M4$ and $M5$. The labor productivity becomes sharply countercyclical and its correlation with labor highly negative.

The simulated moments of our model are then dependent on the presence of monetary shocks. In this theoretical framework, we now discuss the *RBC* proposition and ask whether monetary shocks improve or not the ability of the model to mimic the French and US business cycle?

6.2.4 The Effect of Increasing Returns

Our benchmark model leads to a 17% pure profit share for the US economy, which is higher than the results of the empirical literature. Furthermore, our mark-up calibration is conservative (.2), as it must be

.5 in a model without raw material. These two points raised a problem that has not an unique and simple solution. In our specification, it is clear that any attempt to raise the mark-up (to answer to the second point) will raise the pure profit share (which will not be an answer to the first point). One solution is then to choose an increasing return production function to answer to these two questions: this specification will allow us to increase the mark-up, but not the pure profit share, thanks to the fixed costs.

In model $M7$, we then adopt the following increasing return specification:

$$Y_{j,t} = A_t K_{j,t}^{\alpha} H_{j,t}^{1-\alpha} - F \qquad (6.47)$$

where F is a fixed cost of installation. Such a specification does not imply any particular technical problems, and we solved the economy for such a production function, with a calibrated mark-up value of .5 and a pure profit share of 5% for the US economy. The results of the simulations are not qualitatively different from those of the benchmark model. The results of 20 simulations of the benchmark model are given in the following table:

Table 6.15. Model $M7$
Mark-up = .5, Pure Profit Share = 5%
(US Calibration)

Variable	$\widehat{y}$	$\widehat{c}$	$\widehat{i}$	$\widehat{h}$	$\widehat{x}$	$\widehat{\mu}$	$\widehat{M}$	$\widehat{f}$
S.D.	1.54	.41	5.45	1.91	1.23	2.32	1.59	1.19
S.D./S.D.($\widehat{y}$)	1	.27	3.5	1.2	.82	1.51	1.04	.78
Autocor. order 1	.34	.73	.23	-.05	.33	-.05	.82	-.03
Cor. with $\widehat{y}$	1	.65	.98	.76	.05	-.66	.15	.65
Cor. with $\widehat{h}$	-	-	-	-	-.59	-	-	-

The relative standard deviations are very similar to the constant return specification but the absolute levels of variance are smaller. This is due to the fact that the parameter α is .3 in the constant return specification and .3895 in the increasing return one. In the last case, the economy is less volatile as the weight of the less volatile production factor (capital) is higher in the production function. Furthermore, to get a 5% pure profit share, one must impose an unrealistic level of fixed costs (at the steady state, F must represent 29.82% of gross production ($AK^{\alpha}H^{1-\alpha}$) and is equal to 42.5% of net output (Y)). For these two last reason, we adopt a constant returns to scale technology in our benchmark model.

6.2.5 The Model and the Business Cycle on US and French Data

We computed the business cycle characteristics on the cyclical component of each macroeconomic series, by applying Hodrick-Prescott filter to US and French data[15].

Table 6.16. Cyclical Properties of US Business Cycle
Quarterly Data (CitiBase) 1959-1990

Variable	$\widehat{y}$	$\widehat{c}$	$\widehat{i}$	$\widehat{h}$	$\widehat{x}$	$\widehat{M}$	$\widehat{f}$
S.D.	1.76	1.28	8.47	1.42	.89	1.27	.39
S.D./S.D.($\widehat{y}$)	1	.72	4.81	.80	.50	.72	.22
Autocor. order 1	.85	.86	.81	.84	.52	.72	.24
Cor. with $\widehat{y}$	1	.81	.90	.86	.59	.36	.18
Cor. with $\widehat{h}$	-	-	-	-	.06	-	-

In the United States, the consumption standard deviation is less than the output one, which is less than the investment one. The worked hours standard deviation is close to the output one, and higher than the labor productivity one. All these variables are strongly procyclical, and worked hours-labor productivity correlation is close to zero. Persistence, measured by first order autocorrelation, is quite important, except for labor productivity and inflation[16].

[15] As usual for quarterly data, we choose $\lambda = 1600$. French data are taken from INSEE quarterly data bank and US data from the Citibase. See appendix A for a description of the data.

[16] Some *RBC* studies use *Current Population Survey* data for worked hours and labour productivity, which leads to different standard deviations. The worked hours standard deviation is around 1.7 and the labor productivity one is equal to 1.1. Nevertheless, our computations are in the same range.

Table 6.17. Cyclical Properties of French Business Cycle Quarterly Data (INSEE Base) 1970-1990

Variable	$\widehat{y}$	$\widehat{c}$	$\widehat{i}$	$\widehat{h}$	$\widehat{x}$	$\widehat{M}$	$\widehat{f}$
S.D.	.91	.81	3.64	.83	.65	1.35	.52
S.D./S.D.($\widehat{y}$)	1	.9	4.01	.92	.72	6	.57
Autocor. order 1	.76	.67	.82	.89	.63	.63	.20
Cor. with $\widehat{y}$	1	.63	.80	.71	.45	.18	.15
Cor. with $\widehat{h}$	-	-	-	-	-.35	-	-

We observe on French data the same relative variance of consumption, output and investment, as this feature is common to all OECD countries. Nevertheless, output standard deviation is one half less important than in the US (which means that shocks are less important or that the French economy accommodates them more) and consumption relative standard deviation is higher. All the variables cyclical components are less autocorrelated than in the US, and all correlations with output are weaker.

Worked hours have a standard deviation close to the output one and higher than the labor productivity one, which is similar to the US case. Nevertheless, worked hours-labor productivity correlation is negative (-.35). In both countries, money-output and inflation-output correlation are positive.

We simulate the theoretical model for each country calibration and with purged Solow residual.

Table 6.18. Simulation of the Benchmark Model with US Calibration

Variable	$\widehat{y}$	$\widehat{c}$	$\widehat{i}$	$\widehat{h}$	$\widehat{x}$	$\widehat{\mu}$	$\widehat{M}$	$\widehat{f}$
S.D.	1.86	.58	9.06	1.63	.94	2.53	1.60	1.22
	(.17)	(.08)	(.88)	(.12)	(.11)	(.19)	(.24)	(.1)
S.D./S.D.($\widehat{y}$)	1	.31	4.88	.88	.50	1.37	.85	.66
	(0)	(.0200)	(.15)	(.0666)	(.034)	(.169)	(.159)	(.082)
$AR(1)$	.56	.76	.46	.21	.48	-.03	.82	-.00
	(.0758)	(.065)	(.0812)	(.09)	(.11)	(.0870)	(.030)	(.0872)
Cor. with $\widehat{y}$	1	.80	.97	.86	.46	-.38	.1	.36
	(0)	(.031)	(.0045)	(.019)	(.0948)	(.08)	(.17)	(.09)
Cor. with $\widehat{h}$	-	-	-	-	-.03	-	-	-
					(.12)			

Table 6.19. Simulation of the Benchmark Model with French Calibration

Variable	$\hat{y}$	$\hat{c}$	$\hat{i}$	$\hat{h}$	$\hat{x}$	$\hat{\mu}$	$\widehat{M}$	$\hat{f}$
S.D.	1.16	.47	6.70	1.09	.76	1.75	1.86	1.31
	(.1)	(.06)	(.7)	(.06)	(.07)	(.1)	(.27)	(.1)
S.D./S.D.($\hat{y}$)	1	.40	5.80	.94	.65	1.52	1.62	1.14
	(0)	(.026)	(.36)	(.087)	(.046)	(.163)	(.285)	(.12)
$AR(1)$	.54	.70	.34	.1	.44	.00	.85	.06
	(.09)	(.069)	(.10)	(.09)	(.10)	(.08)	(.04)	(.088)
Cor. with $\hat{y}$	1	.70	.95	.77	.40	-.47	.08	.48
	(0)	(.066)	(.008)	(.03)	(.11)	(.07)	(.15)	(.070)
Cor. with $\hat{h}$	-	-	-	-	-.25	-	-	-
					(.11)			

Does the model provide significant improvements in describing US and French stylized facts when *both* monetary shocks and technology shocks are taken into account?

- First of all, the model reproduces the standard deviation of output in both countries with *estimated* shocks [17]

  This point is remarkable, as these levels are very different from one country to another. The complete model with a *naive* Solow residual produces too high levels of output standard error; the gain with *purged* Solow residual is particularly important on French calibration.

[17] The results of the French simulation with *naive* Solow residual are given in the following table:

Table 6.20. Model $M5'$
Simulation of the Benchmark Model with French Calibration and *naive* Solow Residual

Variable	$\hat{y}$	$\hat{c}$	$\hat{i}$	$\hat{h}$	$\hat{x}$	$\hat{\mu}$	$\widehat{M}$	$\hat{f}$
S.D.	2.06	.53	13.1	1.63	.82	1.75	1.86	1.32
S.D./S.D.($\hat{y}$)	1	.25	6.35	.79	.39	.85	.9	.64
Autocor. order 1	.65	.72	.60	.47	.49	-.01	.85	.04
Cor. with $\hat{y}$	1	.83	.97	.92	.65	-.18	.04	.18
Cor. with $\hat{h}$	-	-	-	-	.32	-	-	-

- Only the benchmark model provides a correct description of the nominal features of the business cycle. Money-output and inflation-output correlations are positive. Unlike others monetarized *RBC* models (for instance Cooley and Hansen [1989]), we reproduce the empirical inflation-output trade-off in the short run.

- The worked hours-labor productivity correlation is well reproducéd in both countries, close to zero for the US and negative for France. This result is strongly related to the presence of monetary (demand) shocks and improves greatly the cyclical properties of traditional *RBC* models.

- Worked hours standard deviation is higher than labor productivity one, which is not the case in a monopolistic model without monetary shocks. We reproduce the variance of these two variables both in United States and in France.

- Mark-up are countercyclical in the model. This stylized fact has been widely studied in the empirical literature and many authors concluded explicitly (Bils [1987] and Morrison [1990] on US data, Morrison [1989] on Canadian data) or implicitly (Hall [1988] on US data) that mark-up are countercyclical[18]. In a model with quasi-fixed factors, Morrison [1990] estimated a value of -.419 for the correlation between mark-up and a measure of capacity utilization. As we do not allow for excess capacity, the equivalent correlation is between mark-up and output. We found a value of -.36, which is in the same range than Morrison [1990].

So, monetary shocks in a monopolistic competition framework with price adjustment costs improve the understanding of some real and nominal aspects of the business cycle without damaging the main results of standard *RBC* models.

[18]We must notice however that Domowitz, Hubbard and Petersen [1987] founded a positive correlation between mark-up and output.

6.2.6 Impulse Responses to Technological and Monetary Shocks

Impulse responses to a technological shock are similar to the traditional *RBC* model ones. A positive shock increases temporarily consumption, real wage, capital, real balances, investment, output, profits and mark-up. The first four variables exhibit an hump-shape response, and the last four are always above their steady state level.

Impulse responses to a monetary shock (Figures 1 to 7[19]) are coherent with previous econometric studies (see Blanchard [1989] and Bec and Hairault [1993] for instance). A 1% shock on the money rate of growth increases instantaneously output by 1% in the US and .8% in France. Investment, worked hours and inflation also react positively. The negative (or slightly positive at the first period in France) response of the interest rate to a monetary growth shock differs from the results of King [1990] (positive response), as money is explicitly in the utility function. At the opposite, profits and mark-up stay under their steady state level during all the adjustment. The low serial correlation of all variables after a monetary shock is a consequence of the low autocorrelation coefficient of the $AR(1)$ process of the monetary growth shock.

6.3 Concluding Comments

Our ambition was not to asses that monetary shocks are the main impulse of the business cycle, but to show that they allow for a better understanding of it in a model which departs from the perfectly competitive and flex-price framework. Our results showed that the New Keynesian perspective (imperfect competition and nominal rigidities) proposes an answer to some empirical puzzles within a *RBC* methodology. As the model is able to mimic two sets of cyclical stylized facts in two different countries (France and the United States), with a suitably redefined measure of the technological impulse in the spirit of Hall [1989], we consider it as a useful step towards a better understanding of the role of demand factors, and particularly monetary

[19] All these impulse responses are presented in appendix B.

shocks, in the business cycle.

Beyond the shortcomings of the *RBC* models, due to a too narrow view of cyclical impulses and a too idealized view of the way the markets work, modern macroeconomics may well benefit from the methodological message of this approach: fully worked out intertemporal computable equilibrium models are worth to be considered seriously[20].

[20] See Danthine and Donaldson [1991] and Hénin [1991] for a similar view.

6.4 Appendix

A. The Data

Table A.1. presents the data code of the series for French and US data.

table A.1.

	databank		Code	
	France	USA	France	USA
Y	Insee	Citibase	PIBT8	GNP82
C	Ocde	Citibase	FRACSMRX	GC82
I	Insee	Citibase	P41TUIP8	GPI82
H	Insee	Citibase	(EFMOA1 × DUMOA1)	(LHEM × LHCH)
X	Insee	Citibase	Y/H	Y/H
P	Ocde	Citibase	Fradefl	GD
M	Ocde	Citibase	FraM1QS	FM1

B. Impulse Responses to a Monetary Growth Shock

Figure 6.1: Monetary Shock (1% Shock on g)

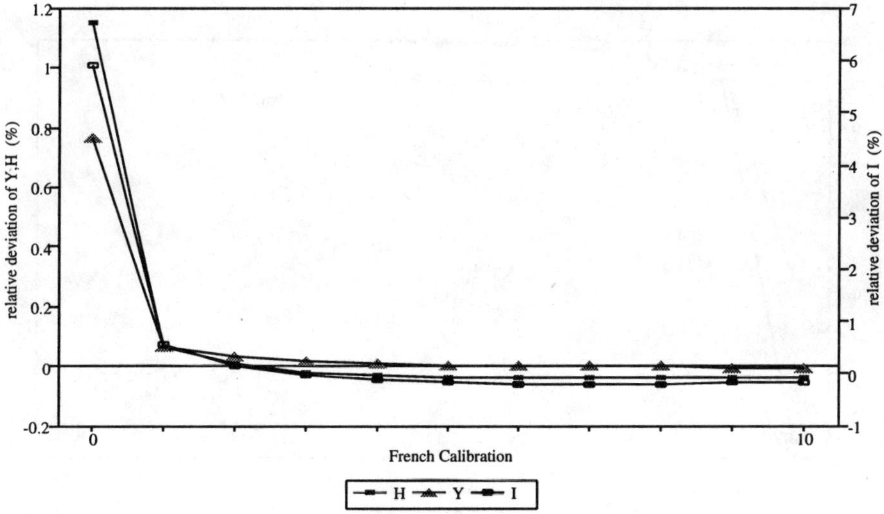

Figure 6.2: Monetary Shock (1% Shock on g)

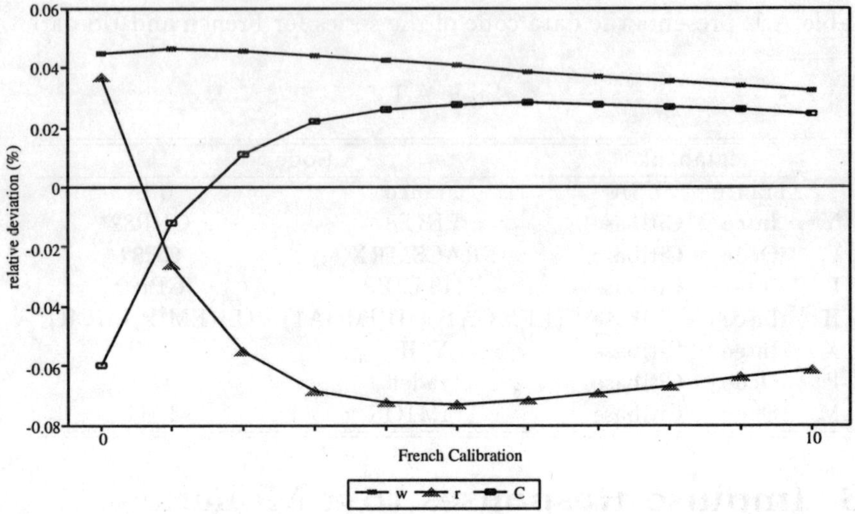

Figure 6.3: Monetary Shock (1% Shock on g)

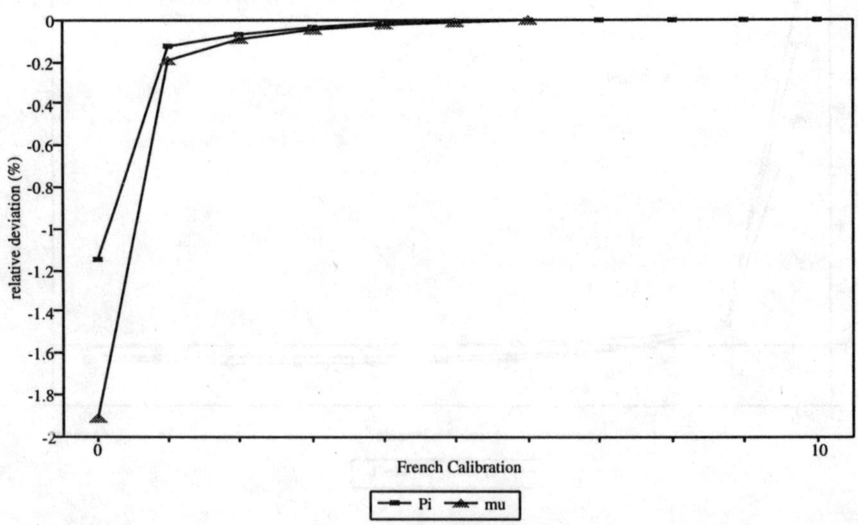

Figure 6.4: Monetary Shock (1% Shock on g)

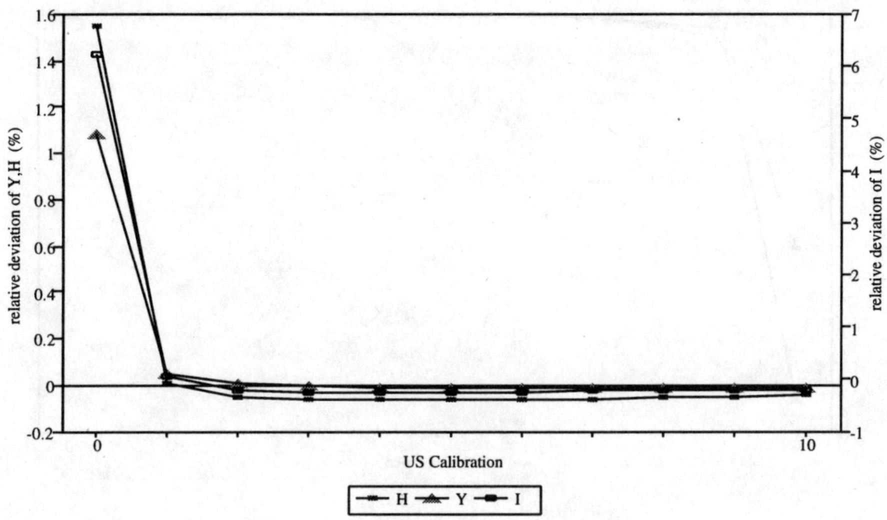

Figure 6.5: Monetary Shock (1% Shock on g)

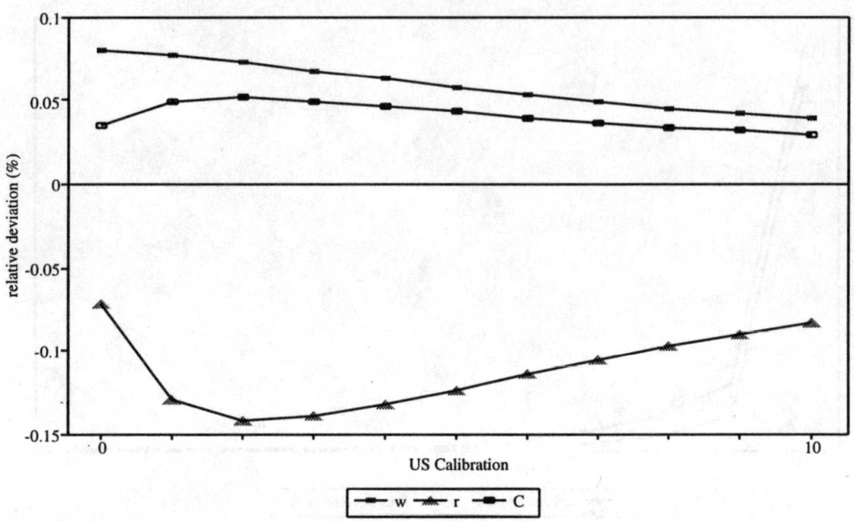

Figure 6.6: Monetary Shock (1% Shock on g)

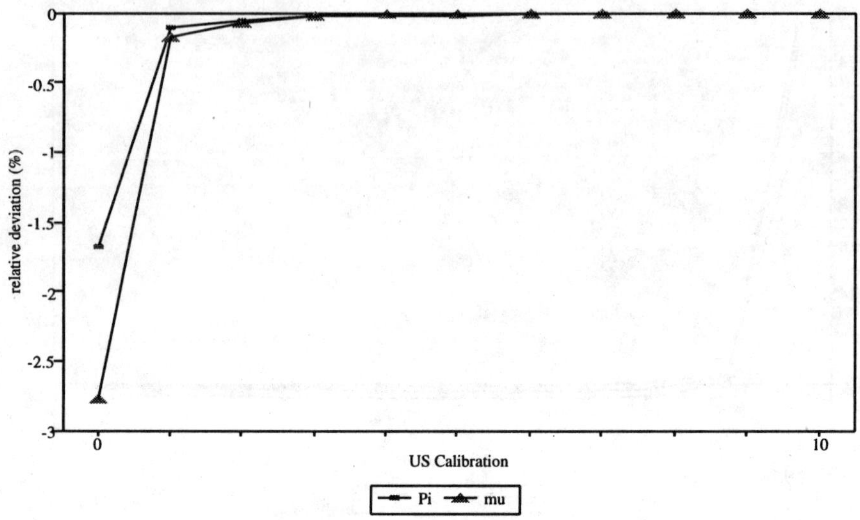

Figure 6.7: Inflation after a Monetary Shock (1% Shock on g)

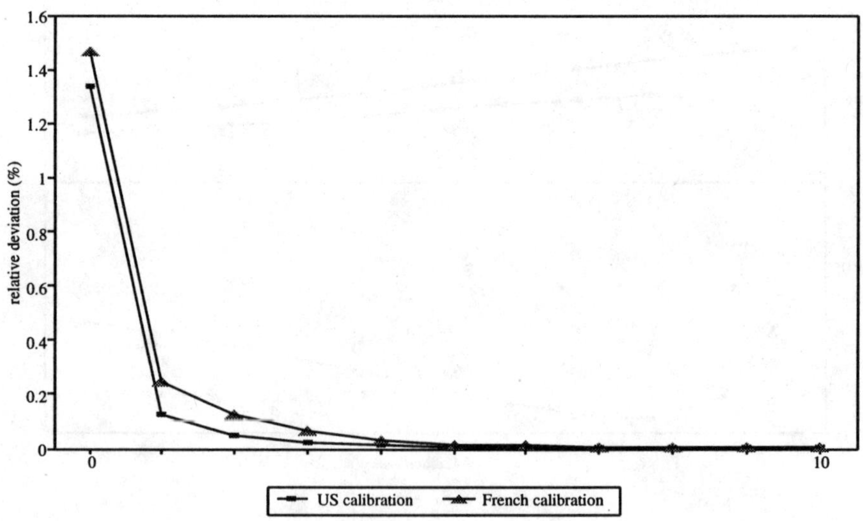

C. Sensibility to the Price Adjustment Cost Parameter ϕ

The existence of nominal rigidities is crucial determinant of the model response to a demand shock, as table C.1. shows how instantaneous responses (the Π matrix) evolve when adjustment costs increase[21]:

Table C.1.

ϕ	0	1/100	1/10	1	5
$\frac{CA(.01)}{Y}$	0%	.0001%	.001%	.01%	.05%
Π_{cg}	-.024	-.023	-.017	.035	.218
Π_{Hg}	-.006	.010	.157	1.545	6.33
Π_{wg}	.002	.003	.010	.080	.323
Π_{rg}	-.004	-.004	-.012	-.072	-.24
Π_{yg}	.005	.007	.110	1.08	4.43
$\Pi_{\Pi g}$	-.005	-.022	-.181	-1.68	-6.85
$\Pi_{\mu g}$	0	.029	-.297	-2.76	-11.2
Π_{ig}	. .090	.155	.737	6.23	25.2
Π_{xg}	.001	-.003	-.047	-.463	-1.90
Π_{fg}	1.410	1.410	1.402	1.340	1.12

The reduction of the mark-up becomes larger with the magnitude of the adjustment costs. The increase in good demand leads to high level of output and low price level when adjustment costs are high. Besides, hours and investment positive response increase with adjustment costs.

Table D.2. shows how variables simulated standard deviations evolve with ϕ (100 simulations).

[21]These results are obtained for the US calibration

Table C.2. Simulated Standard Deviations for Different Values of ϕ (US calibration)

ϕ	0	1/100	1/10	1	5
$\frac{\mathcal{CA}(.01)}{Y}$	0%	.0001%	.001%	.01%	.05%
$\widehat{c}$	.61 (.08)	.59 (.08)	.59 (.08)	.58 (.08)	.59 (.09)
$\widehat{h}$	1.07 (.12)	1.03 (.12)	1.01 (.11)	1.63 (.12)	5.83 (.4)
$\widehat{x}$	.81 (.1)	.78 (.1)	.79 (.11)	.94 (.11)	2.07 (.1)
$\widehat{y}$	1.77 (.2)	1.71 (.2)	1.70 (.2)	1.86 (.17)	4.17 (.28)
$\widehat{i}$	7.97 (.96)	7.7 (.92)	7.66 (.97)	9.06 (.88)	26.98 (4.36)
$\widehat{f}$	1.29 (.08)	1.29 (.08)	1.29 (.08)	1.22 (.1)	1.01 (.07)
$\widehat{\pi}$	1.77 (.2)	1.72 (.2)	1.74 (.2)	2.52 (.2)	6.8 (.5)

Consumption standard deviation is not sensible to ϕ[22], hours, investment, output and labor productivity standard deviations increase with ϕ. Inflation standard deviation is a decreasing function of ϕ.

One must notice that inflation standard deviation is always higher than in the data (1.22 for the US benchmark model and .52 on US data), even with high price adjustment costs (1.2 for $\phi = 5$). This failure of the model is linked to the existence of a substitution effect between money and consumption. In a model with adjustment cost on a real variable (*e.g.* capital), one can arbitrarily reduce the standard deviation of the variable by increasing the adjustment cost. In that model, households arbitrate between money and consumption. Therefore, the elasticity of substitution between money and consumption (σ) is a key parameter in the variance of inflation. For a given σ, the instantaneous response of inflation (and its standard deviation if we simulate the model) is of course a decreasing function of the price adjustment cost parameter ϕ. For a given ϕ, this response is an increasing function of the elasticity

[22] These standard deviation are not exact values but simulated ones. Therefore, one must not interpret small variations of them for different values of ϕ.

of substitution σ (figure 6.8).

Figure 6.8: Instantaneous Response of Inflation to a 1% Monetary Shock as a Function of the Elasticity of Substitution between Money and Consumption σ and of the Size of the Price Adjustment Cost ϕ

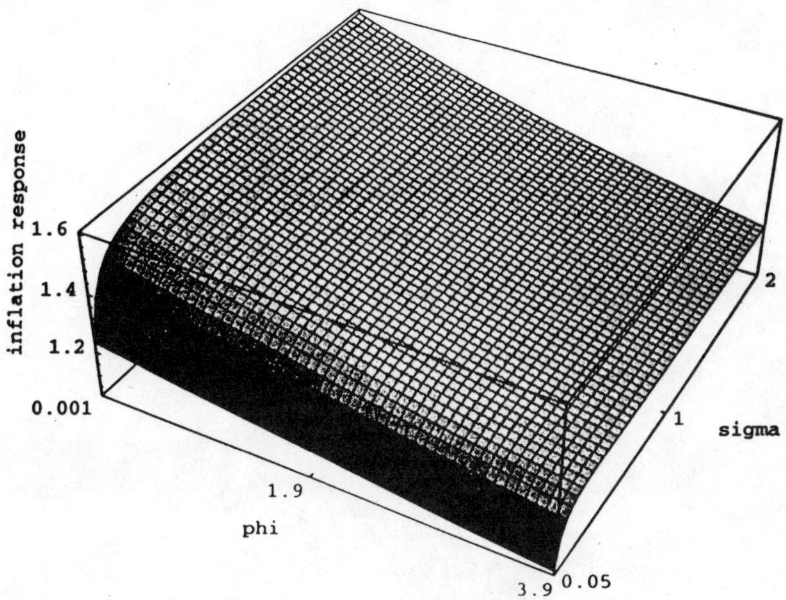

The more money can be substituted to consumption (high values of σ) and the more inflation will be important after a monetary growth shock. As a monetary shock increases the inflationary tax, households substitute consumption to real balances. The higher σ is, the higher is the demand for good and the higher is inflation. This effect dominates the effect of the adjustment cost in the model. If we increase the price adjustment costs, inflation will not be much lower after a monetary shock, but profits will be, as firms incurred higher adjustment costs (see table C.1.).

Bibliography

S. Ambler and L. Phaneuf. Wage Contracts and Business Cycles Models. *European Economic Review*, 36(4):783–800, May 1992.

F. Bec and J.O. Hairault. Supply and Demand Contributions to the Business Cycle: an Empirical Study in the Common Trends Framework. *Annales d'Economie et de Statistiques*, 30:85–120, April/June 1993.

J.P. Benassy. Imperfect Competition, Unemployment and Policy. *European Economic Review*, 31(1/2):417–426, February-March 1987.

G. Bertola and R. Caballero. *Kinked Adjustment Costs and Aggregate Dynamics.* Discussion Paper 465, Columbia University, February 1990. Published in National Bureau of Economic Research Macroeconomics Annual, 1991.

M. Bils. The Cyclical Behavior of Marginal Cost and Price. *American Economic Review*, 77(5):838–854, December 1987.

O. Blanchard and C. Kahn. The Solution of Linear Difference Models under Rational Expectations. *Econometrica*, 48(5):1305–1311, July 1980.

O. Blanchard and N. Kiyotaki. Monopolistic Competition and the Effect of Aggregate Demand. *American Economic Review*, 77(4):647–666, September 1987.

O. Blanchard. A Traditional Interpretation of Economic Fluctuations. *American Economic Review*, 79(5):1146–1164, December 1989.

O. Blanchard. Why does Money Affect Output? A Survey. In B. Friedman and F. Hahn, editor, *Handbook of Monetary Economics*, chapter 15, North-Holland, Amsterdam, 1990.

C. Burnside, M. Eichenbaum and S. Rebelo. *Labor Hoarding and the Business Cycle.* Working Paper 3556, NBER, December 1990.

F. Charpin. *Les effets de l'inflation dans la théorie du cycle de vie.* Working paper 89-02, OFCE, June 1989.

J.O. Cho and T. Cooley. *The Business Cycle with Nominal Contracts.* Working paper , University of Rochester, 1990.

J.O. Cho. *Nominal Wage Contracts.* Working Paper , Western Ontario University, 1990.

J.O. Cho. *Real Business Cycle and Market Structure.* Working Paper , Western Ontario University, 1990.

T. Cooley and G. Hansen. The Inflation Tax in a Real Business Cycle Model. *American Economic Review*, 79(4):733–748, September 1989.

J.P. Danthine and J. Donaldson. Efficiency Wages and the Business Cycles Puzzle. *European Economic Review*, 34(7):1275–301, November 1990.

J.P. Danthine and J. Donaldson. *Risk Sharing, the Minimum Wage and the Business Cycle.* Cahiers de Recherche Economique 9102, Université de Lausanne, 1990.

J.P. Danthine and J. Donaldson. *Methodological and Empirical Issues in Real Business Cycle Theory.* Cahiers de Recherche Economique 9102, Université de Lausanne, 1991.

I. Domowitz, R. Hubbard and B. Petersen. Market Structure and Cyclical Fluctuations in U.S. Manufacturing. *Review of Economics and Statistics*, 70(1):55–66, February 1987.

M. Eichenbaum, L. Hansen and K. Singleton. A Time Analysis of Representative Agent Models of Consumption and Leisure Choice under Uncertainty. *Quarterly Journal of Economics*, 103(1):51–78, February 1988.

C. Evans. Productivity Shocks and Real Business Cycles. *Journal of Monetary Economics*, 29(2):191–208, April 1992.

X. Fairise and F. Langot. Labor Productivity and Business Cycles: Can RBC Models be Saved? *European Economic Review*, 38, October 1994.

R. Gordon. What is New Keynesian Economics ? *Journal of Economic Literature*, 28(3):1115–1171, September 1990.

J.O. Hairault and F. Portier. Monnaie et inflation dans un modèle de cycles réels. *Recherches Econimiques de Louvain*, 59(4):427–461, 1993.

R. Hall. *Increasing Returns: Theory and Measurement with Industry Data.* Working paper , Hoover Institution and Dpt.of Economics, Stanford University and NBER, September 1988.

R. Hall. *Invariance Properties of Solow's Productivity Residual.* Working paper 3034, NBER, July 1989.

G. Hansen. Indivisible Labor and the Business Cycles. *Journal of Monetary Economics*, 16(3):309–327, November 1985.

P.Y. Hénin. Une macroéconomie sans monnaie pour les années 90. *Revue d'Economie Politique*, 99(5):531–596, 1989.

P.Y. Hénin. *Développements de la théorie des cycles réels.* Working paper 9113, CEPREMAP, Paris, 1991.

R. King and C. Plosser. Money, Credit and Prices in a Real Business Cycle. *American Economic Review*, 74(3):363–380, June 1984.

R. King, C. Plosser and S. Rebelo. *Production Growth and Business Cycles: Technical Appendix.* Working paper, University of Rochester, 1987. Revised May 1990.

R. King, C. Plosser and S. Rebelo. Production, Growth and Business Cycles I. *Journal of Monetary Economics*, 21(2/3):196–232, March-May 1988.

R. King. *Money and Business Cycles.* Working paper, University of Rochester, 1990.

N. Kiyotaki. *Macroeconomics of Monopolistic Competition.* Ph.D. dissertation, Harvard University, Cambridge, Mass, 1985.

E. Koenig. Real Money Balances and the Timing of Consumption: An Empirical Investigation. *Quarterly Journal of Economics*, 105(2):399–425, 1990.

F. Kydland and E. Prescott. Time to Build and Aggregate Fluctuations. *Econometrica*, 50(6):1345–1370, November 1982.

J.P. Laffargue, P. Malgrange and T. Pujol. *Une maquette trimestrielle de l'économie française avec anticipations rationnelles et concurrence monopolistique.* Working paper, CEPREMAP, April 1990. Rapport de contrat pour le Commissariat Général au Plan.

J. Long and C. Plosser. Real Business Cycle. *Journal of Political Economy*, 91(1):39–69, February 1983.

G. Mankiw and P. Romer. *New-Keynesian Economics.* Volume 1 and 2, MIT Press, Cambridge, Mass, 1991.

C. Morrison. *Markup Behavior in Durable and Nondurable Manufacturing: A Production Theory Approach.* Working paper 2941, NBER, April 1989.

C. Morrison. *Market Power, Economic Profitability and Productivity Growth Measurement: an Integrated Structural Approach.* Working paper 3355, NBER, May 1990.

C. Nelson and C. Plosser. Trend and Random Walks in Macroeconomic Time Series. *Journal of Monetary Economics*, 10(1):139–162, September 1982.

M. Parkin. The Output-Inflation Trade off When Prices are Costly to Change. *Journal of Political Economy*, 94(1):200–224, February 1986.

F. Portier. *Imperfect Competition, Imperfect Information, Menu Cost and the Neutrality of Money.* Working paper, M.A.D., Université de Paris I, 1991.

R. Rogerson. Indivisible Labor, Lotteries and Equilibrium. *Journal of Monetary Economics*, 21(1):3–16, January 1988.

J. Rotemberg and M. Woodford. *Oligopolistic Competition and the Effect of Aggregate Demand on Economic Activity.* Working paper 3206, NBER, 1989.

J. Rotemberg and M. Woodford. Mark-up and the Business Cycle. In *NBER Macoreconomics Annual*, MIT Press, 1991.

Chapter 7

Nominal Wage Contracts and the Short-Run Dynamics of Real Wages

Xavier Fairise

Abstract

In this chapter, we present a real business cycle model with interrelated adjustment costs and nominal wage contracts. We show that the combination of these two elements allows to reproduce simultaneously productivity-employment and employment-wage correlations close to the stylized facts. In this model, productivity is a good leading indicator of employment fluctuations while wage is a lagged one.

Introduction

The aim of this chapter is to show that nominal wage contracts account for the lagged adjustment of real wage over the cycle. The wage contracts were introduced in the literature by Fischer [1977] and Taylor [1980]. The debate was then different from the one evoked in this chapter. It focused essentially on the implications of the rational expectations hypothesis for economic policy. The relation underlined by Phillips [1958] has for a long time been perceived as giving to the monetary authorities the possibility of a trade-off between inflation and unemployment. The Phillips relation was then considered as stable. However, this belief was challenged by Phelps [1967] and Friedman [1968] who distinguish a long-run and a short-run Phillips curve. The inflation-unemployment trade-off is then possible in the short-run only. The efficiency of monetary policy in the short-run is essentially due to the inertia of adaptative expectations. After all, Lucas [1972] showed that under rational expectations hypothesis and perfect price flexibility, the monetary policy, in so far as it is well expected, has no effect on product and employment, even in the short-run. The aim of the nominal wage contracts introduced by Fischer and Taylor is to show that the rational expectations hypothesis is not inconsistent with a real effect of the monetary policy. Indeed, the wage rigidities implied by the presence of contracts lead to an efficient monetary policy.

Nominal wage contracts were not intended to explain the real wage dynamics with respect to employment. The debate focused on economic policy, and especially the efficiency of monetary policy. Wage contracts were introduced in real business cycle models. The aim is to account for the propagation of nominal shocks in the economy. The studies of Cho [1990], Cho and Cooley [1990] and Cho and Phaneuf [1993] are concerned with this topic. Empirical evidence suggests that wage fluctuations are leaded by employment fluctuations. What kind of mechanism may explain this feature ? The following question comes naturally to mind : Do some wage rigidities similar to *wage contracts* contribute to explain the wage dynamics over the cycle ?

Beyond the economic policy discussions it initiated, the Phillips curve is a wage formation equation. It describes a lagged adjustment process of wages according to the labor market disequilibrium. More importantly, the inertia concerns the nominal wage evolution. When the inflationist pressures are strong, the nominal wages increase with a delay, and the resulting decrease in the real wages induces a momentary fall in unemployment. The nominal wage contracts follow the same intuition; *(i)* they imply a short-run rigidity of nominal wages, and *(ii)* the monetary shocks are important for the employment and (real) wage dynamics.

The wage contracts that will be used in this chapter lead to a working of the labor market opposite to the one implied by the intertemporal substitution hypothesis. According to this assumption, the agents raise (reduce) their labor supply in response to a wage increase (decrease). It implies that the employment fluctuations reflect the optimal agent reaction to the wage changes. In an economy with wage contracts, employment fluctuations do not follow the same explanation. They are induced by changes in the firm labor demand. To clarify our purpose, we quickly describe the wage contracts that are used. The contractual nominal wage, established several periods in advance, is equal to the rational expectation of the wage that would prevail at the labor market equilibrium of an economy without contracts. At a given period, the nominal wage is then fixed, and the real wage essentially depends on the price level resulting itself from the monetary shocks. Employment is then determined by the firm which is always on its labor demand curve. The households accept to work as much as firms want them to, as they specified the wage contracts. In this context, the employment fluctuations essentially depend on the firms behavior. We will also emphasize the contribution of the monetary shocks *via* their effect on the real wage.

It cannot be referred to the wage and employment dynamics without evoking the controversy between Dunlop and Tarshis on the one hand[1], and Keynes on the other hand[2] concerning the pro-cyclicity or contra-cyclicity of real wages. More precisely, the discussions mainly bear on the sign of the instantaneous wage-employment correlation. Contrary to the Keynes's belief, the studies of Dunlop [1938] and Tarshis [1939] conclude in favor of a positive correlation. In fact, the debates around this question are not yet closed. However, beyond these debates, we will argue that the short-run real wage dynamics better emerges from the lagged and advanced wage-employment correlations, and not only from the instantaneous one. The explanation rests on the two following points :

- The contributions that follow the ones of Dunlop and Tarshis do not allow to determine the sign of the employment-wage correlation. It is sometimes positive, zero, or negative. Beyond the controversy about the true sign of this correlation, these contradictory results show the difficulty of giving a reliable evaluation

[1] *Cf.* Dunlop [1938] and Tarshis [1939].
[2] *Cf.* Keynes [1939]

of it.

- The instantaneous employment-wage correlation provides, in itself, only little information about real wage fluctuations over the cycle. Only the study of correlations' profile enables one to analyze the real wage dynamics compared to the employment one. According to this point of view, the sign, weakly positive or negative, of the instantaneous correlation between the wage and the employment does not matter.

The aim of this chapter is to show that nominal wage contracts provide some explanations of the real wage dynamics with respect to the employment. The model developed in this chapter includes interrelated adjustment costs. Nominal wages are not determined by labor market equilibrium, but *on the basis of contracts.* The simulation results show that the model allows to reproduce both the productivity-employment and the employment-wages correlations profiles. The importance of the nominal shocks in the explanation of real wage dynamics also emerges from the model.

This chapter includes three sections. The first section is devoted to the presentation of the model and to the definition of the equilibrium. The model without contract is first presented. It is necessary for the definition of the nominal wage contracts. The contracts are then defined in detail, and the economy with contracts is described. The second section begins by a discussion of the model calibration. The remaining part of the section is devoted to an evaluation of the mechanisms at work in the model. We show how the two assumptions of interrelated adjustment costs and nominal wage contracts allow to dissociate the short-run dynamics of productivity from the real wage dynamics. Finally, in the third section, we discuss the ability of our model to replicate the American and French stylized facts.

7.1 The Model

This section is devoted to a general presentation of the model. We start by a description of the competitive model, without wage contracts. It is an interrelated adjustment costs model in which money is included through a cash-in-advance constraint. The model with wage contracts is then exposed, and the new equilibrium of the economy defined.

7.1.1 The Economic Environment

The Households

The representative household has the following utility function :

$$u(C, 1-N) = \frac{1}{1-\sigma}\left[C^{1-\phi} + d(1-N)^{1-\phi}\right]^{\frac{1-\sigma}{1-\phi}}$$

with $\phi \in]0,1[$ and $\sigma \in]0,1[\cup]1,+\infty[$ and $d > 0$.

The representative household has a time endowment normalized at 1, shared between labor N and leisure L. Finally, C represents its consumption. The C.E.S. term in the utility function can be interpreted as a composite good. This utility function is then a constant risk aversion one, and σ is the relative risk aversion degree. $\frac{1}{\sigma}$ is the intertemporal substitution elasticity of the composite good between two periods.

$\frac{1}{\phi}$ is the instantaneous elasticity of substitution between consumption and leisure. If ϕ tends towards 1, then the C.E.S. bundle tends towards a Cobb-Douglas of the form $C^{\frac{1}{1+d}}(1-N)^{\frac{d}{1+d}}$. One may then interpret the parameter d: It is the weight of leisure relative to consumption in the agent's tastes. Following Kydland and Prescott [1982], this parameter reflects the share of time devoted to market activities — consumption.

The Cash-in-Advance Constraint: The definition of the nominal wage contracts requires the introduction of money in the model.

Here, it is assumed that households are subject to a cash-in-advance constraint, in the line of the nominal wage contracts model of Cho [1990]. This author retains the *"monetarized"* real business cycle model of Cooley and Hansen [1989][3] as a benchmark framework.

[3]Alternatively, it would be possible to submit the firms to a cash-in-advance constraint with respect to investment. However, it seems more likely to assume that households support such a constraint. Their credit possibility is more limited than the firms one. It is possible to refer to Hairault and Portier in chapter 3 of this book for a study of a real business cycles model with a cash-in-advance constraint on consumption and/or investment.

At the beginning of each period t, households possess a money stock m_{t-1}, inherited from the previous period. Moreover, this money stock is increased by a lump-sum transfer of money equal to $M_t - M_{t-1} = (\gamma_t - 1)M_{t-1}$, where M_t is the money supply of the period t. It follows the stochastic process :

$$M_t = \gamma_t M_{t-1}$$

We admit that the logarithm of the growth rate of the monetary stock, γ_t follows an autoregressive process of the form :

$$\log(\gamma_{t+1}) = \rho_\gamma \log(\gamma_t) + (1 - \rho_\gamma) \log(\overline{\gamma}) + \epsilon_{\gamma t}$$

ρ_γ is the persistence parameter, strictly less than 1 in absolute value, and ϵ_γ is the *iid* innovation of the process whose standard deviation is denoted by $\sigma_{\epsilon\gamma}$. Finally, $\overline{\gamma}$ is the mean of the process. Households being supposed to hold in advance the money necessary to purchase a consumption good, they are subject to the constraint :

$$p_t C_t \leq m_{t-1} + (\gamma_t - 1) M_{t-1}$$

where p_t represents the price level at period t.

The Firm

A representative firm products the output using two factors, namely capital K and labor N. Investment I and hiring H are subject to interrelated adjustment costs. In the line of Lucas [1967], the adjustment cost function is homogeneous of degree 1 with respect to capital, labor, investment and hiring. The production technology F, net of the adjustment costs, is described by the function :

$$F(K_t, N_t, I_t, H_t; A_t) = \left(1 - s\frac{I_t}{K_t}\frac{H_t}{N_t}\right) A_t K_t^{1-\alpha} N_t^\alpha - \frac{a}{2}\frac{I_t^2}{K_t} - \frac{c}{2}\frac{H_t^2}{N_t} - I_t$$

a and c are positive, s is a parameter that may be positive or negative. This specification is close to the one of Galeotti and Schiantarelli [1991]. The variable A_t represents the technological shock, its mean A being normalized at 1. The process $\log(A_t)$ is supposed to be autoregressive of order 1, that is :

$$\log(A_t) = \rho_A \log(A_{t-1}) + (1 - \rho_A) \log(A) + \epsilon_{At}$$

ρ_A is the persistence parameter, strictly less than 1 in absolute value, and ϵ_{At} is the *iid* innovation of the process whose standard deviation is denoted by $\sigma_{\epsilon A}$.

Capital and employment are accumulated according to $K_{t+1} = (1-\delta)K_t + I_t$ and $N_{t+1} = (1-\nu)N_t + H_t$ respectively[4]. The capital depreciates at rate δ, and ν represents the quit rate of labor force.

The Government Expenditures

The government expenditures are denoted by G_t. The term $\log(G_t)$ follows an autoregressive process of order 1 :

$$\log(G_t) = \rho_G \log(G_{t-1}) + (1-\rho_G)\log(G) + \epsilon_{Gt}$$

The persistence parameter ρ_G satisfies $|\rho_G| < 1$, and we note $\sigma_{\epsilon G}$ the standard deviation of the innovation ϵ_{Gt} supposed to be *iid*. G is the mean of the process.

At each period, government expenditures are financed by a lump-sum tax exactly equal to their level.

7.1.2 The Competitive Equilibrium of the Economy without Wage Contracts

The Representative Firm Program

The intertemporal maximization program of the firm is :

$$\max_{I_t,H_t} E_0 \sum_{t=0}^{\infty} \rho_t \left[F(K_t, N_t, I_t, H_t; A_t) - \tfrac{w_t}{p_t} N_t\right]$$

$$\text{s.t.} \begin{cases} K_{t+1} &= (1-\delta)K_t + I_t \\ N_{t+1} &= (1-\nu)N_t + H_t \end{cases}$$

ρ_t is the stochastic discount factor of the firm, w_t and p_t are respectively the nominal prices and wages.

The Representative Household Program

The representative household maximizes its intertemporal utility subject to budget and cash-in-advance constraints :

[4]The evolution equation of employment implies that employment is predetermined.

$$\max_{C_t,H_t} E_0 \sum_{t=0}^{\infty} \beta^t u(C_t, 1-N_t)$$

$$\text{s.t.} \left\{ \begin{array}{rcl} C_t + \frac{m_t}{p_t} + E_t\left\{\frac{\rho_{t+1}}{\rho_t}\Psi_{t+1}\right\} & \leq & \Psi_t + \frac{w_t}{p_t}N_t + \frac{1}{p_t}(m_{t-1} + (\gamma_t - 1)M_{t-1}) - G_t \\ C_t & \leq & \frac{m_{t-1}}{p_t} + (\gamma_t - 1)\frac{M_{t-1}}{p_t} \end{array} \right.$$

$\{\rho_t\}$ represents a stochastic pricing kernel for contingent claims, that is a security whose payment at period $t+1$ in terms of period $t+1$ goods is a random variable Ψ_{t+1}. The price of this contingent claim at date t is given by :

$$E_t\left\{\frac{\rho_{t+1}}{\rho_t}\Psi_{t+1}\right\}$$

Moreover, the household is subject to the following non-borrowing constraint :

$$\lim_{j\to\infty} E_t\left\{\rho_{t+j}\Psi_{t+j}\right\} \geq 0$$

In this study, the cash-in-advance constraint is supposed to be always binding, so that we never have to take into account regime switchings during simulation exercises.

Determination of the Equilibrium

The good market equilibrium is reached if the resource constraint is satisfied, that is :

$$F(K_t, N_t, I_t, H_t; A_t) = C_t + G_t$$

At the equilibrium, the equality between the supply of money M_t and the stock of money held by the household m_t is obtained, that is $m_t = M_t$. The household constraint can thus be rewritten as follows :

$$C_t + E_t\left\{\frac{\rho_{t+1}}{\rho_t}\Psi_{t+1}\right\} = \Psi_t + \frac{w_t}{p_t}N_t - G_t$$

$$p_t C_t = M_t$$

Given that the transversality conditions of the firm problem, as well as the non-borrowing constraint of the household, are satisfied, the firm value function and the household budget constraint are integrated. Provided that the good market is expected to be in equilibrium at each future period, the following equality between the firm value and the *ex post* value of the household asset is obtained. This is the capital market equilibrium condition, and we have :

$$\Psi_t = V^F(t)$$

The Competitive Equilibrium: To simplify the computation of equilibrium, the following variables change is adopted : the nominal variables, prices and wages, are deflated by the stock of money in order to get stationary variables. We then define $\tilde{p}_t = \frac{p_t}{M_t}$ and $\tilde{w}_t = \frac{w_t}{M_t}$.

Finally, the computation of equilibrium implies the following kinds of policy rules for consumption (C_t), investment (I_t) and hiring (H_t) :

$$\begin{aligned} C_t &= C_t(K_t, N_t, A_t, G_t, \gamma_t) \\ I_t &= I_t(K_t, N_t, A_t, G_t, \gamma_t) \\ H_t &= H_t(K_t, N_t, A_t, G_t, \gamma_t) \end{aligned}$$

The processes followed by the transformed price and wage are :

$$\begin{aligned} \tilde{w}_t &= \tilde{w}_t(K_t, N_t, A_t, G_t, \gamma_t) \\ \tilde{p}_t &= \tilde{p}_t(K_t, N_t, A_t, G_t, \gamma_t) \end{aligned}$$

Knowing the transformed price and wage process in the competitive economy, it is possible to define wage contracts, and thus, the equilibrium of the wage contracts economy.

7.1.3 The Equilibrium with Nominal Wage Contracts

The Wage Contracts

The Notion of Wage Contracts: The nominal wage contracts proposed by Fischer are grounded on the following hypothesis. Nominal wages are fixed by negotiation, several periods in advance. A contract negotiated at period $t-j$ determines the nominal wage prevailing at period t. The firm holding the right to manage, it is free to set employment at the optimal level, knowing the current period shock. Households satisfy the firm labor demand, whatever the quantity. It is also possible to consider staggered wage contracts : at each period, a fraction of the contracts is negotiated again.

Now, an important question still remains, that is the one of the relevant length of contracts. Fischer [1977] considers successively the case where all the contracts are fixed one period in advance, and the case in which one half of the contracts are negotiated again at each period, the contract length being then two periods. It appears that the one period contracts imply the neutrality of monetary policy. In return, the other type of contracts (of two periods length) leads to a long run effect of nominal shocks. Fischer gives no ground to the length of such contracts. More generally, an important difficulty in the Fischer's analysis comes from the lack of micro-foundations of the type of contracts he introduces.

The study of Gray [1978] provides an explicit derivation of the optimal length of the contracts. The model rests on the two following assumptions. Firstly, there exists a negotiation cost for the new contracts. Secondly, lengthy contracts are by themselves costly because the forecast error is increasing with the horizon. In other words, the lack of precision of the expectations, associated with lengthy contracts, leads to employment levels quite different from the optimal levels. The determination of the optimal contract length thus obeys to a trade-off between the gain of negotiating rarely (each negotiation is costly), and the cost (in terms of sub-optimal employment levels) that lengthy contracts imply. The length of the contracts increase with the negotiation costs and decrease with the variance of the shock.

Specification of the Wage Contracts: The idea to include wage contracts in a real business cycle model is due to Cho [1990][5]. More precisely, the wage contract is defined as follows. The contractual nominal wage w_t^C is determined j periods in advance, namely at period $t-j$. At period t, on the basis of the information available at this time, knowing that the nominal wage is given, the firms determine their labor demand. It is stipulated in the contract that the workers give up to the firm the right to manage. If at date $t-j$, there is agreement about the nominal wage w_t^C, the workers engage to provide at period t the

[5]It is also possible to refer to King [1990]. One has also to mention the contribution of Benassy [1993]. This author includes nominal wage contracts in the model of Long and Plosser [1983]. It appears that non-anticipated monetary shocks have an effect on employment and output.

quantity of labor demanded by the firm. Fischer [1977] admits that the nominal wage is fixed such that the real wage remains unchanged. The definitions retained in the *real business cycle* literature remain in the line of Fischer. The contractual nominal wage is equal to the rational expectation at date $t-j$ of the equilibrium wage for period t. It is necessary to define what one means by *equilibrium wage*, since there exist two possibilities.

1. In his study, Cho [1990] considers that the contractual wage w_t^C corresponds to the expectation, at period $t-j$, of the nominal wage that would clear the labor market at time t in a wage contracts economy.

2. Cho and Cooley [1990] use a variant of the wage contracts previously described. In their model, contractual nominal wages w_t^C correspond to the expectation at period $t-j$ of the nominal wage that would prevail at equilibrium in the *walrasian* model. However, when agents determine the contractual wage w_t^C, they rationally expect that, during the intermediate periods, $t-j+1,...,t-1$, capital accumulation is done in a wage contracts economy framework.

Cho and Cooley [1990] discuss the differences between the two kinds of wage contracts. They assert that the contracts of Cho [1990] are more "efficient". Indeed, the contracts of Cho [1990] are very coherent, in so far as they are defined within the framework of the model. That is not the case for the second category of contracts which are defined at the equilibrium of the walrasian model. However, these two authors use these last contracts because they permit to avoid some important computational difficulties in the determination of the model equilibrium. Moreover, they observe that, quantitatively, there are few differences between these two types of wage contracts.

In this study, contracts corresponding to the ones presented in the second point are used. Formally, the contractual wage w_t^C is defined according to :

$$\log(w_t^C) = E_{t-j}\left\{\log(w_t)\right\}$$

where w_t is the equilibrium wage at period t of the walrasian model.

We also take into account the case of staggered wage contracts, and the definition of Cho and Cooley [1990] is once more retained. The contractual wage is thus defined by the following equation :

$$\log(w_t^C) = \sum_{k=0}^{j} \theta_k E_{t-k} \log(w_t)$$

$\sum_{k=0}^{j} \theta_k = 1$, and θ_k represents the fraction of wages negotiated k periods in advance, with $k = 0, 1, .., j$. The term θ_0 calls for some specific comments : it corresponds to the share of the wages that are competitively established. More generally, these staggered contracts imply that some wages are determined in a competitive environment while others are set by contracts of 1, 2, .. to j periods.

The Representative Household

The representative household program corresponds to the walrasian one with the following new constraint on employment[6] $n_t = N_t$, which reflects the fact that the household provides exactly the labor quantity requested by the firm. The program becomes :

$$\max_{C_t, n_t} E_0 \sum_{t=0}^{\infty} \beta^t u(C_t, 1 - N_t)$$

$$\text{s.t.} \begin{cases} C_t + \frac{m_t}{p_t} + E_t\left\{\frac{\rho_{t+1}}{\rho_t}\Psi_{t+1}\right\} & \leq \Psi_t + \frac{w_t}{p_t} n_t + \frac{1}{p_t}(m_{t-1} + (\gamma_t - 1)M_{t-1}) - G_t \\ C_t & \leq \frac{m_{t-1}}{p_t} + (\gamma_t - 1)\frac{M_{t-1}}{p_t} \\ N_t & = n_t \end{cases}$$

Small 'n' denotes the labor quantity that the household wishes to supply, which usually differs from the one demanded by the firm. Thus, n_t represents the employment level desired by household. One gets optimality conditions of the form :

$$\begin{aligned} u_C(t) - x_t - \mu_t &= 0 \\ u_L(t) - \frac{w_t}{p_t} x_t &= \nu_t \\ \beta \frac{x_{t+1}}{x_t} - \frac{\rho_{t+1}}{\rho_t} &= 0 \end{aligned}$$

[6] n_t represents the household labour supply, and N_t the firm labour demand.

$$x_t = \beta E_t \left\{ \frac{p_t}{p_{t+1}} (x_{t+1} + \mu_{t+1}) \right\}$$

$$\lim_{j\to\infty} E_t \left\{ \beta^{t+j} x_{t+j} \Psi_{t+j} \right\} = 0 \quad \text{and} \quad \lim_{j\to\infty} E_t \left\{ \beta^{t+j} (\mu_{t+j} + x_{t+j}) \frac{m_{t+j}}{p_{t+j}} \right\} = 0$$

with, as in the case of the walrasian model :

$$x_t = V_B^M(t) \quad \text{and} \quad \frac{x_t}{p_t} + \frac{\mu_t}{p_t} = \beta E_t \left\{ V_m^M(t+1) \right\}$$

and ν_t is the multiplier associated to the constraint $N_t = n_t$.

The Firm

The intertemporal maximization problem of the firm is the same as in the competitive model, except that a constraint corresponding to the wage contract is now added :

$$\log(w_t^C) = E_{t-j} \left\{ \log(w_t) \right\}$$

w_t being of the form :$w_t = w(K_t, N_t, A_t, G_t, \gamma_t)$. This expression was obtained by the resolution of the walrasian model. The program becomes :

$$\max_{I_t, H_t} E_0 \textstyle\sum_{t=0}^{\infty} \rho_t \left[F(K_t, N_t, I_t, H_t; A_t) - \frac{w_t}{p_t} N_t \right]$$

$$\text{s.t.} \left\{ \begin{array}{rcl} K_{t+1} &=& (1-\delta) K_t + I_t \\ N_{t+1} &=& (1-\nu) N_t + H_t \\ \log(w_t^C) &=& E_{t-j} \left\{ \log(w_t) \right\} \end{array} \right.$$

Optimality conditions are similar to those of the competitive model. Indeed, such a contract implies that firm is always on its labor demand curve. Thus, one gets :

$$F_I(t) + q_t = 0$$

$$F_H(t) + \lambda_t = 0$$

$$q_t = E_t \left\{ \frac{\rho_{t+1}}{\rho_t} \left(F_K(t+1) + (1-\delta) q_{t+1} \right) \right\}$$

$$\lambda_t = E_t \left\{ \frac{\rho_{t+1}}{\rho_t} \left(F_N(t+1) - \frac{w_{t+1}^C}{p_{t+1}} + (1-\nu) \lambda_{t+1} \right) \right\}$$

$$\lim_{j \longrightarrow \infty} E_t \{\rho_{t+j} q_{t+j} K_{t+j+1}\} = 0 \quad \text{and} \quad \lim_{j \longrightarrow \infty} E_t \{\rho_{t+j} \lambda_{t+j} N_{t+j+1}\} = 0$$

Implicit prices satisfy :

$$q_t = E_t \left\{ \frac{\rho_{t+1}}{\rho_t} V_K^F(t+1) \right\} \quad \text{and} \quad \lambda_t = E_t \left\{ \frac{\rho_{t+1}}{\rho_t} V_N^F(t+1) \right\}$$

Wage is determined by :

$$\log(w_t^C) = E_{t-j} \{\log(w_t)\}$$

The Equilibrium

As in the walrasian model, the following equalities hold at equilibrium.

$$\begin{aligned} F(K_t, N_t, I_t, H_t; A_t) &= C_t + G_t \\ M_t &= m_t \\ \Psi_t &= V^F(t) \end{aligned}$$

In order to compute equilibrium, we deflate nominal variables p_t and w_t^C by M_t, which gives $\widetilde{w}_t^C = \frac{w_t}{M_t}$ and $\widetilde{p}_t = \frac{p_t}{M_t}$. The equation giving the nominal wage can then be rewritten :

$$\log(\widetilde{w}_t^C) = E_{t-j} \{\log(w_t)\} - \log(M_t)$$

We also define $\phi_t = x_t q_t$ and $\psi_t = x_t \lambda_t$. The different optimality conditions may then be rewritten as functions of these variables, and finally give the following system whose solution provides the equilibrium of our economy. This system is :

$$\begin{aligned} (u_C(t) - \mu_t) F_I(t) + \phi_t = 0 \\ (u_C(t) - \mu_t) F_H(t) + \psi_t = 0 \\ \phi_t = \beta E_t \{(u_C(t+1) - \mu_{t+1}) F_K(t+1) + (1-\delta)\phi_{t+1}\} \\ \psi_t = \beta E_t \left\{ (u_C(t+1) - \mu_{t+1})(F_N(t+1) - \frac{\widetilde{w}_{t+1}^C}{\widetilde{p}_{t+1}}) + (1-\nu)\psi_{t+1} \right\} \\ u_C(t) - \mu_t = \beta E_t \left\{ \frac{1}{\gamma_{t+1}} \frac{\widetilde{p}_t}{\widetilde{p}_{t+1}} u_C(t+1) \right\} \\ K_{t+1} = (1-\delta) K_t + I_t \end{aligned}$$

$$N_{t+1} = (1-\nu)N_t + H_t$$
$$F(K_t, N_t, I_t, H_t; A_t) = C_t + G_t$$
$$C_t = \frac{1}{\widetilde{p}_t}$$
$$\log(\widetilde{w}^C_{t+1}) = E_{t-j}\left\{\log(w_{t+1})\right\} - \log(M_{t+1})$$

The contractual nominal wage is determined by the following equation, taken from the competitive model :

$$\log(w^C_t) = E_{t-j}\left\{\log(w(K_t, N_t, A_t, G_t, \gamma_t))\right\}$$

The implicit prices ϕ_t, ψ_t and μ_t are moreover submitted to the terminal conditions :

$$\lim_{j\to\infty} E_t\left\{\beta^{t+j}\phi_{t+j}K_{t+j+1}\right\} = 0$$
$$\lim_{j\to\infty} E_t\left\{\beta^{t+j}\psi_{t+j}N_{t+j+1}\right\} = 0$$
$$\lim_{j\to\infty} E_t\left\{\beta^{t+j}\mu_{t+j}\frac{1}{\widetilde{p}_{t+j}}\right\} = 0$$

The simulation method used is the one of King, Plosser and Rebelo [1988], the system defining equilibrium being log-linearized near the steady state of the model. A rational expectations system is obtained. It is then solved and gives a linear approximation of the optimal policy rules[7]. Each of the models presented here are simulated 100 times for an horizon of 120 quarters, namely 30 years. Before computing the moments, the simulated series are filtered using Hodrick and Prescott method.

7.2 The Mechanisms of the Model

This section is devoted to the inspection of the mechanisms at work in the model. To do it, several variants of the model have been simulated (this exercise is made on the American calibration). To begin, we discuss the implication of the interrelated adjustment costs for the short-run dynamics of productivity (*model CA-C0*). Then, we examine

[7]The resolution of the wage contracts model is more difficult than the one of the usual models. In particular, it is necessary to compute lagged anticipations. A desciption of the method is given in Fairise [1994]

the implications of the assumption of interrelated adjustment costs and nominal wage contracts on the short-run dynamics of productivity and real wage. This evaluation of the model properties rests on simulation results (*models CA-C4a, CA-C4b and CA-CI4b*) and impulse response function analysis. Before discussing the simulation results, we discuss the calibration used for the simulation exercises.

7.2.1 Calibration

We suppose that the French and American economies differ only by their production technologies and the shocks. On the other hand, agents in the two countries are supposed to have the same preferences.

Preference Parameters: The value of the parameter σ, reflecting the willingness of an agent to substitute intertemporally some composite good :

$$\left[C^{1-\phi} + d(1-N)^{1-\phi}\right]^{\frac{1}{1-\phi}}$$

is set at 1.5. It corresponds to the one traditionally retained since Kydland and Prescott [1982]. The parameter d is taken equal to 2 : agents devote one third of their available time to consumption and the two other thirds to leisure. The parameter ϕ is used to set the stationary employment at 0.40. This implies a value of 0.8.

Finally, the discount factor β is as in other studies taken equal to 0.99. All the parameters are summed up in table (7.1).

The adjustment costs function is calibrated such that the adjustment cost of marginal investment represents, at the steady state, 0.15% of the marginal investment price[8], and the marginal adjustment cost of employment is equal to 0.05% of the wage. In practice, the values of s, a and c are chosen so as to respect the preceding proportions.

Other Parameters: The USA and France differ by their production technology and the shocks whose calibration is now discussed.

For the USA, the government expenditures level is chosen such that it represents 21% of output. This corresponds to the share of the

[8]The marginal price of marginal investment is 1, and therefore, one has $s\frac{H}{N}AK^{-\alpha}N^{\alpha} + a\frac{I}{K} = 0.0015$ at the steady state.

Table 7.1: Preferences

σ	ϕ	d	β
1.5	0.8	2	0.99

government expenditures in the American product after World War II. This proportion is of 18.5% in France. The US parameter α is, as it is traditional, taken equal to 0.58. For France, according to Laffargue and Malgrange [1991], the value of α is equal to 0.545. The US depreciation rate δ is equal to 0.025. Concerning the French economy, δ is chosen equal to 0.0125. This value is also taken from Laffargue and Malgrange [1991]. Following Akerlof, Rose and Yellen [1988], the quit rate of the labor force ν is set at 0.06 for the USA. For France, ν is set equal to 0.0245 which corresponds to the annual value reported by Bentolila and Bertola [1990]. Finally, an autoregressive process of order 1 on the Solow residual, the government expenditures and the growth rate of the money stock was estimated on the US and French economy (see Hairault [1992] and Portier [1992]). All the values are summed up in tables (7.2) and (7.3). Five different models are considered, with different

Table 7.2: Technology and Processes of the Shocks : the USA

α	δ	ν	ρ_A	$\sigma_{\epsilon A}$	ρ_G	$\sigma_{\epsilon G}$	ρ_γ	$\sigma_{\epsilon\gamma}$
0.58	0.0025	0.06	0.95	0.009	0.975	0.013	0.377	0.009

Table 7.3: Technology and Processes of the Shocks : France

α	δ	ν	ρ_A	$\sigma_{\epsilon A}$	ρ_G	$\sigma_{\epsilon G}$	ρ_γ	$\sigma_{\epsilon\gamma}$
0.545	0.0125	0.0245	0.987	0.0081	0.985	0.0083	0.50	0.0098

adjustment costs and contracts charasterictics.

- *model CA-C0*: without contract and with adjustment costs (USA [$s = -7.5$]).
- *model CA-C4a* : 4-period contracts and adjustment costs (USA [$s = -7.5$]).

- *model CA-C4b* : 4-period contracts and adjustment costs (USA $[s=-15]$ and France $[s=-25]$).
- *model CA-CI4b* : staggered contracts of 4 periods and adjustment costs (USA $[s=-15]$).
- *model CA-C8* : 8-period contracts and adjustment costs (France $[s=-25]$).

7.2.2 The Walrasian Model with Interrelated Adjustment Costs

The simulations of the walrasian model with interrelated adjustment costs (*model CA-C0*) make clear the implications of that assumption (see tables (7.4), (7.5) and (7.6)). The two-period leading productivity-employment correlation is maximum : the productivity is hence a leading indicator of employment fluctuations. In other words, the model exhibits a leading dynamics of productivity with respect to employment. These results differ from the ones given by a model without adjustment costs. There, the one period leading correlation is maximum[9] (see table (7.7)).

The results are in the line of the ones of Chapter 2, even though, the mechanisms at work are quite different. In the model of chapter 2, the leading dynamics of productivity only arose from the labor adjustment costs. More precisely, the ability of that model to exhibit a leading dynamics of productivity only depended on the labor adjustment cost size. Under the assumption of interrelated adjustment costs, the leading dynamics of productivity is induced by the complementarity[10] of investment and hiring in the adjustment cost technology.

To underline this point, we simulated the model under the assumptions of interrelated and separable adjustment costs. — *i.e.* $s=-7.5$ and $s=0$ —. Let us recall that, in these two cases, the steady state

[9] This is due to the fact that employment is a predetermined variable, as it is indicated by equation $N_{t+1}=(1-\nu)N_t+H_t$. It induces automatically a one period lag of the maximum productivity-employment correlation (see Chapter 2). Without this assumption, the instantaneous correlation would be maximum.

[10] If $s<0$, then the derivative F_{IH} is positive. It follows that the marginal adjustment cost of a factor is a decreasing function of the investment level in the other factors. Then, there are a complementarity between hiring and investment.

marginal adjustment cost of investment represents 0.15% of the marginal investment price and the marginal adjustment cost of employment is equal to 0.05% of the real wage. This implies that the size of the adjustment costs is the same in both models. As we previously mentionned, the interrelated adjustment costs model induces a leading dynamics of productivity (of more than one period), whereas the model with separable adjustment costs gives results similar to the ones without adjustment costs (compare table (7.5), (7.7) and (7.8)). Consequently, the complementarity of investment and hiring in the adjustment cost technology allows to increase the employment inertia without increasing the weight of the adjustment costs. It also allows to increase the lead of productivity with respect to employment[11].

Table 7.4: Model CA-C0

Series	Std	Std/Std$_Y$	corr(Y, X)
Y	1.32	1	1
C	0.87	0.66	0.79
I	3.27	2.53	0.97
N	0.43	0.33	0.67
PR	1.07	0.81	0.96
W	0.82	0.61	0.83

Y : Product, C : Consumption.
I : Investment, N : Employment.
PR : Productivity, W : Real wage.

Concerning the wage dynamics, the instantaneous employment-wage correlation is maximum. Thus, the wage fluctuations follow instantaneously the employment ones. This is coherent with the walrasian labor market of the model. The perfect flexibility of wages ensures that they adjust instantaneously to clear the labor market. The instantaneous

[11]See also Fairise [1994] for a detailled analysis of the interrelated adjustment cost assumption.

Table 7.5: Productivity-Employment Correlations (Model CA-C0)

	-4	-3	-2	-1	0	1	2	3	4
corr(PR_t, N_{t+i})	-0.10	-0.03	0.08	0.23	0.45	0.73	0.75	0.64	0.47

Table 7.6: Employment-Wage Correlations (Model CA-C0)

	-4	-3	-2	-1	0	1	2	3	4
corr(N_t, W_{t+i})	0.17	0.37	0.57	0.72	0.76	0.67	0.54	0.39	0.25

Table 7.7: Productivity-Employment Correlations (Model without adjustment costs)

	-4	-3	-2	-1	0	1	2	3	4
corr(PR_t, N_{t+i})	0.04	0.12	0.21	0.32	0.45	0.79	0.50	0.28	0.10

Table 7.8: Productivity-Employment Correlations (Model with separable adjustment costs)

	-4	-3	-2	-1	0	1	2	3	4
corr(PR_t, N_{t+i})	-0.01	0.09	0.19	0.30	0.44	0.78	0.53	0.30	0.12

employment-wage correlation is then maximum.

7.2.3 The Model with Interrelated Adjustment Costs and Contracts

According to the productivity-employment correlations profile, the model (*model CA-C4a*, see tables (7.9) to (7.11)) exhibits a leading productivity dynamics. This is obviously the effect of the adjustment costs previously discussed. However, we observe that the level of the correlations is lower than in the model without contracts (compare tables (7.5) and (7.10)). This is due to the contracts and will be explained later.

Lagged employment-wage correlations are negative, and leading ones are positive from the second period. The instantaneous employment-wage correlation is significantly negative with a value of -0.16. In other words, the wage short-run dynamics is lagged with respect to the employment one. Such an employment-wage correlation profile is quite different from the one given by the model without contract.

The wage contracts imply a predetermination of the nominal wages,

Table 7.9: Model CA-C4a

Series	Std	Std/Std$_Y$	corr(Y, X)
Y	1.46	1	1
C	1.04	0.71	0.53
I	4.31	2.95	0.92
N	0.98	0.67	0.70
PR	1.04	4.72	0.74
W	2.27	1.57	0.10

Table 7.10: Productivity-Employment Correlations (Model CA-C4a)

	-4	-3	-2	-1	0	1	2	3	4
corr(PR_t, N_{t+i})	0.05	0.04	0.00	-0.02	0.05	0.28	0.37	0.32	0.16

and thus their rigidity. The labor market does not clear automatically. Indeed, the price level adjusts at each time and clears the good market, but nothing ensures that the resulting real wage will equalize labor demand and supply. No mechanism allows an instantaneous adjustment of the real wage to its equilibrium level.

Indeed, starting from a stationary situation, suppose that a monetary shock occurs at time t, and that no other shock appears after period t. Nominal wages are predetermined until $t + j - 1$, and real wages will not clear the labor market at these periods. On the other hand, nominal wages negotiated at date t for $t + j$, knowing the monetary shock, will clear the labor market at this period (we assumed that no new shock occurs after t). Finally, when a shock disturbs the economy, monetary (and real) wages adjust to their equilibrium value with a lag equal to the contract length, which is expressed by the profile of the employment-wage correlations.

We now come back to the explanation of the level of the productivity-

Table 7.11: Employment-Wage Correlations (Model CA-C4a)

	-4	-3	-2	-1	0	1	2	3	4
corr(N_t, W_{t+i})	-0.15	-0.35	-0.49	-0.47	-0.16	0.18	0.41	0.45	0.31

employment correlations that is lower than in the model without contract. The inflationist effect of a monetary shock leads to a decrease in real wage. Consequently, employment increases whereas the mean productivity of labor decreases. This effect contributes to lower the productivity-employment correlations.

Thus, simulation results show how the model generates the productivity and wage short-run dynamics. In the contract model, these two dynamics appear to bo very different (compared to the walrasian model). Productivity leads employment whereas real wage lags. The walrasian model does not possess this feature : there, real wages and employment move together, without lead or lag. However, to have a best understanding of the mechanisms at work in the contract model, it is useful to study some impulse response functions.

Analysis of the Productivity and Wage Dissociation by Mean of the Impulse Response Functions: The analysis of the dissociation between wages and productivity is done by mean of the impulse response functions to the shocks disturbing this economy.

The contributions of the different shocks to the wages and productivity dissociation are not the same. The government spendings effect is very clear (see figures (7.1) and (7.3)). During the contract duration, real wages slightly decrease because of the effect of the government expenditures shock. However, at the time when the nominal wage negotiated when the shock occurred prevails, the real wage is suddenly lowered and progressively goes up. In response to this shock, the short-run behavior of productivity is quite different. It is stable during the contract length, then slightly decreases below its stationary value and comes back in the long-run.

The effect of the monetary shock on the respective dynamics of productivity and wages appears without ambiguity. The monetary shock has a very limited impact on productivity : it decreases a little before going back to the steady state. Wages response is different. The monetary shock induces an important increase in prices, and so a decrease in real wages since the nominal wages are predetermined. When the nominal wages set at the monetary shock date prevail, real wages rise suddenly and are above their steady state level.

These comments show that wage contracts have the effect of dissociating, in the short-run, the respective dynamics of productivity and wage. The contract length plays a major role in obtaining such a result. Indeed, beyond the contract duration, the variables tend to a common trajectory (corresponding to the walrasian model). Thus, it is essentially during the contracts duration that wages and productivity dynamics are separate.

It is also interesting to compare the profile of impulse responses obtained with and without wage contracts (figures (7.2) and (7.1)). After the contract length, the responses profile mainly correspond to the walrasian model. Thus, it is over this period that the dissociation induced by wage contracts is important. This is particularly clear for government expenditures and monetary shocks.

The Effect of a Variation of s: The previous results allow to see that the interrelated adjustment costs and the nominal wage contracts enable us to reverse the wage and productivity dynamics. We have already mentionned the sensitivity of the level of productivity-employment correlations to the wage contracts. Conversely, what is the sensitivity of the employment-wage correlations to an increase in the interrelated term s? In that case, the investment-hiring complementarity is increased. Thus, a simulation of the model was made with $s = -15$, the length of wage contracts remaining 4 periods (*model CA-C4b*, see tables (7.12) to (7.14)). The important point to note is that the increase in the interrelated adjustment term s tends to rise the level : *(i)* of productivity-employment correlations (tables (7.10) and (7.13)), and *(ii)* of employment-wage correlations (tables (7.11) and (7.14)).

Table 7.12: Model CA-C4b

Series	Std	Std/Std$_Y$	corr(Y,X)
Y	1.47	1	1
C	1.20	0.82	0.49
I	4.40	3.01	0.90
N	0.81	0.57	0.70
PR	1.05	0.72	0.84
W	2.51	1.73	0.15

Table 7.13: Productivity-Employment Correlations (Model CA-C4b)

	-4	-3	-2	-1	0	1	2	3	4
corr(PR_t, N_{t+i})	0.01	0.03	0.04	0.08	0.21	0.46	0.54	0.47	0.26

Table 7.14: Employment-Wage Correlations (Model CA-C4b)

	-4	-3	-2	-1	0	1	2	3	4
corr(N_t, W_{t+i})	-0.20	-0.31	-0.37	-0.30	0.003	0.28	0.46	0.47	0.33

The impact on employment-wage correlations is understood as follows. Under the nominal wage contracts assumption, the price effect of a monetary shock induces a decrease in real wage. An increase in employment then arises, and the instantaneous employment-wage correlation is negative. According to our previous discussion, an increase in s rises employment inertia. Thus, in models with contracts, when a monetary shock occurs, the increase in employment associated to the decrease in real wage is smaller when the investment-hiring complementarity is important. The effect of a monetary shock on employment-wage correlations is thus tempered. More precisely, employment adjustment costs limit the negativity of the employment-wage correlations induced by monetary shocks and contracts.

The increase in the productivity-employment correlations also comes from the greater employment inertia. We previously explained why contracts allow to appreciably reduce the productivity-employment correlations. Thus, an increase in the employment inertia leads to diminish the contract effect on the productivity-employment correlations. They then have a higher level.

Staggered Contracts: We consider here the case of staggered wage contracts (*model CA-CI4b*, see tables (7.15) to (7.17)). It is supposed that a quarter of the wages are formed in a competitive manner ($\theta_0 = 1/4$).

The leading dynamics of productivity reproduced by the model is as long as in the preceding models. The correlation reaches its maximum

Table 7.15: Model CA-CI4b

Series	Std	Std/Std$_Y$	corr(Y,X)
Y	1.42	1	1
C	1.12	0.80	0.47
I	4.34	3.07	0.91
N	0.63	0.44	0.75
PR	1.03	0.73	0.92
W	1.64	1.16	0.37

Table 7.16: Productivity-Employment Correlations (Model CA-CI4b)

	-4	-3	-2	-1	0	1	2	3	4
corr(PR_t, N_{t+i})	-0.003	0.05	0.12	0.24	0.43	0.72	0.74	0.57	0.28

value for two leads. However, an increase in the correlation levels can be noticed. Employment-wage correlations also have a profile similar to the one given by the previous models. However, they are higher.

What is the origin of this increase in the correlation levels? Recall that the definition of staggered wage contracts implies that a fraction of the wages are determined in a competitive way. Thus, the staggered wage contracts model is the mean of the walrasian and contract models. Then, the effects working in the staggered contracts model are also a mean of the effects at work in the two extreme models (*model CA-C0 and CA-C4b*). Consequently, the correlations in the model with staggered contracts are between the ones given respectively by the walrasian and the contract models.

Adjustment costs, wage contracts and the smoothness effect: In table (7.18), we give the volatility level of variables when the 4-period contract model does not include adjustment costs.

Table 7.17: Employment-Wage Correlations (Model CA-CI4b)

	-4	-3	-2	-1	0	1	2	3	4
corr(N_t, W_{t+i})	-0.19	-0.11	0.03	0.24	0.53	0.65	0.62	0.44	0.29

Table 7.18: 4-Period Contract Model

Series	Std	Std/Std$_Y$	corr(Y, X)
Y	2.83	1	1
C	1.23	0.43	0.39
I	8.92	3.15	0.97
N	4.08	1.23	0.92
PR	1.86	0.66	-0.49
W	1.83	0.65	-0.42

It is obvious that wage contracts increase volatility levels. For what reason? In the labor market, short-run adjustments are done by quantities exclusively, *i.e.* by employment changes. Consequently, in the labor market, employment is the only variable which "absorbs" the shocks, and an increase in the variability of employment (and other variables) arises. However, in our contract model including adjustment costs, there is a smoothness effect that comes surely from adjustment costs. We then obtain an output variability closer to the one given by standard RBC models.

7.3 Validation

In the previous section, we highlighted the mechanisms at work in the model. We know discuss the ability of our model with interrelated adjustment costs to replicate the data. We first discuss the American and French stylized facts. Secondly, we compare the model predictions with the stylized facts. To finish, we highlight the contribution of the monetary shocks for the short-run dynamics of real wage (*models CA-C4b/m and CA-CI4b/m*).

7.3.1 The Stylized Facts

The Traditional Stylized Facts

The moments concerning the stylized facts traditionally studied in the real business cycle literature for the French and the American economies are reported in tables (7.19) and (7.20).

The product and its two components, consumption and investment,

Table 7.19: The French Stylized Facts

Series	Std	Std/Std$_Y$	corr(Y, X)
Y	0.91	1	1
C	0.81	0.90	0.63
I	3.64	4.01	0.80
N	0.83	0.92	0.71
PR	0.65	0.72	0.45
W	0.72	0.79	0.02

Table 7.20: The American Stylized Facts

Series	Std	Std/Std$_Y$	corr(Y, X)
Y	1.90	1	1
C	1.23	0.64	0.66
I	8.85	4.60	0.81
N	1.49	0.78	0.84
PR	1.03	0.54	0.63
W	1.02	0.52	0.48

call for the following comments. The investment is the most volatile variable, and for the two countries, it is 4 to 5 times more variable than the output. Finally, the consumption is slightly less volatile than the output. However, one may notice that the relative volatility of consumption to output is greater in France than in the USA. Finally, we observe that output, investment, and consumption are significantly more volatile in the USA than in France.

The stylized facts bearing on the three labor market variables suggest the following comments. In level, employment is more variable in the USA than in France. Productivity and wage also have a greater volatility in the USA. However, this feature is less clear than for employment. In both countries, employment is more variable than productivity, and wage is slightly less variable than productivity.

The other stylized facts that are of direct interest bear on the labor market : correlations between productivity and employment on the one hand, and employment and wage on the other hand.

Productivity-Employment Correlations

Productivity-employment correlations for the USA and for France are reported in tables (7.21) and (7.22).

Table 7.21: Productivity-Employment Correlations (France)

	-4	-3	-2	-1	0	1	2	3	4
$\text{corr}(PR_t, N_{t+i})$	-0.34	-0.44	-0.45	-0.40	-0.30	-0.14	0.02	0.14	0.22

Table 7.22: Productivity-Employment Correlations (USA)

	-4	-3	-2	-1	0	1	2	3	4
$\text{corr}(PR_t, N_{t+i})$	-0.25	-0.16	-0.07	0.07	0.11	0.31	0.36	0.33	0.32

In France, the instantaneous productivity-employment correlation is significantly negative with a value of -0.30. Likewise, lagged productivity-employment correlations are negative. Leading productivity-employment correlations have an increasing profile. The one-period leading productivity-employment correlation is negative, the two-period one is close to 0, while the following are positive and increasing. Concerning the USA, productivity-employment correlations profile possesses characteristics similar to the French one. However, some slight differences exist. The instantaneous correlation is slightly positive, and the lagged ones are decreasing and slightly negative. The advanced correlations are firstly increasing, peaking for the two and three periods advanced correlations. In both countries, the time profiles of productivity-employment correlations have the following common properties : *(i)* the lagged correlations present a decreasing profile and are or tend to become negative, and *(ii)* the advanced correlations have an increasing profile and are or become positive. We notice that for the USA, the maximum productivity-employment correlation is the one advanced of two or three periods. In the French economy, it is the four (or five) period advanced correlation that is maximum. This is this last point which constitutes the main difference between France and the USA. In both countries, the general profile of productivity-employment correlations makes clear the lag of employment fluctuations with respect to productivity. In France, employment fluctuations follow productivity ones with a lag of four to five quarters. In the USA, this delay is only of two or three quarters. To sum up, productivity fluctuations constitute a leading indicator of employment fluctuations. The lags thus observed in employment dynamics reveal the inertia of this production factor — *i.e.* its flexibility is limited. This stylized fact, revealed by productivity-employment correlations, corresponds to a *productivity cycle*.

Employment-Wage Correlations

French and U.S. employment-wage correlations are reported in tables (7.23) and (7.24).

Table 7.23: Employment-Wage Correlations (France)

	-4	-3	-2	-1	0	1	2	3	4
corr(N_t, W_{t+i})	-0.43	-0.42	-0.37	-0.30	-0.19	-0.07	0.05	0.20	0.37

Table 7.24: Employment-Wage Correlations (USA)

	-4	-3	-2	-1	0	1	2	3	4
corr(N_t, W_{t+i})	-0.21	-0.06	0.08	0.21	0.19	0.34	0.36	0.32	0.20

From these tables, one may notice that employment-wage correlations have the same profile in the French and American economies. This one is regularly increasing with negative lagged correlations and positive leading correlations. Some differences must however be underlined. The instantaneous employment-wage correlation is slightly negative in France (-0.19) whereas it is slightly positive in the USA. In each country, wages constitute a lagged indicator of employment. Correlations remain negative longer in France than in the USA. They indicate that the lag in wage fluctuations with respect to employment is greater in France than in the USA.

7.3.2 Does the Model Match the Data?

The USA

Here, we compare the simulation results of *model CA-C4b* to the stylized facts, this one performing better than the other models.

Within *model CA-C4b* (see tables (7.12) to (7.14)), the product variability is equal to 1.47. Compared to the stylized facts, this value is more realistic than the one given by a contract model which does not include adjustment costs (see table (7.18) and observe the excessive volatility levels, see also Cho and Cooley [1990]). Finally, by their smoothness effect, adjustment costs allow to improve the capacity of contract models to reproduce the output volatility. A similar observation holds for employment volatility. To begin, observe that this one (0.57) is lower than the empirical one (0.72). However, the smoothness effect of the adjustment costs on the employment variability is less important than in *model CA-C0*, which is due to the *contract effect*, previously discussed, on the volatility level of the variables.

The relative variability of consumption is close to its empirical value. Employment and productivity relative volatilities are not replicated. Compared to the employment, the productivity appears too volatile. Likewise, wage variability is excessive.

The model replicates in a satisfactory way the short-run dynamics of productivity and real wage. The model including both interrelated adjustment costs and nominal wage contracts performs better than the other models (*Cf.* section 7.2). Simulation results of *model CA-C0* (table 7.5) show that interrelated adjustment costs induce a labor productivity cycle. However, the level of the correlations is too high. According to our analysis of the model mechanisms, wage contracts allow to lower the level of the productivity-employment correlations. Finally, the model with contracts and interrelated adjustment costs performs better than the model without contract, in reproducing the productivity cycle.

The model also reproduces the short-run dynamics of real-wage. Wage contracts allow to induce a lagged dynamics of real wage with respect of employment. Moreover, the predictions of the model for the employment-wage correlations are improved by the adjustment costs. To highlight this point, compare the results obtained by *model CA-*

C4a ($s = -7.5$) and *CA-C4b* ($s = -15$) with the stylized facts. The correlation levels given by *model CA-C4b* is higher than with *model CA-C4a* and closer to the stylized facts (see section 7.2 for a justification). Finally, an increase in the investment-hiring complementarity, and therefore in the employment inertia, allows to improve the employment-wage correlations reproduced by the model.

To sum up, the predictions of the model including interrelated adjustment costs and contracts are better than the ones of models that contain only one of these assumptions. As a whole, this is true for the volatility level of some important variables (output and employment) of the model, the productivity cycle and the short-run dynamics of real wage.

- On the one hand, the smoothness effect of adjustment costs on employment volatility is less important than in *model CA-C0*, which is due to the *contract effect* on the variability level of the variables. On the other hand, the adjustment costs leads to volatility level more realistic than the ones usually obtained in contract models (see Cho and Cooley [1990] and Fairise [1994]).

- The interrelated adjustment costs allow to replicate the productivity cycle whereas the nominal wage contracts imply a lagged adjustment of the real wage over the cycle. Moreover, each of these two assumptions helps to improve the model predictions for the other stylized facts.

France

Concerning the model simulated on the French economy, the contract length is of 4 periods and the value retained for s is -25 (see tables (7.25) to (7.27)).

The variability of output, equal to 1.18, is a little greater than the empirical value of 0.91. The relative volatility of consumption, with a value of 0.90, is also close to the stylized facts. As for labor market, employment is too smooth, its variability representing only 0.44 times the output one, and being below the productivity one. Moreover, one may notice that wage volatility is excessive, since it reaches 2.58 times the output one.

Table 7.25: Model CA-C4b (France)

Series	Std	Std/Std$_Y$	corr(Y,X)
Y	1.18	1	1
C	1.06	0.90	0.37
I	4.45	3.79	0.86
N	0.52	0.44	0.57
PR	0.97	0.83	0.90
W	3.01	2.58	0.48

Table 7.26: Productivity-Employment Correlations (Model CA-C4b)

	-4	-3	-2	-1	0	1	2	3	4
corr(PR_t, N_{t+i})	-0.07	-0.06	-0.03	0.04	0.17	0.38	0.46	0.43	0.30

Table 7.27: Employment-Wage Correlations (Model CA-C4b)

	-4	-3	-2	-1	0	1	2	3	4
corr(N_t, W_{t+i})	-0.24	-0.40	0.50	-0.47	-0.19	0.13	0.38	0.46	0.35

Productivity-employment correlations exhibit a productivity cycle. The correlation peaks at two leads, but its size is otherwise comparable to the one and three period advanced correlations. The productivity cycle reproduced by the model has therefore a length comparable to the empirical cycle. However, correlation levels are a little too high.

Employment-wage correlations have an interesting profile. Lagged correlations are negative, and advanced correlations become positive. The instantaneous correlation, significantly negative, corresponds to the empirical value. To sum up, the employment-wage correlations profile reproduced by the model mimics quite well the stylized facts.

It appears that the model matches very badly the French economy. For instance, the employment variability, equal to 0.44, is excessively low. Indeed, to reproduce a productivity cycle having the good length, we impose for s a value of -25. The employment inertia is then enough to replicate the productivity cycle. However, such a value for s alters the ability of the model to reproduce the other stylized facts. The smoothness effect is excessive.

Having in mind our previous discussion about the role of wage contracts on the productivity-employment correlations, an increase in the contract length should allow to reduce their level. It would also allow to increase the employment volatility. As a whole, increasing the contract length should lead to a magnification of the *contract effect* previously analyzed. Finally, the idea of increasing the contract length for the French economy is quite natural. Indeed, it is currently admitted that wage inertia is stronger in France than in the USA. To conclude, we thus analyze the simulation results of the model with 8 periods contracts (*model CA-C8*, tables (7.28) to (7.30)).

Table 7.28: Model CA-C8 (France)

Series	Std	Std/Std$_Y$	corr(Y,X)
Y	1.36	1	1
C	1.24	0.92	0.35
I	5.18	3.83	0.85
N	1.30	0.97	0.68
PR	1.05	0.79	0.43
W	3.79	2.85	-0.22

Table 7.29: Productivity-Employment Correlations (Model CA-C8)

	-4	-3	-2	-1	0	1	2	3	4
corr(PR_t, N_{t+i})	-0.11	-0.22	-0.31	-0.36	-0.35	-0.22	-0.10	0.01	0.10

Table 7.30: Employment-Wage Correlations (Model CA-C8)

	-4	-3	-2	-1	0	1	2	3	4
corr(N_t, W_{t+i})	-0.61	-0.72	-0.76	-0.69	-0.47	-0.19	0.08	0.31	0.49

Increasing contract length allows to improve the model performances with respect to the employment level and the productivity cycle. *Model CA-C8* reproduces some levels of employment and productivity variability that are very satisfactory. As a whole, the levels of the productivity-employment correlations are lower and thus more satisfactory than with *model CA-C4b*. Finally, we will mention a limit of this exercise. If the model performs better with respect to the employment volatility and the productivity cycle, it reproduces some employment-wage correlation that are too negative. The wage volatility is also excessive. However, the model with 8-period contracts seems to work better than the 4-period one. The idea that contract length are longer in France than in the USA is thus supported by our results.

7.3.3 Nominal Shocks and Short-Run Dynamics of Real Wages

In this sub-section, we also expose the simulation results of the model without monetary shocks, which allows us to underline the contribution of the nominal shocks to the short-run dynamics of the real wage. The previous comments suggested the importance of the nominal shocks to obtain our results. Thus, the *models CA-C4b/m* was simulated omitting monetary shocks[12]. The results are reported in tables (7.31) to (7.33). The productivity-employment and the productivity-wages correlations

[12]CA-C4b/m : 4-period contracts and adjustment costs and without monetary shock.

clearly show that when the model does not contain monetary shocks, its predictions are not in accordance with the stylized facts, especially concerning the employment-wages correlations. In our model with nominal wage contracts, the contribution of monetary shocks to the short-run dynamics of the real wages is thus determining.

Table 7.31: Model CA-C4b/m

Series	Std	Std/Std$_Y$	corr(Y, X)
Y	1.41	1	1
C	1.03	0.73	0.51
I	4.23	3.00	0.92
N	0.61	0.43	0.75
PR	1.03	0.73	0.92
W	1.12	0.80	0.55

The hypothesis of nominal wage contracts is essential in the explanation of the short-run dynamics of wages. This assumption of nominal wage contracts only has an effect on the short-run real wages dynamics in so far as the economy is disturbed by monetary shocks. If the money stock increases at a deterministic rate $\overline{\gamma}$, the profile of employment-wage correlations is only slightly influenced by contracts. In fact, monetary shocks and contracts are inseparable :

1. Contracts may constitute a privileged transmission channel of monetary disturbances. Contracts only have a marked effect on the variables dynamics if the economy is affected by monetary shocks.

2. The monetary shocks have a limited impact if there does not exist some support to their propagation. Thus, the adjustment costs model without wage contracts gives similar results to the one simulated by Fairise [1994] that does not include nominal

Table 7.32: Productivity-Employment Correlations (Model CA-C4b/m)

	-4	-3	-2	-1	0	1	2	3	4
corr(PR_t, N_{t+i})	-0.04	0.01	0.09	0.23	0.44	0.75	0.79	0.64	0.33

Table 7.33: Employment-Wage Correlations (Model CA-C4b/m)

	-4	-3	-2	-1	0	1	2	3	4
corr(N_t, W_{t+i})	-0.20	-0.01	0.23	0.52	0.81	0.89	0.79	0.53	0.31

wage contracts. The impact of monetary shocks is very low if no mechanism ensures their transmission.

To show that the nominal shocks really explain the short-run wages dynamics, the employment, the productivity and the wage variances are decomposed . The decomposition variance exercise bears on the *model CA-C4b*. The results are reported in table (7.34).

Table 7.34: Contribution of Monetary Shocks (in %)

Periods	N	P	W
1	00.00	0.00	99.41
2	55.80	0.62	98.41
3	50.84	1.42	96.86
4	44.34	1.94	82.73
5	39.88	1.90	74.24
6	36.29	1.73	67.78
7	33.38	1.55	62.63
8	31.03	1.39	58.41
12	25.37	1.00	46.96
20	21.55	0.72	35.80

At the contracts horizon, namely the four initial periods, the monetary shock explains the totality of wages variance. Twenty periods after the shock, this one explains yet the third of the variance of wages. Beyond the contract length, the monetary shock still has a non negligible effect on wages. This shows that the propagation mechanism induced by the nominal wage contracts exceeds the simple automatic effect existing during the contract length. It remains significantly longer than the contract length.

Concerning the productivity, the situation is quite different. The monetary shock explains a very small share of its total variance. During the contract length, the monetary shock explains almost 50% of the total variance of employment.

The results of the variance decomposition exercise confirm the intuition previously developed on the basis of simulation results and impulse response functions analysis. The nominal shocks explain the main part of real wages short run dynamics.

Conclusion

The aim of this chapter was to show that wage rigidities formalized by wage contracts contributes to the explanation of the short run dynamics of wages relatively to employment. More precisely, our objective was to built a model able to explain simultaneously the productivity and wage dynamics with respect to employment. The basic framework was an interrelated adjustment costs model. Moveover, it was assumed that wages were not determined in a competitive market, but by mean of nominal wage contracts. This idea relates to the keynesian assumption of a nominal wage rigidity.

The simulation of the models provides very promising results and stresses the relevance of the wage contracts assumption. The two main objectives initially fixed are reached, and the model reproduces simultaneously *(i)* the labor productivity cycle, and *(ii)* the employment-wage correlations profile. Moreover, the wage contracts hypothesis proposes an explanation of employment fluctuations which is an alternative to intertemporal substitution, and to its last development — *e.g.* the indivisible labor hypothesis of Hansen [1985]. Employment fluctuations do not reflect the optimal response of labor suppliers to shocks, but are uniquely determined by the firm labor demand behavior. Although there exists adjustment costs, the model reproduces quite well the employment variability. It also appears that the wage contracts hypothesis "resists" as well to adjustment costs as the indivisible labor of Hansen.

Our model also suggests that nominal shocks play an important role in the explanation of the short run dynamics of the real wages. In case of inflationist pressures, nominal wages adjust with lags and real wages temporarily diminishes, whereas employment increases (also temporarily).

Finally, our model seems more relevant in the American case than in the French case. For the USA, the model with interrelated adjustment costs and 4-period nominal wage contracts reproduces the productivity cycle and the short-run dynamics of wages simultaneously. The relative employment volatility is however slightly too high now. Likewise, the output variability predicted by the model is smaller than the empirical one. For the French economy, the model has difficulties to reproduce productivity-employment and employment-wages correlations. When the contracts duration is 4 periods, the productivity cycle is well reproduced, but the employment-wage correlations profile is not satisfactory. Eight-period contracts improve the explanation of the short run dynamics of wages, but the productivity-employment correlations do not coincide with empirical evidence. As a whole, we will retain that the short-run dynamics of wages is consistent with wage contracts that are longer in France than in the USA.

Figure 7.1: Employment, Productivity and Wage — Model CA-C4

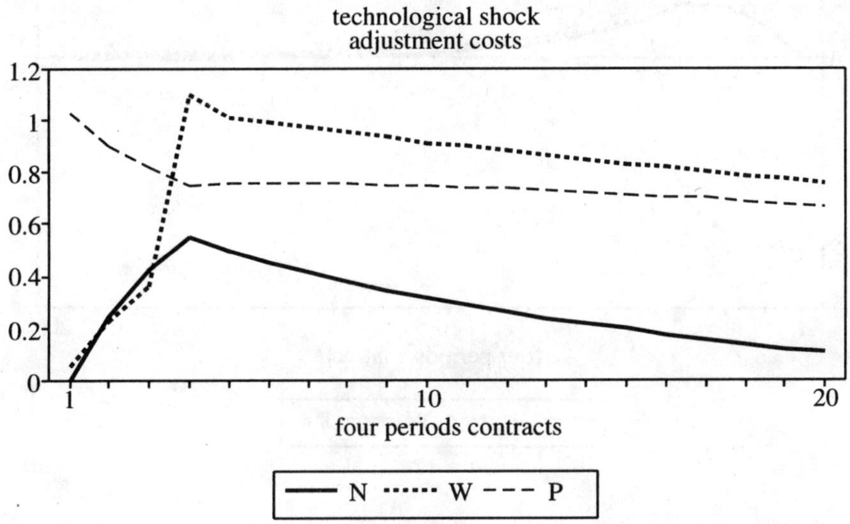

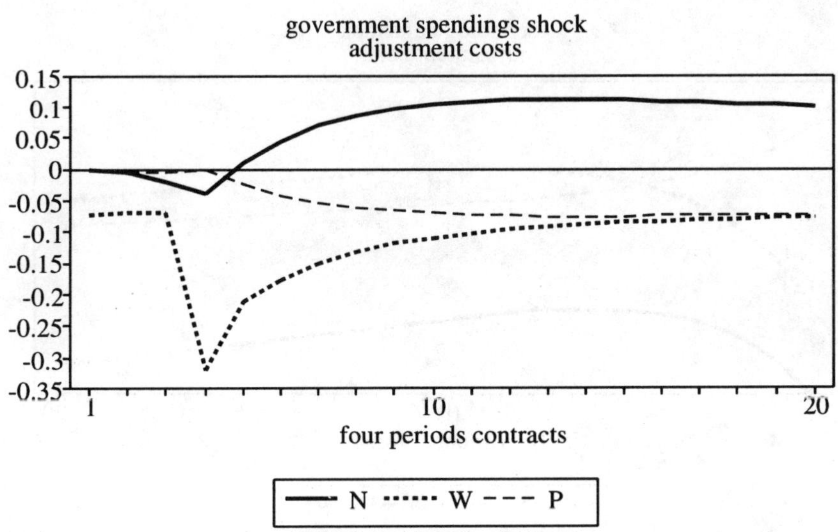

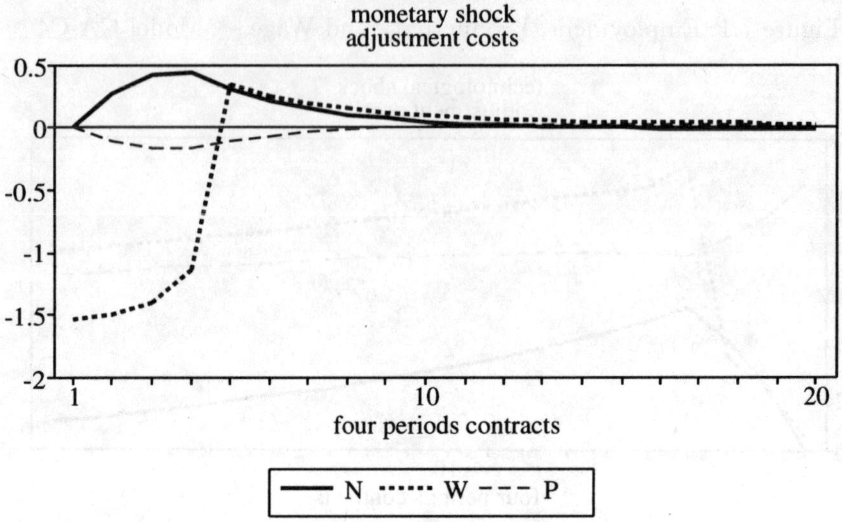

Figure 7.2: Employment, Productivity and Wage — Model CA-C0

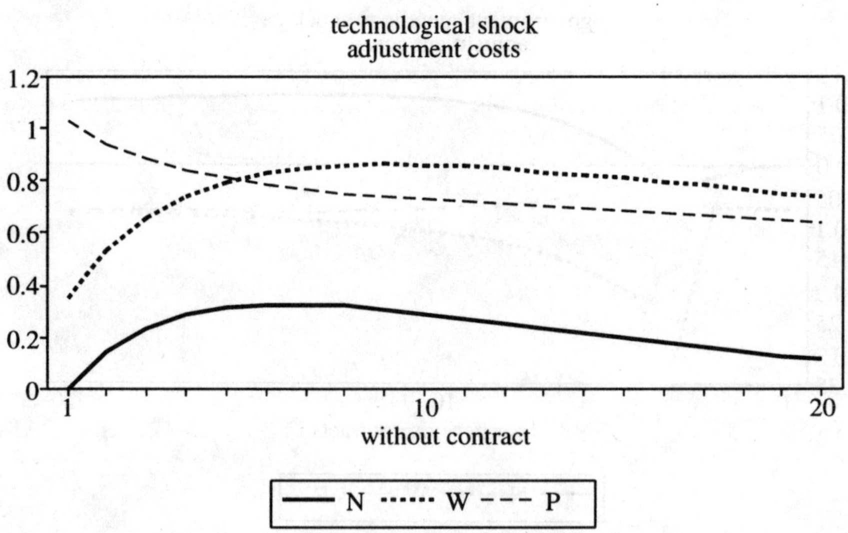

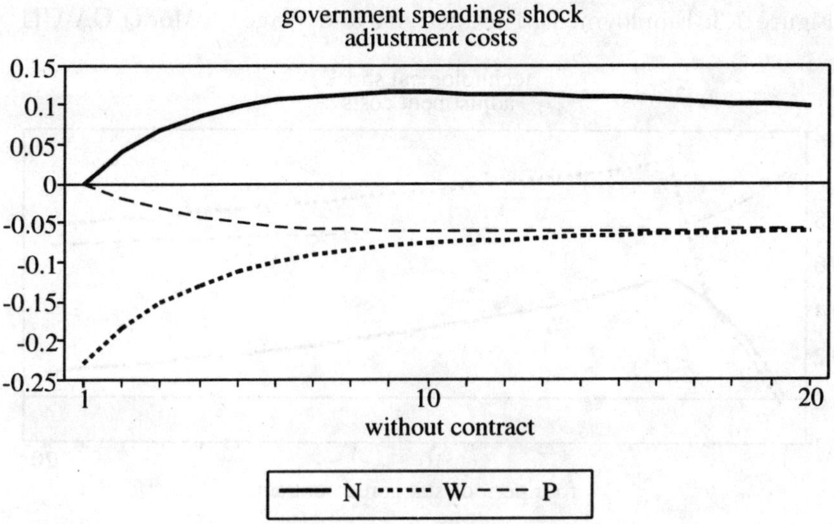
government spendings shock
adjustment costs
0.15
0.1
0.05
0
-0.05
-0.1
-0.15
-0.2
-0.25
1
10
20
without contract
N
W
P

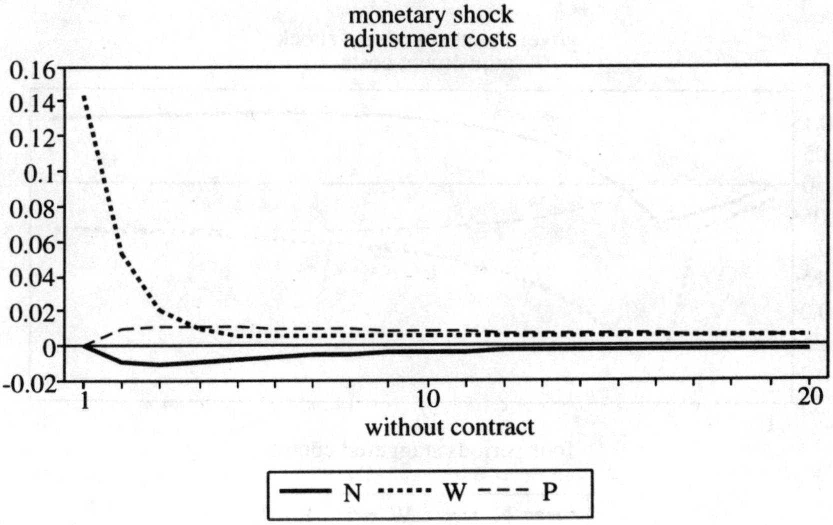
monetary shock
adjustment costs
0.16
0.14
0.12
0.1
0.08
0.06
0.04
0.02
0
-0.02
1
10
20
without contract
N
W
P

Figure 7.3: Employment, Productivity and Wage — Model CA-CI4

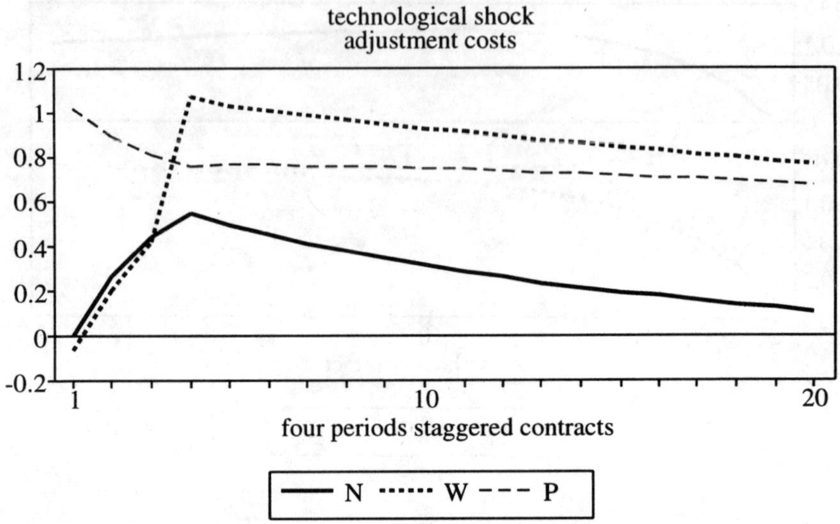

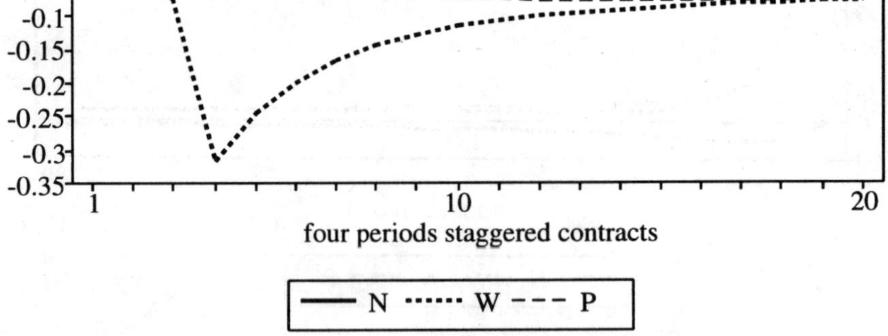

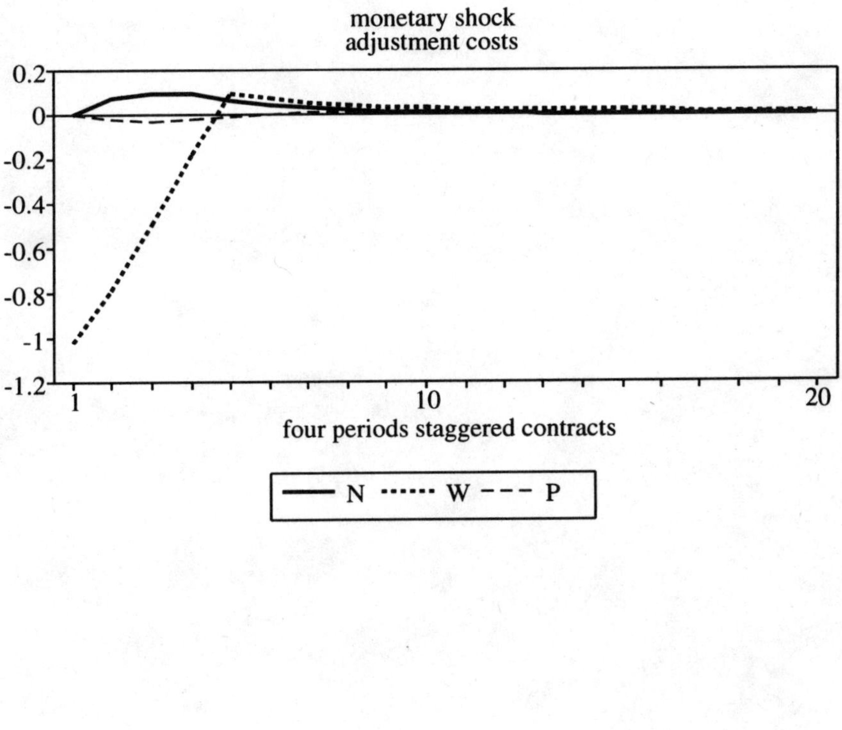
monetary shock
adjustment costs
0.2
0
-0.2
-0.4
-0.6
-0.8
-1
-1.2
1
10
20
four periods staggered contracts
N
W
P

Bibliography

G. Akerlof, A. Rose and J. Yellen. Job Switching and Job Satisfaction in the U.S. Labor Market. *Brooking Papers on Economic Activity*, 2:495–594, 1988.

J.P. Benassy. *Money and Wage Contracts in an Optimizing Model of the Business Cycle.* Working paper 9325, CEPREMAP, 1993.

S. Bentolila and G. Bertola. Firing Costs and Labor Demand : How Bad is Eurosclerosis? *Review of Economic Studies*, 57:381–402, 1990.

C. Burnside, M. Eichenbaum and S. Rebelo. *Labor Hoarding and the Business Cycle.* Working Paper 3556, NBER, December 1990.

J.O. Cho and T. Cooley. *The Business Cycle with Nominal Contracts.* Mimeo 260, University of Rochester, 1990.

J.O. Cho and L. Phaneuf. *A Business Cycle Model with Nominal Wage Contracts and Government.* Working paper, CREFE-RCEEF, 1993.

J.O. Cho. *Money, Nominal Contracts, and the Business Cycle: I. One-Period Contract Case.* Working paper, Queen's University, May 1990.

T. Cooley and G. Hansen. The Inflation Tax in a Real Business Cycle model. *American Economic Review*, 79(4):733–748, September 1989.

J. Dunlop. The Movement of Real Wage and Money Wage Rates. *Economic Journal*, 48:413–434, September 1939.

X. Fairise. *La dynamique de l'emploi et des salaires : un approfondissement de la théorie des cycles réels.* Thèse de doctorat, Université de Paris I, 1994.

S Fischer. Long-Term Contracts, Rational Expectations and the Optimal Money Supply Rule. *Journal of Political Economy*, 85:191–205, 1977.

M. Friedman. The Role of Monetary Policy. *American Economic Review*, 58(1):1–17, 1968.

M. Galeotti and F. Schiantarelli. Generalized Q Models for Investment. *Review of Economics and Statistics*, LXXIII(3):383–392, August 1991.

J. Gray. On Indexation and Contract Length. *Journal of Political Economy*, 86:1–18, 1978.

J.O. Hairault. *L'influence de la monnaie dans les fluctuations économiques : évaluation empirique et fondements théoriques.* Thèse de doctorat, Université de Paris I, 1992.

G. Hansen. Indivisible Labor and the Business Cycles. *Journal of Monetary Economics*, 16(3):309–327, November 1985.

J. Keynes. Relative Movements of Real Wage and Output. *Economic Journal*, 34–51, March 1939.

R. King, C. Plosser and S. Rebelo. Production, Growth and Business Cycles I. *Journal of Monetary Economics*, 21(2/3):196–232, March-May 1988.

R. King. *Money and Business Cycles.* Working paper, University of Rochester, 1990.

F. Kydland and E. Prescott. Time to Build and Aggregate Fluctuations. *Econometrica*, 50(6):1345–1370, November 1982.

J.P. Laffargue and P. Malgrange. *Une maquette trimestrielle de l'économie française avec anticipations rationnelles et concurrence monopolistique.* Working paper , CEPREMAP, 1991.

J. Long and C. Plosser. Real Business Rycle. *Journal of Political Economy*, 91(1):39–69, February 1983.

R. Lucas. Adjusment Costs and the Theory of Supply. *Journal of Political Economy*, 75:321–334, August 1967.

R. Lucas. Expectations and the Neutrality of Money. *Journal of Economic Theory*, 4(2):103–124, April 1972.

E. Phelps. Phillips Curves, Expectations of Inflation, and Optimal Unemployment over Time. *Economica*, 34(135):254–281, 1967.

A.W. Phillips. The Relation between Unemployment and the Rate of Change of Money Wage Rates in the United Kingdom. *Economica*, 25(100):283–299, 1958.

F. Portier. *Les rigidités de prix dans les fluctuations économiques.* Thèse de doctorat, Université de Paris I, 1992.

L. Tarshis. Change in Real and Money Wage. *Economic Journal*, March 1939.

J. Taylor. Aggregate Dynamics and Staggered Contacts. *The Journal of Political Economy*, 88:1–23, 1980.

Chapter 8

Unemployment and Business Cycle : a General Equilibrium Matching Model

François Langot

Abstract

A stochastic intertemporal general equilibrium model is developed where non-walrasian feature allows us to generate permanent unemployment. An uncoordinated search process induces some endogenous turn-over cost. The total rent of a match is shared according to the Nash solution to a bargaining problem. The model is simulated with two exogenous shocks: technological shocks and mismatch shocks. The results clearly show that this propagation mechanism allows us to reproduce some specific labor market stylized facts. Moreover, we show that the main source of labor market dynamics is the aggregate activity disturbances, here the technological shocks.

Introduction

The aim of this chapter is to extend the standard Real Business Cycle methodology to non-walrasian features on labor market. Since Kydland and Prescott's [1982] contribution, the main criticism formulated against these models has to do with their incapability to reproduce the labor market stylized facts. Many authors improve the empirical performances of the walrasian model introducing some specific assumptions on labor supply or labor demand[1]. Moreover, this literature is unable to take into account the unemployment phenomenon, which is an essential problem for the U.S. and more particularly for the French economy where, since the middle of the seventies, the labor market is clearly marked by a high and persistent level of unemployment.

Indeed, it seems to be reasonable to assume that the labor supply is rationed at the equilibrium and hence, to abandon the assumption that labor fluctuations are caused exclusively by the intertemporal substitution mechanism suggested by Lucas and Rapping [1969].

Then, it seems to be worth incorporating non-walrasian considerations on labor market. For this purpose, using the microeconomic analysis of matching models proposed in Pissarides [1990], we develop a stochastic optimization framework where the trade in the labor market is a costly and uncoordinated process. Diamond [1984] or Pissarides [1986] and [1987] have shown that search equilibrium can explain theoretically the persistence and variability of unemployment, and the cyclical behavior of job availability. Moreover, these studies suggested that this representation of the labor market seems to constitute a solution to solve the puzzle of the aggregate wage-employment fluctuations, contrary to the intertemporal labor substitution[2]. In the matching model, a specification of the wage-setting rule is required to close the model. Indeed, the time lags and the transaction costs characterizing the meeting and trade process induce specific quasi-rents. Then, employees have a bargaining power whenever replacing them is costly, the "Insider-Outsider" model provides a rational for a wage in excess of the value of leisure. In order to model this wage determination in bilateral monopoly, we assume that the total rent of a match is shared according to the Nash solution to a bargaining problem. With this wage-setting rule, the equilibrium unemployment exceeds the frictional unemployment, because the wage exceeds that required to compensate the worker for search[3].

[1]For the labour market dynamics, see chapter 2 for different kind of extension of the standard *RBC* model.

[2]See chapter 7 for an alternative approach of the wage setting rule.

[3]This non-walrasian wage-setting rule gives a theoretical support to the endogeneity of the Solow residual. Indeed, the wage is not equal to the marginal productivity of labour and we assume that employees and firms bargain on the efficiency of labour, which can be introduced as hour measurement errors. Then, the Solow

Some New-Keynesian features on labor market are introduced and tested following the *RBC* methodology by Danthine and Donaldson [1990], Mortensen [1990] or Andolfatto [1991][4]. Danthine and Donaldson [1990] construct a stochastic general equilibrium model that incorporates the efficiency wage-setting rule and conjecture that future research, which would fully endogenize the shirking motivation, could solve the wage-employment variability puzzle. Assuming the existence of coordination failure on the labor market, Mortensen [1990] and Andolfatto [1991] develop search equilibrium models and show that such models match the observed data on labor market much better than the standard *RBC* models. However, these two models ignore physical capital inputs and thus the effect of the capital-employment substitution or the endogeneity of the interest rate[5]. Then the natural extension of these models, proposed in this paper, is to "*integrate the search equilibrium description of the labor market into a richer and more realistic model of business fluctuations*" (Mortensen [1990], p5).

In the spirit of the *RBC* literature, the man aim of this chapter is to provide a test of ability of the matching models to explain the observed business cycle stylized facts and more specifically the labor market dynamics. To this end, we calibrate and simulate a stochastic dynamic general equilibrium model in order to test, on U.S. and French data, if the cyclical properties of artificial data generated by the model match the set of cyclical indicators constituted of second order moments[6]. We assume that two exogenous shocks can disturb the economy: aggregate activity shocks, here technological shocks, and a specific labor market shock, interpreted as a mismatch shocks[7]. The quantitative analysis of the model allow us to answer at the following question:

residual fluctuations over-estimate the fluctuations of the technological shock. See Summers [1986] or Mankiw [1989] or chapter 2 for more details about this criticism. See Hall [1989] or Langot [1991] for statistical evidences.

[4]See Rotemberg and Woodford [1989] or chapter for business cycle models with New-Keynesian features on good market.

[5]Indeed, Hénin and Jobert [1993]'s empirical studies show that the physical investment innovation have the main contribution in the decomposition of variance in unemployment forecasting error, particularly on U.S. data.

[6]In order to compare easily our results with the literature, all the second moments are computed on the cyclical component of the data extracted by the Hodrick and Prescott filter.

[7]This disturbance affecting of the matching function is suggested by the empirical studies by Layard, Nickell and Jackman [1991].

Are the sources of the unemployment fluctuations due to structural perturbation on the labor market or to aggregate activity shocks within the business cycle?

The results of the different experiments clearly show that this general equilibrium matching model can reproduce a set of U.S. and French labor market stylized facts without altering the cyclical properties on the other markets, when the model is simulated with only aggregate activity shocks. Moreover, we can solve some labor market puzzles, that walrasian models cannot explain :

- volatility of employment exceeds that of labor productivity,
- labor productivity is an leading indicator of cyclical employment fluctuations. This is what is called the labor productivity cycle.
- the lagged, instantaneous and leading correlations between vacancies and unemployment given by the dynamics around the Beveridge curve,
- the instantaneous correlation between employment and wage, which refers to the Dunlop [1938] and Tarshis [1939] controversy[8].

Moreover, we show that the introduction of specific labor market shocks alter the ability to explain the stylized facts: during the U.S. and French business cycle, unemployment fluctuations seem to be driven by the aggregate activity shocks. These results confirm the previous empirical studies by Blanchard and Diamond [1989] and Jacques and Langot [1993].

In a first section, the market structure, households and firms program are described. The second section is devoted to the computation of the rational expectation general equilibrium. The qualitative analysis and the simulation results for the U.S. and the French economies are presented respectively in the third and fourth section. Concluding remarks are reported in the last section.

[8]See chapter 7 for more details on this point and for an other modelization of the labour market.

8.1 The Model

In order to compute a rational expectation general equilibrium where the wage w and the effort at work l is the output of a bargaining process between a firm and a worker, we must first characterize how firms and households determine their optimal choices for all $\{w_t\}_{t=0}^{\infty}$ and $\{l_t\}_{t=0}^{\infty}$ paths. Given these optimality conditions, we assume that wage and effort are bargained between firms and workers at each period. Then, after a decision of the allocative process on the labor market, the behavior of the individual agents are described. Symmetrically, for the unemployed workers, we assume that search intensity (e_t) is chosen before the optimal choices of the individuals on the good market.

8.1.1 The Labor Market

Following Holt and David [1966], Mortensen [1982] or Pissarides [1990], we assume that trade is a costly and uncoordinated economic activity on the labor market. Hence, without a walrasian labor market structure, the allocation of resource is lead by a search process: we assume that there exists a well-behaved *matching function* linking the number of aggregate hirings H_t with aggregate search behavior of the agents:

$$H_t = X_t h(V_t, e_t U_t) = X_t V_t^{\gamma} (e_t U_t)^{1-\gamma}$$

where, the size of the population being normalized to unity:

- V_t is the vacancy rate reflecting the recruiting effort of the firms,
- $e_t U_t$ is the unemployed workers' aggregate search effort with $U_t = 1 - N_t$ denoting the unemployment rate and e_t denoting the average intensity of unemployed search activity.

The function $h(.,.)$ is assumed to have the standard properties of any neoclassical production function, including constant returns to scale. This assumption is consistent with the estimations of Pissarides [1986] on U.K. data and Blanchard and Diamond [1989] on U.S. data.

Moreover, we assume that the matching function can be affected by a stochastic shock X_t. This shock can be interpreted as a mismatch disturbance. Indeed, the simultaneity of jobs creation and destruction process at a disaggregated level can have a negative impact at the macroeconomic level when the labor input is not perfectly mobile across sectors. The famous empirical study of Lilien [1982] shows the importance of this allocative shock in the unemployment dynamics. Nevertheless, after the Abraham and Katz [1986]'s criticism of this paper, it seems to be interesting to evaluate the relative importance of these shocks. Following Layard, Nickell and Jackman [1991], this allocative shock is referred as a *mismatch* shock. X_t follows the stationary stochastic process:

$$\log(X_{t+1}) = \rho_x \log(X_t) + (1-\rho_x)\log(X) + \epsilon_{xt} \tag{8.1}$$

where $\log(X)$ is the unconditional mean of the process, $|\rho_x| < 1$ and ϵ_{xt} denotes the innovation of the process having standard deviation σ_x.

Implicitly, this function entails a specialization in either trade or production. A firm can have both filled and unfilled jobs, but only the unfilled ones are engaged in the trade process. Symmetrically, only unemployed workers look for jobs.

At each time, vacant jobs and unemployed workers match and move from trade to production. In equilibrium, unemployment persists because at each time some existing jobs disappear, resulting in a flow of new unemployment.

In matching models, the search process implies that from any agent's point of view, moving from vacancy to occupancy or from unemployment to employment, is an uncertain event. The numbers of job vacancies and unemployed workers matched at time t are randomly selected from the sets V_t and U_t. The rate at which job vacancies are filled is given by:

$$q(\theta_t, X_t) = \frac{H_t}{V_t} = X_t h\left(1, \frac{e_t U_t}{V_t}\right) = X_t h\left(1, \theta_t^{-1}\right)$$

where $\theta_t = \frac{V_t}{e_t U_t}$ denotes the *job availability* or the *tightness* of the labor market. Then, the mean vacancy duration of job is $1/q(\theta_t, X_t)$. The transition rate at which unemployed workers i move to employment is $p_{i,t} = e_{i,t}\frac{H_t}{e_t U_t}$, where $e_{i,t}$ is the individual search effort. Given the homogeneity of the matching function, we define the aggregate transition rate to employment as:

$$p(\theta_t, X_t) = \frac{H_t}{U_t} = e_t X_t h\left(\frac{V_t}{e_t U_t}, 1\right) = e_t X_t h(\theta_t, 1) = \theta_t q(\theta_t, X_t)$$

Then, the individual probability to become employed is $p_{i,t} = e_{i,t}\, p(\theta_t, X_t)$. The mean duration of unemployment is $1/p(\theta_t, X_t)$.

With these assumptions about trade in labor market, one shows that the transition rates from vacancy to occupancy $q(\theta_t, X_t)$, and from unemployment to employment $p(\theta_t, X_t)$, depend on the relative number of traders. There are two types of trade externalities.

- First, if V_t increases, θ_t increases, the probability of rationing firms increases. Symmetrically, if $e_t U_t$ increases, θ_t decreases, the probability of rationing unemployed workers increases. These trade externalities are *congestion* externalities.
- Second, if $e_t U_t$ increases, θ_t decreases, the probability of rationing firms decreases. Symmetrically, if V_t increases, θ_t increases, the probability of rationing unemployed workers decreases: there are some *positive trade externality* between traders[9].

At each time t, the number of new matches is determined by the hirings H_t, and the number of quits by the product of the quit rate with the number of current employed workers sN_t.

Then, the employment evolves according to the following process:

$$\begin{aligned} N_{j,t+1} &= (1-s)N_t + q(\theta_t, X_t)V_{j,t} \\ N_{i,t+1} &= (1-s)N_t + e_{i,t}p(\theta_t, X_t)(1-N_t) \end{aligned} \tag{8.2}$$

The only variables an individual controls is the vacancies rate $V_{j,t}$ in a firm j or the intensity $e_{i,t}$ of the search for a unemployed worker i. The unemployment rate U_t is an adjustment variable.

8.1.2 The Firm

Following Pissarides [1986] and [1990], we model the firm as a sufficiently large establishment where the production process requires many workers and the hiring process many job vacancies[10]. Each firm j has access to a constant returns to scale production function to produce an homogeneous good:

[9]Unemployed workers find jobs more easily when the vacancies level is high compared with the workers searching intensity; similarly, the greater is the workers searching intensity, the easier it is for a firm to fill up a vacancy.

[10]This assumption is made by Mortensen [1990]. Andolfatto [1991] assumes that a firm has only one employed worker or one vacancy, following the modeling of the markets proposed in Pissarides [1990]'s first chapter.

$$Y_{j,t} = A_t F(K_{j,t}, N_{j,t} l_t) = A_t K_{j,t}^{\alpha} (N_{j,t} l_t)^{1-\alpha} \tag{8.3}$$

where A_t, $K_{j,t}$, $N_{j,t}$ and l_t denote respectively the level of technology, physical capital, employment stocks and the level effort used by firm j to produce $Y_{j,t}$. A_t follows the stationary stochastic process:

$$\log(A_{t+1}) = \rho_a \log(A_t) + (1 - \rho_a) \log(A) + \epsilon_{at} \tag{8.4}$$

where $\log(A)$ is the unconditional mean of the process, $|\rho_a| < 1$ and ϵ_{at} denotes the innovation of the process having standard deviation σ_a. This technological shock is assumed common to all firms[11].

The wage and effort at work is determined through individual bargaining. Hence, given a price, a level of effort and the realization of stochastic shocks, the firm controls its hiring policy through vacancies. However, the aggregate job availability only determines the rate at which its jobs vacancies are filled. Then, this externality causes a stochastic rationing on the individual hiring policy. Firm accumulates capital $K_{j,t+1}$. The accumulation technology is given by:

$$K_{j,t+1} = (1 - \delta) K_{j,t} + I_{j,t} \tag{8.5}$$

where $I_{j,t}$ is the level of firm's investment.

The dynamic problem of the firm j is to maximize the expected discounted sum $\mathcal{V}_{j,0}$ of its profit flows, conditionally to the information available at time 0:

$$\begin{aligned} \max_{\{I_{j,t}, V_{j,t}\}} E_0[\mathcal{V}_{j,0}(\mathcal{E}_{j,0}, x_0)] &= \max_{\{I_{j,t}, V_{j,t}\}} E_0 \left[\sum_{t=0}^{\infty} \rho_t \Pi_{j,t} \right] \qquad (8.6) \\ \text{s.t. } K_{j,t+1} &= (1-\delta) K_{j,t} + I_{j,t} \\ N_{j,t+1} &= (1-s) N_{j,t} + q(\theta_t, X_t) V_{j,t} \end{aligned}$$

where $\mathcal{E}_{j,0}$ is the given initial conditions for the firm, $\mathcal{E}_{j,0} = \{K_{j,0}, N_{j,0}, w_0, l_0\}$, $x_0 = \{A_0, X_0\}$ and $\Pi_{j,t}$ is the profit flow of the firm j at time t, given w_t and l_t:

$$\Pi_{j,t} = A_t F(K_{j,t}, N_{j,t} l_t) - w_t N_{j,t} l_t - I_{j,t} - \omega V_{j,t} \tag{8.7}$$

[11] With the equation (8.1) and (8.4) we characterize the processes following by the states. Then we can associate at this state vector $x_t = \{A_t, X_t\}$ its conditionnal density function $f(x_{t+1}, x_t)$, and Ω the entire space of possible x.

and ρ_t is the kernel for the profit flow[12]. We can interpret ω as a scale parameter in the adjustment cost. Indeed, the matching process involves some endogenous linear labor adjustment costs: the parameter of this adjustment cost, $\frac{\omega}{q(\theta_t)}$, depends on the labor market fluctuations.

The firm's decision rules are solution to the following Bellman equation:

$$
\begin{aligned}
\mathcal{V}_j(\mathcal{E}_{j,t}, x_t) &= \max_{\{I_{j,t}, V_{j,t}\}} \left\{ \Pi_{j,t} + E_t \left[\frac{\rho_{t+1}}{\rho_t} \mathcal{V}_j(\mathcal{E}_{j,t+1}, x_{t+1}) \right] \right\} \\
\text{s.t. } K_{j,t+1} &= (1-\delta)K_{j,t} + I_{j,t} \\
N_{j,t+1} &= (1-s)N_{j,t} + q(\theta_t, X_t)V_{j,t}
\end{aligned}
$$

8.1.3 The Household

The utility function is chosen so that the consumption-saving decisions are independent of the effort supply on the labor market. The motivation for this choice is to isolate the propagation mechanism induced by the matching process from the intertemporal substitution effect. Then, the instantaneous utility function contingent to the state in the labor market ($a = n, u$, *i.e.* workers are employed or unemployed) is:

$$
U(C^a_{i,t}, l_t, e_t) = \begin{cases} U(C^n_{i,t} - \Gamma(l_t)) = \frac{1}{1-\sigma}\left[C^n_{i,t} - \frac{\eta}{1+\eta} l_t^{(1+\eta)/\eta}\right]^{(1-\sigma)} & \text{if } a = n \\ U(C^u_{i,t} - \Gamma(e_{i,t})) = \frac{1}{1-\sigma}\left[C^u_{i,t} - \frac{\eta}{1+\eta} e_{i,t}^{(1+\eta)/\eta}\right]^{(1-\sigma)} & \text{if } a = u \end{cases}
$$

with $\sigma > 0$ and $\eta > 0$ and where $C^a_{i,t}$ and $e_{i,t}$ denote respectively the consumption contingent to its situation on the labor market ($a = n, u$), and the individual search effort if $a = u$ of an agent i for the period t. The function $\Gamma(.)$ measures the disutility of effort expressed in consumption good unit.

---

[12] Indeed, the dynamic program of the firm can be rewritten as:

$$
\max_{\{I_{j,t}, V_{j,t}\}} E_0 \left[\sum_{t=0}^{\infty} \rho_t \Pi_{j,t} \right] = \max_{\{I_{j,t}, V_{j,t}\}} \sum_{t=0}^{\infty} \int \frac{\rho(x_t)}{\rho(x_0)} \Pi_{j,t}(x_t) dx_t
$$

The pricing kernel of an unit of flow profit at time t, contingent to the state x_t, is the price of time 0 flow profit: $\int \frac{\rho(x_t)}{\rho_0} f(x_{t+1}|x_t) dx_t$. Then, with the normalization $\rho_0 = 1$, we obtain (8.6), where we note $\rho_t = \rho(x_t)$.

Given the evolution of employment, driven by the hiring decision of the infinitely lived firm, the probabilities to be employed and unemployed at each time are N_t and $1 - N_t$. Each unemployed workers can influence individually the probability to become employed by through his search effort. Nevertheless, individual agent can alter the aggregate transition rate to employment[13]. Then, at time 0, each agent does not know its state in the labor market at any time t: hence, he maximizes the discounted sum of its expected instantaneous utilities:

$$\mathcal{U}_{i,t} = \alpha_{i,t} U(C^n_{i,t}, l_t) + (1 - \alpha_{i,t}) U(C^u_{i,t}, e_{i,t})$$

where $\alpha_{i,t}$ is the individual probability of the agent to be employed:

$$\alpha_{i,t} = \begin{cases} (1-s) & \text{if i is employed in } t-1 \\ e_{t-1} p(X_{t-1}, \theta_{t-1}) & \text{if i is unemployed in } t-1 \end{cases}$$

In this economy, we assume that households only get paid for work: unemployed workers get paid nothing by firms. If unemployed workers have a lower income, they save less and their capital will be smaller in the next period. Then, in this case, the entire history of the individuals becomes important to their capital state. To solve this possible heterogeneity, we assume the existence of an insurance market where households will have the opportunity to insure themselves against the uncertainty associated with being either employed or unemployed in any period. They choose the optimal number $B_{i,t}$ of claims corresponding to the unemployment compensation. The price[14] of this insurance is τ_t. Thus, they trade state contingent commodities $B_{i,t}$ at price τ_t. If the worker is unemployed in the current period, these commodities have a return $B_{i,t}$. The optimal choice of $B_{i,t}$ is given by the following program, where we denote $\mathcal{C}^a_{i,t} = \{C^a_{i,t}, B_{i,t}, q^a_i(x_{t+1})\}_{a=n,u}$:

$$\max_{\mathcal{C}^a_{i,t}} E_\tau \left[\mathcal{W}(\mathcal{E}_{i,\tau}(x_\tau), x_\tau)\right] = \max_{\mathcal{C}^a_{i,t}} E_\tau \left[\sum_{t=\tau}^{+\infty} \beta^t \mathcal{U}_{i,t}\right] \quad \forall\, \tau \in [0, \infty[$$

$$s.t \begin{cases} C^n_{i,t} + \tau_t B_{i,t} + \int \frac{\rho(x_{t+1})}{\rho(x_t)} q^n_i(x_{t+1}) f(x_{t+1}|x_t) dx_{t+1} & \le & w_t l_t + d_{i,t} + q_i(x_t) \\ C^u_{i,t} + \tau_t B_{i,t} + \int \frac{\rho(x_{t+1})}{\rho(x_t)} q^u_i(x_{t+1}) f(x_{t+1}|x_t) dx_{t+1} & \le & B_{i,t} + d_{i,t} + q_i(x_t) \\ (1-s)N_t + p_t e_t (1 - N_t) & = & N_{t+1} \end{cases}$$

[13] At general equilibrium, the unemployment is not optimal choice, or volontary decision, as in the model of Hamilton [1988].

[14] This price is a function of the probability that the household works $(1 - s)$ if the worker is employed in $t - 1$, and $e_{t-1} p(X_{t-1}, \theta_{t-1})$ if the worker is unemployed in $(t - 1)$

The pricing kernel $\int \frac{\rho(x_{t+1})}{\rho(x_t)} f(x_{t+1}|x_t)dx_{t+1}$ is the function corresponding to the price, in terms of time t consumption good, of a claim of one unit of the period $t+1$ consumption good contingent on the event in period $t+1$. $q_i^a(x_{t+1})$ $(a = n, u)$ denotes the net amount of the date $t+1$ good which the household i purchases at time t.

Then, it is easy to show that the optimality conditions of this program imply that households insure themselves on their utility level. Given the functional form of the utility function, this result implies that $C_{i,t}^n - \Gamma(l_t) = C_{i,t}^u - \Gamma(e_t)$, $\forall i$. Then, households choose to be fully insured in equilibrium: $B_{i,t} = w_t l_t - [\Gamma(l_t) - \Gamma(e_t)]$. Nevertheless, since the wage is not the price which clears a walrasian labor market, the resolution of this problem does not characterize a Pareto optimum, contrary to the solution proposed in Hansen [1985]. In our case, we have an equilibrium with sub-optimal equilibrium unemployment.

8.2 The Symmetric General Equilibrium

The symmetric general equilibrium is obtained in two steps: first, we compute the optimal search behavior, the wage rate and the on-the-job effort level. Second, we impose market clearing in good and financial markets by requiring individual agents choices to equivalent to their aggregate counterparts.

Then, the symmetric general equilibrium is defined by the set of functions $\{w(\cdot), h(\cdot), e(\cdot), C^n(\cdot), C^u(\cdot), V(\cdot), K(\cdot), N(\cdot)\}$ depending on the state variables $(\mathcal{E}_t, x_t)$ which solve the system of firms and households optimality conditions[15]:

(*i*) $w(\mathcal{E}_t, x_t) = w(\mathcal{E}_i^\star(x_t), \mathcal{E}_{j,t}^\star, x_t)$ and $h(\mathcal{E}_t, x_t) = h(\mathcal{E}_i^\star(x_t), \mathcal{E}_{j,t}^\star, x_t)$ $\forall\ i$ and $\forall\ j$ solve the wage bargaining for the wage rate and the on-the-job effort. $e(\mathcal{E}_t, x_t) = e(\mathcal{E}_i^\star(x_t), \mathcal{E}_{j,t}^\star, x_t)$ solve the Nash equilibrium for the search intensity effort.

(*ii*) $C_t^a = C^a(\mathcal{E}_t, x_t)$ for $a = n, u, o$, $V_t = V(\mathcal{E}_t, x_t)$, $N_t = N(\mathcal{E}_t, x_t)$ and $K_t = (\mathcal{E}_t, x_t)$ solve the set of aggregate firms and households policy rules for given vector: $\{w_t, h_t\}$.

[15] We denote $\mathcal{E}_i^\star(x_t) = \mathcal{E}_i(x_t) \setminus \{w_t, h_t\}$,$\mathcal{E}_{t,j}^\star = \mathcal{E}_{t,j} \setminus \{w_t, h_t\}$ and $\mathcal{E}_t = \{K_t, N_t\}$.

8.2.1 The Wage Bargaining Process and the Search Intensity Decision

Firms and workers are engaged in a costly trade process on the labor market. If a worker is unemployed, he chooses his optimal search intensity in order to maximize his expected income of the labor market. A successful job match yields some economic rent equals to the sum of the firm j and worker i search costs. We assume that this rent is shared according to the Nash solution to a bargaining problem. The bargaining problem is essentially the one of price determination in a bilateral monopoly. Following Pissarides [1990], we assume that individual firms and workers are too small to influence the market. Bargaining output is thus computed by taking the behavior of the other agents on the labor market as given. We assume that the wage and the effort is bargained each period.

The match rent for all firm j is given by the marginal real value of employment, which is given by[16]:

$$\Omega_{j,t}^F = \frac{\partial \mathcal{V}(\mathcal{E}_{j,t}, x_t)}{\partial N_{j,t}} = A_t \frac{\partial F_{j,t}}{\partial N_{j,t}} - w_{i,j,t} l_{i,j,t} + (1-s) E_t \left[\frac{\rho_{t+1}}{\rho_t} \Omega_{j,t+1}^F \right]$$

We assume that household want to maximize its expected actualized sum of gains net of the work disutility. Then, if the negotiation succeed, the worker have:

$$\Psi_{i,t}^n = w_{i,j,t}^n - \Gamma(l_{i,j,t}) + E_t \left[\frac{\rho_{t+1}}{\rho_t} \{(1-s)\Psi_{t+1}^n + s\Psi_{t+1}^u\} \right]$$

The threat point of the household is then the expected actualized sum of the search effort disutility, *i.e.* the disutility if the worker is unemployed:

$$\Psi_{i,t}^u = -\Gamma(e_{i,t}) + E_t \left[\frac{\rho_{t+1}}{\rho_t} \{e_{i,t} p(X_t, \theta_t) \Psi_{t+1}^n + (1 - e_{i,t} p(X_t, \theta_t)) \Psi_{t+1}^u\} \right]$$

The search intensity is chosen in order to maximize $\Psi_{i,t}^u$. Then the optimality condition of search intensity is given by:

$$\frac{\partial \Gamma}{\partial e_{i,t}} = p(X_t, \theta_t)) E_t \left[\frac{\rho_{t+1}}{\rho_t} (\Psi_{t+1}^n - \Psi_{t+1}^u) \right]$$

For the household, the match rent is given by the gap between $\Psi_{i,t}^n$ and $\Psi_{i,t}^u$, denoted $\Omega_{i,t}^M$:

[16] This condition is obtained using the envelope theorem on the firm's problem.

$$\begin{aligned}\Omega^M_{i,t} &= \Psi^n_{i,t} - \Psi^u_{i,t} \\ &= [w_{i,j,t} l_{i,j,t} - \Gamma(l_{i,j,t}) + \Gamma(e_{i,t})] + (1 - s - p_t e_{i,t})\beta E_t \left[\Omega^M_{i,t+1}\right]\end{aligned}$$

The wage and the effort of an employee are derived from the following Nash bargaining criterium:

$$\max_{w_{i,j,t}, l_{i,j,t}} \left(\Omega^F_{j,t}\right)^{1-\xi} \left(\Omega^M_{i,t}\right)^{\xi} \qquad 0 \leq \xi \leq 1$$

The first order conditions are:

$$\frac{\xi}{1-\xi}\Omega^F_{j,t} = \Omega^M_{i,t} \tag{8.8}$$

$$\frac{\xi}{1-\xi}\frac{\Omega^F_{j,t}}{\Omega^M_{i,t}} = -\frac{\frac{\partial^2 F}{\partial N_{j,t}\partial l_{i,j,t}} - w_{i,j,t}}{w_{i,j,t} - \frac{\partial \Gamma}{\partial l_{i,j,t}}} \tag{8.9}$$

Equation (8.8) gives the sharing rule of match rent between the firm and the employee. From the equations (8.8) et (8.9), we obtain the efficiency condition on the equilibrium labor effort:

$$\frac{\partial^2 F}{\partial N_t \partial l_t} = \frac{\partial \Gamma}{\partial l_t} \tag{8.10}$$

Since all workers have the same preferences and all jobs are equally productive, the wage and the effort fixed after the meeting of a firm and a worker is the same in whole the economy. The labor effort is independent of the intertemporal allocative consumption choice, this equilibrium condition is static.

Using the household's optimality condition on search effort and (8.8), the search supply effort for an unemployed worker is given by:

$$\frac{\partial \Gamma}{\partial e_t} = p_t \frac{\xi}{1-\xi}\beta E_t\left[\frac{\lambda_{t+1}}{\lambda_t}\Omega^F_{t+1}\right] \tag{8.11}$$

The equilibrium search effort is given, using the firm's optimality condition on vacancies[17], and the envelope condition on the household which gives the relation between the kernel pricing process and the Lagrange multiplier associated to the household budget constraint, $\frac{\rho_{t+1}}{\rho_t} = \beta\frac{\lambda_{t+1}}{\lambda_t}$, by:

[17]This firm's optimality condition is:

$$E_t\left[\frac{\rho_{t+1}}{\rho_t}\frac{\partial \mathcal{V}_{t+1}}{\partial N_{t+1}}\right] = E_t\left[\frac{\rho_{t+1}}{\rho_t}\Omega^F_{t+1}\right] = \frac{\omega}{q(\theta_t, X_t)}$$

$$\frac{\partial \Gamma}{\partial e_t} = p_t \frac{\xi}{1-\xi} \frac{\omega}{q_t} \tag{8.12}$$

Like the labor effort, the equilibrium search effort is independent of intertemporal substitution consumption/saving mechanism. Using equations (8.8) and (8.12), we obtain the wage-setting rule, knowing that $p_t = \theta_t q_t$:

$$w_t l_t = \xi \left(A_t \frac{\partial F}{\partial N_t} + \omega e_t \theta_t \right) + (1-\xi)(\Gamma(l_t) - \Gamma(e_t)) \tag{8.13}$$

At the symmetric general equilibrium, the wage, the labor effort and the search intensity solutions allow us to select the optimal paths among the possible ones described by the first order conditions for the firms and the households derived for w_t, l_t and e_t given.

The surplus accruing to the firm is given by the following profit equation:

$$\pi_t = A_t \frac{\partial F}{\partial N_t} - w_t l_t \tag{8.14}$$

Then, we can compute the dividend payment accruing to the representative household at each time[18]:

$$\begin{aligned} d_t &= N_t \pi_t - \omega V_t \\ &= (1-\xi) \left[N_t A_t \tfrac{\partial F}{\partial N_t} + \omega \theta_t e_t N_t - N_t(\Gamma(l_t) - \Gamma(e_t)) \right] - \omega \theta_t e_t \end{aligned}$$

Hence, the wage and the on-the-job effort, needed to trade on good and labor markets, are determined. We denote $d_t = \sum_{i=1}^{m} d_{i,t}$, the sum of the dividend received by the m households of this economy.

8.2.2 Rational Expectations Equilibrium

Given the linear homogeneity of the production function it is easy to show that, at symmetric equilibrium, the sum of the m the budget constraint of the households is equivalent to the equilibrium condition on the good market:

$$K_{t+1} = (1-\delta)K_t + A_t F(K_t, l_t N_t) - \omega V_t - N_t C_t^n - (1-N_t) C_t^u$$

Then, the rational expectations general equilibrium is characterized by the following 12 equations:

[18] We use the definition equation of $\theta_t = \frac{V_t}{e_t(1-N_t)}$.

$$\frac{\partial U}{\partial C_t^n} = \lambda_t \tag{8.15}$$

$$\frac{\partial U}{\partial C_t^u} = \lambda_t \tag{8.16}$$

$$\frac{\partial \Gamma}{\partial e_t} = \frac{\xi}{1-\xi}\omega\theta_t \tag{8.17}$$

$$\frac{\partial \Gamma}{\partial l_t} = \frac{\partial^2 F}{\partial N_t \partial l_t} \tag{8.18}$$

$$V_t = e_t\theta_t(1-N_t) \tag{8.19}$$

$$w_t l_t = \xi\left(A_t\frac{\partial F}{\partial N_t} + \omega e_t\theta_t\right) + (1-\xi)(\Gamma(l_t) - \Gamma(e_t)) \tag{8.20}$$

$$\pi_t = (1-\xi)\left(A_t\frac{\partial F}{\partial N_t} - (\Gamma(l_t) - \Gamma(e_t))\right) - \xi\omega e_t\theta_t \tag{8.21}$$

$$K_{t+1} = (1-\delta)K_t + A_t F(K_t, l_t N_t) - \omega V_t - N_t C_t^n - (1-N_t)C_t^u \tag{8.22}$$

$$N_{t+1} = (1-s)N_t + q_t e_t \theta_t (1-N_t) \tag{8.23}$$

$$\lambda_t = \beta E_t\left[\left(1-\delta+A_{t+1}\frac{\partial F}{\partial K_{t+1}}\right)\lambda_{t+1}\right] \tag{8.24}$$

$$\lambda_t\frac{\omega}{q_t} = \beta E_t[\pi_{t+1}\lambda_{t+1}] + \beta E_t\left[(1-s_{t+1})\lambda_{t+1}\frac{\omega}{q_{t+1}}\right] \tag{8.25}$$

$$C_t^n = C_t^u + [\Gamma(l_t) - \Gamma(e_t)] \tag{8.26}$$

The equilibrium dynamic evolution of the employment's implicit price is given by equation (8.25). Indeed, in optimum, $\frac{\omega}{q_t}$ is equal to the marginal value of employment. This condition is equivalent to the "free entry" condition on the labor market when firms can have only one job, filled or unfilled: the firm j creates jobs until the marginal value of employment is equal to the cost of vacancy. Since the matching process involves some endogenous linear labor adjustment costs, the number of job vacancies is a jump variable. The firm chooses its level such that the marginal value of its employment is equal to the cost of vacancy. Hence, the equilibrium dynamic adjustment of the vacancies is given by equation (8.25) which describes the evolution of the marginal value of employment implied by the time consuming search process[19].

Using the functional form of the utility function and equations (8.16) and (8.17), we can find the Frischian consumption demand for a unemployed worker:

$$C_t^u = \lambda_t^{-(1/\sigma)} + \frac{\eta}{1+\eta}\frac{\xi}{1-\xi}\omega\frac{V_t}{U_t}$$

Contrary to the traditional permanent income model where the consumption demand is only a positive function of the wealth, in our model the unemployed consumption demand C_t^u is a negative function of the unemployment rate. This can provide an explanation of the empirical rejection of the traditional permanent income model.

8.2.3 Resolution Method

We cannot obtain an analytical solution to the previous set of equations, which defined a general equilibrium. Then, following King, Plosser and Rebelo [1988] , we log-linearized the system of the efficiency conditions around the deterministic steady state. In a first step, in order to apply this numerical approximation method, we calibrate the model for the U.S. and the French economy. Then, the rational expectations linearized dynamic system is solved.

U.S. Calibration

The parameter β is set such that the subjective annual discount rate value equals 4%, ($i.e.$ $\beta = 1.04^{-0.25} \simeq 0.99$). The coefficient of relative risk aversion σ ranges between 1/3 and 2, following Eichenbaum, Hansen and Singleton [1988]'s estimation: we choose an intermediate value, 1.5. Following Mortensen [1990] we set η equal to 2. This corresponds to the highest value of the elasticity of the transition function into employment obtained by Burdett, Kiefer, Mortensen and Neumann [1984].

[19] This equilibrium condition is computed using evolution of the employment's marginal value of the firm:

$$\frac{\omega}{q_t} = E_t\left[\frac{\rho_{t+1}}{\rho_t}\left(A_{t+1}\frac{\partial F}{\partial N_{t+1}} - w_{t+1}l_{t+1}\right)\right] + E_t\left[(1-s)\frac{\rho_{t+1}}{\rho_t}\frac{\omega}{q_{t+1}}\right]$$

The equilibrium stochastic process of the kernel price is $\frac{\rho_{t+1}}{\rho_t} = \beta\frac{\lambda_{t+1}}{\lambda_t}$, and the wage bargaining output given the profit (8.14); therefore we obtain (8.25).

The technology parameter values are the ones reported by Christiano and Eichenbaum [1992]: $\alpha = 0.64$ and $\delta = 0.025$.

The value of γ is set following the Blanchard and Diamond [1989]'s matching function estimation: 0.6. Following the estimation of Burdett, Kiefer, Mortensen and Neumann [1984] and the calibration of Mortensen [1990], the quit rate s is fixed at 0.15 and the mean employment rate N is fixed at 0.63: this value correspond to the mean of participation. The U.S. vacancies data and the mean employment rate gives the value of the ratio V/U which is equated to 0.1044. In order to determine the steady state value of the parameters ω and ξ consistent with the calibration, we use equations (8.17), (8.18), (8.20) and (8.25). Then, we obtain :

$$\frac{wlN}{Y} = \alpha\left[\xi + (1-\xi)\left(\frac{\eta}{1+\eta}\right)\alpha\right] + \xi\left(\frac{\eta}{1+\eta}\right)\frac{(1-\xi)(1+\eta-\alpha\eta)\alpha\beta p}{[1-\beta(1-s)](1+\eta)+\xi\beta p}$$

This equation in ξ is solved for $\frac{wlN}{Y}$ equal to 0.58, the average labor income retained by King, Plosser and Rebelo [1988]. Equations (8.17), (8.19) and (8.23) allow us to give a value of the parameter of labor adjustment cost ω, if we normalize $X = 1$:

$$\omega = \frac{1-\xi}{\xi}\frac{\left[s\left(\frac{N}{1-N}\right)\left(\frac{1-N}{V}\right)^{\gamma}\right]^{(1+\eta)/\eta(1-\gamma)}}{\left(\frac{V}{1-N}\right)}$$

Then the set of the calibrated parameters is reported in the table 8.1

Table 8.1: U.S. Structural Parameters

β	σ	η	α	δ	γ	s	$V/(1-N)$	N	ξ	ω
0.99	1.5	2	0.64	0.025	0.6	0.15	0.1044	0.63	0.7696	2.771

Contrary to Hansen [1985]'s model, the unemployed workers have a steady state consumption level lower than that of employed workers. Indeed, we have $C^n = 1.3759$ and $C^u = 1.1947$.

French Calibration

The preferences parameters are the same as in U.S. economy. Concerning the technological parameters, the depreciation rate δ and the elasticity of output relatively to employment α are respectively fixed at 0.014 and 0.66, the values estimated by Fève and Langot [1993]. The quit rate s is fixed at 0.13, which correspond to the value reported by Sneesens [1993]. The value of the elasticity of hiring relatively to vacancies $\gamma = 0.58$ correspond to the estimator reported by Fève and Langot [1993]. As for the U.S. economy, the participation rate is calibrated to 0.63. The French vacancies data and the mean employment rate gives the value of the ratio V/U which equals 0.108.

Then, the set of structural parameters is reported in table 8.2

Table 8.2: French Structural Parameters

β	σ	η	α	δ	γ	s	$V/(1-N)$	N	ξ	ω
0.99	1.5	2	0.66	0.014	0.58	0.13	0.108	0.63	0.74	2.95

We use the same method as for the U.S. calibration in order to fixe ξ and ω. As for the U.S. calibration, the unemployed workers have a steady state consumption level lower than the one of the employed workers. For the French economy, we have $C^n = 1.1825$ and $C^u = 1.0543$.

The State Space Form

Following King, Plosser and Rebelo [1988], we use log-linear approximation method (log-linearization) of the optimality condition around the deterministic steady state. Let $\widehat{x}_t = \log\left(\frac{X_t}{X}\right) \simeq \frac{X_t - X}{X}$ where X is the steady state value of X_t, the solution of this linear rational expectations system is given by the following State-Space form:

$$\mathcal{S}_{t+1} = M\mathcal{S}_t + \epsilon_{t+1} \tag{8.27}$$

$$\Theta_t = \Pi\mathcal{S}_t \tag{8.28}$$

with $\mathcal{S}_t = [\widehat{k}_t, \widehat{n}_t, \widehat{a}_t, \widehat{x}_t]'$ $\Theta_t = [\widehat{y}_t, \widehat{c}_t, \widehat{c}_t^n, \widehat{c}_t^u, \widehat{i}_t, \widehat{n}_t, \widehat{y/n}_t, \widehat{u}_t, \widehat{v}_t, \widehat{h}_t, \widehat{l}_t, \widehat{e}_t, \widehat{w}_t, \widehat{\pi}_t, \widehat{r}_t]'$ $\epsilon_t = [0, 0, \epsilon_{a,t+1}, \epsilon_{x,t+1}]'$

We adopt the following notation: $\widehat{y/n}_t$ is the apparent labor productivity, $\widehat{u}_t$ is the unemployment rate, $\widehat{h}_t$ is the hiring rate, $\widehat{w}_t$ is the real wage, $\widehat{\pi}_t$ is the real profit, $\widehat{r}_t$ is the real interest rate.

All the coefficients of the matrix M and Π are non-linear functions of the structural parameters. Equations (8.27) and (8.28) allow us to simulate the cyclical components of the optimal paths, *i.e.* the theoretical cyclical properties of the economy[20].

8.3 Results

The approximation method allows us to study the theoretical properties of the model: indeed we can plot the theoretical Impulse Response Functions (I.R.F.) to the different shocks, and then discuss the propagation mechanism characterizing the model. We discuss only the theoretical properties of the model calibrated on U.S. data.

In a second step, in order to test the model ability to reproduce the U.S. and the French business cycles, we present the simulation results and compare them to the U.S. and French stylized facts.

8.3.1 Impulse Response Functions

We present the I.R.F. to the two shocks to disentangle their respective effects.

Technological Shock

The I.R.F. to the technological shock are reported in figures 8.1 and 8.2. Then, we can see that the instantaneous response of capital and employment are zero because these two variables are predetermined. The technological shock increases the labor return. Indeed, the real wage and the profit respond positively. Hence, firms and unemployment workers are incited to choose a higher search intensity: vacancies and search effort increase. The necessary investment to capture these labor market opportunities are immediately engaged: in the short run, the investment in vacancies is larger than the one in physical capital. The increase in search activity causes an increase of the hirings and then a decrease in unemployment. This result is due to the larger elasticity of

[20] When we simulate the model, we extract the cyclical component of the solution paths using the Hodrick and Prescott filter in order to define the same cyclical component as in the historical data. See King and Rebelo [1993] for the statistical properties of this filter.

Figure 8.1: I.R.F., Technological Shock (1% Shock on a)

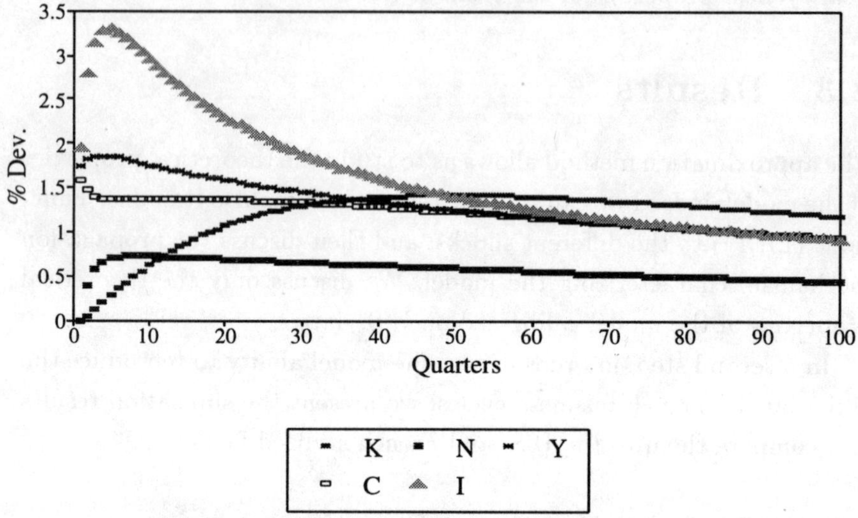

Figure 8.2: I.R.F., Technological Shock (1% Shock on a)

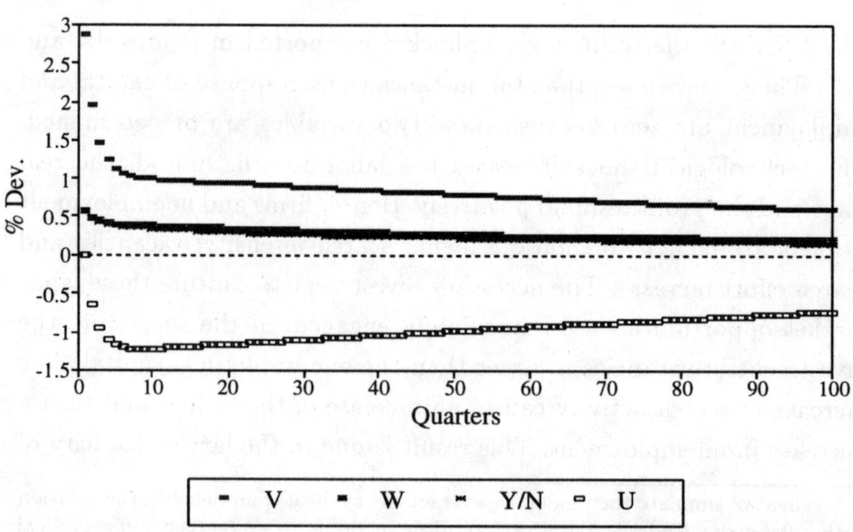

the vacancies relatively to the one of the unemployed search effort: the job availability, measured by θ, increases.

During the transition, the instantaneous jump of vacancies induces an increase of the competition between firms, and then the unemployed workers find a job more easily: the mean duration of vacancy and unemployment are negatively correlated. Then, the dynamic adjustment path, in the $u-v$ space, describes an anti-clockwise loop along the Beveridge curve. The I.R.F. to technological shock are consistent with previous empirical studies (Holt and David [1966] or Hansen [1970]).

The wage dynamics can be interpreted in the following way[21]: the increase in the job availability decreases the mean duration of unemployment and increases the mean duration of vacancies which is equivalent to a lowering of the threat point of the firm during the bargaining process. Hence, the wage instantaneously increases.

Contrary to the traditional *RBC* models, the employment and the labor productivity response do not have the same shape which implies, within these models, the impossibility to reproduce the productivity cycle. On the one hand, employment increases during six quarters and comes back to its stationary value: this result comes from the fact that the matching process is a time consuming process. On the other hand, the labor productivity instantaneously jumps, and monotically decreases to reach eventually the steady state: hence, we obtain a propagation mechanism which is able to reproduce the labor productivity cycle, *i.e.* that the labor productivity is an advanced indicator of employment dynamics.

Mismatch Shock

At an aggregate level, this shock can be interpreted as a variation of the matching efficiency which can be measured by the degree of heterogeneity in the labor market. The I.R.F. of the variables are reported in figures 8.3 and 8.4. For the household, this shock affects instantaneously only the unemployed worker behavior: search effort increases because the probability to find a job increases too. For the same reason, firms increase the number of vacancies. Nevertheless, the larger amplitude of the vacancies response relatively to the search unemployed wor-

[21] See Blanchard [1989] for more details.

Figure 8.3: I.R.F., Mismatch Shock (1% Shock on x)

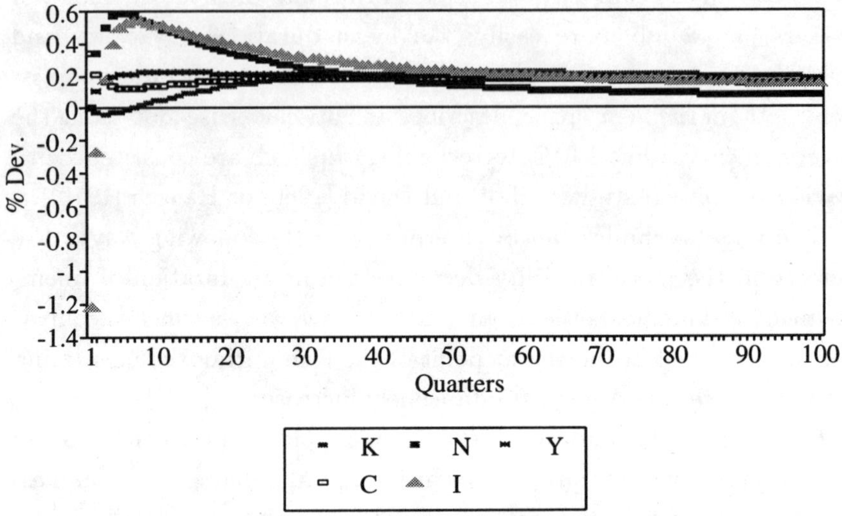

Figure 8.4: I.R.F., Mismatch Shock (1% Shock on x)

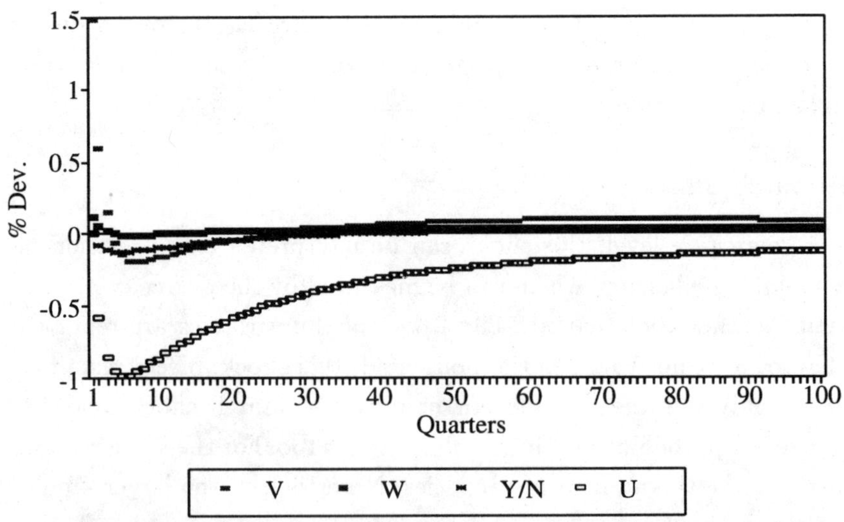

kers one implies an increase in the job availability. Then, as in the case of a technological shock, this disturbance causes an anti-clockwise loop around the Beveridge curve, describing the shift of this relation in the $u - v$ space. This job availability dynamics causes an increase of the real wage, because the threat point shifts in favor of the employees.

Production and hence labor effort have an instantaneous null response. Indeed, the bargaining process implies that the labor effort is negotiated with the "insiders": the labor effort is a solution to equation (8.18) where all the variables are predetermined.

After period $t + 1$, the hired workers become productive and the bargained labor effort increases because the employment/capital ratio increases. The entry of new workers implies a decrease in the workers threat point relatively to the employers one: then the wage comes back to its stationary value. In the short run, employment and labor productivity I.R.F. are in opposite direction, which can imply a decrease in the correlation between employment and labor productivity.

8.3.2 Does the Model Match the U.S. Business Cycle?

The model simulations are, following Kydland and Prescott [1982], a good test of the ability of the model to reproduce the U.S. business cycle and account for the relative importance of aggregate activity shock and specific labor market shocks in the unemployment dynamics. Traditional *RBC* models fail to reproduce the stylized facts on labor market and do not take into account unemployment phenomena. The results of different simulations show how some puzzle on the labor market can be solved and how the cyclical component of unemployment is reproduced by the model.

The U.S. Stylized Facts

Different cyclical characteristic indicators of main macroeconomic series[22] are reported in table 8.3.

At this level, we can summarize the following stylized facts concerning the labor market:

---

[22]The series used are those of the Citibase on the sample 1960-1990. The series are logged and filtered by the Hodrick and Prescott method.

Table 8.3: U.S. Stylized Facts

Variables $\widehat{x}$	$\widehat{y}$	$\widehat{c}$	$\widehat{i}$	$\widehat{n}$	$\widehat{p}$	$\widehat{u}$	$\widehat{v}$	$\widehat{w}$
S.D.	1.76	1.28	8.47	1.42	0.89	11.51	13.76	0.96
S.D./S.D.($\widehat{y}$)	1	0.72	4.81	0.80	0.50	6.54	7.82	0.55
corr($\widehat{x}, \widehat{x}_{-1}$)	0.85	0.86	0.81	0.84	0.52	0.90	0.91	0.84
corr($\widehat{x}, \widehat{y}$)	1	0.81	0.90	0.86	0.59	-0.88	0.92	0.35
corr($\widehat{x}, \widehat{n}$)					0.11			0.21
corr($\widehat{x}, \widehat{u}$)							-0.95	-0.26

- a volatility of labor productivity smaller than that of employment.
- a weakly positive correlation between labor productivity and worked hours.
- a positive correlation between real wage and employment.

We also estimate various cross correlations on the labor market for leads and lags up to one year.

- **Beveridge Curve**: The cross correlation between vacancies and unemployment is negative for all leads and lags, the larger being the instantaneous one. These moments are reported in table 8.4.

Table 8.4: Correlations between U and V corr($\widehat{v}_t, \widehat{u}_{t+i}$)

-4	-3	-2	-1	0	1	2	3	4
-0.20	-0.37	-0.61	-0.83	-0.95	-0.92	-0.77	-0.54	-0.30

- **Labor Productivity Cycle**: the cross correlation between labor productivity has a typically S-shape, that is, a negative correlation for $i \leq 0$ and positive for $j > 1$. The maximum positive correlation between productivity and employment occurs at lead 2 or 3. These moments are reported in table 8.5.

In order to evaluate the relative contributions of the different shocks, we simulate two models:

Table 8.5: The Labour Productivity Cycle corr($\widehat{p}_t, \widehat{n}_{t+i}$)

-4	-3	-2	-1	0	1	2	3	4
-0.26	-0.17	-0.08	0.06	0.11	0.37	0.47	0.47	0.34

(*i*) The model I, or benchmark model, has a single disturbance: the technological shock[23]. The results of the model can be then directly compared to the *RBC* model or to the Danthine and Donaldson [1990]'s efficiency wage model.

(*ii*) The model II has two disturbances: the technological shock and a mismatch shock[24].

The Benchmark Model

The results, reported in table 8.6, show that the model exhibits a weak variability of output and a weak relative variability of investment, as in the traditional *RBC* model. The variability of the consumption better matches the data than the traditional *RBC* models. This can be explained by the sensitivity of unemployed workers consumption to the search effort fluctuations.

The model can reproduce an employment variance higher than the labor productivity one, without introducing the controversial assumption of indivisible labor (Hansen [1985]). Nevertheless, the level of these volatility are lower than the stylized facts, because the matching process acts like a labor adjustment cost.

Table 8.6 shows that the model can generate non-walrasian features on the labor market[25] . The unemployment and the vacancies variabilities are smaller than the historical ones, whereas the correlation between unemployment and output is lower (in absolute value): this suggests that the labor market fluctuations are quite independent

[23]The calibration of this shock follows the estimation of Prescott [1986]: $\rho_a = 0.95$ and $\sigma_{\epsilon a} = 0.72\%$. This calibration is chosen because it is the benchmark of the traditionnal *RBC* models simulations.

[24]The calibration of the specific labour market shock are chosen in order to reproduce the ouput variability in the complet model (model II). We have $\rho_x = 0.5$ and $\sigma_{\epsilon x} = 1\%$ for the mismatch shock.

[25]In the following tables, all numbers between parenthesis are multiplied by 100.

Table 8.6: Model I

Variables $\widehat{x}$	$\widehat{y}$	$\widehat{c}$	$\widehat{i}$	$\widehat{n}$	$\widehat{p}$	$\widehat{u}$	$\widehat{v}$	$\widehat{w}$
S.D.	1.69	1.34	2.83	0.54	0.46	0.91	2.09	0.45
	(0.20)	(0.14)	(0.40)	(0.08)	(0.04)	(0.13)	(0.16)	(0.04)
S.D./S.D.($\widehat{y}$)	1	0.79	1.66	0.32	0.27	0.53	1.24	0.27
	(0)	(1.50)	(5.44)	(1.27)	(1.35)	(4.20)	(7.58)	(1.24)
corr($\widehat{x}, \widehat{x}_{-1}$)	0.71	0.62	0.84	0.85	0.56	0.85	0.41	0.57
	(6.15)	(7.01)	(4.17)	(3.98)	(7.24)	(3.81)	(7.49)	(7.16)
corr($\widehat{x}, \widehat{y}$)	1	0.98	0.95	0.63	0.95	-0.63	0.83	0.96
	(0)	(0.09)	(0.64)	(5.50)	(0.24)	(5.56)	(0.99)	(0.18)
corr($\widehat{x}, \widehat{n}$)					0.37			0.42
					(6.59)			(6.54)
corr($\widehat{x}, \widehat{u}$)							-0.10	-0.42
							(5.89)	(6.58)

of the good market ones. In fact, this result comes from the timing of decisions on the labor market. At time t, the unemployed workers disposable stock during the matching process is U_t. Nevertheless, the hiring flow can determine an unemployment workers stock at the end of the period t. In the model, this stock is denoted U_{t+1}. This one-period lag could appear as being an artefact of the discretization of a model specified in continuous time. Then, the unemployment stock corresponding to the information set available at time t is U_{t+1}, given corr($\widehat{y}_t, \widehat{u}_{t+1}$)=-0.88, which is close to the stylized facts.

The correlation between employment and real wage is divided by two relatively to the one obtained in the standard *RBC* models. Nevertheless, this correlation is greater that the historical one.

Table 8.7: Model I, *UV* Relation corr($\widehat{v}_t, \widehat{u}_{t+i}$)

-4	-3	-2	-1	0	1	2	3	4
0.25	0.24	0.22	0.13	-0.10	-0.58	-0.67	-0.59	-0.46
(9.32)	(9.00)	(7.93)	(6.96)	(5.89)	(1.75)	(4.14)	(7.74)	(8.10)

Concerning the correlation between vacancies and unemployment (table 8.7), the theoretical moments have the same shape as the historical one, but lagged one period. This one-period lag could also appear as being an artefact of the discretization of a flow model. If we adopt the convention that the current unemployment is the unemployment workers stock at the end of the period, the output of the model is closer to the stylized facts.

Table 8.8: Model I, Labour Productivity Cycle corr($\widehat{p}_t, \widehat{n}_{t+i}$)

-4	-3	-2	-1	0	1	2	3	4
-0.20	-0.14	-0.04	0.10	0.36	0.78	0.80	0.67	0.49
(10.86)	(10.22)	(9.06)	(8.61)	(6.59)	(2.20)	(4.72)	(8.02)	(8.56)

Concerning the labor productivity, the shape and the length of the labor productivity cycle is reproduce by the model. These results are close to those obtained in chapter 2 with only one technological shock.

To sum up, this benchmark model better fits the data than the standard *RBC* models. Moreover, we can reproduce the labor productivity cycle. As for the non-walrasian feature of the labor market, we can explain the fluctuations around the Beveridge curve and the weak correlation between real wage and employment. Nevertheless, new difficulties appear: unemployment and vacancies fluctuations generated by the model are too smooth. Consequently, we introduce some specific labor market disturbances.

The Introduction of Mismatch Shocks

The introduction of the mismatch shocks improve the output of the model concerning investment and employment volatilities (see table 8.9). Moreover, unemployment and vacancies variances better match the historical data. Then, if we inspect only the standard deviations, the introduction of the mismatch shock seems to improve the ability of the model to reproduce the data. Nevertheless, this improvement can be avoided only at the price of damaging the correlation between variables directly related to labor market: corr($\widehat{u}, \widehat{w}$), corr($\widehat{u}, \widehat{v}$) and corr($\widehat{v}, \widehat{w}$).

This remark is reinforced by the results relative to the *UV* relation, reported in table 8.10.

The technological and the mismatch shocks have opposite effects on the unemployment and vacancies dynamics. Indeed, an aggregate activity shock drives the unemployment and the vacancies responses in opposite directions, while the mismatch shock drives unemployment

Table 8.9: Model II

Variables $\widehat{x}$	$\widehat{y}$	$\widehat{c}$	$\widehat{i}$	$\widehat{n}$	$\widehat{p}$	$\widehat{u}$	$\widehat{v}$	$\widehat{w}$
S.D.	1.74	1.54	4.37	1.08	0.52	1.86	4.69	0.58
	(0.27)	(0.18)	(0.53)	(0.17)	(0.05)	(0.32)	(0.31)	(0.06)
S.D./S.D.($\widehat{y}$)	1	0.89	2.53	0.63	0.30	1.08	2.74	0.33
	(0)	(5.61)	(19.48)	(8.57)	(3.22)	(19.99)	(35.04)	(3.31)
corr($\widehat{x}, \widehat{x}_{-1}$)	0.72	0.51	0.42	0.72	0.59	0.72	0.16	0.41
	(6.24)	(9.17)	(11.06)	(6.34)	(7.81)	(6.23)	(9.46)	(9.55)
corr($\widehat{x}, \widehat{y}$)	1	0.84	0.67	0.45	0.78	-0.45	0.33	0.74
	(0)	(3.02)	(6.87)	(11.78)	(5.27)	(11.81)	(7.31)	(3.90)
corr($\widehat{x}, \widehat{n}$)					-0.17			0.03
					(14.34)			(12.38)
corr($\widehat{x}, \widehat{u}$)							0.19	-0.03
							(7.56)	(12.32)

Table 8.10: Model II, UV Relation corr($\widehat{v}_t, \widehat{u}_{t+i}$)

-4	-3	-2	-1	0	1	2	3	4
0.18	0.24	0.32	0.33	0.19	-0.51	-0.55	-0.44	-0.28
(10.40)	(7.79)	(7.55)	(7.68)	(7.56)	(1.79)	(5.54)	(8.55)	(11.21)

and vacancies in the same direction. Thus, the introduction of this specific labor market shock lowers the negative link between unemployment and vacancies. These quantitative implications of this general equilibrium framework give some theoretical support of the Blanchard and Diamond [1989] statistical results:

> "As the co-movement of unemployment and vacancies over the postwar period shows, short- and medium-term fluctuations in unemployment have been due mainly to aggregate activity shocks,..., rather that changes in the degree in reallocation intensity"(p50).

The introduction of the mismatch shock induces a decrease of the entire sequence of productivity-employment correlations. The labor productivity cycle generated by the model is thus closer to the stylized facts.

Table 8.11: Model II, Labour Productivity Cycle corr($\widehat{p}_t, \widehat{n}_{t+i}$)

-4	-3	-2	-1	0	1	2	3	4
-0.06	-0.09	-0.14	-0.19	-0.17	0.11	0.25	0.30	0.29
(16.23)	(15.01)	(13.16)	(13.74)	(14.34)	(13.34)	(12.28)	(12.86)	(14.89)

Then, first of all, the non-walrasian labor market assumption helps in reproducing the stylized facts on which the *RBC* literature usually focuses. Second, the model presented in this chapter seems more relevant than the efficiency wages assumption retained by Danthine and Donaldson [1990]. Indeed, their "gift exchange model" can not reproduce an employment variability greater than the labor productivity variability. In their second wage setting rule corresponding to a "shirking model", the employment variability is greater than the output variability, but this model is not explicitly solved.

8.3.3 Does the Model Match the French Business Cycle?

As for the U.S. case, we present the French stylized facts in a first step. Then, we compare the results of the simulation with this set of second moments. We follow the same strategy in order to measure the relative importance of the specific labor market shock in the French business cycle.

The French Stylized Facts

As for the U.S. economy, different cyclical characteristic indicators of main macroeconomic series[26] are reported in table 8.12.

Table 8.12: French Stylized Facts

Variables $\widehat{x}$	$\widehat{y}$	$\widehat{c}$	$\widehat{i}$	$\widehat{n}$	$\widehat{p}$	$\widehat{u}$	$\widehat{v}$	$\widehat{w}$
S.D.	0.91	0.81	3.64	0.83	0.65	7.93	18.31	0.72
S.D./S.D.$(\widehat{y})$	1	0.9	4.01	0.92	0.72	0.11	0.05	0.79
corr$(\widehat{x}, \widehat{x}_{-1})$	0.76	0.67	0.82	0.89	0.63	0.91	0.88	0.71
corr$(\widehat{x}, \widehat{y})$	1	0.63	0.80	0.71	0.45	-0.91	0.87	0.02
corr$(\widehat{x}, \widehat{n})$					-0.30			-0.19
corr$(\widehat{x}, \widehat{u})$							-0.70	0.29

This table shows that the French labor market stylized facts are not the same as the U.S. one:

- a negative correlation between labor productivity and hours worked.
- a weakly negative correlation between real wage and employment.

We estimate also various cross correlations on the labor for leads and lags up to one year.

- **Beveridge Curve**: The cross correlation between vacancies and unemployment is negative for all leads and lags, the larger being the instantaneous. These moments are reported in table 8.13.
- **Labor Productivity Cycle**: the cross correlation between labor productivity has a typically S-shape, that is, a negative correlation for $i \leq 1$ and positive for $j > 2$. The maximum positive

[26]The series used are those of the INSEE data bank on the sample 1960-1990. The series are logged and filtered by the Hodrick and Prescott method.

Table 8.13: Correlations between U and V corr$(\widehat{v}_t, \widehat{u}_{t+i})$

-4	-3	-2	-1	0	1	2	3	4
0.19	-0.05	-0.41	-0.56	-0.70	-0.68	-0.62	-0.46	-0.22

correlation between productivity and employment occurs at lead 5 (see chapter 2). These moments are reported in table 8.14.

Table 8.14: The Labour Productivity Cycle corr$(\widehat{p}_t, \widehat{n}_{t+i})$

-4	-3	-2	-1	0	1	2	3	4
-0.34	-0.44	-0.45	-0.40	-0.30	-0.14	0.02	0.14	0.22

As for the U.S. economy, we simulate two models in order to evaluate the relative contributions of the different shocks:

(*i*) The model I (benchmark model) has only a technological shock[27].

(*ii*) The model II has two impulses: the technological shock and a mismatch shock[28].

The Benchmark Model

As for the U.S. economy, the table 8.15 shows that the model implies a weak relative variability of investment, whereas the relative variability of consumption seems to better match the data than *RBC* models (see chapter 1 and 2): this result comes from the dependence of aggregate consumption to search effort fluctuation.

As for the U.S. economy, all the labor market variabilities exhibited by the model are too smooth. Nevertheless, the relative volatilities are qualitatively well reproduced: the variability of employment is higher than that of productivity and the variability of vacancies is higher than

[27]The calibration of this shock follows the estimations of discussed in chapters 1 et 2: $\rho_a = 0.975$ and $\sigma_{\varepsilon a} = 0.38\%$. This calibration is chosen in order to reproduce the output volatility in the complet model.

[28]The calibration of the specific labour market shock are the same as for the U.S. economy: $\rho_x = 0.5$ and $\sigma_{\varepsilon x} = 1\%$.

Table 8.15: Model I

Variables $\widehat{x}$	$\widehat{y}$	$\widehat{c}$	$\widehat{i}$	$\widehat{n}$	$\widehat{p}$	$\widehat{u}$	$\widehat{v}$	$\widehat{w}$
S.D.	0.93	0.72	1.75	0.31	0.76	0.52	1.25	0.27
	(0.12)	(0.08)	(0.28)	(0.04)	(0.08)	(0.07)	(0.11)	(0.03)
S.D./S.D.($\widehat{y}$)	1	0.78	1.89	0.33	0.81	0.56	1.36	0.28
	(0)	(1.30)	(7.40)	(1.37)	(2.66)	(4.79)	(6.42)	(1.20)
corr($\widehat{x}, \widehat{x}_{-1}$)	0.74	0.65	0.87	0.86	0.59	0.87	0.48	0.61
	(4.52)	(5.74)	(2.15)	(2.41)	(6.45)	(2.33)	(7.52)	(6.18)
corr($\widehat{x}, \widehat{y}$)	1	0.98	0.93	0.63	0.94	-0.64	0.82	0.96
	(0)	(0.09)	(0.82)	(4.38)	(0.21)	(4.36)	(0.99)	(0.16)
corr($\widehat{x}, \widehat{n}$)					0.36			0.41
					(5.24)			(5.21)
corr($\widehat{x}, \widehat{u}$)							-0.11	-0.41
							(4.54)	(5.24)

the unemployment one. The correlation between real wage and unemployment have the opposite sign relatively to the historical one. The positive correlation between unemployment and real wage in the data can be explained by the rigidity on the French labor market: the real wage is weakly sensitive to past unemployment and an increase in real wage implies an increase in unemployment in future periods. Then this stylized fact shows that the shifts of the Phillips curve are more important that the adjustments around this curve in order to explain the joint unemployment-wage dynamics. Nevertheless, a technological shock can only causes a dynamics around the Phillips curve. Thus, the model can reproduce the French correlations between wage and unemployment[29].

Like in the U.S. economy, the correlation between employment and wage are not matched by the model. This comes from the unicity of the shock and form the wage setting which gives too much importance of the marginal labor productivity fluctuations.

Concerning the correlation between vacancies and unemployment (table 8.16), the shape of the correlation shows that the vacancies are a leading indicator of unemployment fluctuations. Nevertheless, the theoretical correlation are lagged one period, as for the U.S. economy.

Since the labor productivity cycle is longer in France, the theoretical

[29]See Fève and Langot [1993] for more details on this point and for a solution of this puzzle.

Table 8.16: Model I, UV Relation corr$(\widehat{v}_t, \widehat{u}_{t+i})$

-4	-3	-2	-1	0	1	2	3	4
0.36	0.35	0.29	0.15	-0.11	-0.55	- 0.69	-0.65	-0.55
(7.96)	(7.89)	(7.19)	(5.63)	(4.54)	(1.44)	(3.59)	(6.58)	(7.42)

moments generated by the model do not reproduce this stylized fact, contrary to the results obtained on U.S. data (see table 8.17). As it is showed in chapter 2, it seems to be difficult to reproduce this stylized fact on French data.

Table 8.17: Model I, Labour Productivity Cycle corr$(\widehat{p}_t, \widehat{n}_{t+i})$

-4	-3	-2	-1	0	1	2	3	4
-0.29	-0.22	-0.09	0.08	0.36	0.75	0.82	0.72	0.56
(8.38)	(8.40)	(7.84)	(6.56)	(5.24)	(1.57)	(3.64)	(6.10)	(6.84)

These first results shows that this non-walrasian model match better the data than the *RBC* with only technological shock presented in chapter 1 and 2. Nevertheless, as for U.S. economy, it seems to be difficult to reproduce unemployment, vacancies and real wages second order moments.

The Introduction of Mismatch Shocks

Does the model perform better if we introduce a labor market specific shock, as the mismatch shock? Like in the U.S. economy, the theoretical moments of investment and employment better match the stylized fact if we introduce the mismatch shock.

Except these two variances, table 8.18 shows that introducing a mismatch shock does not improve the output of the model. This can be interpreted as a relative small impact of labor market specific shock on French short run fluctuations.

The results reported in table 8.19 reinforced this conclusion. Indeed, the cross-correlations between unemployment and vacancies generated by the model are dominated by the mismatch shock which implies the strong positive correlation between unemployment and vacancies. Nevertheless, as it is showed by Jacques and Langot [1993], the joint

Table 8.18: Model II

Variables $\widehat{x}$	$\widehat{y}$	$\widehat{c}$	$\widehat{i}$	$\widehat{n}$	$\widehat{p}$	$\widehat{u}$	$\widehat{v}$	$\widehat{w}$
S.D.	0.91	1.00	4.51	0.91	0.96	1.55	4.55	0.49
	(0.12)	(0.09)	(0.48)	(0.11)	(0.12)	(0.15)	(0.35)	(0.03)
S.D./S.D.($\widehat{y}$)	1	1.08	4.92	0.99	1.04	1.69	4.98	0.54
	(0)	(8.57)	(46.71)	(9.92)	(11.93)	(19.65)	(55.70)	(5.50)
corr($\widehat{x}, \widehat{x}_{-1}$)	0.71	0.39	0.19	0.69	0.63	0.70	0.14	0.26
	(6.23)	(6.97)	(7.51)	(3.79)	(7.38)	(4.05)	(6.74)	(6.91)
corr($\widehat{x}, \widehat{y}$)	1	0.63	0.44	0.45	0.52	-0.44	0.14	0.44
	(0)	(5.79)	(7.37)	(10.48)	(7.90)	(10.49)	(8.80)	(7.56)
corr($\widehat{x}, \widehat{n}$)					-0.51			-0.09
					(9.74)			(8.58)
corr($\widehat{x}, \widehat{u}$)							0.25	0.10
							(5.71)	(8.78)

unemployment-vacancies dynamics is largely explained by shocks on the good market at the business cycle frequency.

Table 8.19: Model II, *UV* Relation corr($\widehat{v}_t, \widehat{u}_{t+i}$)

-4	-3	-2	-1	0	1	2	3	4
0.15	0.21	0.30	0.37	0.25	-0.49	-0.53	-0.37	-0.23
(7.56)	(9.52)	(7.68)	(6.83)	(5.71)	(2.00)	(4.01)	(7.61)	(8.68)

Like in the U.S. economy, the introduction of the mismatch shock decrease the level of all the correlations between employment and productivity.

Table 8.20: Model II, Labour Productivity Cycle corr($\widehat{p}_t, \widehat{n}_{t+i}$)

-4	-3	-2	-1	0	1	2	3	4
0.01	-0.07	-0.22	-0.40	-0.51	-0.23	0.01	0.12	0.18
(14.85)	(16.73)	(15.42)	(13.24)	(9.74)	(8.84)	(9.60)	(9.85)	(11.62)

These simulations show that this model perform better on U.S. data than on French data. This result can be due to the fact that the business cycle of a European country like France can not be explained in a model that does not take into account the interaction with foreign countries.

8.4 Concluding Comments

This paper extends the standard *RBC* literature by introducing unemployment-vacancies dynamics and wage bargaining in intertemporal framework. Using the *RBC* methodology, we show that the introduction of non-walrasian features in the labor market improves the empirical performance of standard *RBC* models along many dimensions. It accounts for unemployment phenomenon and gives theoretical backgrounds within an intertemporal general equilibrium framework, to the fluctuations observed around the Beveridge curve. The lack of a walrasian auctioneer induces a costly and uncoordinated trade process. These transaction costs generate specific rents which are shared through a bargaining process. Under these assumptions, the model generates involuntary and persistent unemployment. Indeed, the non-walrasian wage exceeds that required to compensate the unemployed worker disutility to search for a job. This wage-setting rule seems to match better the data: the correlation between real wage and employment is well reproduced contrary to the case where the wage is equal to the marginal productivity of labor. Moreover the simulation results give some quantitative evidence on the main impulse source of the labor market dynamics: only the aggregate activity shock explain the unemployment-vacancies fluctuations during the business cycle. These implications of the model correspond to empirical results of Blanchard and Diamond [1989] and Jacques and Langot [1993] obtained using the V.A.R. methodology.

Nevertheless, an important problem still remains: the correlation between unemployment and vacancies is not negative enough. The introduction of specific labor market disturbances does not solve this problem. A modification in the timing decision or the endogeneization of labor market participation seems to be a way out of this problem. Indeed, Langot and Pucci [1993] show that the pro-cyclicity of the participation rate can explain, in this type of model a strong negative correlation between unemployment and vacancies.

Concerning the specificity of the European countries, the results suggest that a essential dimension is forgotten in the modelling of the French economy. Fève and Langot [1993] show the importance of the openness of this economy in order to explain the French business cycle and more particularly the unemployment, vacancies and real wage dynamics.

Bibliography

K. ABRAHAM AND L. F. KATZ. Cyclical Unemployment : Sectoral Shifts or Aggregate Disturbances ? *Journal of Political Economy*, 94:507–522, 1986.

D. ANDOLFATTO. *Business Cycles and Labor Market Search.* Working paper, University of Waterloo, October 1991.

O. BLANCHARD AND P. DIAMOND. The Beveridge Curve. *Brookings Papers on Economic Activity*, 1:1–76, 1989.

O. BLANCHARD. A Traditional Interpretation of Economic Fluctuations. *American Economic Review*, 79(5):1146–1164, December 1989.

K. BURDETT, N. KIEFER, D. MORTENSEN AND G. NEUMANN. Earnings, Unemployment, and the Allocation of Time over Time. *Review of Economic Studies*, 51, 1984.

L. CHRISTIANO AND M. EICHENBAUM. Current Real Business Cycle Theories and Aggregate Labor-Market Fluctuations. *American Economic Review*, 82(3):430–450, 1992.

J.P. DANTHINE AND J. DONALDSON. Efficiency Wages and the Business Cycles Puzzle. *European Economic Review*, 34(7):1275–301, November 1990.

P. DIAMOND. *A Search-Equilibrium Approach to the Micro Foundations of Macroeconomics.* The MIT Press, Cambridge Mass., 1984.

J. DUNLOP. The Movements of Real and Money Wages Rates. *Economic Journal*, 48:413–434, 1938.

M. EICHENBAUM, L. HANSEN AND K. SINGLETON. A Time Series Analysis of Representative Agent Models of Consumption and Leisure Choice under Uncertainty. *Quarterly Journal of Economics*, 103(1):51–78, 1988.

P. FÈVE AND F. LANGOT. *The R.B.C. Model through Statistical Inference.* Cahiers ECO & MATHS 93.08, MAD, Université de Paris I, 1993. Revised 1994, Forthcoming in Journal of Applied Econometrics.

R. HALL. *Invariance Properties of Solow's Productivity Residual.* Working paper 3034, NBER, 1989.

J. Hamilton. A Neoclassical Model of Unemployment and the Business Cycle. *Journal of Political Economy*, 96(3):593–617, 1988.

B. Hansen. Excess Demand, Unemployment, Vacancies, and Wages. *Quaterly Journal of Economics*, 1–23, 1970.

G. Hansen. Indivisible Labor and the Business Cycles. *Journal of Monetary Economics*, 16(3):309–327, 1985.

C. Holt and M. David. The Concept of Jobs Vacancies in a Dynamic Theory of the Labor Market. In NBER, editor, *The Mesurement and Interpretation of Job Vacancies*, Colombia University Press, New York, 1966.

P.Y. Hénin and T. Jobert. Profits, investissement et chômage. In P.Y. Hénin, editor, *La persistance du chômage*, Economica, Paris, 1993.

J.F. Jacques and F. Langot. La dynamique de la courbe de Beveridge. In P.Y. Hénin, editor, *La persistance du chômage*, Economica, Paris, 1993.

R. King and S. Rebelo. Low Frequency Filtering and the Real Business Cycles. *Journal of Economic Dynamics and control*, 17(1/2):207–232, 1993.

R. King, C. Plosser and S. Rebelo. Production, Growth and Business Cycles I. *Journal of Monetary Economics*, 21(2/3):196–232, March-May 1988.

F. Kydland and E. Prescott. Time to Build and Aggregate Fluctuations. *Econometrica*, 50(6):1345–1370, November 1982.

F. Langot and M. Pucci. *Participation, Unemployment and Business Cycles : A General Equilibrium Model.* Cahiers ECO & MATHS 93.42, MAD, Université de Paris I, 1993.

F. Langot. Composantes sectorielles et nationales dans l'évolution du résidu de solow. *Annales d'Economie et Statistiques*, 24:133–154, October-December 1991.

R. Layard, S. Nickell and R. Jackman. *Unemployment, Macroeconomic Performance and the Labour Market.* Oxford University Press, 1991.

D. Lilien. Sectoral Shifts and Cyclical Unemployment. *Journal of Political Economy*, 90:777–793, 1982.

R. Lucas and L. Rapping. Real Wages, Employment and Inflation. *Journal of Political Economy*, 77(5):721–754, September/October 1969.

G. Mankiw. Real Busines Cycles: a New Keynesian perspective. *Journal of Economic Perspectives*, 3(3):79–90, Summer 1989.

D. Mortensen. The Matching Process as a Noncooperative/Bargain Game. In J. McCall, editor, *The Economics of Information and Uncertainty*, University of Chicago Press, 1982.

D. Mortensen. *Search Equilibrium and Real Business Cycles.* Working paper , Northwestern University, August 1990.

C. Pissarides. Unemployment and Vacancies in Britain. *Economic Policy*, 3:498–559, October 1986.

C. Pissarides. Seach, Wages Bargains and Cycles. *Review of Economic Studies*, 54:473–483, July 1987.

C. Pissarides. *Equilibrium Unemployment Theory.* Basil Blackwell, 1990.

E. Prescott. Theory Ahead of Business Cycle Measurement. *Carnegie Rochester Conference Series on Public Policy*, 25:11–44, Autumn 1986.

J. Rotemberg and M. Woodford. *Oligopolistic Competition and the Effect of Aggregate Demand on Economic Activity.* Working paper 3206, NBER, 1989.

H. Sneesens. *Courbe de Beveridge et demande de qualification.* Working paper, IRES, Université de Louvain, February 1993.

L. Summers. Some Skeptical Observations on Real Business Cycles Theory. *Federal Reserve Bank of Minneapolis Quaterly Review*, 10:23–27, Autumn 1986.

L. Tarshis. Changes in Real and Money Wages. *Economic Journal*, 49:150–154, March 1939.

Chapter 9

Business Cycle and Endogenous Growth : Learning by Doing versus Rationalizing

Fabrice Collard

Abstract

Endogenous growth models are mainly concerned with the studying of the long run properties without making explicit the cyclical dynamics of the economy. This chapter presents a cyclical growth model in which the physical capital accumulation is augmented with a human capital accumulation process, including a *learning by doing effect* and a *rationalizing* of the productive activity mechanism. The growth rate is then endogenous and keeps the trace of business cycle fluctuations. The model is able to explain the cycle-growth integration. Analyzing the dynamics of the model, we show that transitory shocks exert a permanent effect, whose sign depends on the relative magnitude of the learning by doing and rationalizing mechanisms. We then seek a calibration allowing one to match, in a quite encouraging manner, the cyclical pattern of the historical fluctuations of the french and U.S. economies.

Introduction

During the fifties and the sixties, Solow [1956]'s model has emerged as the unified framework for growth theory. The traditional model assumes that there exists an exogenous growth rate, sum of the population and the Harrod neutral technical progress growth rates. The interest is mainly focused on the analysis of the long run growth path, and the convergence to the steady-state. The cyclical properties are rarely studied[1]. On the contrary, in the eighties, on the spur of the Real Business Cycle (R.B.C) theory, the debate shifted on the board of the cycle analysis. The canonical *RBC* model abstracts from growth and focuses on the analysis of fluctuations, which are interpreted as the result of optimal responses of agents facing exogenous real shocks. The dichotomy between cycles and growth is thus maintained[2].

Each of these approaches predicts a trend stationary representation of time series. This implies that the economy cannot permanently deviate from its equilibrium growth path after a shock. However Nelson and Plosser [1982] and Stulz and Wasserfallen [1985] concluded to the existence of a unit root in the process of the main aggregates so that transitory shocks exert a permanent effect on the dynamics of the economy. These results pointed out the need to reformulate the growth-cycles integration.

In parallel, the end of the eighties have seen a renewal in the growth literature under the impulse of endogenous growth theorists. The growth rate is then endogenized and depends on the structural parameters of the model, notably the processes of the shocks altering the economy. This class of models allows for the growth-cycles integration, in so far as the growth rate is affected by the short run fluctuations. However, the interest has focused on long run properties of the model. The sign of the persistence of the different shocks constitutes a crucial stake for the macroeconomic analysis. The literature seems to privilege the existence of alternative models specific to each thesis. On the one hand, some, invoking the existence of learning by doing effects (Stadler [1990], Hercowitz and Sampson [1991]) or positive externalities Romer [1986], assume that the shocks have a positive long run impact on the dynamics, that is to say that negative shocks persistently rush the economy in a permanent recession. On the other hand, others, placing their reliance on reallocation effects (Gali and Hammour [1991]) or Research

[1]See King and Rebelo [1993]b

[2]It is noteworthy that the *RBC* model is built on the optimal growth model, so that the growth-cycles integration could have been studied in that setting.

and Development activities (Aghion and Saint-Paul [1991]), defend the thesis of a negative persistence of shocks, there exists a "Virtue of bad times" (Aghion and Saint-Paul [1991]). The aim of this chapter is then to present a formulation able to account for the two effects within a common framework in order to characterize their cyclical and dynamical implications.

We develop a cyclical growth model in the line of Stadler [1990]. Stadler proposed an equilibrium cycle model in which the technical progress is endogenized through a learning by doing mechanism. He then illustrates how transitory shocks (technological *and* monetary shocks) affect the long run dynamics of the output. One disputable feature of his analysis is that the growth rate of output is non stationary, which is not supported by the data. In the present chapter, sustained growth comes from a human capital accumulation process, which combines a learning by doing mechanism and a rationalizing of productive activity effect, transiting through the average labor productivity. This modeling has the advantage not to impose the domination of an effect on the other. The returns to scale in the technology and the human capital accumulation are assumed to be constant with respect to the reproducible factors, which allows for the existence of sustained growth.

As the human capital accounts for the trend component of technology, the technological shock fits the exogenous stationary component of the Solow residual. Since the long run growth rate of the economy, the human capital growth rate, is endogenous, the model achieves the growth-cycles integration. The hypothesis of endogenous growth implies that the processes of the main series exhibit the unit root property. Each impulse affecting the short run activity is then likely to alter the long run path of the economy. The model therefore provides a natural theoretical framework to gauge the long run neutrality of transitory shocks :

Have government expenditures shocks a long run impact on the dynamics of the economy? or are they, as Blanchard and Quah [1989] assume, neutral? If the neutrality property is rejected, do they exert a positive effect on the long run dynamics, as the Kaldor-Veerdorn law assumes or, on the contrary, do they imply a loss of global wealth leading the economy to a lower growth path?

In order to answer at these questions, the model is calibrated and simulated, allowing for the study of responses to each shock. A sensibility analysis to the parameter ruling the magnitude of each effect is also conducted. The ability of the model to match the cyclical feature of french and U.S. economy is then evaluated. Two filtering methodologies are envisaged, the Hodrick and Prescott [1980]'s filter and the Log-differentiation.

The first section describes the model, focusing on the properties of the human capital accumulation process. The second section shows the computation of the competitive equilibrium, and presents the simulation methodology. The third section then analyses the dynamics of the model and the impulse response functions in order to display the internal mechanisms. Finally, the simulation results are presented and briefly commented.

9.1 Presentation of the Model

We retain the benchmark framework defined by King and Rebelo [1988]. However, our model deviate from theirs in several aspects. The human capital accumulation differs from the one propounded by Lucas [1988] and King and Rebelo, since it does not constitute an autonomous production sector. It rests on a *learning by doing* and a *rationalizing* of productive activity phenomenon. This specification is alike to Stadler [1990]'s.

9.1.1 The Households

The economy is populated by many identical infinitely-lived individuals acting in a competitive world. The population is normalized to unity and we assume there exists a representative agent with preferences over goods and leisure represented by :

$$U = E_0 \left\{ \sum_{t=0}^{\infty} \beta^t u(C_t, 1 - n_t; G_t) \right\}$$

where β is the discount factor, C_t is private consumption in period t, and n_t is the number of hours worked. The instantaneous utility function of the representative household is given by :

$$u(C_t, 1 - n_t; G_t) = \log(C_t + \nu G_t) + \theta(1 - n_t)$$

The choice of the households in terms of leisure is characterized by a Hansen [1985]'s specification, so that the leisure intertemporal substitution elasticity is infinite. This can be interpreted as the existence of indivisibilities in hours worked[3]. θ is the marginal utility of leisure. G_t denotes the government expenditures, which as in Barro [1981] affects the utility of households. The parameter ν is crucial in the determination of the impact of different shocks on the variables.

- If $\nu = 0$ then the marginal utility of private consumption remains unchanged after a government expenditures shock, which effect only operates through wealth effects.

- If $0 < \nu < 1$ then the marginal utility of private consumption diminishes less after a government expenditures unit shock than after a unit increase in consumption.

- If $\nu = 1$ then private consumption and government expenditures are perfect substitutes. A positive government expenditures shock then implies a complete crowding out on private consumption, the other variables remaining unchanged.

In each period, individuals face the intertemporal wealth constraint:

$$C_t + T_t + \int_{\Omega} \frac{\rho_{t+1}(\omega_{t+1})}{\rho_t} B_{t+1}(\omega_{t+1}) d\mu(\omega_{t+1}|\omega_t) \leq B_t + w_t n_t H_t$$

where T_t, B_t denote respectively lump sum taxes, wealth and w_t the wage rate. Ω is the information set including the whole history of the shocks and the state variables. $\omega \in \Omega$ then denotes an event and $\mu(.)$ the conditional associated measure. Then, $\int_{\Omega} \frac{\rho_{t+1}(\omega_{t+1})}{\rho_t} B_{t+1}(\omega_{t+1}) d\mu(\omega_{t+1}|\omega_t)$ represents the price in period t of a contingent claim which insures a payment B_{t+1} in period t whatever the state of Nature is.

At the aggregate level, the resources constraint states that the total use of commodity cannot exceed the total output. Using the government budget constraint, one gets :

$$C_t + I_t + G_t \leq Y_t$$

[3]See Hansen [1985] and chapter 2 for further details.

9.1.2 The Government Expenditures

The government consumption G_t evolves according to the stochastic growth component of the model, the human capital, and an exogenous stationary component. It is assumed that the individual observes the government expenditures process, without discriminating between the permanent and the stationary components. The stationary component is assumed to follow an exogenous first order autoregressive process :

$$\log(g_t) = \rho_g \log(g_{t-1}) + (1-\rho_g)\log(\bar{g}) + \varepsilon_{g,t}$$

with $0 < \rho_g < 1$, $E(\varepsilon_g) = 0$ and $E(\varepsilon_g^2) = \sigma_g^2$. $\log(\bar{g})$ denotes the unconditional mean of the process.

9.1.3 The Firms

The good, to be accumulated and consumed, is produced according to a technology, represented by the following production function :

$$Y_t = A_t F(K_t, n_t H_t) = A_t K_t^{\alpha}(n_t H_t)^{1-\alpha}, \quad 0 < \alpha < 1$$

where K_t and H_t are respectively the predetermined physical capital stock and human capital stock. The returns to scale are constant with respect to the paid factors, K_t and $(n_t H_t)$, as well as the reproducible factors K_t and H_t. A_t is a technological shock assumed to follow an exogenous stationary first order autoregressive process :

$$\log(A_t) = \rho_a \log(A_{t-1}) + (1-\rho_a)\log(\bar{A}) + \varepsilon_{a,t}$$

with $0 < \rho_a < 1$, $E(\varepsilon_a) = 0$ and $E(\varepsilon_a^2) = \sigma_a^2$. $\log(\bar{A})$ denotes the unconditional mean of the process.

It is noteworthy that A_t cannot be assimilated to the *naive* Solow residual :

$$\begin{aligned}\log(RES_t) &= \log(Y_t) - \alpha\log(K_t) - (1-\alpha)\log(n_t) \\ &= \log(A_t) + (1-\alpha)\log(H_t)\end{aligned}$$

As in Chapter 2, $\log(RES_t)$ differs from the technological shock, but, there, the wedge is a non stationary process, H_t. As H_t follows an integrated process the model can account for the non stationarity in the Solow residual. Assuming the equality between the technological shock and the Solow residual innovation would lead to overestimate the persistence of the shock. In such an intertemporal framework, it is well known[4] that the elasticity of the variables of interest with respect to shocks are very sensitive to the persistence parameter : the more the technological shock is persistent the stronger the wealth effect. However A_t can be assimilated to the stationary component of a given trend-cycle decomposition of the Solow residual.

9.1.4 Accumulation Processes

The physical capital accumulation process is traditionally given as :

$$K_{t+1} = I_t + (1 - \delta_K)K_t, \quad 0 < \delta_K < 1$$

where δ_K is the constant depreciation rate of the physical capital.

The human capital accumulation process follows :

$$H_{t+1} = \Phi \overline{\left(\frac{Y_t}{n_t}\right)}^{\psi} (n_t H_t)^{1-\psi} + (1-\delta_H)H_t, \quad \Phi > 0,\ 0 \leq \psi \leq 1,\ 0 \leq \delta_H \leq 1$$

where δ_H is the constant depreciation rate of the human capital. The evolution of human capital depends on productivity and the efficient hours worked, extending Stadler [1990]'s formulation. In the symmetric equilibrium, H_{t+1} is homogenous of degree one with respect to (Y_t, H_t). As Y_t exhibits constant returns to scale with respect to (K_t, H_t), the human capital accumulation is homogenous of degree one with respect to the reproducible factors. That property together with the constant returns to scale in the technology with respect to the reproducible factors, implies that the model generates an endogenous sustained growth.

The human capital accumulation does not constitute a particular sector. In Lucas [1988], the human capital relies on a formal education phenomenon[5], but this mechanism is relevant in a long run analysis. We do not think that formal education is a good representation of human capital accumulation at the business cycle frequency. Here, the human capital is linked to the business cycle.

The term in $(n_t H_t)$ represents a learning by doing effect. It is the by product of experiment,that is effective within the activity phases.

---

[4] See Chapter 1

[5] In the sense of *learning or doing* like in Lucas [1988].

The higher the efficient employment the more knowledge increases, – *i.e.* the global productivity grows. Contrary to a tradition initiated by Arrow [1962], this effect is not treated as an externality since, in this model, learning by doing represents the productivity gains incorporated in the worker : the individual knows that by offering an additional unit of work, he will accumulate work experience, that is to say his future wealth.

An opposite mechanism usually appears in the "learning or doing" models, where the formation constitutes an activity alternative to production. An increase in hours spent in current production can negatively alter the growth rate. The human capital formation process is also able to account for productive recessions. Many mechanisms are usually associated with that idea. Gali and Hammour [1991] and Saint-Paul [1992] assume the existence of a reallocation of labor force within the business cycle, while Aghion and Saint-Paul [1991] attribute this "virtue of bad times" to a research-development (R&D) activity. During bad times one part of the labor force is reallocated to another sector (formation or R&D), because the opportunity cost of this activity is much lower, so that the future global productivity increases. This approach is named *opportunity cost* by Saint-Paul [1992]. Here, such a phenomenon is captured by the term in $\overline{\left(\frac{Y_t}{n_t}\right)}$, which is the translation of the productivity gains of the work post, so that it is not embodied in the worker. It then appears as an externality, so that optimum and competitive equilibrium do not coincide. As the average productivity of hours is a decreasing function of hours worked, the negative effect of employment transits through this rationalizing mechanism. In recession times, the staff cut allows the economy to maintain the previous level of average productivity so that the human capital keeps on growing. As Gali and Hammour [1991] notes :

> "Recessions have a "cleaning-up" effect that causes less productive jobs to be closed down. This can happen either because those jobs become unprofitable, or because recessions provide an excuse for firms to close them down in the context of formal or informal worker-firms arrangements. As a consequence, the average productivity of jobs will rise." (Gali and Hammour [1991], p. 15)

The net effect of hours worked is summed up in table (9.1)

Table 9.1: Net Impact of Hours Worked in the Symmetric Equilibrium

$\psi < \frac{1}{1+\alpha}$	$\frac{\partial H_{t+1}}{\partial n_t} > 0$	domination of learning by doing
$\psi = \frac{1}{1+\alpha}$	$\frac{\partial H_{t+1}}{\partial n_t} = 0$	neutrality of hours worked
$\psi > \frac{1}{1+\alpha}$	$\frac{\partial H_{t+1}}{\partial n_t} < 0$	domination of rationalizing

This rationalizing effect also incorporates a capital effect, which is pro-cyclical while employment effect is counter-cyclical, so that capital plays a moderating role in the human capital process. There can exist parametrization such that the impact of rationalizing is positive.

9.2 Solving the Model

This section is devoted to the computation of the decision rules of each agent and the characterization of the competitive equilibrium. As the model includes an externality in the human capital process, the equivalence between the equilibrium and the Pareto optimum is no more satisfied.

9.2.1 The Representative Firm Problem

The firm maximizes its intertemporal profit, by mean of choosing the level of investment and employment. It then solves the Bellman's equation :

$$\begin{aligned} V^F(\Delta_t^F) &= \max_{(I_t, n_t H_t)} \{A_t F(K_t, n_t H_t) - w_t n_t H_t - I_t \\ &\quad + \textstyle\int_\Omega \frac{\rho_{t+1}(\omega_{t+1})}{\rho_t} V^F(\Delta_{t+1}^F(\omega_{t+1})) d\mu(\omega_{t+1}|\omega_t)\} \\ s.t.\ K_{t+1} &= I_t + (1-\delta_K)K_t \end{aligned}$$

$\Delta_t^F = (K_t, A_t, g_t)$ the state vector. ρ_t is the stochastic pricing kernel for contingent claims[6].

The optimality conditions are :

$$q_t = 1 \tag{9.1}$$

[6]We will note $E_t(X_{t+i}) = \int_\Omega X_{t+i}(\omega_{t+i})\, d\mu(\omega_{t+i}|\omega_t)$.

$$w_t = (1-\alpha)\frac{Y_t}{n_t H_t} \tag{9.2}$$

$$q_t = E_t\left\{\frac{\rho_{t+1}}{\rho_t}\left(\alpha\frac{Y_{t+1}}{K_{t+1}} + q_{t+1}(1-\delta_K)\right)\right\} \tag{9.3}$$

$$\lim_{j\to\infty} E_t\left\{\rho_{t+j}q_{t+j}K_{t+j+1}\right\} = 0 \tag{9.4}$$

where the implicit price verifies : $q_t = E_t\left\{\frac{\rho_{t+1}}{\rho_t}V_K^F(\Delta_{t+1}^F)\right\}$. As the physical capital accumulation is not submitted to adjustment costs, the system (9.1)-(9.4) describes a factor demand behavior. It can then be shown[7] that the value of the firm verifies :

$$V^F\left(\Delta_{t+1}^F\right) = K_{t+1}$$

the expected value of the firm is given by its capital stock.

9.2.2 The Household Problem

The representative household maximizes his intertemporal utility subject to his intertemporal budget constraint and the human capital accumulation process. He solves the following Bellman's equation :

$$V^M(\Delta_t^M) = \max_{(C_t,n_t)}\left\{u(C_t, 1-n_t; G_t) + \beta\int_\Omega V^M(\Delta_{t+1}^M(\omega_{t+1}))d\mu(\omega_{t+1}|\omega_t)\right\}$$

$$s.t.\left\{\begin{array}{rcl} C_t & + & G_t + \int_\Omega \frac{\rho_{t+1}(\omega_{t+1})}{\rho_t}B_{t+1}(\omega_{t+1})d\mu(\omega_{t+1}|\omega_t) \leq B_t + w_t n_t H_t \\ H_{t+1} & = & \Phi\left(\frac{Y_t}{n_t}\right)^{\psi}(n_t H_t)^{1-\psi} + (1-\delta_H)H_t \end{array}\right.$$

where $\Delta_t^M = (B_t, H_t, A_t, g_t)$ is the state vector.
The optimality conditions then follows[8].

$$u_c(t) = x_t \tag{9.5}$$

$$u_l(t) = x_t w_t H_t + (1-\psi)z_t\left(\frac{H_{t+1}-(1-\delta_H)H_t}{n_t}\right) \tag{9.6}$$

$$\beta x_{t+1} = \frac{\rho_{t+1}}{\rho_t}x_t \tag{9.7}$$

$$\begin{aligned} z_t = \beta E_t\Big\{ & w_{t+1}n_{t+1}x_{t+1} \\ & + z_{t+1}\left((1-\psi)\left(\frac{H_{t+2}-(1-\delta_H)H_{t+1}}{H_{t+1}}\right) + 1 - \delta_H\right)\Big\} \end{aligned} \tag{9.8}$$

[7] For a proof in a more general framework see Fairise [1993]
[8] $u_x(t)$ denotes the marginal utility of good x in period t.

$$\lim_{j\to\infty} E_t \left\{\beta^{t+j} x_{t+j} B_{t+j+1}\right\} = 0 \tag{9.9}$$

$$\lim_{j\to\infty} E_t \left\{\beta^{t+j} z_{t+j} H_{t+j+1}\right\} = 0 \tag{9.10}$$

The implicit prices verify : $x_t = V_B^M(\Delta_t^M)$ and $z_t = \beta E_t \left\{V_H^M(\Delta_{t+1}^M)\right\}$.

(9.5) and (9.7) mean that each extra unit of consumption increases the individual's current utility by $E_t\left\{\frac{\rho_{t+1}}{\rho_t} u_c(t)\right\}$ but lowers its future utility by $\beta E_t(u_c(t+1))$. These equations then describe the consumption-saving individual's behavior.

(9.6) tells that offering one extra hour of work increases individual's wealth by $w_t x_t H_t$ and his human capital valuation by the second right hand side term. But that lowers his utility by $u_l(t)$. This equation rules the behavior of supply of hours. It is noteworthy that in this model the cost in utility is constant, θ.

(9.6) and (9.8) tell that each additional hour worked leads to an increase in consumption utility of $H_t w_t u_c(t)$ at the price of an utility cost $u_l(t)$. That also increases the end of period human capital by $(1-\psi)(H_{t+1} - (1-\delta_H)H_t)/n_t$. The household can then consume additional goods, whose utility value is given by $w_{t+1} n_{t+1} u_c(t+1)$. The second effect relies on ψ. If $\psi = 0$, the learning by doing effect implies that the individual has accumulated further skill that allows him to offer less hours. Then he gains $u_l(t+1)$, but loss $H_{t+1} w_{t+1} u_c(t+1)$. The sign of these terms are reversed in the case $\psi = 1$, but transits only through the externality.

(9.9) and (9.10) give terminal conditions for the problem.

9.2.3 The Competitive Equilibrium

In an equilibrium, the resources constraint is satisfied, so that :

$$Y_t = C_t + I_t + G_t$$

The symmetric equilibrium condition imposes that :

$$\overline{\left(\frac{Y_t}{n_t}\right)} = \left(\frac{Y_t}{n_t}\right)$$

In equilibrium, the transversality conditions are both satisfied. It can then be shown that the individual's wealth is given by the value of the firm :

$$B_{t+1} = E_t \left\{ \frac{\rho_{t+1}}{\rho_t} V^F(\Delta^F_{t+1}) \right\}$$

This equation expresses the capital market equilibrium. Noting $\Lambda_t = x_t q_t$ and $M_t = z_t q_t$, the following definition can be stated.

Definition 1: *The competitive equilibrium of the economy is a set of policy rules :*

$$\begin{aligned} C_t &= C(K_t, H_t, A_t, g_t) \\ I_t &= I(K_t, H_t, A_t, g_t) \\ n_t &= n(K_t, H_t, A_t, g_t) \end{aligned}$$

such that :

$$u_c(t) = \Lambda_t \tag{9.11}$$

$$u_l(t) = (1-\alpha)\Lambda_t \frac{Y_t}{n_t} + M_t \left((1-\psi)\Phi\overline{\left(\frac{Y_t}{n_t}\right)}^{\psi} H_t^{1-\psi} n_t^{-\psi} \right) \tag{9.12}$$

$$\Lambda_t = \beta E_t \left\{ \Lambda_{t+1} \left(\alpha \frac{Y_{t+1}}{K_{t+1}} + 1 - \delta_K \right) \right\} \tag{9.13}$$

$$M_t = \beta E_t \left\{ \Lambda_{t+1} \alpha \frac{Y_{t+1}}{H_{t+1}} + M_{t+1} \left((1-\psi)\Phi\overline{\left(\frac{Y_{t+1}}{n_{t+1}}\right)}^{\psi} n_{t+1}^{1-\psi} H_{t+1}^{-\psi} + 1 - \delta_H \right) \right\} \tag{9.14}$$

$$K_{t+1} = A_t F(K_t, n_t H_t) - C_t - G_t + (1-\delta_K) K_t \tag{9.15}$$

$$H_{t+1} = \Phi\overline{\left(\frac{Y_t}{n_t}\right)}^{\psi} (n_t H_t)^{1-\psi} + (1-\delta_H) H_t \tag{9.16}$$

$$\lim_{j\to\infty} E_t \left\{ \beta^{t+j} \Lambda_{t+j} K_{t+j+1} \right\} = 0 \tag{9.17}$$

$$\lim_{j\to\infty} E_t \left\{ \beta^{t+j} M_{t+j} H_{t+j+1} \right\} = 0 \tag{9.18}$$

This system differs from the system of optimality conditions that characterizes the Pareto optimum, since the latter would take into account the effect of the choice of employment, physical and human capital on growth transiting through the rationalizing effect.

9.2.4 Simulation Methodology

Stationarization and State-Space Form

This model is non-stationary as it does not possess a steady state. But the two types of capital are cointegrated, so that $\log(K_t/H_t)$ is a stationary variable. We can then define a transformed economy that possesses a steady state. Each variable is stationarized, removing the common stochastic trend, H_t, from its process[9]. As in the standard *RBC* analysis, the model is log-linearized, and solved according to the methodology described in chapter 1. We then obtain the following state-space form :

$$\begin{pmatrix} \widehat{k}_{t+1} \\ \widehat{\gamma}_{t+1} \\ \widehat{A}_{t+1} \\ \widehat{g}_{t+1} \end{pmatrix} = \begin{pmatrix} \pi_{kk} & \pi_{k\gamma} & \pi_{ka} & \pi_{kg} \\ \pi_{\gamma k} & \pi_{\gamma\gamma} & \pi_{\gamma a} & \pi_{\gamma g} \\ 0 & 0 & \rho_a & 0 \\ 0 & 0 & 0 & \rho_g \end{pmatrix} \begin{pmatrix} \widehat{k}_t \\ \widehat{\gamma}_t \\ \widehat{A}_t \\ \widehat{g}_t \end{pmatrix} + \begin{pmatrix} 0 \\ 0 \\ \varepsilon_{a,t+1} \\ \varepsilon_{g,t+1} \end{pmatrix}$$

$$\begin{pmatrix} \widehat{c}_t \\ \widehat{n}_t \\ \widehat{y}_t \\ \widehat{i}_t \\ \widehat{y/n}_t \end{pmatrix} = \begin{pmatrix} \pi_{ck} & \pi_{c\gamma} & \pi_{ca} & \pi_{cg} \\ \pi_{nk} & \pi_{n\gamma} & \pi_{na} & \pi_{ng} \\ \pi_{yk} & \pi_{y\gamma} & \pi_{ya} & \pi_{yg} \\ \pi_{ik} & \pi_{i\gamma} & \pi_{ia} & \pi_{ig} \\ \pi_{y/nk} & \pi_{y/n\gamma} & \pi_{y/na} & \pi_{y/ng} \end{pmatrix} \begin{pmatrix} \widehat{k}_t \\ \widehat{\gamma}_t \\ \widehat{A}_t \\ \widehat{g}_t \end{pmatrix}$$

where π_{ij} denotes the instantaneous elasticity of variable i to variable j. The main series can then be recover, noticing that :

$$(S) \quad \log(X_t) = \widehat{x}_t + \log(H_t) + \log\left(\frac{X}{H}\right) = \widehat{x}_t + \sum_{j=0}^{t} \gamma_t + \log(X)$$

In order to conduct the dynamic analysis and the simulations, the model has to be calibrated.

US Calibration

Table 9.2: Calibration Parameters : USA

β	ν	n^*	α	δ_K	γ
0.9926	0.2	0.4	0.42	0.025	1.0035
ψ	δ_H	ρ_a	σ_a	ρ_g	σ_g
0.635	0.01	0.95	0.008	0.97	0.02

Preferences: The individual is assumed to discount time at a rate of 3% per year, which implies a value of β equal to $(1.03)^{-\frac{1}{4}} = 0.9926$.

[9]We will note $x_t = \frac{X_t}{H_t}$ and $\gamma_{t+1} = \frac{H_{t+1}}{H_t}$.

The parameter ν is fixed to a value of 0.2 according to an estimation by Aschauer [1985]. The parameter θ is chosen such that in equilibrium, the individual devotes 40% of its total time endowment to work.

The share of government expenditures in U.S. G.N.P is evaluated at 21%, which corresponds to the average value estimated for the post-war period. The parameters defining the government expenditures process retained are the one estimated by Christiano and Eichenbaum [1988], $\rho_g = 0.97$ and $\sigma_g = 0.02$.

Technology: The labor share in output, $1-\alpha$, is fixed at 58%, average value of wage in U.S. G.N.P between 1948-1986. The depreciation rate of physical capital is fixed at 0.025, which corresponds to an annual rate of 10%. The persistence parameter of the technological shock is $\rho_a = 0.95$ with a standard deviation $\sigma_a = 0.008$.

The long run growth factor of human capital is fixed at the value of $\gamma = 1.0035$ per quarter.

The parameter ψ is obtained using the human capital accumulation law. As $\log(RES_t) = \log(A_t) + (1+\alpha)\log(H_t)$, we assimilate $\log(H_t)$ to the trend component of Solow residual, $\log(res_t^T)$. Then, approximating the human capital accumulation, we estimate :

$$\frac{\Delta \log\left(res_t^T\right)}{1-\alpha} = \psi \log\left(\frac{y_t}{n_t}\right) + (1-\psi)\log(n_t)$$

where $\log\left(res_t^T\right)$ is obtained by the Hodrick-Prescott filter and y_t/n_t is the average productivity of hours worked, stationarized by res_t^T[10]. The estimation leads to $\psi = 0.635$. Φ is chosen so that in steady state $\gamma = 1.0035$. The depreciation rate of human capital is fixed at a value of $\delta_H = 0.01$ per quarter.

French Calibration

Preferences: The individual is assumed to discount time at a rate of 4% per year, which implies a value of β equal to $(1.04)^{-\frac{1}{4}} = 0.99$.

[10]This result is maintained if we consider the following regression :

$$\frac{\Delta \log(res_t)}{1-\alpha} = \psi \Delta \log\left(\frac{Y_t}{n_t}\right) + (1-\psi)\log(n_t)$$

The parameter ν is fixed to the same value retained in the U.S. economy. The parameter θ is chosen such that in equilibrium, the individual devotes 42% of its total time endowment to work. The share of government expenditures in french G.N.P is evaluated at 22%, which corresponds to the average value estimated for the 1970-1990 period. The parameters defining the government expenditures process retained are estimated on government expenditures data purged from the human capital component[11] : $\rho_g = 0.986$ and $\sigma_g = 0.006$.

Table 9.3: Calibration Parameters : France

β	ν	n^*	α	δ_K	γ
0.99	0.2	0.42	0.46	0.0125	1.0067
ψ	δ_H	ρ_a	σ_a	ρ_g	σ_g
0 / 0.734	0.01	0.98	0.009	0.986	0.006

Technology: The labor share in output, $1-\alpha$, is fixed at 54%, average value of wage in french G.N.P between 1970-1990 (See Laffargue, Malgrange and Pujol [1990]). The depreciation rate of physical capital is fixed at 0.0125, which corresponds to an annual rate of 5%. The persistence parameter of the technological shock is fixed at a value of $\rho_a = 0.98$ with a standard deviation $\sigma_a = 0.009$. These values are consistent with those retained in other *RBC* models on french data.

The long run growth factor of human capital is fixed at the value of $\gamma = 1.0067$ per quarter.

The value of ψ is obtained using the procedure defined for the U.S. economy. Whereas the estimation of the first equation leads to $\psi = 0$, that is to say that the growth process is essentially driven by a learning by doing mechanism, if we consider the following regression :

$$\frac{\Delta \log\left(res_t^T\right)}{1-\alpha} = \psi \Delta \log\left(\frac{Y_t}{n_t}\right) + (1-\psi)\log(n_t)$$

The estimation leads to $\psi = 0.734$, which implies a rationalizing effect. The two values of ψ will be considered in what follows. Φ is chosen so

[11] The obtention of such a series is discussed in the next paragraph.

that in steady state $\gamma = 1.0067$. The depreciation rate of human capital is fixed at a value of $\delta_H = 0.01$ per quarter as in the U.S. economy.

9.3 Analysis of the Dynamics

This section is devoted to the study of the transitional dynamics and the propagation mechanisms of the shocks in the theoretical model. The existence of a sustained growth implies that the different shocks have effects that persist in the long run[12] even if, contrary to Romer [1986], the growth rate is stationary.

9.3.1 Transitional Dynamics

We consider a 1% deviation of K_t/H_t from its steady-state value. This implies a dynamic adjustment to the steady state in the transformed model that characterized the transitional dynamics. After such a "shock", the output, in the transformed economy, also deviates positively. Then, by a wealth effect, consumption and leisure tend to grow. This implies a loss in hours worked. Further, as the capital stock rises, the wage rate increases whereas the interest rate diminishes. The fall of the latter reinforces the wealth effect in so far as future consumption appears less attractive. It also tends to depreciate saving, thus affecting investment negatively. The instantaneous effect on hours worked is negative since the expected discounted future wages are going up, the individuals then transfer hours worked to the future. The instantaneous increase in wages thwarts this phenomenon. Nevertheless, the net effect on hours worked is negative in this model.

In the U.S. benchmark calibration, $\psi < \frac{1}{1+\alpha}$ the learning by doing effect dominates the dynamics of the growth rate. Since hours worked respond negatively to a unit deviation of K_t/H_t, the growth rate should fall in relation to its steady state value. But the calibration of the model is such that ψ is chosen close to the value that cancels the effect of hours worked on the growth rate. As the magnitude of the response of physical capital stock is higher than the one of hours worked, the total impact on growth is positive in the short run. The french calibration ($\psi = 0.734$) implies the domination of the rationalizing mechanism, so

[12] The graphs are reported in appendix.

that the growth rate responds positively. As it converges positively to its steady state value, human capital stays durably on a higher steady state growth path. By equation (S) , consumption, investment, output and productivity reach a higher steady state growth path.

It is noteworthy that the speed of adjustment to the new path is low. This is partly due to the fact that individuals know that by offering more hours worked they participate to the increase in long run productivity. Hence they expect a future wealth gain, which will be partially devoted to leisure. The virtuous circle of learning by doing is then weakened. This phenomenon is totally effective in the pure learning by doing case.

It then appears that the value of the parameter ψ is crucial in the determination of the long run impact of any shock on the dynamics. Tables (9.4), (9.5) and figures (9.1), (9.2), (9.3), (9.4)[13] illustrate this point.

Table 9.4: USA : 1% Increase in (K_t/H_t)

ψ	0	0.635	$\frac{1}{1+\alpha}$	1
IRF(∞)	-0.2198	0.0731	0.0889	0.1513
IRF(∞) whithout G	-0.1669	0.0744	0.0869	0.1397

Table 9.5: France : 1% Increase in K_t/H_t

ψ	0	$\frac{1}{1+\alpha}$	0.734	1
IRF(∞)	-0.5697	0.1506	0.1688	0.2548
IRF(∞) whithout G	-0.3953	0 1465	0.1909	0.2338

As $\psi \to 0$, the learning by doing effect completely dominates the dynamics of human capital. Then, since the response of hours worked to a positive deviation in K_t/H_t is negative, the growth rate deviates negatively from its steady state value. In the long run, the interest variables rest on a lower steady state growth path.

[13]plain line : $\psi = 0$, pecked line : ψ =estimated value, alternate : $\psi = \frac{1}{1+\alpha}$, dotted line : $\psi = 1$

Figure 9.1: USA : Response of Y_t/n_t to a 1% Deviation in (K_t/H_t)

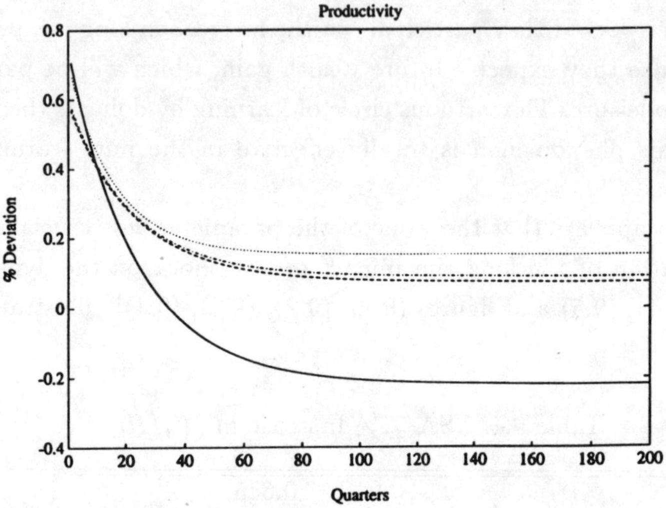

Figure 9.2: USA : Response of γ_t to a 1% Deviation in (K_t/H_t)

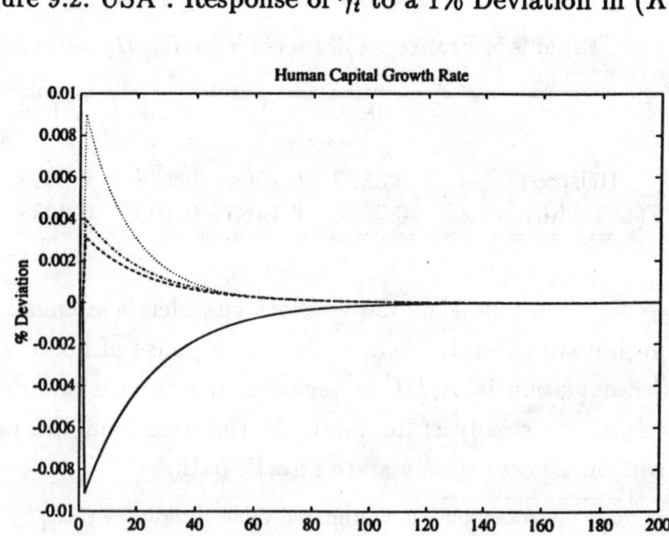

Figure 9.3: France : Response of Y_t/n_t to a 1% Deviation in K_t/H_t

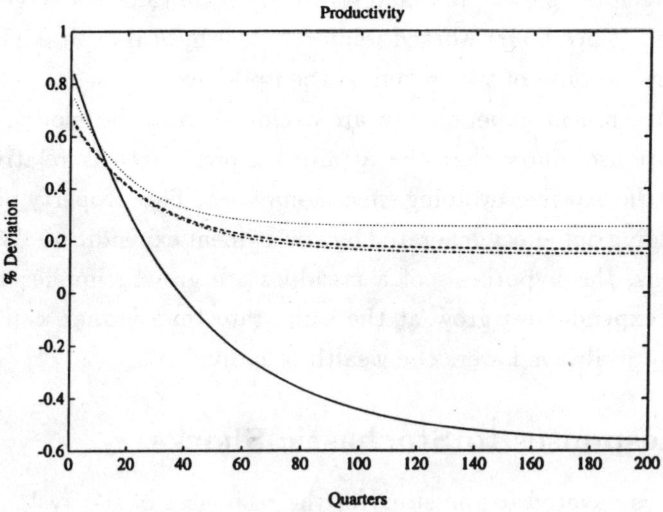

Figure 9.4: France : Response of γ_t to a 1% Deviation in K_t/H_t

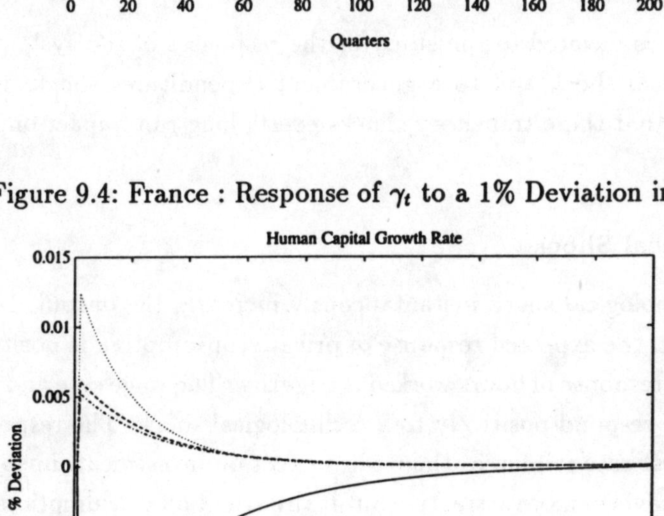

When $\psi = \frac{1}{1+\alpha}$, hours worked do not play any direct role in the dynamics of growth rate of human capital. Therefore, a positive gap in K_t/H_t implies an increase in the growth rate, whose dynamics is traced on the one of K_t/H_t. Hence, the interest variables deviate positively from their steady state growth path. Finally, when $\psi \to 1$, the rationalizing effect dominates the dynamics. As hours worked react negatively, the gap between the growth rate and its steady state value converges to zero positively, since hours worked reinforce the physical capital effect. The long run response of the system is then positive.

When government expenditures are excluded from the model, the long run responses show that the attained growth path is relatively higher when the learning by doing effect dominates. This property point out the crowding out effect generated by government expenditure. Whatever happens, the hypothesis of a steady state growth implies that government expenditures grow at the same rate than human capital. Consequently it always lowers the wealth of individuals.

9.3.2 Responses to Stochastic Shocks

This section is devoted to the study of the responses of the system to a technological shock and to a government expenditures shock. It is noteworthy that these transitory shocks exerts long run impact on the dynamics.

Technological Shock

A unit technological shock instantaneously increases the output. By a wealth effect, the expected response of private consumption is positive, whereas the response of hours worked is negative. The wage rate and the interest rate respond positively to a technological shock. The response of the interest rate reinforces the wealth effect on investment, in so far as it makes savings more attractive but it thwarts it on consumption. In this model, the wealth effect gets the upper hand of substitution effect so that consumption responds positively. The specification of the utility function in terms of leisure is such that the intertemporal elasticity of substitution of hours worked is infinite, so that hours respond according to a substitution effect. The response is then positive. Besides the direct effect of technological shock on the growth rate, through the productivity term, the domination of learning by doing leads to a positive response of growth rate in the short run. As the technological shock is transitory, its direct effect disappears in the dynamics, since the internal transitional dynamics of the model takes over. Then, after 20 quarters, the response of hours worked becomes negative in the U.S. so that its direct effect on growth should be negative. But as it has been noticed the value of ψ implies that the dynamics of growth is determined by the physical capital stock. In so far as the response of this latter is positive at the horizon of 20 quarters, the growth rate converges to its steady state positively. Then, in the long run, the steady state growth path attained is higher. The same phenomenon holds in France. The magnitude of the negative impact of the response of hours worked on the growth rate is not sufficient to break the direct positive impact of the technological shock transiting through the productivity gains component, because of decreasing return with respect to hours.

Once again, the response of the system is dependent on the value of ψ, as it can be seen in tables (9.6), (9.7) and figures (9.5), (9.6), (9.7), (9.8).

Table 9.6: USA : 1% Technological Shock

ψ	0	0.635	$\frac{1}{1+\alpha}$	1
IRF(∞)	-0.1600	0.3325	0.3600	0.4715
IRF(∞) without G	0.0145	0.3500	0.3688	0.4496

Table 9.7: France : 1% Technological Shock

ψ	0	$\frac{1}{1+\alpha}$	0.734	1
IRF(∞)	-1.0374	0.9523	1.0021	1.2425
IRF(∞) without G	-0.1080	0.9937	1.0268	1.1975

As $\psi \to 0$ the instantaneous response of the growth rate is positive since hours worked increase. But, in the U.S., at an horizon of 15 quarters, its response becomes negative. It then converges to its stationary state by negative values. That leads to a negative long run response

Figure 9.5: USA : Response of Y_t/n_t to a 1% Shock in A_t

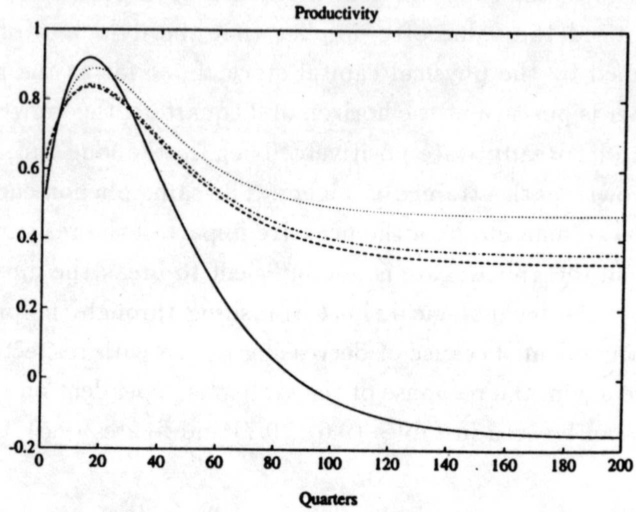

Figure 9.6: USA : Response of γ_t to a 1% Shock in A_t

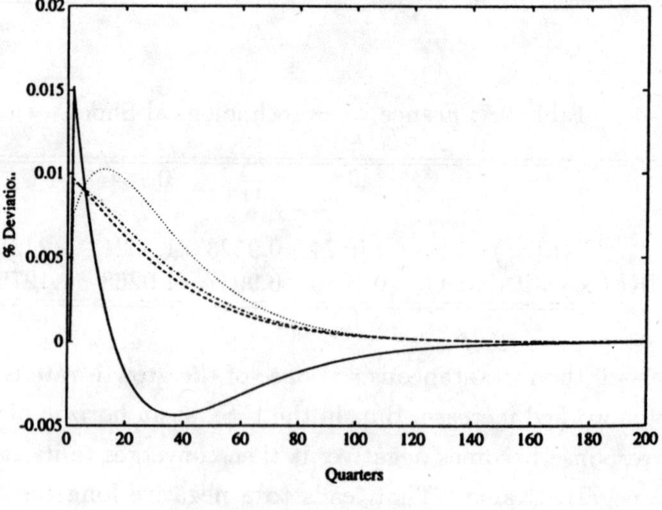

Figure 9.7: France : Response of Y_t/n_t to a 1% Shock in A_t

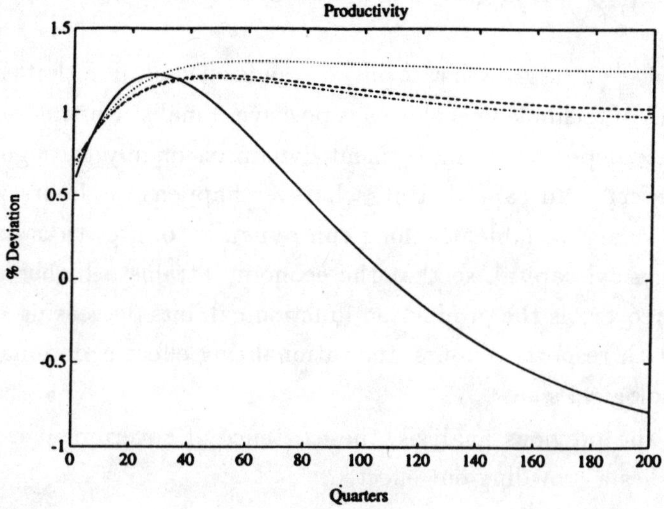

Figure 9.8: France : Response of γ_t to a 1% Shock in A_t

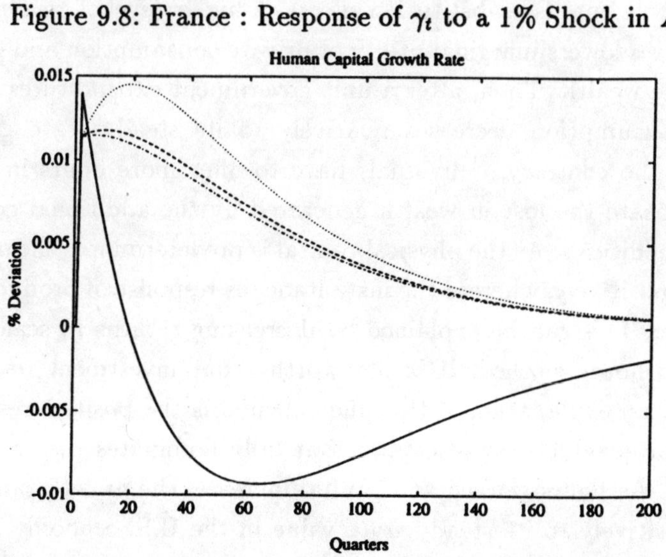

of the whole system. This phenomenon relies on the domination of the substitution effect in the behavior of individuals in terms of hours worked and on the existence of government expenditure, which, reducing the wealth, leads to a larger response of hours worked. A technological gain can then generate a relative loss of wealth in the long run even in the case of pure learning by doing. This is also observed in the French economy.

As $\psi = \frac{1}{1+\alpha}$, the growth rate only depends on capital so that the long run impact of technological shocks is positive. Finally, when $\psi \to 1$, the growth rate depends on employment dynamics, mainly through rationalizing effect, and capital. But, whatever happens, as hours worked are a stationary variable, the long run dynamics of growth is dominated by physical capital, so that the economy attains a higher growth path. Moreover, as the production function exhibits decreasing returns to scale with respect to hours, the rationalizing effect is dominated by the technological shock.

As in the previous analysis, the existence of government expenditures implies a crowding out effect.

Government Expenditure Shock

In this model $\nu = 0.2$ so that government expenditures have not only wealth effects but also substitution effects. A higher level of government expenditures lowers marginal utility of private consumption and lowers the private wealth. Then, after a unit government expenditures shock private consumption decreases relatively to its steady state growth path. On the contrary, individuals have to offer more hours in order to compensate the loss in wealth generated by the additional government expenditures. As the physical capital is predetermined, the output responds positively, whereas the instantaneous response of productivity is negative. This can be explained by decreasing returns to scale with respect to hours worked. It is noteworthy that investment responds positively, an explanation of this phenomenon is the positive response of marginal productivity of capital that fully dominates the crowding out effect. As hours worked and capital increase, the growth rate converges positively to its steady state value in the U.S. economy. Then, the long run effect of an increase in government expenditure on the system is positive. But it must be noticed that the magnitude of its impact is very slight, as figure (9.9) shows. The case of the french economy is quite different, since for the case $\psi = 0.734$ the rationalizing mechanism dominates. Then, as hours worked increase, the human capital growth rate respond negatively in the short run. But, as investment increases, this leads to an increase in the physical capital stock. At an horizon of 25 quarters, the response of the growth rate becomes positive, so that the long run effect is positive.

As previously, tables (9.8), (9.9) and figures (9.9), (9.10), (9.11), (9.12) illustrate the impact of parameter ψ on the growth dynamics.

Table 9.8: USA : 1% Government Expenditures Shock

ψ	0	0.635	$\frac{1}{1+\alpha}$	1
IRF(∞)	0.1481	0.0096	0.0026	-0.0249
IRF(∞) with $\nu = 0$	0.1877	0.0124	0.0033	-0.0318

Figure 9.9: USA : Response Y_t/n_t to a 1% Shock in G_t

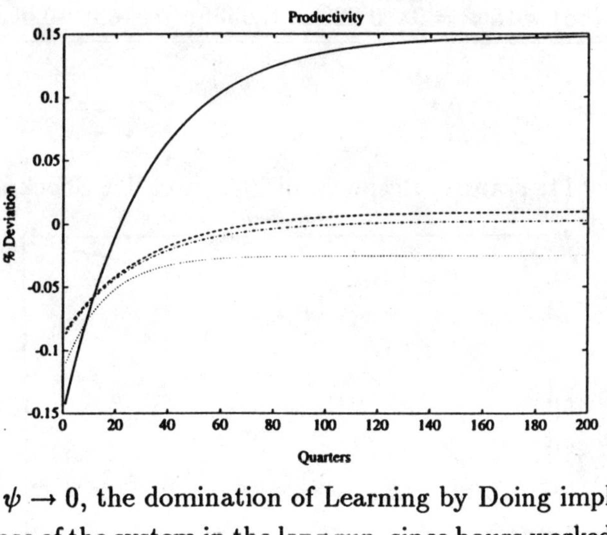

When $\psi \to 0$, the domination of Learning by Doing implies a positive response of the system in the long run, since hours worked increases. A government intervention, as long as it remain exogenous[14], can then

[14]For an analysis of endogenous behavior of government within the *RBC* framework, see Ambler and Paquet [1990] and Ambler and Paquet [1992].

Figure 9.10: USA : Response of γ_t to a 1% Shock in G_t

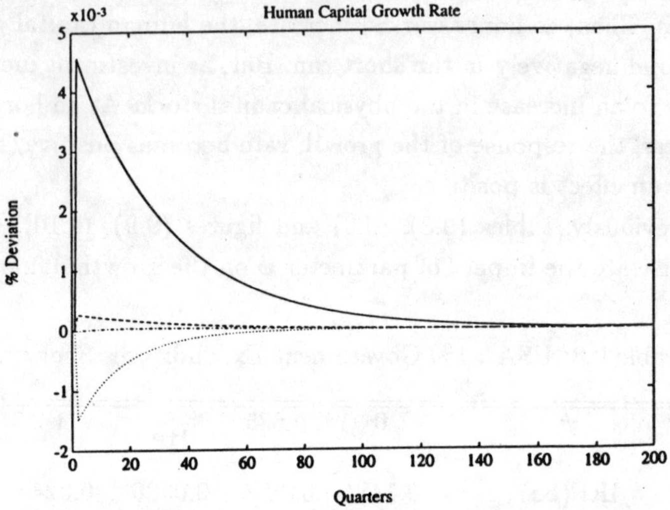

Table 9.9: France : 1% Government Expenditures Shock

ψ	0	$\frac{1}{1+\alpha}$	0.734	1
IRF(∞)	0.6525	0.0266	0.0131	-0.0487
IRF(∞) with $\nu = 0$	0.8298	0.0335	0.0163	-0.0623

Figure 9.11: France : Response of Y_t/n_t to a 1% Shock in G_t

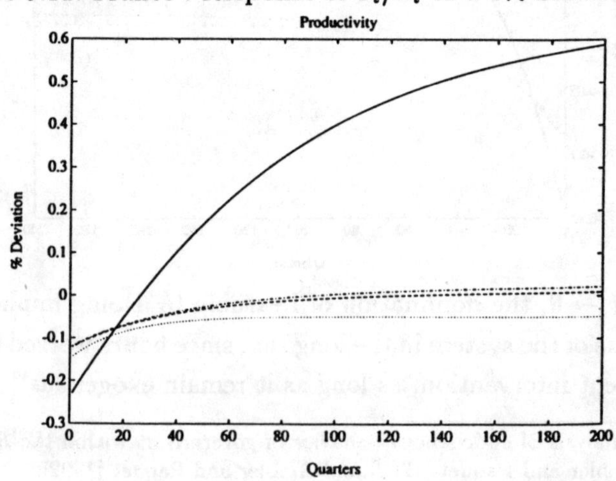

Figure 9.12: France : Response of γ_t to a 1% Shock in G_t

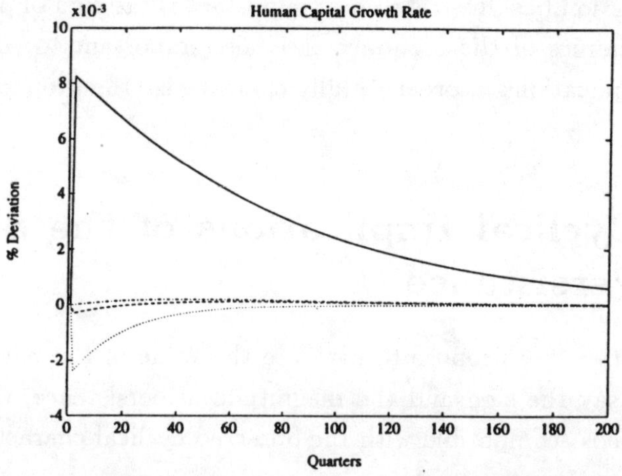

help to restore growth when the economy faces a recession phase. As $\psi = \frac{1}{1+\alpha}$, the dynamics of growth is driven by the physical capital stock, since its response to a government expenditures shock is positive, the long run impact on the system is positive. Finally, when $\psi \to 1$, the rationalizing effect leads to a negative response of the rate of growth, since hours worked increase. But contrary to the case of a technological shock, the response of physical capital is not sufficient to thwart this effect. The long run effect is then negative. That means that there exists a curative virtue of crisis when the rationalizing effect dominates. When the demand for commodities is low (*i.e.* a negative expenditure shock), hours worked diminish relatively to their steady state. This phenomenon is associated to a rationalizing effect that leads to an increase in productivity, which is not internal to individuals. As the gains of productivity persist, the rationalizing leads the economy to a higher steady state growth path.

It is noteworthy that when government expenditure exerts only a wealth effect ($\nu = 0$) the magnitude of long run impact is larger. The explanation of this phenomenon relies on the instantaneous impact of hours worked which is higher in the case $\nu = 0$. Since the marginal utility of private consumption decreases after a unit government expenditures shock, the magnitude of the response of private consumption is higher in the case $\nu = 0.2$. This implies that in the equilibrium, output is lower than in the case $\nu = 0$. Hence hours worked are lower in the case $\nu = 0.2$ than $\nu = 0$. It can also be observed that the magnitude of the response is slightly greater in France than in the USA

This section has illustrated how important is the sign of persistence in the dynamics of the economy. It is also important to consider its cyclical implications in order to fully characterize the properties of the model.

9.4 Cyclical Implications of the Sign of Persistence

In this section, we propose to evaluate the value of the parameter ψ, that is to say the sign and the magnitude of persistence, that seems to be the most compatible with the observed cyclical characteristics of the U.S. economy.

9.4.1 Stochastic Simulation Methodology

As it is fully described in Chapter 1 the model is simulated. We firstly generate 100 two-dimensional gaussian sample of 120 innovations $(\varepsilon_a, \varepsilon_g)$ with mean 0 and standard error σ_a and σ_g). Then the processes of A_t and g_t are built up, so that the time series can be constructed. It can be shown that the process of variable $\log(X)$ is given by :

$$A(L)\Delta\log(X_t) = B(L)\begin{pmatrix} \varepsilon_{a,t} \\ \varepsilon_{g,t} \end{pmatrix} + \tau$$

where[15] $A(L) = (1-\mu_1 L)(1-\rho_a L)(1-\rho_g L)$, $\tau = \log(\gamma)(1-\mu_1)(1-\rho_a)(1-\rho_g)$ and $B(L) = \begin{pmatrix} \theta_{0a} + \theta_{1a}L + \theta_{2a}L^2 + \theta_{3a}L^3 \\ \theta_{0g} + \theta_{1g}L + \theta_{2g}L^2 + \theta_{3g}L^3 \end{pmatrix}$.

As $A(L)$ and $B(L)$ have all their roots greater than unity in modulus, it is clear that the underlying processes of the variables of interest in level are non stationary[16].

In order to focus on the cyclical properties of the model, the time series are filtered so as to eliminate the growth component. Two filters are considered, that correspond to two views of the cycle.

[15] μ_1 is the eigenvalue attached to K_t/H_t. μ_1 and $\{\theta_{ij}\}_{i=\{1,2,3\}j=\{a,g\}}$ are complicated functions of the structural parameters of the model.

[16] Except for hours worked and growth rate of human capital.

Mintz [1969] introduced the distinction between "deviation cycles" and "step cycles". The former corresponds to the traditional view of fluctuations, the business cycle is defined as the gap between the historical time series and their long run trend. This view is suitable for models that relies an exogenous long run trend. "Deviation cycles" are then based on the adjustment of indicators for their long run trend. It then depends on the definition of this trend. In the *RBC* framework, it is traditionally defined by the growth component of the Hodrick and Prescott [1980]'s filter[17]. The latter considers that the cycle is defined as the growth rate of series. This is suitable for an endogenous growth model whose growth rate has its own dynamics. The business cycle is then fully characterized by the way the growth rates of the main aggregates evolves and are linked.

First of all, the log-differentiation filter is considered. Then the Hodrick and Prescott [1980]'s filter is studied. We characterize the cycle by the examination of second order moments, in the line of the real business cycle methodology.

9.4.2 Simulation Results

The French Economy

As table (9.10) shows, the model shall reproduce a variability of hours worked and productivity less than that of output, and a greater variability of investment and consumption. It must also generate a low degree of persistence of cyclical components. The aggregates are all pro-cyclical but the correlations between series and output are low. However, the correlation between productivity growth and the increase in hours worked is quite null.

The value $\psi = 0.734$ seems to correspond to an optimal parametrization of the model. The artificial economy is able to order correctly the relative variabilities of productivity, investment and hours worked. Nevertheless, the volatility of consumption is under-reproduced in spite of the presence of government expenditure shocks, that reinforces the volatility of series[18]. The permanent income hypothesis seems not to be

[17]See King and Rebelo [1993]a for its spectral properties

[18]The results obtained simulating the model with only technological shocks and then only government expenditures shocks confirm this assertion.

Table 9.10: France : $\Delta \log$ Filter

Moments	Historical	$\psi = 0$	$\psi = \frac{1}{1+\alpha}$	$\psi = 0.734$	$\psi = 1$
$\sigma_{\widehat{y}}$	0.72	1.33	1.20	1.20	1.22
$\sigma_{\widehat{c}}/\sigma_{\widehat{y}}$	1.05	0.39	0.56	0.56	0.56
$\sigma_{\widehat{i}}/\sigma_{\widehat{y}}$	2.77	2.70	2.45	2.45	2.47
$\sigma_{\widehat{n}}/\sigma_{\widehat{y}}$	0.48	0.64	0.49	0.50	0.53
$\sigma_{\widehat{y/n}}/\sigma_{\widehat{y}}$	0.89	0.44	0.53	0.53	0.50
$AR(1)_{\widehat{y}}$	0.18	-0.01	-0.02	-0.02	-0.003
$AR(1)_{\widehat{c}}$	-0.09	0.09	0.03	0.02	0.04
$AR(1)_{\widehat{y/n}}$	0.01	0.1	0.02	0.02	0.04
$Corr(\widehat{c},\widehat{y})$	0.46	0.94	0.95	0.95	0.94
$Corr(\widehat{n},\widehat{y})$	0.30	0.95	0.97	0.97	0.97
$Corr(\widehat{y/n},\widehat{y})$	0.04	0.90	0.98	0.98	0.96
$Corr(\widehat{y/n},\widehat{n})$	-0.02	0.73	0.90	0.90	0.87

supported on the french economy. The relative variability of productivity is underestimated whatever the filter used, as table (9.11) shows. In the case, not reported here, of divisible work, this relative volatility is well reproduced for $\psi = 0$. This lack of variability for productivity can be partly explained by the parametrization of the model that leads to a too great smoothing effect of productivity.

It is noteworthy that the more ψ increases, the more hours worked are volatile whereas the less is productivity[19]. This phenomenon relies on the domination of the rationalizing effect : in order to preserve a level of productivity, that is to say to smooth productivity, the firm are led to hire and fire jobs, which increases hours worked volatility. This phenomenon does not play in the case of pure learning by doing, but hours worked are more volatile because of the intertemporal behavior of hours worked supply : individual knows that offering more hours worked today will lead to a higher level of wealth tomorrow. It then seems that the cases of pure learning by doing or pure rationalizing better match the relative volatility of these two aggregates.

The autocorrelations are quite well reproduced when we focus on

[19]We abstract from the case $\psi = 0$.

Table 9.11: France : Hodrick-Prescott Filter

Moments	Historical	$\psi = 0$	$\psi = \frac{1}{1+\alpha}$	$\psi = 0.734$	$\psi = 1$
$\sigma_{\widehat{y}}$	1.03	1.45	1.33	1.29	1.35
$\sigma_{\widehat{c}}/\sigma_{\widehat{y}}$	0.81	0.41	0.59	0.58	0.57
$\sigma_{\widehat{i}}/\sigma_{\widehat{y}}$	3.15	2.68	2.45	2.44	2.46
$\sigma_{\widehat{n}}/\sigma_{\widehat{y}}$	0.72	0.65	0.49	0.50	0.54
$\sigma_{\widehat{y/n}}/\sigma_{\widehat{y}}$	0.73	0.44	0.54	0.54	0.51
$AR(1)_{\widehat{y}}$	0.79	0.66	0.67	0.66	0.66
$AR(1)_{\widehat{c}}$	0.64	0.69	0.68	0.68	0.68
$AR(1)_{\widehat{y/n}}$	0.68	0.70	0.68	0.68	0.69
$Corr(\widehat{c},\widehat{y})$	0.59	0.91	0.93	0.93	0.92
$Corr(\widehat{n},\widehat{y})$	0.69	0.93	0.96	0.96	0.95
$Corr(\widehat{y/n},\widehat{y})$	0.69	0.86	0.97	0.96	0.95
$Corr(\widehat{y/n},\widehat{n})$	-0.05	0.63	0.86	0.85	0.80

the $\Delta \log$ filter. This is partly imputable to mechanism that are at work in the model. As it generates an endogenous growth, stationary shocks affect the long run dynamics in a permanent manner. The variables are then integrated of order 1 ($I(1)$), and their ARMA representation is dominated by the non stationary component. Then the $\Delta \log$ filter removes the rest of the dynamics and the autocorrelations are significantly null. This phenomenon is a generic property of most of endogenous growth models. In the case of the Hodrick-Prescott filter this does not occur because this filter operates in a quite different way, so that some dynamics stays in the processes of the time series[20].

The sign of correlations between output and the other aggregates is in accordance with the observed cyclical pattern of the french economy. But some problems still exist in terms of magnitude. This phenomenon is encountered in other *RBC* models on french data.

The US Economy

Table (9.12) shows that the U.S. economy displays a variability of consumption, hours worked less than that of output, and a greater variabi-

[20]It can even generate a spurious cycle.

lity of investment and productivity. As in France, the degree of persistence is low. The aggregates are also all pro-cyclical but the correlations between series and output are low. Finally, the correlation between productivity growth and the increase in hours worked is negative.

Table 9.12: USA : Δ log Filter

Moments	Historical	$\psi = 0$	$\psi = 0.635$	$\psi = \frac{1}{1+\alpha}$	$\psi = 1$
$\sigma_{\widehat{y}}$	1.14	1.41	1.24	1.24	1.33
$\sigma_{\widehat{c}}/\sigma_{\widehat{y}}$	0.52	0.39	0.54	0.53	0.49
$\sigma_{\widehat{i}}/\sigma_{\widehat{y}}$	2.54	2.49	2.43	2.42	2.45
$\sigma_{\widehat{n}}/\sigma_{\widehat{y}}$	0.80	0.84	0.66	0.68	0.76
$\sigma_{\widehat{y/n}}/\sigma_{\widehat{y}}$	1.36	0.37	0.44	0.43	0.38
$AR(1)_{\widehat{y}}$	0.41	-0.01	-0.03	-0.02	-0.01
$AR(1)_{\widehat{c}}$	0.16	0.08	0.05	0.07	0.04
$AR(1)_{\widehat{y/n}}$	0.08	0.11	0.05	0.07	0.08
$Corr(\widehat{c},\widehat{y})$	0.45	0.55	0.59	0.56	0.56
$Corr(\widehat{n},\widehat{y})$	0.58	0.93	0.94	0.94	0.94
$Corr(\widehat{y/n},\widehat{y})$	0.57	0.59	0.86	0.84	0.74
$Corr(\widehat{y/n},\widehat{n})$	-0.72	0.26	0.63	0.61	0.47

The value $\psi = 0.635$ allows to match the U.S. economy in a quite satisfying way. The artificial economy is able to order correctly the relative variabilities of consumption, investment and hours worked. Nevertheless, the volatility of investment and hours worked are underestimated. The relative variability of productivity is widely underestimated. However, this misestimation appears to rely on the filter used. As table (9.13) shows, in the case of the Hodrick-Prescott filter this volatility is well reproduced. The good reproduction of the variability of productivity in that case is linked on the specification of the process of human capital accumulation and the presence of the government expenditure shock. A technological shock leads to a greater volatility of productivity, but the human capital accumulation leads to a smoothing phenomenon. The government shock has a negative influence on the dynamics of productivity that reinforces the smoothing effect.

The results concerning the volatility of hours worked can be explained in the same framework as in France.

Table 9.13: USA : Hodrick-Prescott Filter

Moments	Historical	$\psi = 0$	$\psi = 0.635$	$\psi = \frac{1}{1+\alpha}$	$\psi = 1$
$\sigma_{\widehat{y}}$	1.76	1.72	1.53	1.53	1.67
$\sigma_{\widehat{c}}/\sigma_{\widehat{y}}$	0.72	0.42	0.58	0.57	0.53
$\sigma_{\widehat{i}}/\sigma_{\widehat{y}}$	4.81	2.47	2.41	2.41	2.43
$\sigma_{\widehat{n}}/\sigma_{\widehat{y}}$	0.80	0.83	0.66	0.68	0.77
$\sigma_{\widehat{y/n}}/\sigma_{\widehat{y}}$	0.50	0.41	0.46	0.45	0.41
$AR(1)_{\widehat{y}}$	0.85	0.68	0.68	0.68	0.68
$AR(1)_{\widehat{c}}$	0.86	0.74	0.73	0.72	0.74
$AR(1)_{\widehat{y/n}}$	0.52	0.75	0.72	0.72	0.75
$Corr(\widehat{c},\widehat{y})$	0.81	0.54	0.56	0.56	0.54
$Corr(\widehat{n},\widehat{y})$	0.86	0.91	0.92	0.92	0.93
$Corr(\widehat{y/n},\widehat{y})$	0.59	0.57	0.83	0.82	0.70
$Corr(\widehat{y/n},\widehat{n})$	0.10	0.37	0.56	0.55	0.39

The autocorrelations are badly reproduced when we focus on the $\Delta\log$ filter. As it has been explained in the french case, this result can be attributed to the endogenous status of growth. Then it can be seen that the autocorrelations are slightly underestimated except for productivity. This latter case is explainable by the smoothing effect implied by the formulation of the human capital process, based on the persistence of gains in productivity.

The sign of correlations between output and the other aggregates is in accordance with the observed cyclical pattern of the U.S. economy. But some problems still exist in terms of magnitude. It appears that extreme values for ψ (pure Learning by doing and in a worse manner pure rationalizing) allow to obtain the correlation productivity-output and the correlation productivity-hours worked. As $\psi \rightarrow 1$, these correlations diminish. This effect is partly explained by the rationalizing effect : when activity is low, firms will fire in order to preserve the level of productivity attained, so that the direct correlation between productivity and hours worked implied by the pure rationalizing effect is negative. It is clear that this effect lowers the correlations productivity-output and productivity-hours worked. Nevertheless, it seems that they are better reproduced in the case of pure Learning by doing. As it has already been noticed, the Learning by doing mechanism leads to an intertemporal effect in hours worked supply. When individual offer an additional hour they expect the future wealth it induces, so that the elasticity of hours worked supply to a shock is higher in this model than in a standard *RBC* model, and the correlation between productivity and hours worked is lower. Finally, this effect is reinforced by the presence of the government expenditures shock.

This model of cyclical growth improve on some points the explicative power of standard *RBC* models without altering other features.

9.5 Concluding Comments

Taking into account a process of human capital accumulation, transiting through a learning by doing and a rationalizing effect, allows one to endogenize the growth rate of the economy in the long run as well as in the short run. Then, growth and fluctuations are intimately linked and the model achieves the integrated view of cycles and growth.

The endogeneity of productivity gains acts as a propagation and amplification canal of transitory shocks within the business cycle. Technological shocks, but government expenditures shocks as well, exerts a permanent effect on the long run dynamics of the economy. The sign of this impact depends on the relative weight of learning by doing and rationalizing effects in the human capital accumulation, given by the parameter ψ. However, allowing for a role of the physical capital stock in the human capital process leads to moderate the magnitude of the negative link between activity and productivity put forward by certain recent analysis. This model then provides an explicit representation of persistence in so far as it allows to study its sources.

The simulation also enables to confront the model to the facts. It then appears that it constitutes a good tool to match the french and U.S. cyclical pattern. But, the results are more encouraging for U.S.A than for France[21]. One more time, the parameter ψ appears to be crucial in the reproduction of the main characteristic of the business cycle.

[21] This result is in accordance with others studies, as shown in chapter 1

However, some difficulties remain. The model is excessively sensitive to the value of ψ. Nevertheless the confrontation of the moments generated by the artificial economy to the data seems to confirm the existence of a positive persistence.

Even though the view of growth in terms of a representative agent adopted here presents a synthetic interest, it implies the loss of more structural aspects of the cycle that interact with growth, such as demand externalities or phenomenons that are the concern of an analysis in terms of heterogenous agents, such as inter-sectoral reallocation. These mechanisms provides incentive to go beyond representative agents and constitute a very stimulating line of research .

9.6 Appendix

A. USA : Transitional Dynamics

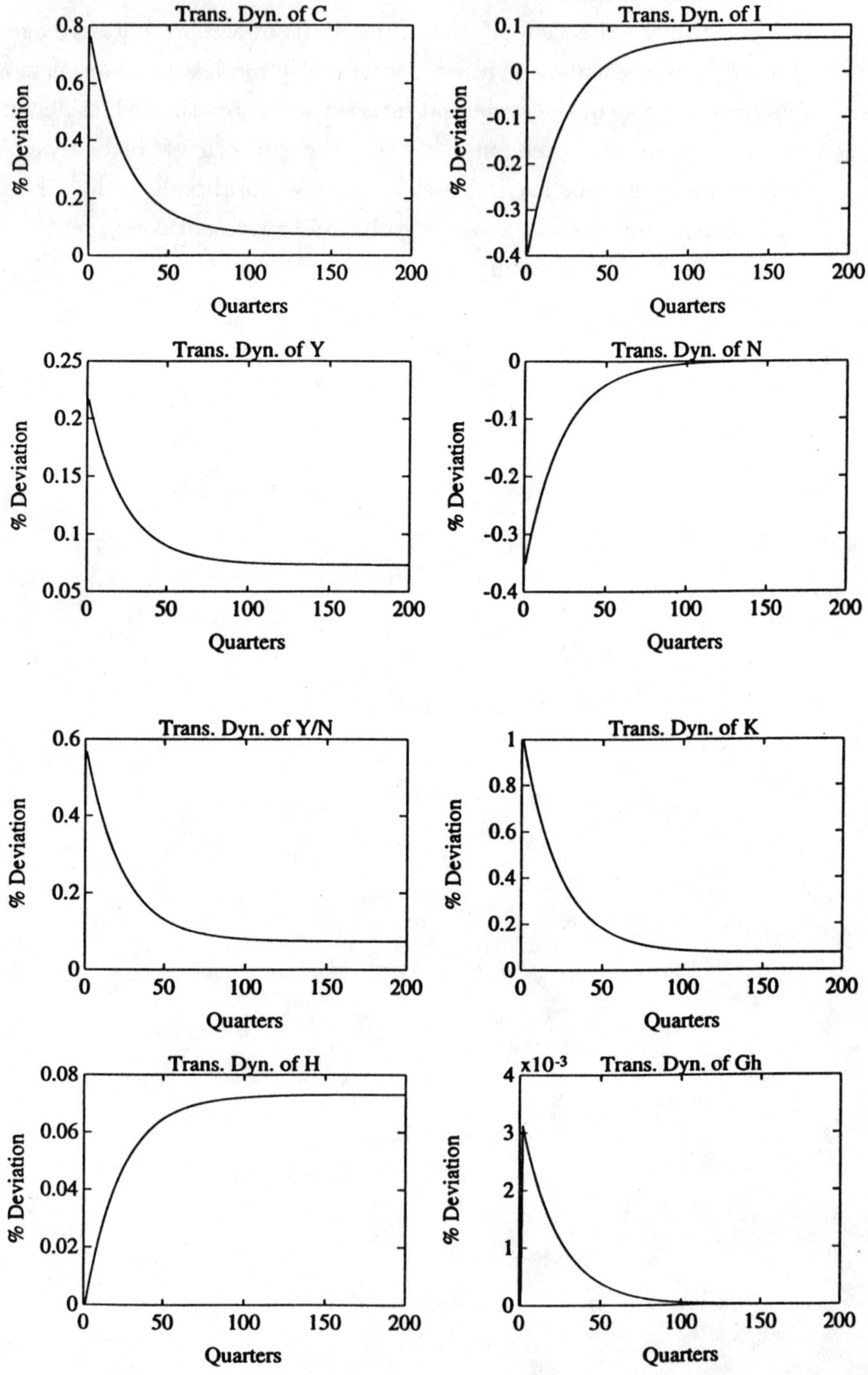

B. USA : Technological Shock

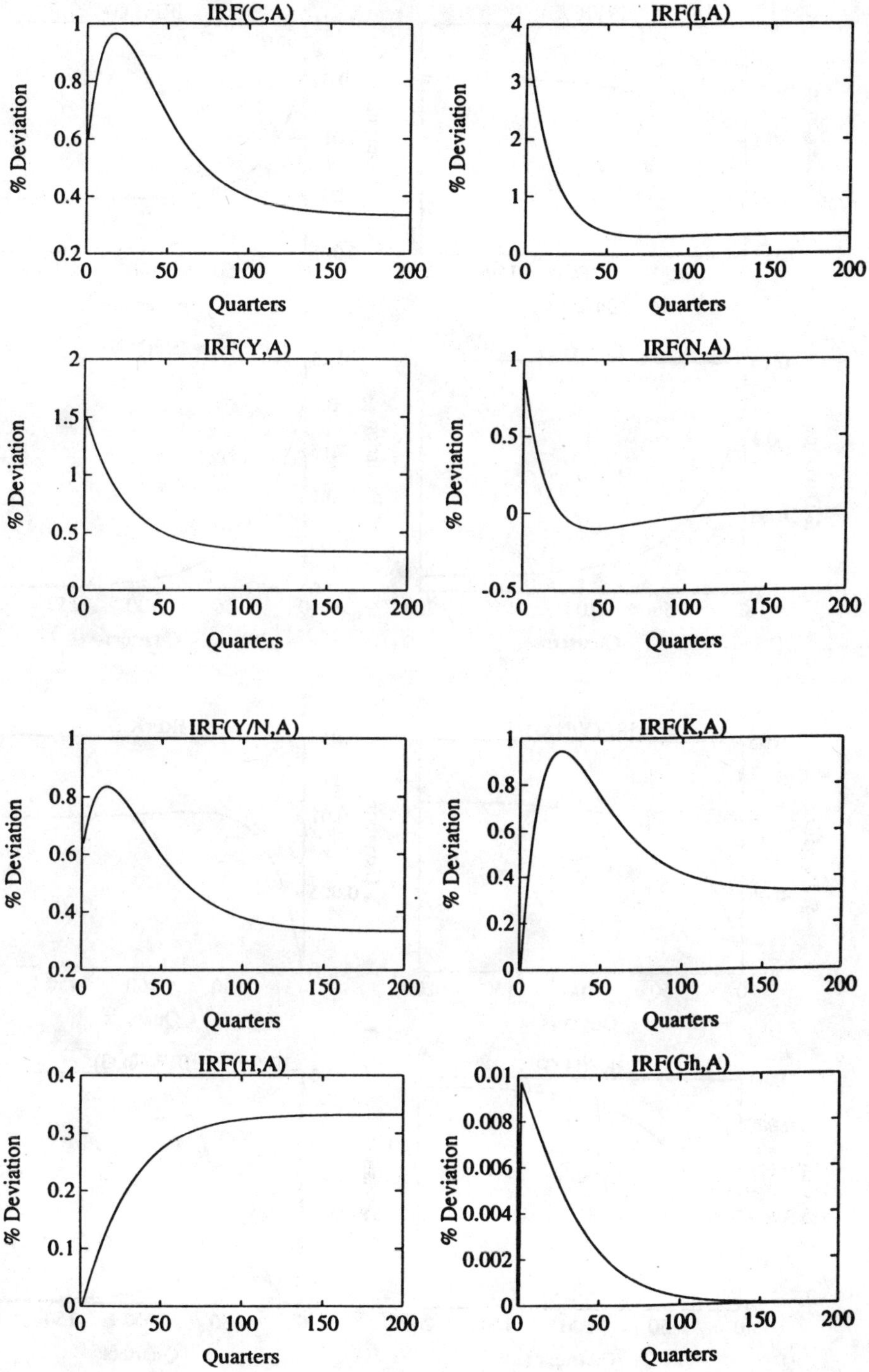

C. USA : Government Spending Shock

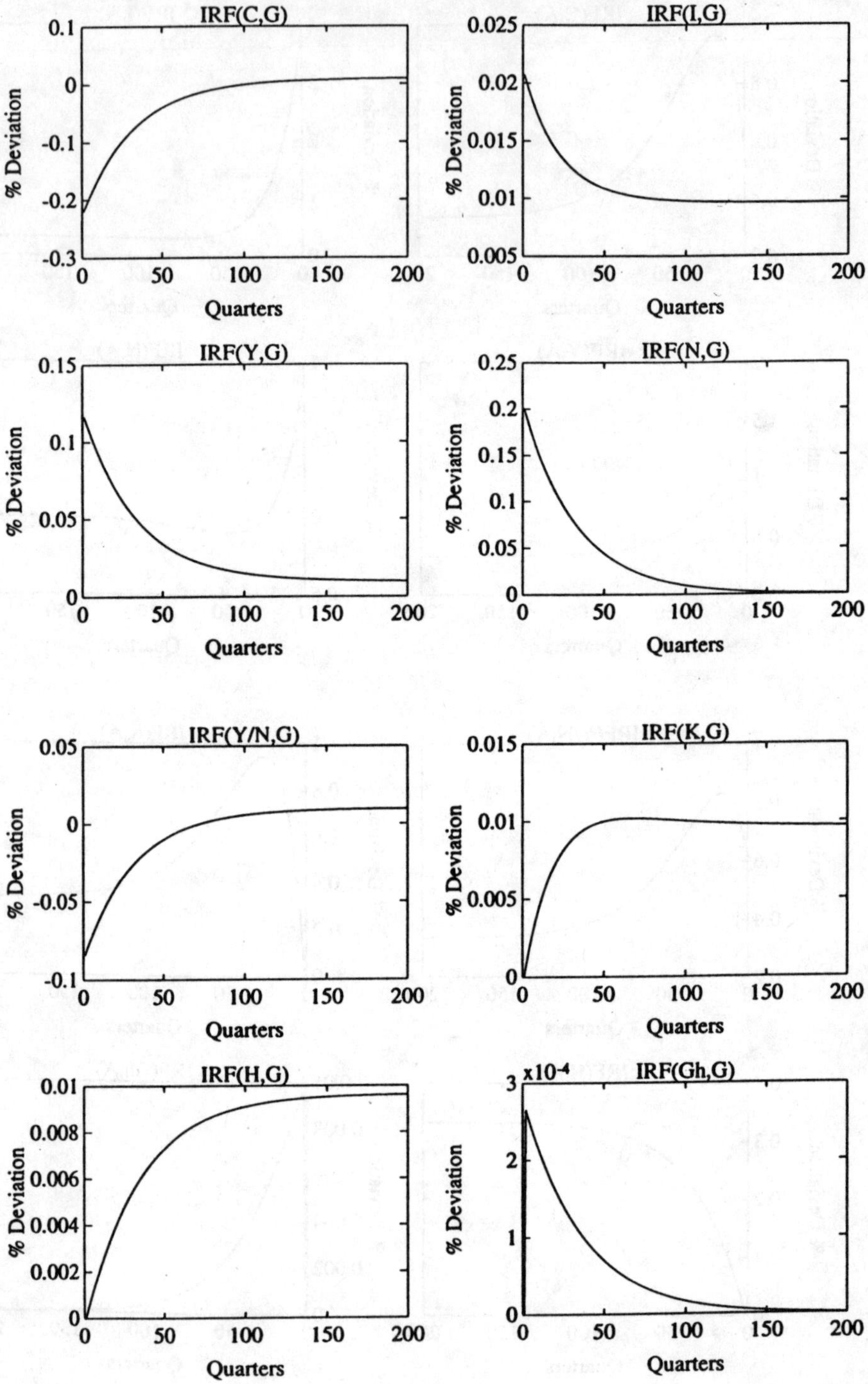

D. France : Transitional Dynamics

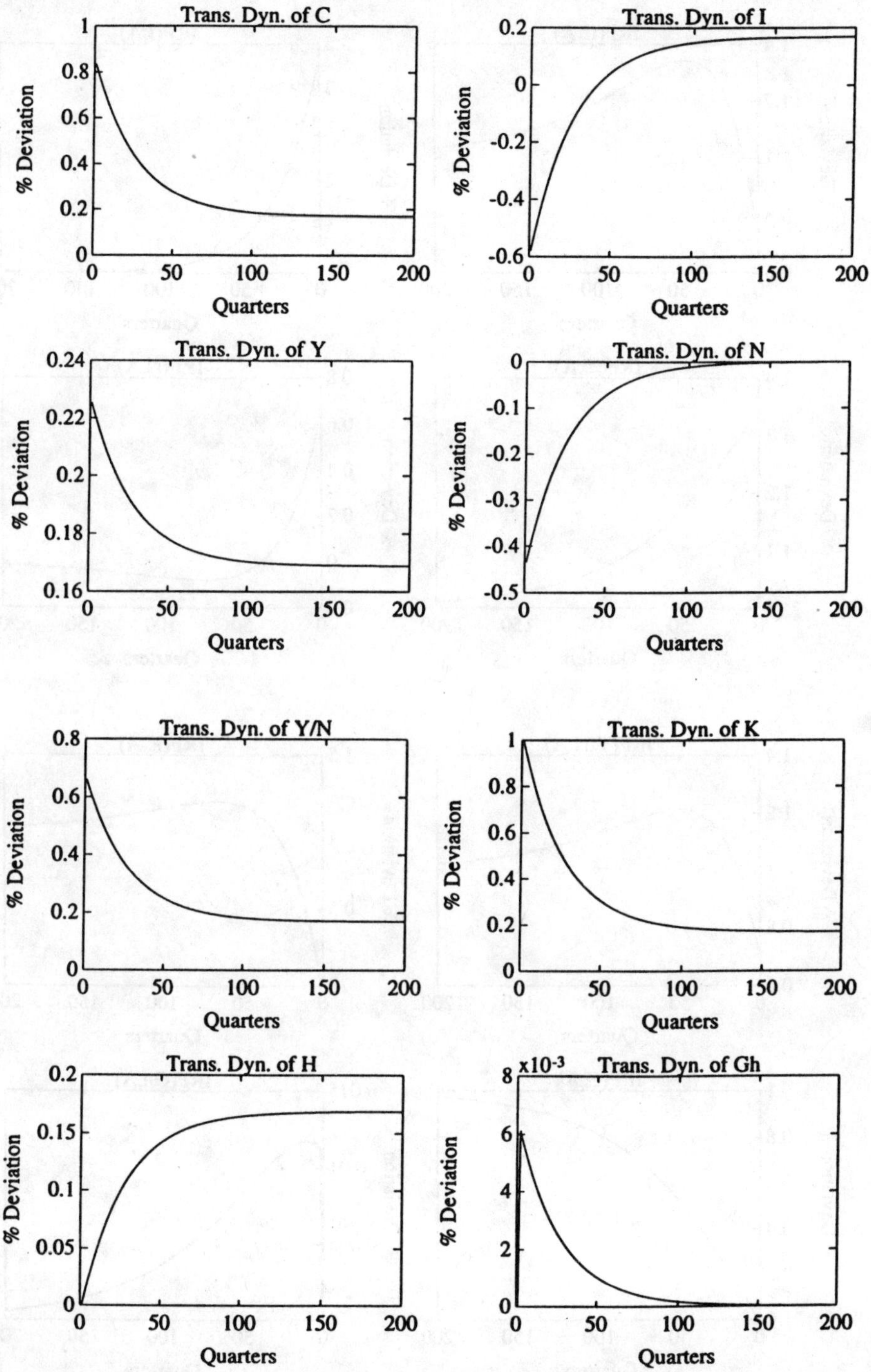

E. France : Technological Shock

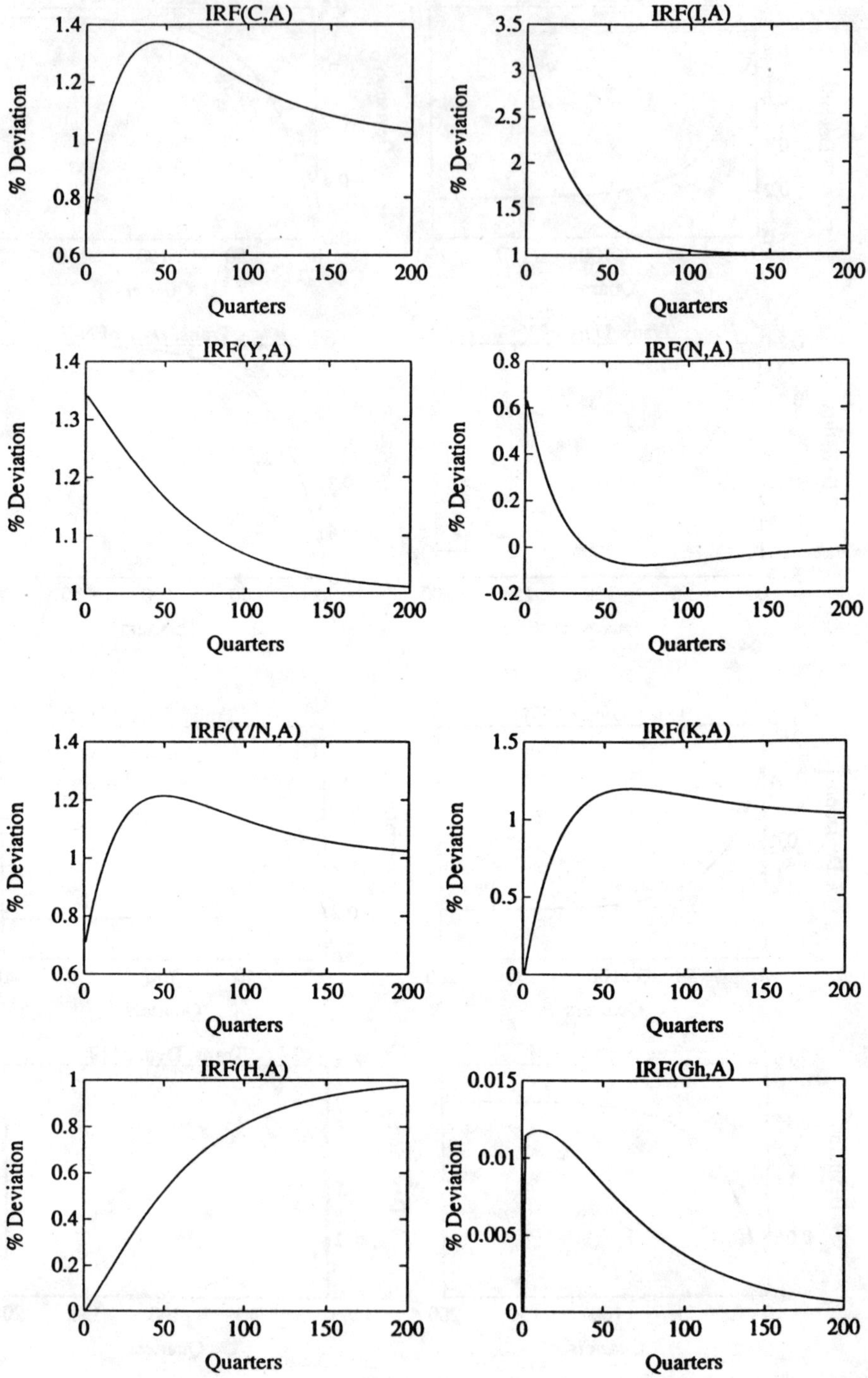

F. France : Government Spending Shock

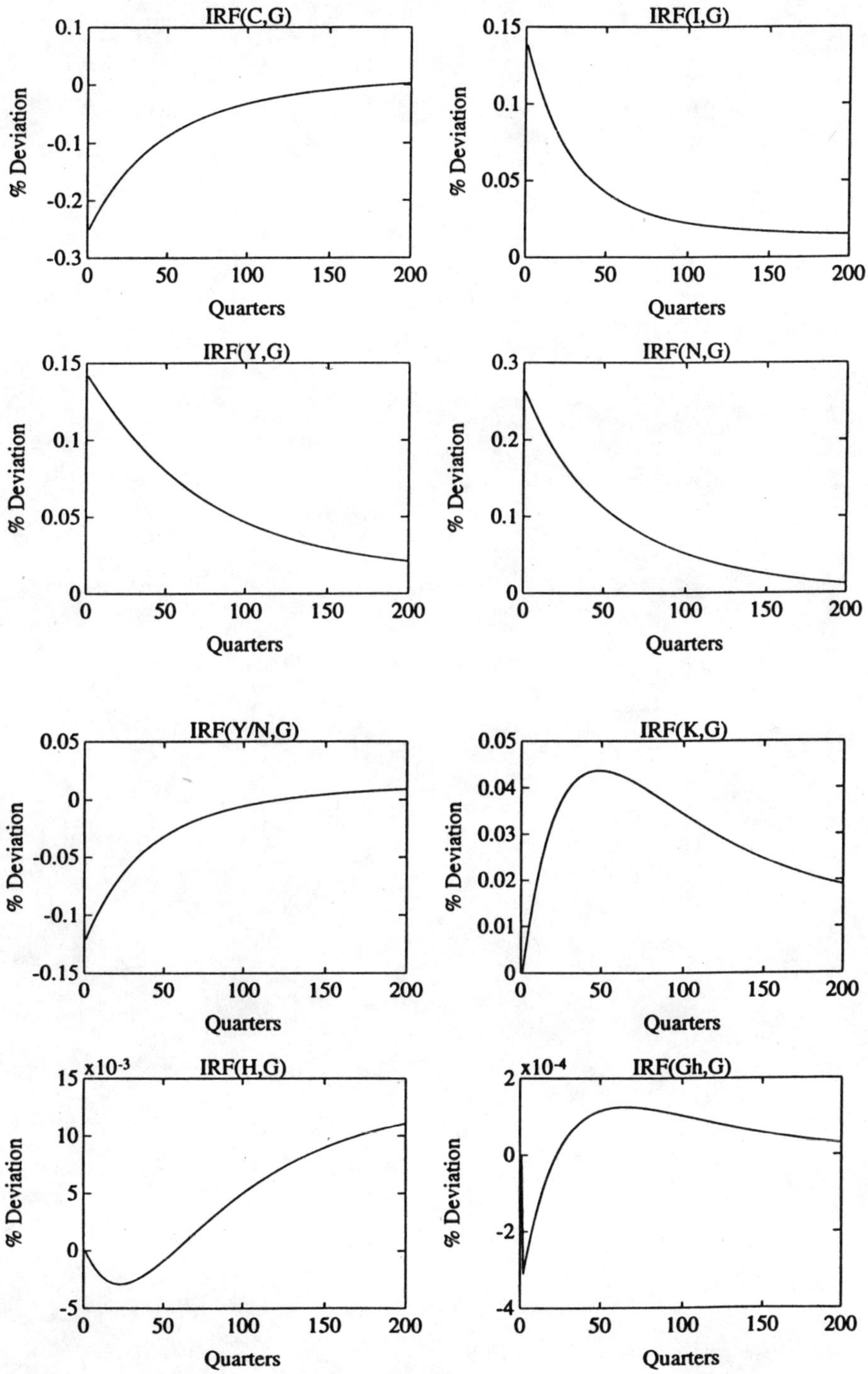

Bibliography

P. Aghion and G. Saint-Paul. *On the Virtues of Bad Times.* Working paper 578, CEPR, 1991.

S. Ambler and A. Paquet. *Fiscal Spendings Shocks, Real Business Cycles and Stabilization Policies.* Working paper 51, Université du Québec à Montréal, 1990.

S. Ambler and A. Paquet. *The Government as Engine of Growth and of Cyclical Fluctuations.* Working paper , Université du Québec à Montréal, 1992.

K. Arrow. The Economic Implications of Learning by Doing. *Review of Economic Studies*, 80:155–173, 1962.

D. Aschauer. Fiscal Policy and Aggregate Demand. *American Economic Review*, 75:117–127, 1985.

R. Barro. Output Effects of Government Purchases. *Journal of Political Economy*, 89(6):1086–1121, 1981.

O. Blanchard and D. Quah. The Dynamic Effects of Aggregate Demand and Supply Disturbances. *American Economic Review*, 79(4):655–673, September 1989.

L. Christiano and M. Eichenbaum. *Is Theory Really Ahead of Measurement? Current Real Business Cycle Theory and Aggregate Market Fluctuations.* Working paper 2700, NBER, 1988.

X. Fairise. *Un modèle de cycles réels avec coûts d'ajustements croisés.* Cahiers ECO & MATHS 93.109, MAD, Université de Paris I, 1993.

J. Gali and M. Hammour. *Long Run Effects of Business Cycles.* Working paper , Columbia University, May 1991.

G. Hansen. Indivisible Labor and the Business Cycles. *Journal of Monetary Economics*, 16(3):309–327, November 1985.

Z. Hercowitz and M. Sampson. Output Growth, the Real Wage, and Employment Fluctuations. *American Economic Review*, 81(5):1215–1237, 1991.

R. Hodrick and E. Prescott. *Post-War U.S. Business Cycles: an Empirical Investigation.* Mimeo , Carnegie-Mellon University, November 1980.

R. King and S. Rebelo. *Business Cycles with Endogenous Growth.* Working paper , Universisty of Rochester, 1988. unpublished manuscript.

R. King and S. Rebelo. Low Frequency Filtering and Real Business Cycles. *Journal of Economic Dynamics and Control*, 17():207–231, 1993.

R. King and S. Rebelo. Transitional Dynamics and Economic Growth in the Neoclassical Model. *American Economic Review*, 83(4):908–931, September 1993.

J.P. Laffargue, P. Malgrange and T. Pujol. *Une maquette trimestrielle de l'économie française avec anticipations rationnelles et concurrence monopolistique.* Working paper, CEPREMAP, April 1990. Rapport de contrat pour le Commissariat Général au Plan.

R. Lucas. On the Mechanisms of Economic Development. *Journal of Monetary Economics*, 22():3–42, 1988.

I. Mintz. *Dating Postwar Business Cycles. Methods and their Application to Western Germany, 1950-1967.* NBER (Distributed by Columbia University Press), New-York, 1969.

C. Nelson and C. Plosser. Trend and Random Walks in Macroeconomic Time Series. *Journal of Monetary Economics*, 10(1):139–162, September 1982.

P. Romer. Increasing Returns and Long Run Growth. *Journal of Political Economy*, 94:1002–1037, 1986.

G. Saint-Paul. Productivity Growth and the Structure of the Business Cycle. *European Economic Review*, 37, May 1992.

R. Solow. A Contribution to the Theory of Economic Growth. *Quarterly Journal of Economics*, 70(1):65–94, February 1956.

G. Stadler. Business Cycle Models with Endogenous Growth. *American Economic Review*, 80(4):763–778, 1990.

R. Stulz and W. Wasserfallen. Macroeconomic Time series, Business Cycles and Macroeconomic Policies. *Carnegie Rochester Conference Series on Public Policy*, 22:9–54, 1985.

Chapter 10

Statistical Evaluation of the RBC Model

Patrick Fève & François Langot

Abstract

The aim of this paper is to test, on French data, the main *RBC* proposition according to which technological innovations are sufficient for a calibrated neoclassical growth model to mimic the business cycle. An intertemporal optimization model with a stationary technology shock and non time-separability in consumption and leisure is developed. Using the Generalized Method of Moments, we estimate the structural parameters and then, test using statistical grounds the model's ability to reproduce the cyclical features of the French economy. We propose an extension of Eichenbaum [1991]'s methodology to show the limit of calibration-simulation methods: as in standard macroeconometric models, the stochastic simulation takes into account the sampling uncertainty on estimated structural parameters. The model is estimated on quarterly data from 1951 to 1989. While the tests do not reject the assumption of balanced growth, they point out the model's inability to reproduce the French business cycle.

Introduction

The analysis of impulse and propagation mechanisms as explanations of economic fluctuations is one of the most discussed issue in macroeconomics. During the eighties, the Real Business Cycle theory deeply renewed this debate. This theory describes the essentials of the business cycle from a set of indicators, as suggested by Lucas [1977] (set of second order moments). In this view, the volatility of macroeconomic data would be the result of optimal responses to technology innovations of a representative agent in a Walrasian framework.

On the basis of the results obtained from the simulation of various *RBC* models, Prescott [1986] and Hansen [1988] consider that 70% to 100% of output fluctuations could be explained, despite some difficulties concerning the reproduction of the labor market.

Whatever the different extensions proposed to this method of analysis [1], an essential criticism addressed to these theoretical papers concerns their validation procedure. As d'Autume pointed out:

> "Considering the calibration and simulation methods as the equivalent of an econometric approach is very excessive because the observation procedure is not codified enough as to evaluate its discriminating power."(d'Autume [1992], p.15)

In macroeconomics, the procedure of testing theories by testing their implications rather than their assumptions relies on the methodology espoused by Friedman [1953]. According to him, every theoretical model is incomplete and is necessarily an abstraction, a simplification and it can never be realistic. Every model is an inaccurate descriptive representation of reality. A selection criterion between models can be simplicity:

> "A hypothesis is important if it explains such by little, that is, if it abstracts the common and crucial elements from the mass of complex and detailed circumstances surrounding the phenomena to be explained and permits valid predictions on the basis of them alone." (Friedman [1953], p. 14)

According to Friedman, a selection criterion between alternative hypotheses equally consistent with available evidence must be to some extent arbitrary, though there is agreement that a relevant way is suggested by the criterion of simplicity and "fruitfulness": theory is more

[1] For example, imperfect competition, price rigidity and monetary shocks (Hairault and Portier in chapter 6 of this book), labor hoarding and government expenditures shocks (Burnside, Eichenbaum and Rebelo [1993], Fairise and Langot [1994]). See Hénin [1991] or McCallum [1989] for different surveys of this literature.

"fruitful" the more precise the resulting predictions, the wider the area within which the theory yields predictions, and the more numerous additional lines for further research it suggests.

> "Theory is thus to be judged by its predictive power for the class of phenomena which it is intended to explain. Only factual evidence can show whether it is right or wrong or, better, tentatively accepted as valid or rejected [...]. The only relevant test of validity of a hypothesis is comparison of its predictions with experience." (Friedman [1953], pp. 8-9)

Factual evidence can never prove a hypothesis, but can only confirm it. If it fails to disprove it, theory can be considered as a useful explanation, and we can conclude that, in reality, individuals behave as if they were obeying the explicit rules of the model.

Indeed, a theory whose justification is its quantitative implications, must propose statistical tests allowing a quantitative evaluation of the validity of these propositions. According to Eichenbaum, an empirical study must answer to the following question:

> "Convincing structural empirical work ought to address the question: Does the model succeed quantitatively in accounting for those features of the data it was designed to shed light on? But good empirical work also ought to tell us just how loudly the data speak in favor of a given hypothesis." (Eichenbaum [1991], p. 624)

In this paper, we test the standard proposition of the *RBC* theory, that is: is the model able to reproduce the second order moments of the macroeconomic data?

An econometric validation method allows us to measure the effect of uncertainty on *RBC* prediction. We do not follow the usual calibration-simulation *RBC* methodology here: we estimate and test in a unified framework the structural parameters and the cyclical properties of the model.

Since the papers of Eichenbaum [1991], Christiano and Eichenbaum [1992] and Burnside, Eichenbaum and Rebelo [1993], econometric methods, such as Generalized Method of Moments have been used to estimate stochastic growth models and test their cyclical counterparts[2].

[2]See Altug [1989] for an alternative estimation method.

Moreover, looking at confidence intervals, obtained through estimation, shows the limits of the calibration exercises for the validation of the theoretical model.

The aim of this paper is to test, on French data, the propagation mechanisms of the standard *RBC* model and to evaluate the impact of technology shocks on economic fluctuations. Thus, the paper is an attempt to find an answer to the two following questions through statistical inference:

- Is the neoclassical growth model with a technology shock able to reproduce the cyclical behavior of the French economy?
- Is the computation of theoretical model implications sensitive to small perturbations in the structural parameters?

To this end, it is necessary to develop estimation and evaluation methods for an *RBC* model. In order to achieve this purpose, we estimate by the Generalized Method of Moments the structural parameters of a growth model, where the technological perturbation follows a stationary process. This estimation method enables us to measure statistically the ability of the model to mimic the French short term economic fluctuations. Moreover, it provides a measure of uncertainty of the importance of the technology shocks and of the estimated parameters. Thus, we get a measure of the structural parameters uncertainty given by the covariance matrix of the estimated parameters. Following Fair [1984], we use the sample uncertainty to take into account the admissible perturbations on structural parameters. This constitutes a statistical test of the *RBC* theory, contrary to the usual calibration and simulation method[3]. In the estimation step, we test some structural assumptions of the model. The results show that the balanced growth hypothesis cannot be rejected, although the non time-separability of leisure hypothesis is strongly rejected. These tests give information on the relevance of the model specification.

On the basis of the same statistical criterion, we cannot reject the hypothesis that the model reproduces a variance of the cyclical component of the output not significantly different from the observed one. The

[3]We can notice that Hairault [1992] parametrizes on French data the canonical model of King, Plosser and Rebelo [1988] and can only show qualitatively the failures of the model in its attempt to replicate economic fluctuations.

other cyclical dimensions generated by the theoretical model cannot be accepted. In the case where uncertainty on the estimated parameters is neglected, but where sample uncertainty is taken into account, the proportion of output volatility explained by technological shocks lies between 85% and 145%. As in validation procedure of macroeconometric models, we analyze the effects of parameters uncertainty on impulse response functions and *ex-post* forecasts.

In a first section, the canonical *RBC* model proposed by King, Plosser and Rebelo [1988] augmented with non time-separability in consumption and leisure is described. The second section is devoted to estimation and testing methods for the structural parameters of the model and of the second order moments of the cyclical components of the data. The empirical results are presented in the last section.

10.1 The Canonical Real Business Cycle Model

We present the resolution of an intertemporal growth model in a stochastic environment. We then state the Euler equations, from which it is possible to estimate the structural parameters and to calculate the theoretical second order moments.

First, we derive the optimality conditions. Second, we present the solution method proposed by King, Plosser and Rebelo [1988], which allows us to compute the co-variations of the theoretical cyclical components of the variables, using the estimated structural parameters.

10.1.1 The Model

Throughout the paper, the standard hypothesis of the neoclassical general equilibrium model will be maintained: perfect price flexibility and complete and competitive markets. In the economy, there is a large number of identical households and firms. In this setting, we can study the behavior of a representative agent.

The representative agent's preferences are defined by the following utility function:

$$u = u(C_t^\star, L_t^\star)$$

where $C_t^\star$ and $L_t^\star$ are respectively the services flows, in period t, resulting from contemporaneous and past decisions on consumption and leisure. The non time-separability on leisure, introduced in a similar model by Kydland and Prescott [1982], is here extended to all goods which provide satisfaction. In this way, service flows provide utility and can be written using lag polynomials on the decision variables C_t and L_t:

$$C_t^\star = C_t + \sum_{\tau=1}^{\infty} \omega_\tau^c C_{t-\tau}$$

$$L_t^\star = L_t + \sum_{\tau=1}^{\infty} \omega_\tau^l L_{t-\tau}$$

where $0 \leq \omega_\tau^c < 1$ and $0 \leq \omega_\tau^l < 1$. Following Kydland and Prescott [1982] or Hotz, Kydland and Sedlacek [1988], these expressions can be written as follows:

$$\begin{aligned} C_t^\star &= C_t + aG_t \\ L_t^\star &= L_t + bH_t \end{aligned}$$

The laws of motion of G_t and H_t are given by:

$$G_t = (1-\eta^G)G_{t-1} + C_{t-1} = \sum_{\tau=1}^{\infty}(1-\eta^G)^{\tau-1}C_{t-\tau}$$

$$H_t = (1-\eta^H)H_{t-1} + L_{t-1} = \sum_{\tau=1}^{\infty}(1-\eta^H)^{\tau-1}L_{t-\tau}$$

where $0 < \eta^G \leq 1$ and $0 < \eta^H \leq 1$. In this specification, the parameters a and b measure the relative influence of consumption and leisure past decisions on the household instantaneous utility. The parameters η^G and η^H measure the rate at which the instantaneous utility discounts the past consumption and leisure choices. The parameters a and b may be interpreted as the substitutability or the complementarity between contemporaneous and past decisions.

- For consumption
  - if $0 > a$, contemporaneous consumption is complementary with past consumption decisions. Thus we have "habit formation", *i.e.* the consumption decisions are persistent.
  - if $0 < a$, contemporaneous consumption is substitutable with past consumption decisions. The present consumption decisions have durable effects on utility.

- The demand for contemporaneous leisure can be interpreted as labor demand for domestic production[4]: the household produces goods $L_t^\star$ with a linear production technology[5] with two factors L_t and H_t.
  - if $0 > b$, the two domestic production factors are complementary, which implies persistence in the choice of leisure demand. In this case, the leisure demand used in the domestic production can be interpreted as the time devoted to education[6].
  - if $0 < b$, the two domestic production factors are substitutable, which implies that the leisure demand decision generates a durable effect on the household utility. In this case, the leisure demand can be interpreted as the time spent on holidays[7].

In each period, the household must choose to allocate, on the one hand, his time endowment T_0 between leisure L_t and work N_t and, on the other hand, his income Y_t between consumption C_t and investment I_t:

$$L_t + N_t \leq T_0$$

$$C_t + I_t \leq Y_t$$

The household accumulates capital, which is rented to the firms. Let the depreciation rate be δ. The stock of capital law of motion is given by:

$$K_{t+1} = (1-\delta)K_t + I_t$$

A representative firm produces an output Y_t of a single homogeneous good with a technology described by the following production function :

$$Y_t = A_t K_t^\alpha (X_{Nt} N_t)^{1-\alpha} = A_t F(K_t, X_{Nt} N_t)$$

---

[4]See Kydland [1984] et Hotz, Kydland and Sedlacek [1988] for a more detailed analysis.

[5]Benhabib, Rogerson and Wright [1991] propound an explicit model of domestic production with a specific technology shock.

[6]Knowledge accumulation is indeed necessary to fully exploit the education expenditures, which are represented here by the leisure purchase.

[7]We can reasonably think that a expenditure spent on holidays can have durable effects on the agent's welfare.

where A_t, K_t, N_t and X_{Nt} are respectively the technology shock, the stock of capital, the hours worked and the growth rate of the labor augmenting technical progress.

With this hypothesis of Harrod neutrality, the balanced growth necessary conditions are satisfied: X_{Nt} is deterministic and grows at the rate γ_x.

The technology shock follows a stationary autoregressive stochastic process of the form :

$$\log(A_t) = \rho_a \log(A_{t-1}) + (1-\rho_a)\log(A) + \epsilon_{at}$$

where $\log(A)$ is the mean of the process, $|\rho_a| < 1$ and ϵ_{at} is the process innovation of a standard-deviation $\sigma_{\epsilon a}$. This technology shock is evaluated as the computation of the total factor productivity proposed by Solow [1957].

In this economy, the two welfare theorems hold. Hence, Pareto optima can be decentralized. Looking for an equilibrium can be reduced to solving the social planner's problem:

$$\max_{\{C_t,N_t\}} E_0 \left[\sum_{t=0}^{\infty} \beta^t u(C_t^\star, L_t^\star)\right]$$
$$s.t \quad C_t + I_t \leq A_t F(K_t, X_{Nt} N_t)$$

where β is the subjective discount rate and E_0 the expectation conditional on available information in period 0.

In the class of utility functions compatible with a balanced growth path[8], we retain the same log-separable functional form as in Christiano and Eichenbaum [1992]:

$$u(C_t^\star, L_t^\star) = \theta \log(C_t^\star) + (1-\theta)\log(L_t^\star)$$

where θ measures the relative weight of consumption in the household's instantaneous utility.

Because the utility and technology functional forms are compatible with a balanced growth path, the problem can be written in terms of transformed variables. Letting $X_{Nt} = \gamma_x^t$, we define:

$$c_t = C_t/\gamma_x^t \ , \ c_t^\star = C_t^\star/\gamma_x^t \ , \ g_t = G_t/\gamma_x^t \ , \ k_t = K_t/\gamma_x^t \ , \ y_t = Y_t/\gamma_x^t \ , \ i_t = I_t/\gamma_x^t$$

[8] See King, Plosser and Rebelo [1987].

In order to obtain a stationary problem, we rewrite the utility function and the budget constraint, where $\kappa = \sum_{t=0}^{+\infty} \beta^t \log(\gamma_x^t)$:

$$\max_{\{c_t, N_t\}} \kappa + E_0 \sum_{t=0}^{\infty} \beta^t \{\theta \log(c_t^\star) + (1-\theta)\log(L_t^\star)\}$$

$$s.t \quad \gamma_x k_{t+1} = (1-\delta)k_t + A_t F(k_t, N_t) - c_t$$

The social-planning problem can be written in a recursive form. The solution satisfies the Bellman equation:

$$\mathcal{V}(k_t, g_t, H_t, A_t) = \max_{\{c_t, N_t\}} \theta \log(c_t^\star) + (1-\theta)\log(L_t^\star) + \beta E_t\left[\mathcal{V}(k_{t+1}, g_{t+1}, H_{t+1}, A_{t+1})\right]$$

$$s.t. \quad \begin{cases} \gamma_x k_{t+1} &= (1-\delta)k_t + A_t F(k_t, N_t) - c_t \\ g_{t+1} &= c_t \\ c_t^\star &= c_t + \frac{a}{\gamma_x} g_t \\ H_{t+1} &= N_t \\ L_t^\star &= T_0 - N_t + b(T_0 - N_{t-1}) \end{cases}$$

The optimality conditions are given by the first order conditions, the envelope conditions, the stock of capital law of motion and the transversality conditions associated with each of the state variables (k_t, g_t, H_t):

$$\begin{aligned} \frac{\partial u_t}{\partial c_t} &= \lambda_t - \mu_t \\ \frac{\partial u_t}{\partial N_t} &= -\lambda_t A_t F'_{N_t} + \nu_t \\ \lambda_t &= \beta E_t\left[\left(1 - \delta + A_{t+1}\frac{\partial F_{t+1}}{\partial k_{t+1}}\right)\lambda_{t+1}\right] \\ \mu_t &= \beta E_t\left[\frac{a}{\gamma_x}\frac{\partial u_{t+1}}{\partial g_{t+2}}\right] \\ \nu_t &= \beta E_t\left[b\frac{\partial u_{t+1}}{\partial H_{t+2}}\right] \\ \lim_{t\to+\infty} E_0\left[\beta^t \lambda_t k_{t+1}\right] &= 0 \\ \lim_{t\to+\infty} E_0\left[\beta^t \mu_t g_{t+1}\right] &= 0 \\ \lim_{t\to+\infty} E_0\left[\beta^t \nu_t H_{t+1}\right] &= 0 \end{aligned}$$

where:

$$\lambda_t = E_t\left[\frac{\beta}{\gamma_x}\frac{\partial\mathcal{V}(k_{t+1},g_{t+1},H_{t+1},A_{t+1})}{\partial k_{t+1}}\right]$$

$$\mu_t = E_t\left[\beta\frac{\partial\mathcal{V}(k_{t+1},g_{t+1},H_{t+1},A_{t+1})}{\partial g_{t+1}}\right]$$

$$\nu_t = E_t\left[\beta\frac{\partial\mathcal{V}(k_{t+1},g_{t+1},H_{t+1},A_{t+1})}{\partial H_{t+1}}\right]$$

With these optimality conditions and after eliminating the multipliers associated to the constraints, we obtain the Euler equations, which can be used for the model estimation:

$$E_t\left[\beta\left(1-\delta+\alpha\frac{Y_{t+1}}{K_{t+1}}\right)\left(\frac{\frac{\partial u_{t+1}}{\partial C_{t+1}}}{\frac{\partial u_t}{\partial C_t}}+\beta\frac{\frac{\partial u_{t+2}}{\partial C_{t+1}}}{\frac{\partial u_t}{\partial C_t}}\right)-\right. \tag{10.1}$$

$$\left.\beta\left(\frac{\frac{\partial u_{t+1}}{\partial C_t}}{\frac{\partial u_t}{\partial C_t}}\right)-1\right] = 0 \tag{10.2}$$

$$E_t\left[\beta\left(1-\delta+\alpha\frac{Y_{t+1}}{K_{t+1}}\right)\left(\frac{Y_t/N_t}{Y_{t+1}/Nt_{+1}}\right)\left(\frac{\frac{\partial u_{t+1}}{\partial N_{t+1}}}{\frac{\partial u_t}{\partial N_t}}+\beta\frac{\frac{\partial u_{t+2}}{\partial N_{t+1}}}{\frac{\partial u_t}{\partial N_t}}\right)-\right.$$

$$\left.\beta\left(\frac{\frac{\partial u_{t+1}}{\partial N_t}}{\frac{\partial u_t}{\partial N_t}}\right)-1\right] = 0 \tag{10.3}$$

$$E_t\left[\frac{\partial u_t}{\partial N_t}+\beta\frac{\partial u_{t+1}}{\partial N_t}-(1-\alpha)(Y_t/N_t)\left(\frac{\partial u_t}{\partial C_t}+\beta\frac{\partial u_{t+1}}{\partial C_t}\right)\right] = 0 \tag{10.4}$$

The relation (10.1) implies an expected intertemporal substitution of consumption goods strictly proportional to the expected marginal return of capital (the same argument is valid for the leisure equation (10.3)). The relation (10.4) implies a leisure marginal disutility equal to leisure marginal productivity, expressed in terms of consumption marginal utility.

10.1.2 Solution Method

The *RBC* model uses the propagation mechanism of the neoclassical growth model in order to explain the macroeconomic fluctuations due to technological impulses. The theoretical second order moments are obtained from simulations of optimal paths.

An analytical solution to the model is possible only in the unrealistic case of immediate capital depreciation [9]. Following King, Plos-

[9] See Long and Plosser [1983] or McCallum [1989].

ser and Rebelo [1988], we use a linear approximation method (log-linearization) around the deterministic steady state of the optimality conditions[10]. Let $\widehat{x}_t = \log\left(\frac{x_t}{\bar{x}}\right) \simeq \frac{x_t - \bar{x}}{\bar{x}}$. The log-linearized optimality conditions can be written in the matrix form[11]:

$$M_{cc}\begin{bmatrix}\widehat{c}_t\\ \widehat{N}_t\end{bmatrix} = M_{cs}\begin{bmatrix}\widehat{k}_t\\ \widehat{g}_{t-1}\\ \widehat{H}_{t-1}\\ \widehat{\lambda}_t\\ \widehat{\mu}_t\\ \widehat{\nu}_t\end{bmatrix} + M_{ce}\begin{bmatrix}\widehat{A}_t\end{bmatrix} \tag{10.5}$$

and

$$\begin{aligned}[M_{ss0} + M_{ss1}L]\begin{bmatrix}\widehat{k}_{t+1}\\ \widehat{g}_{t+1}\\ \widehat{H}_{t+1}\\ \widehat{\lambda}_{t+1}\\ \widehat{\mu}_{t+1}\\ \widehat{\nu}_{t+1}\end{bmatrix} &= [M_{sc0} + M_{sc1}L]\begin{bmatrix}\widehat{c}_{t+1}\\ \widehat{N}_{t+1}\end{bmatrix}\\ &+ [M_{se0} + M_{se1}L]\begin{bmatrix}\widehat{A}_{t+1}\end{bmatrix}\end{aligned} \tag{10.6}$$

This recursive system, under the rational expectations hypothesis, is solved following the method proposed by Blanchard and Kahn [1980]. We obtain a system which determines the evolution of the state variables' deviation from the steady state equilibrium as well as the other macroeconomic variables' deviation from this equilibrium:

$$\begin{bmatrix}\widehat{k}_{t+1}\\ \widehat{g}_{t+1}\\ \widehat{H}_{t+1}\\ \widehat{A}_{t+1}\end{bmatrix} = M\begin{bmatrix}\widehat{k}_t\\ \widehat{g}_t\\ \widehat{H}_t\\ \widehat{A}_t\end{bmatrix} + \begin{bmatrix}0\\ 0\\ 0\\ \epsilon_{at+1}\end{bmatrix} \tag{10.7}$$

and

---

[10]There are other solution methods for such models: Christiano and Eichenbaum [1992] use the second order linear approximation method of the objective function used by Kydland and Prescott [1982]. See Danthine, Donaldson and Mehra [1989] or Dotsey and Mao [1992] for an analysis of various approximation methods.

[11]See appendix 10.5 for an explicit writing of this system.

$$\begin{bmatrix} \widehat{y}_t \\ \widehat{c}_t \\ \widehat{N}_t \\ \widehat{i}_t \\ \widehat{y/N}_t \end{bmatrix} = \Pi \begin{bmatrix} \widehat{k}_t \\ \widehat{g}_t \\ \widehat{H}_t \\ \widehat{A}_t \end{bmatrix} \tag{10.8}$$

where $\widehat{y/N}_t$ denotes deviations of the labor productivity from the stationary equilibrium, which corresponds here to real wage deviations[12].

All the coefficients of the matrix M and Π are non-linear functions of structural parameters. The equations (10.7) and (10.8) allow us to simulate the cyclical components of optimal paths: these two equations link the structural parameters to the model's second order moments, which characterize its cyclical properties.

10.2 Estimation Method, Testing and Stochastic Simulation

The Generalized Method of Moments estimator has been used in various empirical studies, which try to estimate the structural parameters in the Euler equation. Early empirical studies were mostly concerned with intertemporal choices in partial equilibrium: the issue was then to test the model's specification from the first order moments, through over-identifying restrictions. The theory can give to the econometrician a set of over-identified restrictions, which can be tested by the G.M.M.: this indirect test of the model specification has been used in empirical papers on the Euler equations.

This methodology was first used to study household consumption behavior on quarterly U.S. data (Hansen and Singleton [1982], Dunn and Singleton [1983]). Then, different studies extended the model to the labor supply in the intertemporal choices of the household (Mankiw, Rotemberg and Summers [1985], Benabou [1985], Eichenbaum, Hansen and Singleton [1988])[13] and the firm's demand for factors (Sha-

[12]With the production function used in this paper, labor marginal and average productivity are equivalent in terms of deviations from equilibrium.

[13]The papers on consumption have been extended in many dimensions: non time-separability (Constandinides and Ferson [1989], Braun, Constandinides and Ferson [1992]), cash-in-advance constraint (Finn, Hoffman and Schlagenhauf [1990]), money in the utility function (Poterba and Rotemberg [1987]), domes-

piro [1986], Burda [1991]). Here we do not impose over-identifying restrictions (except in the case of the balanced growth hypothesis test) for two main reasons:

- Another evaluation methodology of intertemporal optimization models has been studied by Christiano and Eichenbaum [1992] and Burnside, Eichenbaum and Rebelo [1993]. These authors propose to estimate intertemporal general equilibrium models with the G.M.M. as well as a test methodology in the spirit of the *RBC* theory. The test of the model tries to answer the following question: can the estimated model reproduce from a statistical viewpoint the estimated second order moments of the observed data? In order not to have two specification tests of the model (over-identifying restriction and cyclical properties), we choose to estimate a just-identified model: the only possible test is then about the model's ability to reproduce the business cycle.

- The main difficulty in testing the over-identifying restrictions is that it is clearly impossible to discriminate between the various assumptions in this model: utility specification, rational expectations, instruments validity...

The structural parameters are obtained by fixing first order moments at their empirical values.

In this section, we present the estimation method of the first and second order moments of the model with the Generalized Method of Moments and we extend the stochastic simulation to the case of parameter uncertainty.

10.2.1 Implementing the Generalized Method of Moments

The model developed in the previous section requires the estimation of the following structural parameters vector:

$$\Psi_1 = \{\delta,\ \alpha,\ a,\ b,\ \theta,\ \rho_a,\ \overline{A},\ \gamma_x,\ \sigma^2_{\epsilon a},\ \overline{Y},\ \gamma_Y,\ \overline{C},\ \gamma_C,\ \overline{I},\ \gamma_I\}$$

---

tic and foreign consumptions (Feve [1992]).

where $\overline{A}$, $\overline{Y}$, $\overline{C}$ and $\overline{I}$ are respectively the average levels over the sample of total factors productivity, output, consumption and investment in deviation from deterministic trend.

The parameters β and T_0 are not estimated: T_0 is fixed to 1428 per quarter (or equivalently to 16 hours per day) and the parameter β is set so as to imply a 4% annual subjective discount rate (*i.e.* $\beta = (1.04)^{-0.25}$).

If the estimated neoclassical growth model is a good description of agents' behavior, its cyclical properties must be consistent with those of the French economy. Following the Kydland and Prescott [1982] methodology, the cyclical features are calculated by the application of the filter proposed by Hodrick and Prescott [1980] [14]. We are interested in a set of second order moments of the cyclical component of the data generated by the model, under the null hypothesis that the model is "true". Hence, the test of the second order moments bears on a vector of six parameters Ψ_2 defined by:

$$\Psi_2 = \left\{\sigma_y, \frac{\sigma_c}{\sigma_y}, \frac{\sigma_i}{\sigma_y}, \frac{\sigma_n}{\sigma_{y/n}}, \sigma_n, corr(y/n, n)\right\}$$

where σ_x is the standard deviation of the cyclical component of the variable x for $x = \{y, c, i, n, y/n\}$ and $corr(y/n, n)$ the instantaneous productivity-hours correlation.

Unconditional Moments and the Estimation of Ψ_1

We present here how to estimate $\widehat{\Psi}_1$, which represents the unconditional moments Ψ_1, by the Generalized Method of Moments.

The parameter δ is obtained through the capital accumulation equation $K_{t+1} = (1-\delta)K_t + I_t$. This parameter corresponds to an unconditional expectation of $1 - K_{t+1}/K_t + I_t/K_t$:

$$E\left[\delta - \left(1 - \frac{K_{t+1}}{K_t} + \frac{I_t}{K_t}\right)\right] = 0 \tag{10.9}$$

The utility function used in this study has the following form:

$$u(C_t + aC_{t-1}; N_t + bN_{t-1}) = \theta \log(C_t + aC_{t-1}) + (1-\theta)\log((T_0 - N_t) + b(T_0 - N_{t-1})$$

[14]The cyclical properties of this filter have been analyzed by King and Rebelo [1993].

The Euler equations of the consumption and leisure decisions (intertemporal substitution equations (10.1) and (10.3), and a substitution equation between consumption and leisure (10.4)) allow us to identify α, a, b and θ.

We impose a supplementary orthogonality condition on the intertemporal equation of consumption (see the relation (10.11)) in order to obtain an estimable just-identified form[15].

$$E\left[\beta\left(1-\delta+\alpha\frac{Y_{t+1}}{K_{t+1}}\right)\left(\frac{C_t+aC_{t-1}}{C_{t+1}+aC_t}+\beta a\frac{C_t+aC_{t-1}}{C_{t+2}+aC_{t+1}}\right)-\beta a\left(\frac{C_t+aC_{t-1}}{C_{t+1}+aC_t}\right)-1\right] = 0 \quad (10.10)$$

$$E\left[\beta\left(1-\delta+\alpha\frac{Y_{t+1}}{K_{t+1}}\right)\left(\frac{C_t+aC_{t-1}}{C_{t+1}+aC_t}+\beta a\frac{C_t+aC_{t-1}}{C_{t+2}+aC_{t+1}}\right)-\beta a\left(\frac{C_t+aC_{t-1}}{C_{t+1}+aC_t}\right)-1\right]\left(\frac{C_{t-1}}{C_{t-2}}\right) = 0 \quad (10.11)$$

$$E\left[\beta\left(1-\delta+\alpha\frac{Y_{t+1}}{K_{t+1}}\right)\left(\frac{Y_t/N_t}{Y_{t+1}/N_{t+1}}\right)\left(\frac{(1+b)T_0-(N_t+bN_{t-1})}{(1+b)T_0-(N_{t+1}+bN_t)}+\beta b\frac{(1+b)T_0-(N_t+bN_{t-1})}{(1+b)T_0-(N_{t+2}+bN_{t+1})}\right)-\beta b\left(\frac{(1+b)T_0-(N_t+bN_{t-1})}{(1+b)T_0-(N_{t+1}+bN_t)}\right)-1\right]N_{t-1} = 0 \quad (10.12)$$

$$E\left[\left[\frac{(1-\theta)}{((1+b)T_0-(N_t+bN_{t-1}))}\right]+\beta b\left[\frac{(1-\theta)}{((1+b)T_0-(N_{t+1}+bN_t))}\right]-(1-\alpha)(Y_t/N_t)\left(\left[\frac{\theta}{(C_t+aC_{t-1})}\right]+\beta a\left[\frac{\theta}{(C_{t+1}+aC_t)}\right]\right)\right] = 0 \quad (10.13)$$

For a parameter α of the production function, we estimate the parameters of the Solow residual Z_t. The process followed by Z_t is given by:

$$Z_t = A_t X_t^{1-\alpha} = A_t \gamma_x^{(1-\alpha)t}$$

$$A_t = A_{t-1}^{\rho_a}\overline{A}^{1-\rho_a}exp(\epsilon_t)$$

[15] The orthogonality conditions uses as instrumental variables the lagged consumption and leisure, defined as state variables in the model.

where ϵ_{at} is a white noise process with zero mean and variance equal to $\sigma^2_{\epsilon a}$.

The estimation of the four parameters $\{\rho_a, \overline{A}, \gamma_x, \sigma^2_{\epsilon a}\}$ of the Solow residual process requires the following equations:

$$E[z_t - (1-\alpha)t\log(\gamma_x) - \log(\overline{A})] = 0 \quad (10.14)$$

$$E[z_t - (1-\alpha)t\log(\gamma_x) - \log(\overline{A})](t/T) = 0 \quad (10.15)$$

$$\begin{aligned} E[(z_t - (1-\alpha)t\log(\gamma_x)) - (1-\rho_a)\log(\overline{A}) - \\ \rho_a(z_{t-1} - (1-\alpha)(t-1)\log(\gamma_x))] \\ (z_{t-1} - (1-\alpha)(t-1)\log(\gamma_x) - \log(\overline{A})) &= 0 \end{aligned} \quad (10.16)$$

$$\begin{aligned} E[((z_t - (1-\alpha)t\log(\gamma_x) - \log(\overline{A})) - \\ \rho_a(z_{t-1} - (1-\alpha)(t-1)\log(\gamma_x) - \log(\overline{A}))^2 - \sigma^2_{\epsilon a}] &= 0 \end{aligned} \quad (10.17)$$

with $z_t = \log(Y_t) - \alpha\log(K_t) - (1-\alpha)\log(N_t)$

The mean and growth rate of output, consumption and investment are obtained from the six following equations:

$$E[\log(Y_t) - \log(\overline{Y}) - t\log(\gamma_Y)] = 0 \quad (10.18)$$

$$E[\log(Y_t) - \log(\overline{Y}) - t\log(\gamma_Y)](t/T) = 0 \quad (10.19)$$

$$E[\log(C_t) - \log(\overline{C}) - t\log(\gamma_C)] = 0 \quad (10.20)$$

$$E[\log(C_t) - \log(\overline{C}) - t\log(\gamma_C)](t/T) = 0 \quad (10.21)$$

$$E[\log(I_t) - \log(\overline{I}) - t\log(\gamma_I)] = 0 \quad (10.22)$$

$$E[\log(I_t) - \log(\overline{I}) - t\log(\gamma_I)](t/T) = 0 \quad (10.23)$$

In order to make the estimation method clearer, we define the vector X_t,

$$\begin{aligned} X_t = &\left(\frac{K_{t+1}}{K_t}, \frac{I_t}{K_t}, \frac{Y_{t+1}}{K_{t+1}}, \frac{C_{t+2}}{C_{t+1}}, \frac{C_{t+1}}{C_t}, \frac{C_t}{C_{t-1}},\right. \\ &\left. N_{t+2}, N_{t+1}, N_t, N_{t-1}, \frac{Y_t}{C_t}, \frac{Y_t}{Y_{t+1}}, \frac{N_{t+1}}{N_t}, Y_t, C_t, I_t\right) \end{aligned}$$

With these notations, we can summarize the relations (10.9) to (10.23) by the following form:

$$E\ H^1[X_t, \Psi_1] = 0 \qquad \text{for} \quad t = 1...T \tag{10.24}$$

The function $H^1(.,.)$ is a vector of dimension 15 (See appendix 10.5).

Unconditional Moments and Estimation of Ψ_2

Following Christiano and Eichenbaum [1992], the G.M.M. estimator of $\widehat{\Psi}_2$, representing the unconditional moments Ψ_2, is obtained from the cyclical components of the data after using the Hodrick and Prescott filter. With this filter, the mean of the cyclical component is equal to zero.

The parameters of Ψ_2 can be estimated from the following restrictions that the second order moments must satisfy:

$$E[y_t^2 - \sigma_y^2] = 0 \tag{10.25}$$

$$E[n_t^2 - \sigma_n^2] = 0 \tag{10.26}$$

$$E\left[y_t^2\left(\frac{\sigma_c}{\sigma_y}\right)^2 - c_t^2\right] = 0 \tag{10.27}$$

$$E\left[y_t^2\left(\frac{\sigma_i}{\sigma_y}\right)^2 - i_t^2\right] = 0 \tag{10.28}$$

$$E\left[(y/n)_t^2\left(\frac{\sigma_n}{\sigma_{y/n}}\right)^2 - n_t^2\right] = 0 \tag{10.29}$$

$$E\left[\left(\frac{\sigma_n^2}{\sigma_n/\sigma_{y/n}}\right) corr(y/n, n) - (y/n)_t n_t\right] = 0 \tag{10.30}$$

We determine six unconditional moments from which it is possible to estimate the six second order moments of the vector Ψ_2. We summarize the relations (10.25) to (10.30) by the following form:

$$E\ H^2[x_t, \Psi_2] = 0 \qquad \text{for} \quad t = 1...T \tag{10.31}$$

The function $H^2(.,.)$ is a six-dimensional vector of functions (See appendix 10.5), where the vector x_t is defined by:

$$x_t = \{y_t, c_t, i_t, n_t, (y/n)_t\}$$

This vector represents the data obtained after the use of the Hodrick and Prescott [1980] filter for the usual value [16] of $\lambda = 1600$.

The Generalized Method of Moments

Let $\Psi = [\Psi_1, \Psi_2]$ be a 21-dimensional vector, representing all the estimated moments. The function H, representing all the restrictions that the unconditional moments must verify, includes H^1 and H^2:

$$E\ H([X_t, x_t]', \Psi) = 0 \tag{10.32}$$

The joint writing of these unconditional moments involves the simultaneous estimation of the structural parameters (Ψ_1) and of the empirical moments of the cyclical components (Ψ_2). We define the function $g_T(\Psi)$ of dimension 21. This function represents the empirical counterpart of (10.32).

$$g_T(\Psi) = \frac{1}{T}\sum_{t=0}^{T} H([X_t, x_t]', \Psi)$$

The writing of the model guarantees the stationarity of the variables in the Euler equations. Because Ψ has the same size as the function $g_T(\Psi)$, the model is just-identified. Hence, we can estimate the true value of Ψ^0 by choosing a value of Ψ which minimizes the following objective function:

$$J_T = g_T(\Psi)' W_T g_T(\Psi)$$

where W_T is a symmetric positive definite distance matrix that may depend on sample information. Hansen [1982] shows that W_T converges almost surely to $W_0 = S_0^{-1}$, a limit constant full rank matrix of the covariance of estimation errors. W_T is a consistent estimator of the inverse of the matrix S_0 defined by:

$$S_0 = \sum_{i=-q}^{q} E[H([X_{t+i}, x_{t+i}]', \Psi), H([X_{t+q-i}, x_{t+q-i}]', \Psi)']$$

where q is the order of the MA part of the errors in (10.32). The asymptotic covariance matrix of the estimator is given by:

$$\Sigma = (D_0' W_0^* D_0)^{-1} \quad \text{with} \quad D_0 = E\left[\frac{\partial g_T(\Psi)}{\partial \Psi'}\right]$$

[16] See Prescott [1986] or Danthine and Donaldson [1991] for a justification and an interpretation of this value.

The main difficulty concerning this estimation method is to compute the matrix W_T, especially when the errors vector follows a moving average of order q, with $q \geq 1$. In order to obtain a positive definite covariance matrix, we use the computation method proposed by Newey and West [1987]b[17]:

$$\widehat{S}_T = \widehat{\Omega}_T + \sum_{j=1}^{q} w(j,q)[\widehat{\Omega}_j + \widehat{\Omega}_j']$$

with $w(j,q) = 1 - \frac{j}{q+1}$ and $\widehat{\Omega}_j = \frac{1}{T}\sum_{t=j+1}^{T} \widehat{h}_t \widehat{h}_{t-j}$

The covariance matrix is robust both to heteroskedasticity and serial correlation.

10.2.2 Testing

Since $g_T(.)$ has the same dimension as Ψ, the minimal value of the objective function should be identically zero[18].

We use the likelihood ratio test described in Newey and West [1987]a. The test statistic is:

$$QLR = T[J_T(\widehat{\Psi}_c) - J_T(\widehat{\Psi}_{nc})]$$

where $J_T(\widehat{\Psi}_c)$ and $J_T(\widehat{\Psi}_{nc})$ are the objective functions of the constrained and unconstrained models respectively. We use the same distance matrix W_T for the two alternatives in order to measure the influence of the constraint on the objective function only. The statistic is asymptotically distributed as a χ^2 with as many degrees of freedom as constraints.

We can test the balanced growth hypothesis in a stochastic model of deterministic growth:

$$\gamma_x = \gamma_Y = \gamma_C = \gamma_I$$

The statistic follows a $\chi^2(3)$. We test the existence of a *deterministic* common trend between output, investment, consumption and labor augmenting technical progress.

In order to test the ability of the model to reproduce the cyclical features of the economy, we set the second order moments to be equal to the theoretical moments.

[17]Another matrix computation is proposed by Eichenbaum, Hansen and Singleton [1988].

[18]This results from the just-identification of the model.

Given a set of estimated values for Ψ_1, our model implies particular values for Γ, a vector of second order moments obtained by the model simulations. We represent this relationship *via* the function $\Phi(.)$, depending on the matrix M and Π:

$$\Phi(\widehat{\Psi}_1) = \Gamma$$

In the vector Ψ, we select the moments we want to test. Let A denote a selection matrix:

$$A\widehat{\Psi} = \widehat{\Gamma}$$

Let J_c be the restricted objective function, defined by:

$$J_c(\Psi) = \Phi(\widehat{\Psi}_1) - A\widehat{\Psi}$$

with $J_c(\Psi^0) = 0$, under the null hypothesis. We apply the likelihood ratio test described previously[19].

10.2.3 Parameter Uncertainty and Stochastic Simulations

The main benefit from estimating *RBC* models is to provide a measure of the parameter uncertainty, *via* the covariance matrix of the estimated parameters. It is then interesting to exploit the sample uncertainty in the stochastic simulation of the theoretical model. Usually, the stochastic simulations of *RBC* models take into account the stochastic properties of the innovations only (technology, government expenditures, money supply ...). The use of calibration for the structural parameters of the model allows only the consideration of deterministic and constant parameters.

In this paper, we consider an extension of the usual *RBC* methodology, *via* the introduction of a new source of uncertainty, that is structural parameter uncertainty. We can see in our methodology an analogy with the stochastic simulations of macroeconometric models as described in Fair [1984][20]. Fair presents four levels of uncertainty in the simulation of a model: residuals, parameters, exogenous variables and

[19]Christiano and Eichenbaum [1992] use a Wald test. Since this test may be a bad approximation to the asymptotic distribution in finite sample size, we did not use it.

[20]This methodology is described in chapters 7 and 9 of Fair [1984].

specification. In an estimated *RBC* model, there are only two sources of uncertainty: the stochastic process of the exogenous technological shocks and the estimated parameters.

Let Ψ_1, the structural parameters have mean $\widehat{\Psi}_1$ (the estimated parameters) and covariance matrix $\widehat{\Sigma}$. The parameter uncertainty appears *via* the covariance matrix of the estimated parameters. Hansen [1982] and Gourieroux and Monfort [1989] show that the estimator $\widehat{\Psi}_1$ is asymptotically normal:

$$\sqrt{T}(\widehat{\Psi}_1 - \Psi_1) \rightsquigarrow \mathcal{N}(0, \widehat{\Sigma})$$

If $\widehat{\Sigma}$ is a consistent estimator of Σ, an estimator of the covariance matrix of the estimated parameters in small sample size is obtained by dividing $\widehat{\Sigma}$ by the number of observations less the number of estimated parameters $(T - k)$. Given this covariance matrix, we use the following methodology for the stochastic simulation of the model.

- In a first step, the ith drawing of $\widehat{\Psi}_1$, $\widehat{\Psi}_{1,i}$, is:

  $$\widehat{\Psi}_{1,i} = \widehat{\Psi}_1 + \widehat{\Gamma}\xi_i \quad \text{for} \quad i = 1, ..., n$$

  where $\widehat{\Gamma}$ is the Cholesky decomposition of $\widehat{\Sigma}$ ($\widehat{\Sigma} = \widehat{\Gamma}\ \widehat{\Gamma}'$), ξ_i is a vector of drawings from an independent standard normal distribution and n is the number of parameter simulations.

- In a second step, for the ith drawing of $\widehat{\Psi}_1$, and so for i^{th} drawing of $\widehat{\sigma}_{\epsilon a}$, we obtain a jth drawing of $\widehat{\epsilon}_{a,s}$, $\widehat{\epsilon}_{a,s,j}$:

  $$\widehat{\epsilon}_{a,s,j}(i) = \widehat{\sigma}_{\epsilon,a,i}\mu_{s,j} \quad \text{for} \quad s = 1, ..., T \quad \text{and} \quad j = 1, ..., m$$

  where $\mu_{s,j}$ is a vector of dimension T (T is the length of the stochastic simulation) of drawings from an independent standard normal distribution and m is the number of simulations of the productivity shocks. This second step corresponds to the standard simulation methodology of *RBC* models, when the structural parameters are not stochastic, *i.e.* when the number of simulations is equal to one and $\widehat{\Sigma} = 0$.

The methodology used here requires the computation of a double loop during the simulation: the first loop generates the random parameters (n stochastic simulations) and the second loop generates the productivity shocks, for a particular realization of the standard-deviation of these productivity shocks (m stochastic simulations in this second loop). Since for one realization of the parameters we compute m productivity shocks over the length T, the model must be simulated $m \times n$ times in order to calculate the theoretical moments of the model.

The matrix M and Π are non-linear functions of the estimated parameters. Since this transformation is a continuously differentiable function, we can analyze its effect in terms of large sample theory by applying the convergence theorems for functions of random variables. Following Rao [1965], the asymptotic distribution of parameters of the state-space form is:

$$\sqrt{T}\left[\Omega(\widehat{\Psi}_1) - \Omega(\Psi_1)\right] \rightsquigarrow \mathcal{N}(0, \Delta\Sigma\Delta')$$

where $\Omega(.)$ denotes the non-linear transformation necessary to obtain the state-space form and $\Delta = \frac{\partial\Omega(\Psi_1)}{\partial\Psi_1}$. We can obtain this asymptotic distribution analytically or numerically. In this study, we use only a numerical approximation.

With this methodology, it is possible to take into account the whole sample size uncertainty, because we allow cross-correlation among coefficients and disturbances to influence the model measure of uncertainty. By this mean, we want to measure the influence of the sample size uncertainty, *via* the parameter uncertainty and the technology shocks.

10.3 Empirical Results

The model is estimated on quarterly French data from 1951:1 to 1989:2. We use the data bank constructed by Laroque, Ralle, Salanié and Toujas-Bernate [1990] from the quarterly national account. All the data are seasonally adjusted [21]. Contrary to Christiano and Eichenbaum [1992] and Burnside, Eichenbaum and Rebelo [1993], we do not decompose consumptions data over the whole sample into durable and non-durable goods. Unavailability of disaggregated data is not a problem because we introduce non time-separability to consumption. Output is obtained by adding up consumption and investment. All the data are per capita and employment is the product of the number of workers by hours worked.

[21]See appendix 10.5 for a data description.

10.3.1 Estimation of the Structural Parameters Ψ_1

When computing the covariance matrix, we take into account an $MA(1)$ process for the errors in the Euler equations, following the method proposed by Newey and West [1987]b with a window equal to one[22]. The matrix is also robust to serial correlation and heteroskedasticity. The use of the G.M.M. estimator requires the stationarity of the model and the Euler equations are written in a stationary form. The estimation results are reported in table 10.1.

Table 10.1: Estimation of Ψ_1

Structural parameters		Growth parameters	
δ	0.011	$\overline{Y}$	7.031
	$(0.14\ 10^{-3})$		(0.136)
α	0.252	γ_Y	1.00905
	$(0.45\ 10^{-2})$		$(0.24\ 10^{-3})$
a	0.273	$\overline{C}$	5.816
	(0.540)		(0.086)
b	-0.867	γ_C	1.00905
	(0.880)		$(0.19\ 10^{-3})$
θ	0.234	$\overline{I}$	1.204
	(0.083)		(0.053)
$\overline{A}$	0.036	γ_I	1.00909
	$(0.31\ 10^{-3})$		$(0.50\ 10^{-3})$
γ_x	1.0092		
	$(0.65\ 10^{-4})$		
ρ_a	0.863		
	(0.039)		
$\sigma_{\varepsilon a}$	0.011		
	$(0.11\ 10^{-2})$		
Test			
$a = 0$	0.254	$(\gamma_x = \gamma_Y =$	5.758
P-value	(0.614)	$\gamma_C = \gamma_I)$	(0.124)
$b = 0$	0.126		
P-value	(0.723)		

The standard-errors of the estimated parameters are given in parenthesis.

The model estimation shows clearly that the estimated growth rates (γ_x, γ_Y, γ_C, γ_I) are very close. The augmenting labor growth rate is

[22]The theoretical model implies this length for the moving average process of the errors. We estimate the model with windows of different lengths and the results are not qualitatively affected.

greater than that of investment, which in turn is larger than those of consumption and output. A test of the restrictions ($\gamma_x = \gamma_Y = \gamma_C = \gamma_I$) is accepted and so is the null hypothesis of balanced growth.

The estimation of the parameter of non time-separability on consumption shows the presence of durability (the service flows of the lagged consumption term is positive). This result is not surprising since we use total household consumption. With US aggregate consumption data, habit formation is dominated by a durability effect. According to Singleton [1990], when the non time-separability is studied in two-good models (non-durable goods and durable goods), an habit formation effect for the non-durable goods and a durability effect for durable goods appear, for plausible value of the subjective discount rate.

The parameter b for leisure is negative. It means that there is an intertemporal complementarity in the leisure behavior. The agent must choose today a sufficiently large level to balance the negative impact of the lagged leisure on the current services of leisure. In other words, $(T_0 - N_t)$ must be approximately greater than 3/4 of $(T_0 - N_{t-1})$. It follows that increases in hours will occur in a relatively gradual way, while decreases in hours are unrestricted. One must notice that the standard-errors associated with the parameters a and b are quite large and the test of $a = 0$ and $b = 0$ is accepted. The results are close to those obtained by Constandinides and Ferson [1989] on consumption, where the non time-separability parameter is evaluated with an important uncertainty.

On US data, the estimation of the Kydland and Prescott [1982] model performed by Altug [1989] shows that the standard-error of the parameter of non time-separability on consumption and leisure is large.

The autoregressive parameter of the Solow residual is quite small, compared to the value obtained by Hairault in Chapter 1 of this book ($\rho_a = 0.98$) for a model calibrated on French data[23]. This weak persistence could increase the intertemporal substitution effect relative to the wealth effect, and hence could increase the instantaneous responses of the macroeconomic variables to technological shocks. However, the estimated standard-error of the technological shocks is the same as those obtained in other studies on *RBC* model.

[23]In various models, Hairault and Portier [1993], Fairise and Langot [1994] and Fairise, Hénin and Langot [1992] calibrate the model with a ρ_a larger than 0.95.

Figure 10.1: Joint Distribution of ρ_a and $\sigma_{\epsilon a}$

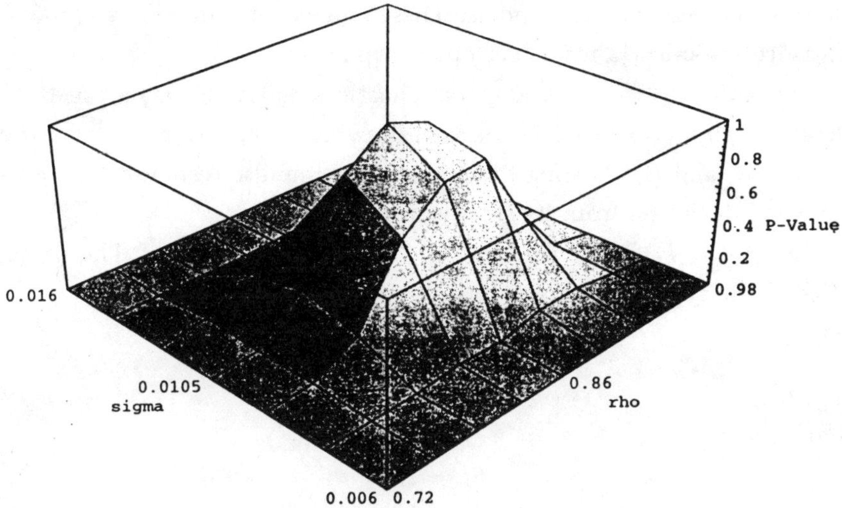

In order to obtain the set of admissible values for the structural parameters of the technological shock (ρ_a and $\sigma_{\epsilon a}$), we test different restrictions on these two parameters. We represent in the figure 10.1 the P-value of the test which follows a χ^2 with two degrees of freedom. The results show unambiguously that usual calibrations for ρ_a are rejected by the data.

10.3.2 Statistical Tests of the *RBC* Propositions

To analyze the quantitative implications of the *RBC* theory, we study the empirical statistical properties of a variety of moments of interest. Particularly, we discuss the sensitivity of the model's prediction about structural parameter uncertainty. Then, we propose two evaluation methods of the theoretical model: first, the calculation of the confidence intervals of the impulse response functions and second, a formal econometric test concerning the second order moments reproduced by the model.

Impulse Response Functions Analysis

We analyze the impulse response functions by stochastic simulations on parameters, in the same spirit as the traditional multiplier analysis in macroeconometric models. These stochastic simulations allow to measure the uncertainty effect on multipliers[24].

We only use the first loop (stochastic simulation on parameters) described in section 10.2.3. For each drawing of $\widehat{\Psi}_1$ ($\widehat{\Psi}_{1,i}$), we form the matrix M_i and Π_i allowing to compute the impulse response functions for a 1% deviation from its steady state value.

Let $S_t = \left[\widehat{k}_t, \widehat{g}_t, \widehat{H}_t, \widehat{A}_t\right]'$ and $\Theta_t = \left[\widehat{y}_t, \widehat{c}_t, \widehat{N}_t, \widehat{i}_t, \widehat{y/N}_t\right]'$. The dynamics of the system are given by:

$$S_{t+1} = M_i S_t$$

and

$$\Theta_t = \Pi_i S_t$$

This experiment is replicated n times and we compute 95% confidence intervals.

We present the results for output in figure 10.2.

Figure 10.2: I.R.F. of Output (Confidence Interval at 95%)

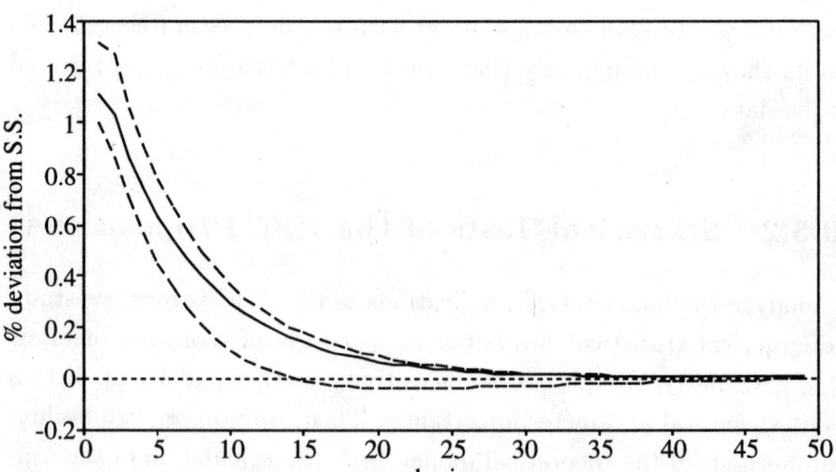

[24]See Fair [1984] or Bianchi, Brillet and Calzolari [1984].

This exercise enables us to measure statistically the mean adjustment lag of output to a technological shock. We can evaluate the horizon at which the impulse response function is not significantly different from zero. Figure 10.2 shows that the model returns to steady state around the 13th period.

The mean lag of the output response can be explained by the persistence of the technological shock and the propagation mechanism. We can not reject the hypothesis that the mean lag of the output response is only twice that of the technological shock[25]. The impulse response functions are the only way to analyze the dynamic theoretical properties of the model. As can be seen from the confidence bands in figure 10.2, these properties seem rather insensitive to admissible perturbations on the structural parameters.

Estimation of the Cyclical Characteristics Ψ_2 and Tests of the Theoretical Model

We now test the model's ability to mimic the cyclical features of the French economy. The test is proposed to answer the following two questions:

- *Is the propagation mechanism of the technological shocks able to generate macroeconomic series whose second order moments are statistically equivalent to their empirical counterparts?*
- *Are the theoretical moments sensitive to parameters uncertainty?*

Taking into account sample uncertainty (*i.e.* uncertainty on the measure of stylized facts) answers the first question. A formal calibration test answers the second one.

For this purpose, following *RBC* theorists, we analyze the percentage of the output variance that the model accounts for. Then, we compute the ratio λ representing the variance of the model under the assumption that $\widehat{\Psi}_1 = \Psi_1$ divided by its empirical counterpart:

$$\lambda = \sigma^2_{ym}(\widehat{\Psi}_1)/\sigma^2_{yd}$$

[25] The latter is 6.3 quarters. The lower bound of the confidence interval is zero at the 13th period.

where $\sigma^2_{ym}(\widehat{\Psi}_1)$ denotes the theoretical variance of the output and σ^2_{yd} the output variance estimated from the data. Moreover, we test if the value of $\sigma^2_{ym}(\widehat{\Psi}_1)$ is statistically equal to its empirical counterpart, σ^2_{yd}. This corresponds to the test of the null hypothesis that the components of the vector $\widehat{\Psi}_2$, representing the output variance, are constrained to be equal to their theoretical value implied by the model[26].

Since Ψ_1 and σ^2_{yd} are not known with certainty, λ is a stochastic variable, subject to sampling uncertainty. This statistic allows one to measure the percentage of the output variance which can be explained by the theoretical model. Then, we can test the proposition of Prescott [1986], which states that a *RBC* model accounts for 70% of the variance of output[27]. The model estimation, giving a measure of sampling uncertainty, enables one to quantify the uncertainty on the model's ability to reproduce the output variance. In order to evaluate statistically the *RBC* model, we simulate it with three degrees of uncertainty concerning the structural parameters: simulation with parameter uncertainty and technological shocks (both), simulation with parameter uncertainty except on the parameters of non time-separability in consumption and leisure and technological shocks (both except a and b) and simulation with technological shocks only (residuals). These various statistics are reported in tables 10.2 and 10.3.

Table 10.2: Estimation of the Output Variability

	Both	Both except a and b	Residuals	Historical data
σ_y	0.0153	0.0150	0.0151	0.0142
	(0.25 10^{-2})	(0.15 10^{-2})	(0.15 10^{-2})	(0.1 10^{-2})
	[0.47]	[0.50]	[0.50]	
λ	1.18	1.13	1.13	
	(0.404)	(0.230)	(0.230)	

Standard error in parenthesis.
P-Value of the statistic J_c in brackets.

The different simulations give the same results concerning the mean of the second order moments produced by the theoretical model. Since the value of λ is the same in the three simulation experiments, the test

[26] This restriction is tested by the statistic J_c described in section 10.2.2.

[27] Hansen [1988] show for various process of the technological shock that the *RBC* model accounts for 75% to 100% of output fluctuations.

concerning the ability of the model to reproduce the output variance will be the same in the three cases. In each case, the null hypothesis of equality between theoretical and empirical variances is accepted for a small P-value. An interesting exercise is to evaluate statistically the admissible range of λ at a critical size of 5%. We thus obtain a confidence interval for the model's ability to mimic the output variance, given the sampling uncertainty concerning the measure of the historical variance.

Figure 10.3: Distribution of λ

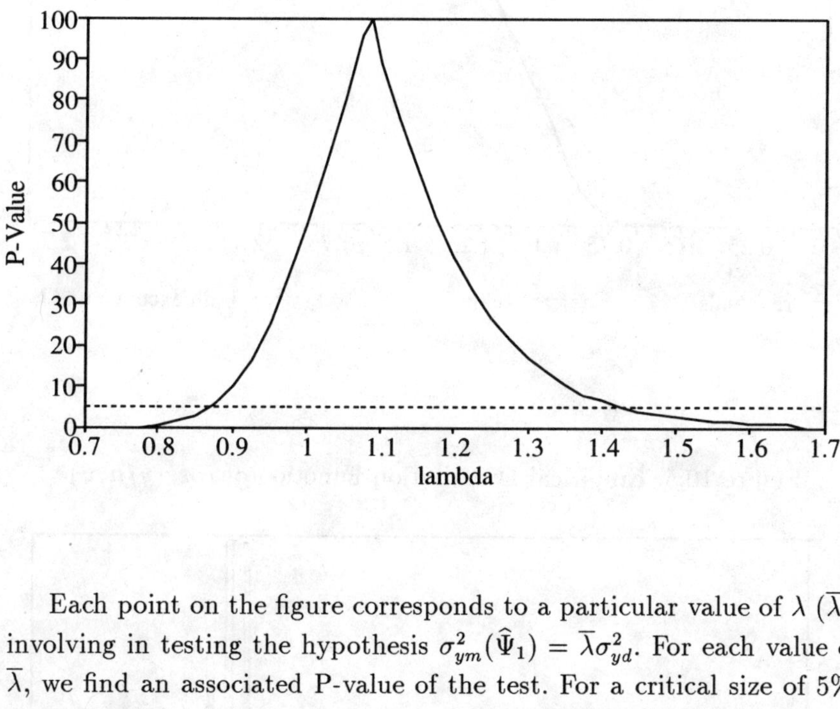

Each point on the figure corresponds to a particular value of λ ($\overline{\lambda}$), involving in testing the hypothesis $\sigma^2_{ym}(\widehat{\Psi}_1) = \overline{\lambda}\sigma^2_{yd}$. For each value of $\overline{\lambda}$, we find an associated P-value of the test. For a critical size of 5%, the technological shocks can explain from 85% to 145% of the empirical output variance.

The previous statistical tests account for sampling uncertainty, but the theoretical second order moments are independent of uncertainty concerning the measure of the structural parameters. The introduction of parameter uncertainty does not modify the statistical test of Ψ_2 (the test is based on sampling uncertainty), but it allows for an evaluation of the dispersion of the second order moments calculated by the model. For example, we compute the empirical cumulative distribution function of

λ in the three simulations experiments. We can see in the figure 10.4 that λ is more dispersed when the model is simulated with stochastic parameters and technological shocks.

Figure 10.4: Empirical Cumulative Distribution Function of λ

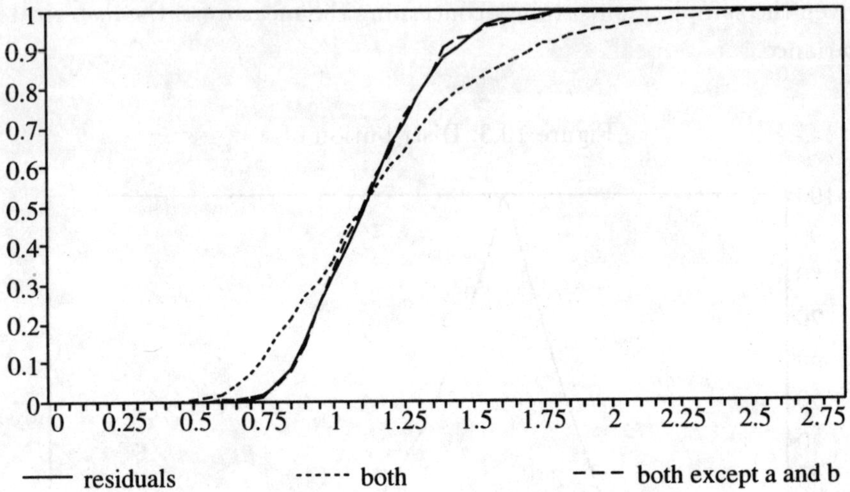

Figure 10.5: Empirical Distribution Function of $corr(y/n, n)$

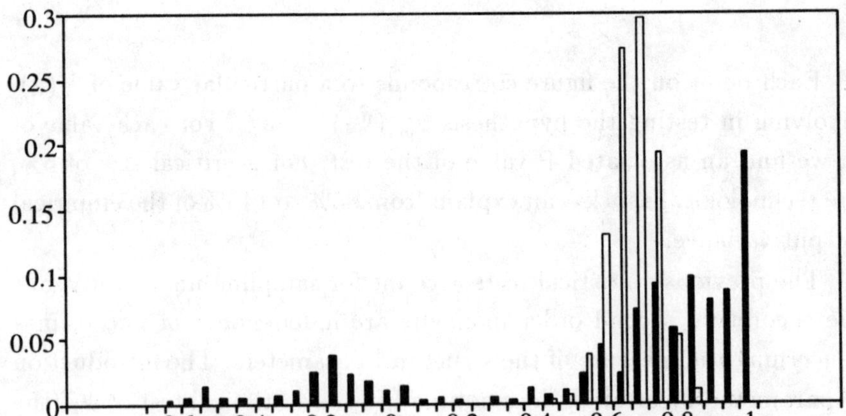

This result shows the usefulness of the estimation of the structural parameters in such models, for we can now compute the theoretical moments dispersion given by the covariance matrix of estimated parameters during the simulations. To illustrate this, we consider a stylized fact that standard *RBC* models cannot reproduce: the correlation between hours and productivity. It appears that the dispersion of this correlation produced by the theoretical model is very large when the structural parameters are stochastic (see figure 10.5).

Table 10.3: Estimation of Ψ_2

	Both	Both except a and b	Residuals	Historical data
σ_c/σ_y	0.3396	0.3528	0.3518	0.765
	(0.097)	(0.020)	(0.021)	(0.029)
	[0]	[0]	[0]	
σ_i/σ_y	4.709	4.570	4.573	3.108
	(0.347)	(0.080)	(0.084)	(0.191)
	[0]	[0]	[0]	
$\sigma_n/\sigma_{y/n}$	0.279	0.226	0.226	0.685
	(0.127)	(0.007)	(0.007)	(0.051)
	[0]	[0]	[0]	
σ_n	0.0128	0.0130	0.0130	0.008
	($0.19\ 10^{-2}$)	($0.14\ 10^{-2}$)	($0.14\ 10^{-2}$)	($0.4\ 10^{-3}$)
	[0]	[0]	[0]	
$corr(y/n, n)$	0.606	0.653	0.655	-0.049
	(0.428)	(0.058)	(0.061)	(0.10)
	[0.317]	[0]	[0]	

Standard error in parenthesis.
P-Value of the statistic J_c in brackets.

The historical correlation between hours and productivity is not significantly different from zero and the statistical test rejects the null hypothesis of the equality between the estimated and simulated correlation when the parameters are not stochastic. In the presence of parameter uncertainty, we see that the historical correlation is included in the confidence interval of the simulated correlation. These results show that taking into account parameter uncertainty makes the computation of the theoretical moments less precise.

In order to complete the previous results, we report in table 10.3 various second order moments calculated by the model. In each case, the statistical test based on sampling uncertainty rejects the assumption of equality between theoretical and empirical moments. The illustrative exercise described for the correlation between hours and productivity could be reproduced for the other theoretical moments, when the model is simulated with parameter uncertainty.

Ex-Post Simulations

Following Prescott [1986], we evaluate the predictive accuracy of the model with respect to the short term fluctuations. Then, we propose to answer to following question:

How well does the RBC model fit the data?

To this end, we use a traditional criterion to judge the *ex-post* forecasts of the model, that is, the root mean square error ($RMSE$).[28]

Figure 10.6: Forecast of Cyclical Part of Output

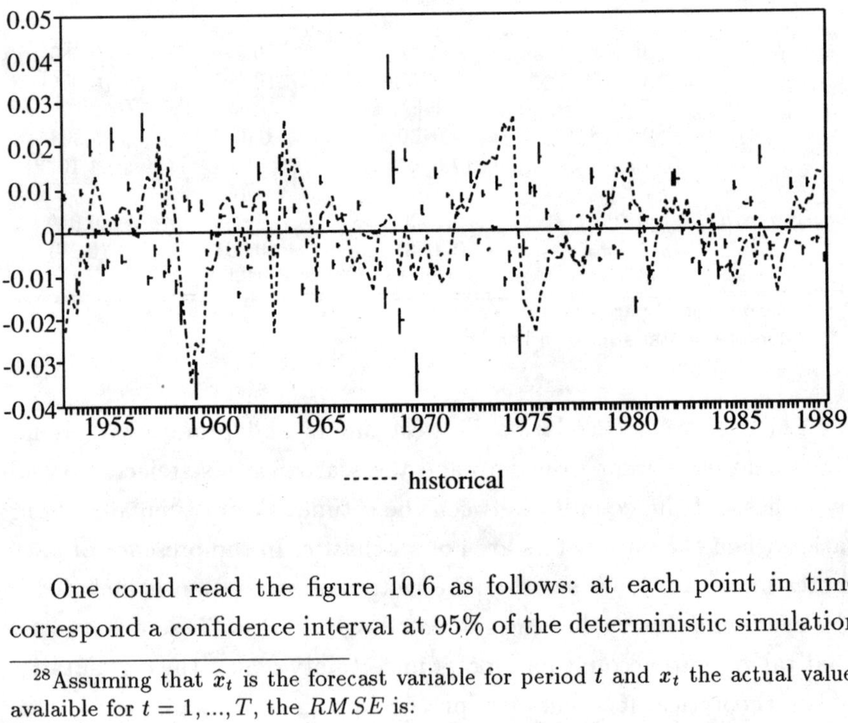

One could read the figure 10.6 as follows: at each point in time correspond a confidence interval at 95% of the deterministic simulation

[28]Assuming that $\widehat{x}_t$ is the forecast variable for period t and x_t the actual value, avalaible for $t = 1, ..., T$, the $RMSE$ is:

$$RMSE = \sqrt{\frac{1}{T}\sum_{t=1}^{T}(x_t - \widehat{x}_t)^2}$$

(represented by a vertical interval on the diagram) and the deterministic simulation (represented by a point in this interval). The deterministic simulation of the cyclical part of the output shows large forecast error in the second part of the sixties and the model do not fit the data very well over the first part of the sample size. It appears that the simulation errors due to parameter uncertainty are small relative to the forecast errors of the model.

A lot of econometric studies analyze short term fluctuations with time series models, such as an ARIMA model. The accuracy of the theoretical model is then compared to the accuracy of an "a-theoretical" model. To this end, we estimate the following AR(4) model:

$$\widehat{y}_t^{HP} = \sum_{i=1}^{4} \beta_i \widehat{y}_{t-i}^{HP} + \epsilon_t$$

where $\widehat{y}_t^{HP}$ is the cyclical component of the output extracted by the HP filter. The estimated parameters are:

$$\widehat{\beta}_1 = 0.70\ (0.081), \quad \widehat{\beta}_2 = 0.09\ (0.100), \quad \widehat{\beta}_3 = -0.05\ (0.100), \quad \widehat{\beta}_4 = -0.13\ (0.081)$$

where the standards errors are in parentheses. The Box-Pierce statistic based on twenty lag has a P-value equal to 11.7%. The $RMSE$ for the deterministic simulation of the model is equal to 0.0143 and is equal to 0.0145 when we incorporate parameter uncertainty. The $RMSE$ for the ex-post simulation of the AR(4) model is only equal to 0.0109. At this level of the econometric evaluation of the *RBC* model, it appears clearly that such a model is unable to forecast the short term fluctuations in output very well.

10.4 Concluding Comments

At the beginning of the eighties, the Nelson and Plosser [1982] and Kydland and Prescott [1982] contributions suggested that economic fluctuations can be explained by technological shocks.

The recent developments in time series, Glachant and Hairault [1991], Quah [1992] and Lippi and Reichlin [1992] show clearly the shortcomings of an analysis in an univariate framework.

Concerning the *RBC* methodology, we can have some doubts about the usual validation method because there is no statistical inference on the structural parameters and on the model's ability to mimic the cyclical component of the data. The use of G.M.M. allows us to estimate in the first step the structural parameters and in a second step to test the standard *RBC* proposition.

This study shows clearly the model's inability to reproduce the cyclical component of the French data over the last forty years. We extend Eichenbaum [1991]'s methodology by taking into account the parameter uncertainty during the stochastic simulations of the model. This exercise allows us to assess how well calibrated model *via* the estimation of the structural parameters represents economic fluctuations and to measure the uncertainty of outcomes in such models *via* the uncertainty on parameters. To this end, we analyze the impulse response functions, the *ex-post* simulations and second order moments and we show that the proposition of the *RBC* literature is statistically rejected. Then the use of calibration methods in validation procedure must be used carefully.

10.5 Appendix

A. The State-Space Form

Let:

$$A1 = \frac{N}{(1+b)(T_0 - N)} \quad ; \quad \phi = \frac{\gamma}{\gamma - (1-\delta)} \quad ; \quad \eta_A = \frac{\gamma - \beta(1-\delta)}{\gamma}$$

$$Y/K = \frac{\gamma - \beta(1-\delta)}{\alpha\beta} \quad ; \quad s_i = \frac{(\gamma - (1-\delta))\alpha\beta}{Y/K} \quad ; \quad s_c = 1 - s_i$$

$$M_{cc} = \begin{bmatrix} -\frac{1}{1+(a/\gamma)} & 0 \\ 0 & -A1 - \alpha(1+\beta b) \end{bmatrix}$$

$$M_{cs} = \begin{bmatrix} 0 & \frac{a/\gamma}{1+(a/\gamma)} & 0 & \frac{\gamma+\beta a}{\gamma} & -\frac{\beta a}{\gamma} & 0 \\ -\alpha(1+\beta b) & 0 & A1 & -(1+\beta b) & 0 & -\beta b \end{bmatrix}$$

$$M_{ce} = \begin{bmatrix} 0 \\ -(1+\beta b) \end{bmatrix}$$

$$M_{ss0} = \begin{bmatrix} \phi s_i & 0 & 0 & 0 & 0 & 0 \\ 0 & 1 & 0 & 0 & 0 & 0 \\ 0 & 0 & 1 & 0 & 0 & 0 \\ (\alpha-1)\eta_A & 0 & 0 & 1 & 0 & 0 \\ 0 & \frac{a/\gamma}{1+(a/\gamma)} & 0 & 0 & 0 & 0 \\ 0 & 0 & bA1 & 0 & 0 & 0 \end{bmatrix}$$

$$M_{ss1} = \begin{bmatrix} -(\phi-1)s_i - \alpha & 0 & 0 & 0 & 0 & 0 \\ 0 & 0 & 0 & 0 & 0 & 0 \\ 0 & 0 & 0 & 0 & 0 & 0 \\ 0 & 0 & 0 & -1 & 0 & 0 \\ 0 & 0 & 0 & 0 & 1 & 0 \\ 0 & 0 & 0 & 0 & 0 & 1 \end{bmatrix}$$

$$M_{sc0} = \begin{bmatrix} 0 & 0 \\ 0 & 0 \\ 0 & 0 \\ 0 & -(1-\alpha)\eta_A \\ -\frac{1}{1+(a/\gamma)} & 0 \\ 0 & -A1 \end{bmatrix}$$

$$M_{sc1} = \begin{bmatrix} -s_c & 1-\alpha \\ 1 & 0 \\ 0 & 1 \\ 0 & 0 \\ 0 & 0 \\ 0 & 0 \end{bmatrix}$$

$$M_{se0} = [0\ 0\ 0\ -\eta_A\ 0\ 0]'$$

$$M_{se1} = [1\ 0\ 0\ 0\ 0\ 0]'$$

B. Representation of H^1

The function H^1 represents the vector of following functions:

$$\begin{aligned}
H_1^1 &= E\left[\delta - \left(1 - \frac{K_{t+1}}{K_t} + \frac{I_t}{K_t}\right)\right] \\
H_2^1 &= E\left[\beta\left(1-\delta+\alpha\frac{Y_{t+1}}{K_{t+1}}\right)\left(\frac{(C_t/C_{t-1})+a}{(C_{t+1}/C_t)+a}\left(\frac{C_{t-1}}{C_t}\right)+\right.\right. \\
&\quad \left.\beta a\frac{1+a(C_{t-1}/C_t)}{(C_{t+2}/C_{t+1})+a}\left(\frac{C_t}{C_{t+1}}\right)\right)- \\
&\quad \left.\beta a\left(\frac{(C_t/C_{t-1})+a}{(C_{t+1}/C_t)+a}\left(\frac{C_{t-1}}{C_t}\right)\right)-1\right] \\
H_3^1 &= E\left[\beta\left(1-\delta+\alpha\frac{Y_{t+1}}{K_{t+1}}\right)\left(\frac{(C_t/C_{t-1})+a}{(C_{t+1}/C_t)+a}\left(\frac{C_{t-1}}{C_t}\right)+\right.\right. \\
&\quad \left.\beta a\frac{1+a(C_{t-1}/C_t)}{(C_{t+2}/C_{t+1})+a}\left(\frac{C_t}{C_{t+1}}\right)\right)- \\
&\quad \left.\beta a\left(\frac{(C_t/C_{t-1})+a}{(C_{t+1}/C_t)+a}\left(\frac{C_{t-1}}{C_t}\right)\right)-1\right]\left(\frac{C_{t-1}}{C_{t-2}}\right) \\
H_4^1 &= E\left[\beta\left(1-\delta+\alpha\frac{Y_{t+1}}{K_{t+1}}\right)\left(\frac{Y_t/N_t}{Y_{t+1}/N_{t+1}}\right)\left(\frac{(1+b)T_0-(N_t+bN_{t-1})}{(1+b)T_0-(N_{t+1}+bN_t)}+\right.\right. \\
&\quad \left.\beta b\frac{(1+b)T_0-(N_t+bN_{t-1})}{(1+b)T_0-(N_{t+2}+bN_{t+1})}\right)- \\
&\quad \left.\beta b\left(\frac{(1+b)T_0-(N_t+bN_{t-1})}{(1+b)T_0-(N_{t+1}+bN_t)}\right)-1\right](N_{t-1}) \\
H_5^1 &= E[(1-\theta)/((1+b)T_0-(N_t+bN_{t-1}))+ \\
&\quad \beta b[(1-\theta)/((1+b)T_0-(N_{t+1}+bN_t))]- \\
&\quad (1-\alpha)\left(\frac{Y_t/N_t}{C_t}\right)([\theta/(1+a(C_{t-1}/C_t))]+\beta a[\theta/((C_{t+1}/C_t)+a])] \\
H_6^1 &= E[z_t-(1-\alpha)t\log(\gamma_x)-\log(\overline{A})] \\
H_7^1 &= E[z_t-(1-\alpha)t\log(\gamma_x)-\log(\overline{A})](t/T) \\
H_8^1 &= E[(z_t-(1-\alpha)t\log(\gamma_x)-\log(\overline{A}) \\
&\quad -\rho_a(z_{t-1}-(1-\alpha)(t-1)\log(\gamma_x)-\log(\overline{A})]\times \\
&\quad (z_{t-1}-(1-\alpha)(t-1)\log(\gamma_x)-\log(\overline{A}))
\end{aligned}$$

$$\begin{aligned}
H_9^1 &= E[(z_t - (1-\alpha)t\log(\gamma_x) - \log(\overline{A}) - \\
&\quad \rho_a(z_{t-1} - (1-\alpha)(t-1)\log(\gamma_x) - \log(\overline{A}))^2 - \sigma_\epsilon^2]
\end{aligned}$$

$$H_{10}^1 = E[\log(Y_t) - \log(\overline{Y}) - t\log(\gamma_Y)]$$

$$H_{11}^1 = E[\log(Y_t) - \log(\overline{Y}) - t\log(\gamma_Y)](t/T)$$

$$H_{12}^1 = E[\log(C_t) - \log(\overline{Y}) - t\log(\gamma_C)]$$

$$H_{13}^1 = E[\log(C_t) - \log(\overline{Y}) - t\log(\gamma_C)](t/T)$$

$$H_{14}^1 = E[\log(I_t) - \log(\overline{I}) - t\log(\gamma_I)]$$

$$H_{15}^1 = E[\log(I_t) - \log(\overline{I}) - t\log(\gamma_I)](t/T)$$

C. Representation of H^2

The function H^2 represents the vector of following functions:

$$H_1^2 = E[y_t^2 - \sigma_y^2]$$

$$H_2^2 = E[n_t^2 - \sigma_n^2]$$

$$H_3^2 = E\left[y_t^2\left(\frac{\sigma_c}{\sigma_y}\right) - c_t^2\right]$$

$$H_4^2 = E\left[y_t^2\left(\frac{\sigma_i}{\sigma_y}\right) - i_t^2\right]$$

$$H_5^2 = E\left[(y/n)_t^2\left(\frac{\sigma_n}{\sigma_{y/n}}\right) - n_t^2\right]$$

$$H_6^2 = E\left[\left(\frac{\sigma_n^2}{\sigma_n/\sigma_{y/n}}\right) corr(y/n, n) - (y/n)_t n_t\right]$$

D. Data Appendix

C_t: Real households consumption in goods and services (1980FF); I_t: Real fixed private investment (1980FF).; EFF_t: Total employment except financial sector (in thousand); DD_t: Hours worked per week except financial sector; K_t: Capital stock; POP_t: Civilian labor force, total, (in thousand).

Bibliography

S. ALTUG. Time-to-Build and Aggregate Fluctuations: Some New Evidence. *International Economic Review*, 30(4):889–920, November 1989.

R. BENABOU. Le modèle d'optimisation dynamique de la consommation et de l'offre de travail: un test sur données françaises. *Annales de l'INSEE*, 57:75–97, 1985.

R. BENHABIB, R. ROGERSON AND R. WRIGHT. *Homework in Macroeconomics II: Aggregate Fluctuations.* Working paper 3344, NBER, 1991.

C. BIANCHI, J.L. BRILLET AND G. CALZOLARI. Ananlyse et mesure d'incertitude en prévision d'un modèle économétrique. application au modèle Mini-DMS. *Annales de l'I.N.S.E.E.*, 54:31–62, April-June 1984.

O. BLANCHARD AND C. KAHN. The Solution of Linear Difference Models under Rational Expectations. *Econometrica*, 48(5):1305–1311, July 1980.

P. BRAUN, G. CONSTANDINIDES AND W. FERSON. *Time Nonseparability in Aggregate Consumption : International Evidence.* Working paper 4104, NBER, June 1992.

M. BURDA. Monopolistic Competition, Costs of Adjustment, and the Behavior of European Manufacturing Employment. *European Economic Review*, 35(1):61–79, january 1991.

C. BURNSIDE, M. EICHENBAUM AND S. REBELO. Labor Hoarding and the Business Cycle. *Journal of Political Economy*, 101(2), 1993.

L. CHRISTIANO AND M. EICHENBAUM. Current Real Business Cycle Theories and Aggregate Labor Market Fluctuations. *American Economic Review*, 82(3):430–450, June 1992.

G. CONSTANDINIDES AND W. FERSON. *Habit Persistence and Durability in Aggregate Consumption: Empirical Tests.* Mimeo, University of Chicago, 1989.

J.P. DANTHINE AND J. DONALDSON. *Methodological and Empirical Issues in Real Business Cycle Theory.* Cahiers de Recherche Economique 9102, Université de Lausanne, 1991.

J.P. Danthine, J. Donaldson and R. Mehra. On some Computational Aspect of Equilibrium Business Cycle Theory. *Journal of Economic Dynamics and Control*, 13(3):449–470, July 1989.

A. d'Autume. *Quelle place place pour la macroéconomie.* Cahiers ECO & MATHS 93.100, MAD, Université de Paris I, 1992.

M. Dotsey and C. Mao. How Well Do Linear Approximation Methods Work? The Production Tax Case. *Journal of Monetary Economics*, 29(1):25–58, February 1992.

K. Dunn and K. Singleton. An Empirical Analysis of the Pricing of Mortage-Backed Securities. *The Journal of Finance*, 38(2):613–623, May 1983.

M. Eichenbaum, L. Hansen and K. Singleton. A Time Analysis of Representative Agent Models of Consumption and Leisure Choice under Uncertainty. *Quarterly Journal of Economics*, 103(1):51–78, February 1988.

M. Eichenbaum. Real Business Cycle Theory: Wisdom or Whimsy? *Journal of Economic Dynamics and Control*, 15:607–626, 1991.

R. Fair. *Specification, Estimation and Analysis of Macroeconometric Models.* Harvaard University Press, 1984.

X. Fairise and F. Langot. Labor Productivity and Business Cycles: Can RBC Models be Saved? *European Economic Review*, 38, October 1994.

X. Fairise, P.Y. Hénin and F. Langot. Les modèles de cycle réel peuvent-ils expliquer les fluctuations de l'emploi et de la productivité? *Economie et Prévision*, 106:23–40, 1992.

P. Feve. *Consommation de biens domestiques et étrangers dans un modèle d'optimisation intertemporelle.* Working paper, MAD, Université de Paris I, 1992.

M. Finn, D. Hoffman and D. Schlagenhauf. Intertemporal Asset-Pricing Relationship in Barter and Monetary Economies. *Journal of Monetary Economics*, 25(3):431–451, June 1990.

M. Friedman. *Essays in Positive Economics.* University of Chicago Press, 1953. Chicago and London.

J. Glachant and J.O. Hairault. *Have Unit Roots in GNP Process Economic Implications ?* Cahiers ECO & MATHS 91.04, MAD, Université de Paris I, 1991.

C. Gourieroux and A. Monfort. *Statistique et modèles économétriques.* Economica, Paris, 1989. 2 Vol.

J.O. Hairault and F. Portier. Monnaie et inflation dans un modèle de cycles réels. *Recherches Econimiques de Louvain*, 59(4):427–461, 1993.

J.O. HAIRAULT. Présentation et évaluation du courant des cycles réels. *Economie et Prévision*, 106(5):1–22, 1992.

L. HANSEN AND K. SINGLETON. Generalized Instrumental Variables Estimation of Nonlinear Rational Expectations Models. *Econometrica*, 50(5):1269–1286, September 1982.

L. HANSEN. Large Sample Properies of Generalized Method of Moments Estimators. *Econometrica*, 50(4):1029–1054, July 1982.

G. HANSEN. *Technical Progress and Aggregate Fluctuations.* Mimeo , University of California, Santa Barbara, 1988.

R. HODRICK AND E. PRESCOTT. *Post-War U.S. Business Cycles: an Empirical Investigation.* Mimeo , Carnegie-Mellon University, November 1980.

J. HOTZ, F. KYDLAND AND G. SEDLACEK. Intertemporal Preferences and Labour Supply. *Econometrica*, 56(2):335–360, March 1988.

P.Y. HÉNIN. *Développements de la théorie des cycles réels.* Working paper 9113, CEPREMAP, Paris, 1991.

R. KING AND S. REBELO. Low Frequency Filtering and the Real Business Cycles. *Journal of Economic Dynamics and Control*, 17(1/2):207–232, January-March 1993.

R. KING, C. PLOSSER AND S. REBELO. *Production Growth and Business Cycles: Technical Appendix.* Working paper, University of Rochester, 1987. Revised May 1990.

R. KING, C. PLOSSER AND S. REBELO. Production, Growth and Business Cycles I. *Journal of Monetary Economics*, 21(2/3):196–232, March-May 1988.

F. KYDLAND AND E. PRESCOTT. Time to Build and Aggregate Fluctuations. *Econometrica*, 50(6):1345–1370, November 1982.

F. KYDLAND. Labor Force Heterogeneity and the Business Cycle. *Canergie Rochester Conference series*, 21():1173–208, 1984.

G. LAROQUE, P. RALLE, B. SALANIÉ AND J. TOUJAS-BERNATE. *Construction d'une base de données trimestrielles longues.* Working paper , INSEE, 1990.

M. LIPPI AND L. REICHLIN. On Persistence of Shocks to Economic Variables: a Common Misconception. *Journal of Monetary Economics*, 29(1):87–93, February 1992.

J. LONG AND C. PLOSSER. Real Business Cycles. *Journal of Political Economy*, 91(1):39–69, February 1983.

R. LUCAS. Understanding Business Cycles. In K. Brunner and A. Meltzer, editor, *Stabilization of the Domestic and International Economy*, Carnegie Rochester Conference Series on Public Policy, North-Holland, Amsterdam, 1977.

G. MANKIW, J. ROTEMBERG AND L. SUMMERS. Intertemporal Substitution in Macroeconomics. *Quarterly Journal of Economics*, 100:225–251, February 1985.

B. MCCALLUM. Real Business Cycles Models. In R. Barro, editor, *Modern Business Cycle Theories*, Harvard University Press, Boston, 1989.

C. NELSON AND C. PLOSSER. Trend and Random Walks in Macroeconomic Time Series. *Journal of Monetary Economics*, 10(1):139–162, September 1982.

W. NEWEY AND K. WEST. Hypothesis Testing with Efficient Method of Moments Estimation. *International Economic Review*, 28(3):703–708, October 1987.

W. NEWEY AND K. WEST. A Simple, Positive Definite, Heteroscedasticity and Autocorrelation Consistent Covariance Matrix. *Econometrica*, 55(3):703–708, May 1987.

J. POTERBA AND J. ROTEMBERG. Money in the Utility Function: an Empirical Implementation. In *New Approaches to Monetary Economics*, Barnett, W. et Singleton, K., 1987.

E. PRESCOTT. Theory Ahead of Business Cycle Measurement. *Carnegie Rochester Conference Series on Public Policy*, 25:11–44, Autumn 1986.

D. QUAH. The Relative Importance of Permanent and Transitory Components: Identification and some Theoretical Bounds. *Econometrica*, 60(1):107–118, January 1992.

C. RAO. *Linear Statistical Inference and its Applications.* John Wiley, Princeton, 1965.

M. SHAPIRO. The Dynamic Demand for Capital and Labor. *Quaterly Journal of Economics*, 51:513–529, August 1986.

K. SINGLETON. Spécification and Estimation of Intertemporal Asset Pricing Models. In B.M. Friedman and F.H. Hahn, editor, *Handbook of Monetary Economics*, Elsevier Science Publishers, New-York, 1990.

R. SOLOW. Technical Change and the Aggregate Production Function. *Review of Economics and Statistics*, 39(3):312–320, August 1957.

List of Contributors

Frédérique Bec,
University of Lille II and M.A.D., University of Paris I

Catherine Bruno,
Observatoire Français des Conjonctures Economiques

Fabrice Collard,
M.A.D., University of Paris I

Xavier Fairise,
University of Cergy-Pontoise and M.A.D., University of Paris I

Patrick Fève,
University of Evry, C.R.E.S.T. and M.A.D., University of Paris I

Jean-Olivier Hairault,
University of Lille I and M.A.D., University of Paris I

Pierre-Yves Hénin,
C.E.P.R.E.M.A.P. and M.A.D., University of Paris I

François Langot,
University of Paris IX and M.A.D., University of Paris I

Franck Portier,
University of Rouen, C.E.P.R.E.M.A.P. and M.A.D., University of Paris I

Springer-Verlag and the Environment

We at Springer-Verlag firmly believe that an international science publisher has a special obligation to the environment, and our corporate policies consistently reflect this conviction.

We also expect our business partners – paper mills, printers, packaging manufacturers, etc. – to commit themselves to using environmentally friendly materials and production processes.

The paper in this book is made from low- or no-chlorine pulp and is acid free, in conformance with international standards for paper permanency.

Printing: Weihert-Druck GmbH, Darmstadt
Binding: Buchbinderei Schäffer, Grünstadt